T0304140

INSTITUTIONAL INTERACTION

Directions in Ethnomethodology and Conversation Analysis

Series Editors
David Francis, Manchester Metropolitan University
Stephen Hester, University of Wales, Bangor

Ethnomethodology and Conversation Analysis are cognate approaches to the study of social action that together comprise a major perspective within the contemporary human sciences. This perspective focuses upon naturally occurring talk and interaction and analyses the methods by which social activities are ordered and accomplished.

This major new book series will present current work in EM/CA, including research monographs, edited collections and theoretical studies. It will be essential reading for specialists in the field as well as those who wish to know more about this major approach to human action.

Also in the Series

Beyond the Black Box
Talk-in-Interaction in the Airline Cockpit
Maurice Nevile
ISBN 0 7546 4240 2

Institutional Interaction
Studies of Talk at Work

ILKKA ARMINEN
University of Tampere, Finland

Routledge
Taylor & Francis Group

LONDON AND NEW YORK

First published 2005 by Ashgate Publishing

2 Park Square, Milton Park, Abingdon, Oxon, OX14 4RN
711 Third Avenue, New York, NY 10017, USA

Routledge is an imprint of the Taylor & Francis Group, an informa business

First issued in paperback 2016

British Library Cataloguing in Publication Data
Arminen, Ilkka
    Institutional interaction. : studies of talk at work -
    (Directions in ethnomethodology and conversation analysis)
    1. Conversation analysis 2. Corporations - Sociological
    aspects 3. Business communication
    I.Title
    302.3'46

Library of Congress Control Number: 2005927748

ISBN 13: 978-0-7546-4285-5 (hbk)
ISBN 13: 978-1-138-26667-4 (pbk)

Contents

List of Figures and Charts

Figures

Charts

Series Editors' Preface

We are extremely pleased to include Ilkka Arminen's *Institutional Interaction: Studies of Talk at Work* as the second volume in our series Directions in Ethnomethodology and Conversation Analysis. The book presents a timely and comprehensive overview of a burgeoning domain of inquiry in social science. Institutional interaction has developed over the last decade or so into the principal field of research within the conversation analytic tradition. It has proved a rich source for the application of the methodological approach of conversation analysis to the study of social action and interaction.

Arminen's work is the first book-length examination of the analysis of institutional interaction. It presents a comprehensive and systematic introduction to the field. This alone would be sufficient to qualify it as a significant contribution to our series. However, the book has many additional strengths. First it locates clearly and informatively the study of institutional interaction within the research tradition of conversation analysis, originating in the work of Harvey Sacks and Emmanuel Schegloff. It shows how key concepts and methods from that tradition have been extended and applied. Second, it brings together the elements of the methodological programme for the study of institutional talk, as outlined in a number of previous publications, notably Drew and Heritage's *Talk at Work* and Boden and Zimmerman's *Talk and Social Structure*. Thirdly, the book shows how the methodological approach previously outlined has been applied in the study of social interaction in specific institutional contexts. These include, among others, school classrooms, medical consultations, courts of law and the use of technology in organizational settings. In this way the book establishes the continuing vitality of the conversation analytic research tradition, demonstrates the substantive scope of its application to the analysis of institutional interaction, and confirms its theoretical potential for understanding the organization and production of institutional life.

In these ways, Arminen's book will be of great interest to several audiences. The relevance of conversation analysis for the social sciences is now widely appreciated. From its original home in the discipline of sociology, conversation analytic research is now pursued across a wide range of other disciplines. Those new to the field of conversation analysis will find the breadth of Arminen's coverage and clarity of exposition extremely welcome and useful. He articulates very succinctly the theoretical perspective of conversation analysis and explains how this perspective provides a distinctive conception of the relationship between social actions and their contexts. More seasoned practitioners will appreciate the insightful manner in which methodological issues in the field are discussed. In particular, the book makes clear the multi-dimensionality of the organization of institutional interaction. In this way, Arminen's book provides a useful link to ongoing debates within ethnomethodology and conversation analysis regarding the various dimensions of analysis that may be necessary for an adequate understanding of the production of institutional interaction. Far from focusing exclusively on sequential aspects of institutional talk, Arminen shows how the sequential dimension of talk-in-interaction is linked with other organizational orders, such as the categorical order of social interaction, to provide for the accomplishment and intelligibility of institutional activities.

The study of institutional talk is a relatively new field of inquiry. As such, it is perhaps unsurprising that its concepts and methods are still evolving. There can be no doubt that it provides a most fruitful context for the application of conversation analytic ideas in all their variety. It allows one to appreciate and explore the complex and layered character of talk-in-interaction, something that Sacks himself emphasized. The excitement of working within this developing field is conveyed most effectively by Arminen's book.

Stephen Hester and David Francis
June 2005

Acknowledgements

Initially, David Silverman gave fruitful feedback on the basic idea. I am grateful to Helena Kangasharju, Doug Maynard, Anssi Peräkylä, Johanna Ruusuvuori and Sanna Vehviläinen for reading and commenting on one or more chapters of the manuscript. I have also received helpful suggestions from anonymous reviewers. Nely Keinänen has helped me to clarify and improve the style and language of my arguments.

The teachers and colleagues at the Linguistic Institute summer courses at Santa Barbara in 2001 provided much-needed stimulation at the middle stages of writing this book. Writing skills were acquired at York, England, during my postgraduate studies under the supervision of Paul Drew and Tony Wootton. I have also greatly benefited from my visit to UCSB and the opportunity to discuss my work with Gene Lerner, Tom Wilson and Don Zimmerman. I am grateful to Chuck Goodwin, who generously gave permission for some of his materials to be reused in this book. Last but not least, I thank Manny Schegloff for his supportive remarks.

In Chapters 1, 2 and 9 I have used parts of my articles published in *Discourse and Society* and in *Acta Sociology*, my thanks to the publisher.

This book is dedicated to my daughter Reetu who was born about the same time as the idea of this book.

Mansessa 2.2.04

Preface

It was not until the 1960s that a systematic science to study conversation and interaction started to develop. This branch of science has been named conversation analysis (CA) (ten Have 1999; Hutchby and Wooffitt 1998). The key idea of CA, still distinguishing it from most other approaches, is that it studies the sequential accomplishment of actions in interaction. In other words, CA analyzes actions through their relationships to the preceding (and the following) actions. This time-bound fabric of social actions is the focus of conversation analytical studies, and distinguishes CA from most other fields, which conceptualize their objects in achronic terms.[1]

Most CA studies are systematic analyses of the emergence of interactional patterns and of their contribution to ongoing social actions. Importantly, CA always examines individual cases; it is never about speech in general, though the findings may be generalizable. This is the basis of the unique adequacy of CA findings: they can always be pinned down to the observable details of interaction, thus enabling them both to be specific and to accumulate. CA can be used to examine any kinds of interactional objects, such as what kinds of rhetorical tropes invite applause from an audience (Atkinson 1984) or what kinds of moves disrupt the ordinary course of an interview, leading to a fierce clash (Schegloff 1988/89; Clayman and Whalen 1988/89).

Initially, CA studies did not differentiate between ordinary, mundane interactions, and particular, specific interactions in institutional settings. Harvey Sacks, the pioneer of CA, had been analyzing calls to a suicide prevention center when he got the idea of performing systematic, empirical analyses of sequential phenomena (I will return to the origins of CA in Chapters 1 and 6). In these circumstances, the delivery of talk may have been fateful for suicidal callers, but Sacks focused on details of talk that were salient both for the accomplishment of institutional tasks and also for the institution of interaction itself.

Later, the internal logic of the emerging science of conversational interaction demanded that the focus be narrowed solely to interaction itself. In the 1970s and 80s, the emphasis was on the analysis of "trivial", everyday interactions (see Heritage 1984a, 238–239). In these early phases of CA, interactions involving "institutional" identities, such as doctor/patient, interviewer/interviewee, teacher/pupil, etc., were purposefully avoided (ibid.). For a similar reason, much CA work in the 1970s, in particular, concentrated on recorded telephone calls; these were useful because the visual side of interaction was deliberately cut off. Telephone calls provided superb material to examine conversational interaction without the added complexities of gazes, gestures, and other visual aspects of interaction.[2] Later still, CA research integrated the visual aspects of face-to-face interaction with the sequential analysis of interaction (see Goodwin 1981; Heath 1986). Originally, however, the deliberately narrow focus on "trivial" interaction enabled researchers to formulate a cumulative science tracing the elementary features of interaction significant for all kinds of interactions, not just for particular kinds. These elementary invariances, upon which all forms of interaction are built, include turn-taking (Sacks et al. 1974), preference organization (Pomerantz 1984), repair organization (Schegloff et al. 1977), and sequence organization[3] (Schegloff 1995).

Regardless of whether it is focusing on mundane or institutional settings, CA is characterized by strict empiricism; it avoids idealizations. There is a pragmatic basis for this empiricism; only recordings tend to be of sufficient quality to allow detailed examination of interactional action. Ethnographic notes, informants' recollections, invented examples or experimentally-manipulated actions lack or distort details of natural situated interaction (Heritage 1984a, 236). Only rarely are verbal or written descriptions adequate to explore the sequential composition of interaction (cf. Holstein 1993).[4] For this reason, interviews are not an adequate technique to collect data. Invented examples, in turn, are only as good as the researcher's intuition. On the whole, human memory does not seem able to store longer sequences of interaction, and therefore recordings seem to be almost the only reliable way to gather data on interactional sequences. Experimental settings may transpose interaction in unpredictable ways, so their relation to "natural" interactional processes is unclear. Experimental data, however, is used on occasion (e.g. Maynard and Zimmerman 1984; Arminen 2002a) if the analysis focuses on interactional processes that the experimental design leaves intact; this, however, may be difficult to know. Consequently, so-called "naturally-occurring" interactions provide the bulk of the data in CA studies.

As Psathas (1995, 2) has said, "the term conversation analysis is a misnomer".[5] In terms of theory, Sacks was not interested in conversations themselves. Instead, recordings turned out to be valuable because they could be studied again and again, and they also enabled others to look at exactly the same data and find what they needed (Sacks 1992a, 619–623). Recorded conversations were just a means to build a primitive science whose findings could be corrected. Conversations provided material through which a human science could deal with the concrete details of actual events. As a whole, CA is not only interested in conversational talk, but in the organization of actions in interaction. The sequential organization of actions includes their syntactic, semantic, prosodic, pragmatic, and social[6] aspects of interaction insofar (and only insofar) as they are accountably relevant for the achievement of action. Generally, CA studies social actions from the sequential point of view to reverse-engineer[7] their composition, meaning and hidden rationality.

This book focuses on talk and interaction in institutional contexts, i.e., contexts where the interacting parties orient to the goal-rational, institutionalized nature of their action. Early on, CA studies observed that interaction in institutional settings was somehow specialized, that it differed from mundane interaction. Study of a sequential course of interaction at work provides a back door to understanding work processes. Speech is a pervasive medium of intersubjective actions in institutional environments and contexts as well; so analyzing sequential details amounts to a respecification of institutional processes.

In an early paper on turn-taking, Sacks, Schegloff, and Jefferson (1974) discussed the possibility of doing comparative studies on different systems of turn-taking. Turn-taking is a system which allocates slots of speaking time between parties, organizing the activity the parties are oriented to. In "ordinary conversations" turn-taking is co-ordinated turn-by-turn, locally without any predesigned arrangements. By contrast, in "formal speech-exchange systems", such as courtrooms, classrooms, and ceremonies, turn-allocation is based on a predesigned order, thereby realizing an institutional order in which parties are oriented to performing institutional tasks as displayed by their commitment to the predesigned turn order. In this way, the analysis of talk-in-interaction in institutional settings aims at specifying the very format through which the institutional practice is talked into being. More recent studies of institutional interaction, however, have mostly focused on "quasiconversational" institutional interaction, whose specificity does not lie in formal turn-taking, but in factors such as turn-design, lexical choices, sequential organization etc.[8] (ten Have 1999, 168).

Nowadays, there is a well-established tradition for the study of institutional interaction in conversation analysis (for overviews, see Boden and Zimmerman 1991; Drew and Heritage 1992a; Heritage 1997; Drew and Sorjonen 1997). The study of institutional interaction aims at explicating the ways in which institutional tasks are carried out in various settings through the management of talk-in-interaction. In particular, Drew and Heritage (1992a) have edited a key collection of studies on institutional interaction which provides a systematic exploration of this distinctive field.

In terms of institutional interaction, CA's reverse-engineering program aims to identify the unique "fingerprint" of each institutional practice (ibid.). Significantly, this fingerprint is not the outcome of analysis, but its starting point. By examining this fingerprint, CA studies how specific institutional tasks, identities, and inferences are achieved. Therefore, analysis of institutional interaction ultimately examines elaborate issues, such as the strategic aspects of interaction, the achievement of collaboration, or procedures whereby participants' differing perspectives are brought into alignment. In this respect, studies of institutional interaction are very close to Sacks' original idea of studying members' methodical ways of accomplishing social tasks in interaction.

The study of institutional interaction is essentially comparative, whereby institutional practices are compared with their counterparts in everyday interactions. This comparative approach aims at defining the specificity of a particular type of institutional interaction. The analyst demonstrates the ways in which the context plays a role in a particular aspect or a segment of interaction, thus allowing us to examine the role the institution has in and for the interaction in the setting. Schegloff (1991) has called this "defining the procedural relevance of context" (to be discussed in Chapter 2), with the aim of providing criteria and a toolkit against arbitrary invocation of a countless number of extrinsic, potential aspects of context.

In all, CA provides a fine-grained machinery to account for a sequential flow of interaction in any context. However, recovering the embodied meaning of interactional practices may depend on an analyst's ability to recognize the participants' situated competencies which inform their activities. At best, studies of institutional interaction are context-sensitive, displaying the role of local, tacit knowledge in the maintenance of an institutional practice. This context-sensitivity also improves and enhances their applicability.

The aim of this book is to provide a systematic introduction to the study of institutional interaction for those interested in communication within organizations, information systems and goal-oriented interaction. CA, as I shall emphasize, studies talk as a way of doing things: the study of institutional interaction focuses on how institutions and organizations are talked into being. This approach is both pragmatic, in its focus on the practical details of communication in work settings, as well as intellectual, through its ethnomethodological underpinnings (to be discussed in Chapter 1).

This book consists of two parts. The first part discusses the theory and methods of CA, focusing on studies of institutional interaction, while the second part takes up the basics of institutional interaction in selected fields.

In Chapter 1, I discuss the theoretical framework of CA as well as its applicability to the analysis of institutional interaction. I will focus on Sacks' original idea to discern methodical practices of doing social activities and compare this approach to other types of studies. Chapter 2 discusses the specificity of institutional interaction as a particular research object. I suggest that although most general principles of CA apply to the scrutiny of institutional interactions and practices, a separate set of concerns arise when we focus particularly on the *institutional* nature of interaction. CA can increase our understanding of institutional practices by respecifying their interactional substratum and in that way concretize, broaden, detail, and even correct our understanding of institutional practices. Chapter 3 provides a hands-on account of how data is handled and managed in an actual research process. In theoretical terms, I emphasize the resemblance between the analytic procedures in CA and the principles of analytic induction. I also address the reliability and validity of CA studies.

In the second part of the book I describe the fundamental patterns of interaction arising out of the parties' orientation to constitutive institutional tasks. The basic factors shaping these types of institutional interaction include 1) managing the interface between the client and the professional, 2) transmitting knowledge and skills, 3) pursuing conflicting interests, 4) conciliating interest conflicts and 5) meeting the challenges of information technologies.

Chapter 4 discusses the fact that an institutional encounter takes place at the crossroads of the client's and professional's perspectives. The professional may need to elicit the client's perspective in order to tailor the delivery of the professional perspective. The client's ownership of experience is particularly crucial in therapeutic, medical and counseling interactions.

Chapter 5 focuses on the transmission of knowledge and skills; this is of course the task of pedagogic institutions, but is also a prominent process in any expert system. In classrooms, pedagogic exchange has been taking place for hundreds of years, and robust patterns, such as the teaching cycle and exam questions, have survived.

Chapter 6 addresses strategic aspects of interactions. In interaction, a strategic actor may try to get something done without "doing" it. For instance, a person may avoid providing help without refusing to provide help by treating the request as a joke. Strategic interaction has its basis in everyday life. In institutional settings, the strategic nature of interaction is important in settings where impression management is salient for parties as in media and legal settings. Cross-examinations are particularly attuned to strategic displays.

Chapter 7 discusses negotiation as a form of strategic interaction in which the goal is to reach an agreement or a compromise between the parties' interests. At the core of a negotiation is a bargaining sequence in which a speaker formulates a position and a recipient aligns or misaligns with it. Sequential analysis of negotiations sheds light on these sequences by analyzing what happens both before and after them.

Chapter 8 deals with the challenges of the increasing computerization and digitalization of institutional (and everyday) environments. Using comparative analyses, CA can address the modifications that technical artifacts bring to institutional settings; much research in this area has focused on the control rooms of technical systems such as air traffic control or subways. CA can even participate in the technology design process through specifying the human and interactional requirements for technological environments.

The final chapter addresses future directions of CA research. For example, an increasing interest concerns comparative studies addressing the historical, cultural, and linguistic differences of sequential practices. Another important direction will be the quantification of findings, as this will be critical for comparative and evaluative studies. CA will also increasingly do applied studies aiming to satisfy pragmatic criteria. Also, studies on technology will become more prominent in CA, as technology is increasingly affecting the ways in which people interact, both inside and outside institutions.

In short, this book will provide you with a clear introduction to the major areas of institutional interaction (a set of exercises to train your skills in analyzing talk at work are available at http://www.uta.fi/laitokset/sosio/project/ivty/english/sivut/exercises.html). CA may help us to learn to pay attention to the details of interaction that matter, and allow us to examine the sequential orchestration of activities upon which the intersubjective understanding of social actions relies.

Notes

1   In this respect, discourse analysis, with which CA is sometimes confused, is a heterogeneous field. Some discourse studies are purely achronic in their conceptualisation of objects, though recently some branches of discourse analysis have increasingly adopted the principles of CA and resemble it (see Edwards and Potter 2001).

2   Current work on mobile calls shows that landline telephone calls also have other specific features which are tied to the limits and possibilities of their enabling technology.

3   Following Schegloff (1995), we can make a distinction between sequential organization and sequence organization. Sequential organization is a broader term that concerns the ordering and positioning of any actions and utterances. Sequence organization concerns courses of action that have been realized through talk. Much CA work is about sequence organization. Currently there is not yet any systematic overview of sequential organization. This will be one of the major theoretical challenges for researchers on interaction. This book mostly focuses on sequence organization, but not exclusively. I address sequential order explicitly, in particular, in Chapters 6, 8 and 9.

4   Though, for instance, Schegloff and Pomerantz, two well known scholars of conversational interaction, use field notes occasionally. Ethnography can be important data source, though occasionally unreliable (see Clavarino et al. 1995).

5   Perhaps ironically, in a booklet entitled "Conversation Analysis – The Study of Talk-in-Interaction".

6   CA is interested in the basic properties of (verbal) interaction that amount to social actions. These include the linguistic grammar, meaning of items in talk and actions, voice quality of talk, types of activities and the emerging relationship between parties in action.

7   The term "reverse-engineering" came to my knowledge through Daniel Dennett (1991). Originally, the term comes from a special field of engineering that deciphers how complex structures, such as pyramids or gothic churches, were built in the first place.

8   These include the ways turns at talk are formulated, words chosen, and the following turns interlinked.

The whole of *Capital* is written according to the following method: Marx analyses a single living "cell" of capitalist society – for example, the nature of value. Within this cell he discovers the structure of the entire system and all of its economic institutions. He says that to a layman this analysis may seem a murky tangle of tiny details. Indeed, there may be tiny details, but they are exactly those which are essential to "micro-anatomy". Anyone who could discover what a "psychological" cell is – the mechanism producing even a single response – would thereby find the key to psychology as a whole.

L.S. Vygotsky (from unpublished notebooks)

Chapter 1

Conversation Analysis and its Applications

> Were the loosest and freest conversation to be transcribed, there would immediately be observed something which connected it in all its transitions. Or where this is wanting, the person who broke the thread of discourse might still inform you, that there had secretly revolved in his mind a succession of thought, which had gradually led him from the subject of conversation.
>
> (Hume, 1777)

Though the idea that conversations are orderly is undoubtedly old, the systematic study of conversational interactions is somewhat new. Conversation Analysis (CA), which is just over thirty years old, describes the competencies and procedures involved in the production of any type of social interaction. In comparison to many sociological approaches, CA is an exact and empirical enterprise, avoiding immature theoretical speculations and informed by a set of theoretical propositions. In this chapter, I will discuss the basic principles of CA and its application, in particular, to the study of institutional interactions and practices (for overviews of CA, see Hutchby and Wooffitt 1998; ten Have 1999; Silverman 1998). In discussing the working principles of the discipline, I will also consider their potential relevance for the study of action in institutional settings, and will also address some disputes concerning the applicability of CA. I will then compare CA with other methodologies. At the end of this chapter, I will briefly return to the issues of how CA might be applied for practical purposes.

In institutional contexts, CA discerns the ways in which talk is specialized and reduced to accomplish the tasks at hand. CA studies do not generally rely on ethnographic knowledge, but the analysis of some institutional settings may require contextual knowledge in order to make sense of realms distinct from everyday life. CA uses inductive logic so its reliability is based on analytic induction (to be discussed more in Chapter 3), but in some specific cases statistical evidence plays a role.

The distinctiveness of CA as a social scientific approach derives from its object of analysis. CA studies conversational turns and interactional moves in their sequences.

It analyzes how a turn treats a previous turn, and what implications it poses for the next ones. CA treats talk and social interaction as a sufficient object for analysis, rather than as a window to wider social processes or as a medium for data collection (Hutchby and Wooffitt 1998, 21). That CA's data collection methods rely on the tape-recording of actual interactions emphasizes the role of social interaction as an autonomous reality *sui generis*. Traditionally, sociologists have not seen the study of talk in its own right as a relevant enterprise. Paradoxically, the very fact that it is impossible to ever achieve a strictly formal analysis of conversation makes it a worthy human science (ten Have 1999, 196–197). That is, a conversation cannot be represented with a closed set of formal rules, which would allow infallible prediction of the n ext possible conversational move, or the set of next possible moves. Instead, every subbsequent conversational move renews our understanding of the prior move so that each turn both orients to a preceding context but also recreates the context anew (Heritage 1984a, 242). Therefore, a purely formal context-free description of a conversation remains impossible. Instead, conversation analysis amounts to discerning the participants' intersubjective understanding of the course of conversation as it evolves moment by moment, as the participants orient themselves to the social action. Consequently, however tiny the details of a conversation, they are the building blocks of the architecture of intersubjectivity upon which the accomplishment of social actions, simple and complex, rests.

1.1   Basic Ideas

The basic idea of CA is so simple that it is difficult to grasp: CA studies what an utterance does in relation to the preceding one(s) and what implications an utterance poses for the next one(s). As Hutchby and Wooffitt (1998, 15) put it, the *next-turn proof procedure* is the most basic tool in CA (see Sacks et al. 1974). That is, the next turn provides evidence of the party's orientation to the prior turn, there and then. This methodic procedure is CA's gateway to the participants' own understandings as they are revealed during actual interaction, thereby providing material for analytic explication. For example, consider this brief exchange between E and M (transcription simplified).

(1) [NB:VII:2] (Heritage 1984a, 236; ten Have 1999, 4)

1 E: e-that <u>Pa</u>:t isn' she a do:[:ll?]
2 M: [iYe]h <u>i</u>sn't she pretty,

In using the next-turn proof procedure, we should be able to say something about E's turn with the help of M's turn. Let us begin with the obvious. M's turn is designed as an answer, but a particular kind of an answer, an assessment. CA then proceeds with a comparative approach through which the specificity of the data instance is explicated. The comparison can be imaginary in the first place. If we wished to work empirically, we would collect parallel cases to find regularities through which similar kinds of actions are accomplished. Here, however, let us be content with an imaginary comparison, a kind of game where the analyst tries to locate an observation within his/her knowledge/imagination, thus sketching out the meaning of an actual course of interaction through comparison with imaginary cases. A proper demonstration would be based on an empirical collection of parallel/similar cases with whose help regularities would be spelled out. Let us proceed. Notice how M continues her answer after the response token "yeah" and in so doing treats her "yeah" as an insufficient response to E's action. At this point, you should be able to see a hermeneutical circle at work. The *next-turn proof procedure* means that a reflexive relationship exists between adjacent turns: the next turn is used as an analytic resource for making sense of the prior turn, which, for its part, has provided the sequential implications that have made the next turn relevant.

M's turn suggests that E has invited M to produce a second assessment. In other words, despite its grammatical form, an assessment that is delivered through a yes-no question format does not work like an ordinary question. That is, M does not treat E's utterance as a straightforward question but as an invitation to assess the person E herself has described as a doll. Moreover, M's assessment is a specific kind of assessment compared to E's prior assessment: it is weaker and narrower, downgraded, which suggests that M does not agree that strongly with E. Now, just as we are about to close our analysis (at least for the moment), we are on the verge of sociological/sociopsychological findings. The situation is rather juicy: E and M are talking about the third party, Pat, and a particular type of relationship is emerging between E and M. E has invited M to participate in a joint appreciation of Pat, but M has declined the invitation with a mild response, and a gulf between their perspectives has been opened. E has provided an assessment, whose upgraded quality M has made plain through her mitigated second.

But, a reader may protest, is this all pure speculation? Can we say anything about the validity of this reading? Maybe Arminen got it all wrong? Is there any way to test and check the accuracy of the analysis? Actually, CA allows its findings to be tested through the very same *next-turn proof procedure* (Heritage 1984a, 256–257). We can examine the turn following M's turn to see whether our explication of the interaction fits with the parties' sense of the ongoing interaction as they reveal it turn-by-turn. We might even imagine the set of alternatives that E would use to counter M's downgraded assessment. In this way, even if we are not able to make infallible predictions of the next turns, we can give an accountable description of the course of the conversation and of its potential next moves. Further, proper empirical research would be based on a collection of cases, whose analysis should amount to invariable regularity.[1] Here, we have the chance to check our skills simply by imagining how the exchange will continue, and then looking at the extended sequence of the exchange (see Heritage 1984a, 236; ten Have 1999, 4).

(1) ((continuation)) [NB:VII:2] (Heritage 1984a, 236; ten Have 1999, 4)

```
3                (.)
4    E:      Oh: she's a beautiful girl.=
5    M:      =Yeh I think she's a pretty gir[l.
6    E:                                      [En' that Reinam'n::
```

Any time you feel that you have a better account of the sequence than one that has been given, please feel free to develop it further, and check it against sequence of data. The adequacy of this kind of analysis is not primarily theory-bound. The analysis is not supposed to be measured against any theoretical account of interaction, but against the reality of recorded interactions and their transcriptions.

Hutchby and Wooffitt (1998, 38–39) make a useful analytic distinction between "sequential order" and what they call "inferential order", though sequential and inferential orders do presuppose one another. That is, the parties' inferential work – the kinds of implications and inferences participants draw about each other's talk and conduct to make sense and to hold each other morally accountable – allows them to build sequences of action upon which this inferential work rests. Sequential order means the "describable ways in which turns are linked together into definite sequences" (ibid.), and its analysis provides the backbone of CA. However, this sequential order is tied to the inferential order, hence the sequential analysis touches also upon the inferential order. In the final instance, the inferential order is the basis for everyday semiotics. This becomes plain in everyday life, but can also be seen in literature. For example, in Shakespeare's *Twelfth Night*, Viola, disguised in male clothes, interprets Olivia's way of speaking as a sign of her psychological state:

> She made good view of me; indeed, so much
> That, as methought, her eyes had lost her tongue,
> For she did speak in starts distractedly.
> She loves me, sure ... (2.2.18–21)

The distinction between different "orders" opens up the multidimensionality of the CA research object. Essentially, CA is about the organization of interaction, about the syntactic, semantic, and prosodic qualities through which turns are designed, and about the pragmatic connections between turns.[2] Furthermore, as Hutchby and Wooffitt (1998, 39) stress, these concerns interplay with normative and inferential properties of talk through which participants orient to the sense and implications of their interaction. The multilayered orderliness of talk makes it a "deep" object, so that even a seemingly innocent or insignificant property of talk may become relevant when looked at from another angle. CA's programmatic stance suggests that we should not *a priori* assume the irrelevance of any detail of talk; instead, we should try to find *order at all points*, as Sacks said (1992a, 484; Hutchby and Wooffitt 1998, 17–22). This methodological canon creates the possibility of unlimited new findings, but also makes the research process a never-ending quest. We may think of CA as the reverse engineering of an immense complex of intersubjectivity. Deciphering this enigmatic structure requires that the analyst be highly-skilled in observing, detailing, describing and systematicizing this fractal-like multitude.

On an analytical level it may be helpful to distinguish between different styles of doing CA. The analysis may focus on the sequential order, paying only minimal attention to the inferential properties of talk. For instance, we could have concentrated on the properties of E's and M's turn-design and on the relationship between turns, passing over the potential social implications of their exchange; or, we could have analyzed the properties of Olivia's turn-beginnings, such as breaths and other aspirations including laughter and laugh tokens, recognizable contexted-silences, coughs, "y'knows", "uh" in all its varieties, cut-offs, re-beginnings, re-directions, etc. (Schegloff 1996a, 103). CA demands a disciplined approach, with the analyst not jumping to sociological or psychological conclusions, falling into immature theoretical speculations, or relying on everyday assumptions. Paul ten Have (1999, 107) goes so far as to make a distinction between "pure" and "applied" CA, arguing the former should concentrate "on talk 'itself', rather than its 'context'". To my mind, however, this strict division and the whole notion of "pure" CA is misleading and inadvisable. Moreover, separating talk from its context goes against all the basic ideas of CA, according to which the context-renewing properties of talk amount to the endogenous construction of context, as parties orient to the "context" through the management of talk-in-interaction as an observable part of doing social actions in the context (to be discussed more in the next chapter). A more sensible way to address the issue of the applicability of CA is to stress that CA allows, and even necessitates, the selection of the focus of analysis, which may be more closely connected to the sequential or inferential properties of talk and action.

As a whole, CA is a technology to access the orientations of the members of a culture, and to avoid implausible constructive theorizing. CA is a program of "reverse engineering" which analyzes interactional practices in order to articulate and respecify the generic building blocks of social interaction. The results obtained illuminate ways in which social and institutional realities are occasioned, maintained, and managed with the help of the organization of talk-in-interaction (Heritage 1984a, 233–292; Drew and Heritage 1992b; Pomerantz and Fehr 1997).[3] The findings of CA are both "uniquely adequate" in that they provide a context-sensitive understanding of a specific instance of interaction (Psathas 1995, 45–53), and are "generically informative" in that they illuminate constitutive features of talk-in-interaction, which enable intersubjective understandings across both language and culture (Sacks et al. 1974).

In the final instance, CA studies social actions. As Schegloff (1991, 46) and Peräkylä (1995, 17) have argued, talk amounts to action as the interactants create and sustain intersubjective understanding about what is going on and what they are doing. Talk in all its occasions, i.e., talk-in-interaction, is the primordial site at and through which the actors construct a sense of the ongoing event, and negotiate a role for their participation in it. Consequently, talk amounts to action. Talk and social actions are not two separate plenums, but talk is a medium for orchestrating activities through which the sense of these activities is made intersubjectively available.

A corollary to the fact that talk amounts to action is the fact that talk is reflexively tied to its context. "Specifically, it is assumed that the significance of any speaker's communicative action is doubly contextual in being both *context-shaped* and *context-renewing*" (Heritage 1984a, 242). First of all, every utterance is context-shaped since recipients rely on their understanding of the immediate context of the action to make sense of it. We can discuss this with the help of a data extract from Sacks's original corpus, the so-called New Year's Eve Call:

(2) [SPC:NYE:1964:1–2:Sacks Transcript]

```
 1    Caller:   I can't call any of my friends or anybody cause they're just
 2              gonna say oh that's silly or that's stupid I guess
 3    Desk:     Uh huh
 4    Caller:   I guess what you really want is someone to say yes I really
 5              understand why you want to commit suicide I do believe you
 6              I would too
 7    Desk:     Uh huh. Well tell me about it
 8    Caller:   Bou I a funny thing I know it's emotionally immature
 9              except that doesn't help
10    Desk:     Uh huh
11    Caller:   I've got a date coming in a half hour and I ((sob))
12    Desk:     I see
13    Caller:   I can't go through with it I can't go through with the
14              evening I can't ((sniffle))
15    Desk:     Uh huh
16→           Caller:   You talk. I don't want to talk
17    Desk:     Uh huh
18    Caller:   ((laugh sob)) It sounds like a real professional uh huh uh
19              huh uh huh ((sniffle))
20    Desk:     Well perhaps you want to tell me uh why you feel like
21              committing suicide
```

Here, the caller relates her personal problems and the agent responds with a series of "minimal responses", which we can roughly[4] characterize as continuers allocating the turn back to the caller. After the agent's fifth minimal response, however, the caller requests that the agent speak for a change: *"You talk. I don't want to talk"* (marked with an arrow). Through her request, the caller displays that from her point of view the agent's previous turn[5] *"Uh huh"* was not sufficient, and did not provide grounds for her to proceed further. Instead it made relevant a request to ask the agent to talk for a change. In this fashion, the request characterized the previous turn as having been insufficient, and something more substantial would have been due at that point. The fact that the agent's *"Uh huh"* was taken as an insufficient response also demonstrates that the caller's preceding turn *"I can't go through with it I can't go through with the evening I can't ((sniffle))"* had accomplished a context that made relevant a range of responses to which *"Uh huh"* did not belong.[6] Here, the caller herself had oriented to the fact that the turns of talk at the interaction are context-shaped. With the help of her turn *"I can't go through with it I can't go through with the evening I can't ((sniffle))"* a context was built up in which a troubled recipient was expected to express some reciprocity, minimally to take a turn. We may still want to add that it was not so much the quality of a single turn that could be characterized as a "request for help", or even an "outcry for help" (note the sniffling in the voice), but it is the turn in its collaboratively constructed context which amounts to the action that we might call a request for help. That is, the caller had been relating her problems for a while, and in the course of that process the emotional intensity had grown, as the start of sniffling indicates. This whole process, the growing of emotional intensity, seems to have made relevant a respective change in the mood of the reception, which, however, did not take place.[7] This extract demonstrates that speakers attend to the sense of the context they have created. Here the recipient's failure to design his actions according to the context in question became accountable, and in this way the sense of the context was made consequential for the interaction in question. Thus, we can see that turns *are* context-shaped: rather than an invention of a conversation analyst, this shaping is the members' own methodological principle through which the intersubjective orderliness of interaction is accomplished and sustained.

This extract also helps us pay attention to the context-renewing force of the interactants' contributions. Here the agent produces a series of neutral, minimal responses; we might think that they would not as such be in any serious sense consequential for the interaction in question, but simply provide a chance for the other party to go on. However, the very fact that a series of neutral responses was produced becomes itself accountable and thereby consequential for the context. The caller ends up challenging the agent who does nothing but grunt *"((laugh sob)) It sounds like a real professional uh huh uh huh uh huh ((sniffle))"*. We may note that the interactants cannot escape the sequential implicativeness of the interaction, and their own contributions always add, deliberately or not, something to the framework in whose terms an ongoing action will be understood. Neither can the interactants avoid taking part in a context that their actions reflexively constitute. A withdrawal from interaction, for instance, is itself a social fact and an action that transposes the sense of the ongoing event.[8]

Finally, the extract also shows the normative character of talk-in-interaction. After the agent did not respond to the caller's request to talk, the agent's non-responsiveness

8   *Institutional Interaction*

becomes not only accountable, that is, noticeable and reportable, but also normatively sanctionable, a matter to complain about: *"((laugh sob)) It sounds like a real professional uh huh uh huh uh huh ((sniffle))"*, and the agent is put into the position of responding to the original request. In this manner, the interactants treat each other's behavior as normatively sanctionable, and the regulative patterns of talk-in-interaction become normatively constituted. Through this normative underpinning the talk-in-interaction becomes an institution in its own right, and the interactants orient to its patterns as a normative standard. The principles discussed briefly above can be summarized in the following figure.

• Talk and other actions in interaction are sequentially organized and ordered

• The relationships between turns and other moves in interaction are the key resource both for participants and analysts in deciphering the sense of ongoing action

• Participants orient to this sequential order and through this orientation realize the normative orderliness of social actions

• Analysis focuses on real-life instances of interactions (since memorized or invented examples tend to lose or transpose significant details of actions)

Figure 1.1 Principles of CA (see Hutchby and Wooffitt 1998; ten Have 1999)

To sum up, CA treats interaction as a structurally-orchestrated enterprise. Contributions in interaction are sequentially implicative: they delimit the range of possible next contributions by making some types of actions conditionally relevant.[9] In this way, the context of interaction is endogenously constructed and becomes an orderly achievement. The participants orient themselves to this orderliness of interaction, and their orientations provide the basis of the intersubjectivity of social action and the orderly course of interaction. Indeed, participants treat the orderly course of interaction as a normative standard, so departures from regulative patterns of interaction are sanctionable, which reflexively maintains the very institution of talk-in-interaction. In the following chapters we will see that these basic principles of interaction also apply in institutional contexts, albeit in a modified form.

1.2   Theoretical Background

The emphasis on studying talk as a way of *doing* links CA to ethnomethodological sociology (Garfinkel 1967). We can characterize ethnomethodology as an empirical research program drawing its inspiration from the phenomenological philosophy of Husserl and Schutz (Heritage 1984a: 37–74). Ethnomethodology transposed phenomenological inquiries about the appearance of phenomena in the social world onto studies of the members' methods of doing *being-in-the-world*. The spectrum of ethnomethodological inquiries covers topics such as jazz improvisation (Sudnow 1978), Gödel's theorem (Livingston 1986), and aboriginals' forms of life (Liberman 1985; for further studies, see Garfinkel 2002). In all its studies, ethnomethodology concentrates on the methods of *doing*, if nothing else then on just *doing being ordinary* – in other words, how people manage their conduct to give an impression of being more-or-less like everybody else (Sacks 1992b, 215–221). Another phenomenological underpinning is the idea of "bracketing", where the question of what the world "really" is is closed off and the inquiry instead concerns the appearance of the world and how it is constructed as it appears to us (Kusch 1989). The idea of bracketing informs both the theory and practice of conversation analysis. First, CA inquiries suspend knowledge about the external context of interaction,[10] and study the way participants make the context relevant for themselves in the course of an ongoing interaction. In this way, CA studies the endogenous construction of context. The idea is not to build upon existing scientific or everyday knowledge of the research object, but rather to examine the research object itself as an achievement of the participants. In terms of practice, the first step in exploring data is simply to listen to or watch the tapes with the help of transcripts. Such unselective and unmotivated data exploration allows the analyst to notice features and possible phenomena without a theory-driven pre-selection of the focus. Thus, no phenomena are precluded prior to inspection of the materials, thereby enabling the analyst to find phenomena through scrutiny of the materials themselves. Consequently, the analysis focuses on the construction of social realities and practices (Pomerantz and Fehr 1997; ten Have 1999, 99–126).

Conversation analysis can also be seen as being inspired by or being part of a broad intellectual movement that has been called "the linguistic turn" of the 20th century. This linguistic turn emphasizes that philosophical problems – whether involving sociological, psychological or epistemological concerns – are essentially questions about language, or at least they depend upon language (Rorty 1967/1992). Accordingly, the linguistic turn transformed language into the most fundamental object of philosophy and the human sciences. In the social sciences, philosophies of ordinary language, speech act theory and Wittgenstein's later work became particularly influential. Ordinary language philosophy and speech act theory (Austin 1962) examined the constitutive role of language, seeing language not as a mere representation of the external world, its mirror, but as the medium of meaning making, bringing meaningfulness to social reality. Austin's speech act theory explored the performative power of utterances which do not just "picture" something but constitute the very fact, such as naming someone or something, wedding people, and sentencing defendants. Many of these concerns informed Harvey Sacks's early article "Sociological description" (1963), where he wondered about the infinitude of descriptions and their power to ascribe meaning to the objects of description, causing Sacks to puzzle over what a "true" scientific description might be. CA has subsequently responded to this concern with the idea that "the procedural relevance" of participants' actions should inform the methodology to ascribe the sense for the ongoing action the participants themselves orient to (Schegloff 1991). CA has remained faithful to the idea of studying the constitutive power of language (use) in other respects as well, as can be seen in formulations about actions, practices, and even institutions which are "talked into being" (Heritage 1984a, 290), or talk as the medium of work, "talk at work" (Drew and Heritage 1992b). More fundamentally, the whole idea of a comparative approach to analysing institutional practices is based on the view that comparing ordinary and institutional talk can reveal the set of linguistic and interactional arrangements constituting the sense of the institutional practice in question. For example, "courtroom-ness" is constituted through a set of reductions and specializations in a set of interactional conventions used in a courtroom. In his late philosophy, Wittgenstein (1958) suggested that there is an internal relationship between language games and forms of life, such that words get their meaning only as part of a particular "language-game". Just as different games have different rules, so do all lexical items have different meanings in different games. Further, the set of language games constitute particular forms of life, so that if we are to understand a form of life we have to recognize the rules of its language games. From this perspective CA can be grasped as the empirical scrutiny of language games which enables an understanding of forms of life. Levinson (1992) has further suggested the study of "activity types" that inform participants' use of language in a speech event, such as a classroom, job interview, or police interrogation. Through respecifying the nature of the activity type we can accordingly deepen our understanding of the social practice in question.

The third set of influences in CA comes from the ethnography of speech and Erving Goffman. Dell Hymes (1964, 1972) introduced the idea of communicative competence in his ethnography of speaking. The focus on speech event and communicative competence allowed a shift of focus from an a-historical, ideal grammar and the ideal speaker to the study of actual speech. Further, communicative competence broadened the scope of research in acknowledging pragmatic, situational and social aspects language use instead of mere linguistic competence, the target of Chomskyan linguistics. Hymes claimed that speakers need to have more than grammatical competence to be able to communicate effectively; they have to orient to the conventions of how language is used by members of a culture to accomplish their purposes. CA has continued the empirical study of communicative competence and the tacit social structures which enable social interaction and language use. Further inspiration for the study of situated social action came from the sociologist Erving Goffman. Throughout his career Goffman promoted acceptance of the face-to-face domain, what he later started to call the "interaction order" (Goffman 1983a). Already in 1964, Goffman (1964) argued that the sociological actor/structure debate neglected situations, which he saw as an autonomous structure mediating between actors and structures. Situations structure actions, amounting to a coercive power over actors. The analytical focus on the interaction order as an autonomous dimension for social analysis is a systematic development of this train of thought. The analysis of talk-in-interaction follows this path, treating interaction as an emergent property that cannot be reduced either to the actors' psychological states or to macroscopic social structures that are not made relevant in the situation. Goffman (1974) has also been directly relevant to the development of studies on institutional interaction. Frame analytical concepts have been used for specifying the participation framework in various institutional contexts (see Maynard 1984; Clayman 1992; Peräkylä 1995).

Many of these influences came together in ethnomethodology. The key for early ethnomethodology was the topic/resource shift (Zimmerman and Pollner 1970). The reservoir of tacit everyday knowledge normally taken for granted by the social sciences was to be opened for research. The fundamental properties of social action were to be turned into the object of study. In short, ethnomethodology aimed to respecify the foundations of social actions through analyzing situated practices at the face-to-face level (Button 1991). Consequently, CA emerged as an offshoot of ethnomethodology, developing into a systematic study of all interactional social behavior which prototypically is verbally mediated and hence called "talk-in-interaction" (Silverman 1998). CA builds on a view that everyday talk forms the bedrock for intersubjective understanding and consequently for all social actions including institutionally distinct forms of action (Heritage 1984a). Hence, the study of talk itself became the bedrock of social analysis, which thus attempted to go beyond common sense through a more fine-grained analysis of social actions than that accessible to social actors at the level of everyday reasoning. The ethnomethodological bedrock of CA can be summarized with the following figure (see also Clayman and Maynard 1995):

PRINCIPLES OF ETHNOMETHODOLOGY

A. The meaning of a social phenomenon is equivalent to methodic procedures through which participants sustain the sense of a given phenomenon

B. Language use and social actions are indexical, i.e., their understanding is bound to the context of their achievement

C. The social order is the participants' methodic achievement

D. Rules and regularities are resources for interpretations and guide the participants as sources of understanding

---

METHODIC IMPLICATIONS FOR RESEARCH

1. Naturalism: Studies concentrate on real events, i.e., naturally occurring data

2. Non-ironical stance—the participants' own actions and orientations are the source of meaning: a researcher does not possess superior knowledge a priori. (The referential truthfulness of participants' understandings is bracketed – they are analysed as situated actions.)

3. Observational science: Studies focus on what can be observed (hidden rationalities or meanings may be inferred from the observational entities).

Figure 1.2 Aspects of the Ethnomethodological Program Relevant to CA[11]

As a whole, studies of social interaction have established the existence of face-to-face behavior as an emergent social fact. Perhaps the strongest formulation is Harvey Sacks' phrase "order-at-all-points", which can be taken as the methodical principle of conversation analysis (Sacks 1992a and b). That is, social interaction may be approached as a systematically organized whole; even the smallest details should not a priori be seen as irrelevant. In this way, Sacks and his colleagues managed to establish a new autonomous field of study (Sacks et al. 1974; Schegloff and Sacks 1973). After the new field was established, questions about its relationship to other subjects started to evolve. In terms of the social sciences, a particularly significant focus of study is institutional interaction. Institutional interaction stands at the crossroads of two institutional realms[12] (Peräkylä 1997a). On the one hand, interaction order is an interface between the institution and its users; on the other hand, by definition institutional interaction is connected to the macroscopic social order as it appears in institutions.

1.3   Origins and Development

In recent years there has been growing consensus on the origins of CA, even of its very moment of discovery (for instance, Hutchby and Wooffitt 1998; ten Have 1999; Silverman 1998). In particular, David Silverman (1998) offers the first book-length introduction to Harvey Sacks' iconoclastic thought experiments which, among others, paved the way for CA. Sacks originally studied law at Columbia and Yale in the 1950s. Through his encounters with Erving Goffman and Harold Garfinkel, Sacks became involved in studies of sociology. Although both Goffman and Garfinkel were important teachers of face-to-face behavior and everyday reasoning processes, gradually Goffman and Sacks parted ways. Sacks obtained his PhD only after Goffman agreed to resign from his evaluation committee in 1966

(Silverman 1998, 28), for Goffman found Sacks's reasoning in his prospective doctoral thesis circular and a-sociological. This part of Sacks's early work, before he became interested in the analysis of conversation, has been known as "membership categorization analysis" (Silverman 1998, 74–97). Notably, it is this early work which has sparked the most debate, perhaps even more than conversation analysis (Jayyusi 1984; Schegloff 1992a). Goffman was himself critical of the then emerging conversation analysis, though his final book *Forms of Talk* (1981) is at least topically very close to conversation analysis.

In 1963 Sacks was working with Garfinkel at the Center for the Scientific Study of Suicide at UCLA. For one study, a set of calls to a suicide prevention center was recorded. One task for personnel was to try to obtain the caller's name, as out of professional cautiousness, they avoided asking the caller's name directly. In most cases, the call takers were successful in getting the caller's name by giving their name first. But then Sacks came across one call-opening (see Silverman 1998, 98–99; Hutchby and Wooffitt 1998, 18–20; ten Have 1999, 13–15) which ran like this (transcription simplified):

(3) (Sacks 1992a, 6)

A: This is Mr Smith, may I help you
B: I can't hear you.
A: This is Mr <u>Smith</u>.
B: Sm<u>i</u>th.

In this case, the caller, B, reports a hearing problem, leading to a trajectory where the place for a reciprocal giving of names never materialized. Instead, the solution to the caller's hearing problem made it relevant for the call-taker to acknowledge the caller's hearing with an item, such as "yes", and then to return to the opening of activity "may I help you". (Unfortunately, Sacks did not show how this call went on, but the course described above seems to be the regular pattern, see Sacks 1992a, 6–76.) Since the call-taker could not at this point ask the caller's name directly, the reporting of a hearing problem had in effect prevented him from getting it.

Thus, Sacks encountered a puzzle. Was this trajectory just a plain accident, or was there something more to it? At this point, what he felt was a "wild" possibility occurred to him. Could talk be analyzed as being composed of methodical ways of doing things up to this level of detail, rather than just a string of propositions? Could talk be reduced to a set of methods and procedures through which given tasks were performed? Here the reporting of a hearing problem was a methodic solution to "avoiding giving your name without refusing to do so". After this discovery, Sacks started to apply the new methodology to the set of materials he had. His lectures from 1964 (published in 1992a) allow us to follow his meditations, such as "how to get someone's name without asking for it" (give yours), "how to avoid giving help without refusing to give it" (treat the circumstance as a joke), "how to get help for suicidalness without requesting it" (ask "how does this organization work"), etc.

It took about ten years for the key ideas of CA to become crystallized. Much of the early development took place through collaboration between Gail Jefferson, Emanuel Schegloff, and Harvey Sacks. A series of early CA papers culminated in the publication of a paper on turn-taking in conversation by Sacks, Schegloff, and Jefferson in 1974, before Sacks was tragically killed in a car accident in 1975. In the late 1970s, researchers began focusing on interactions in institutional settings. Atkinson's and Drew's *Order in Court* (1979) was the first published monograph which systematically adopted a comparative perspective through which meaning in institutional practice was spelled out through a series of detailed comparisons to linguistic practices in ordinary talk. Since then this comparative perspective has remained the bedrock of the study of institutional talk and action.

Another development was the adoption of a collection-based research practice, in which a prospective phenomenon occurring either in ordinary talk or in institutional practices is examined through a collection of cases that allow deciphering of the interactional regularities. A set of key essays that enabled the formation of a standardized research practice was published in 1984 under the title *Structures of Social Actions*. The title itself was informative, as it bore an intertextual link to Talcott Parsons' *The Structure of Social Action* (1937), undermining the idea of the existence of a "single structure of social action", and instead referring to the empirical polyphonous constitution of social actions at the level of intersubjective reality.

As soon as a standardized research practice was established, applied uses of the CA research procedure started to emerge. Though Lucy Suchman's *Plans and Situated Action: The Problem of Human-Machine Communication* (1987) was not immediately widely noticed among CA practicioners, it is a pioneering work in several respects. Not only did it open a new field addressing human-machine interaction, but it also paved the way for design-oriented applied studies that now serve as a resource for systems design in information technology (Arminen 2002b). Moreover, Suchman's study is also salient theoretically in that it illuminates human nature and cognition in action in contrast to fabricated, mechanical designs. In an increasingly technologically-saturated world, these are quintessential questions concerning the nature of human agency.

Finally, in the 1990s conversation analysis not only matured into a "normal science",[13] but also diversified. Studies of institutional interaction have clearly become one of the central research fields in CA. Drew and Heritage (1992a) collected some major articles amounting to a normative standard in the scrutiny of institutional talk at work. Moreover, even though conversation analysis started within the social sciences, it has also gained a position among linguistics. The emergence of so-called interactional linguistics, studying the intersection of grammar and interaction, has also sharpened knowledge about linguistic structures in interaction among CA practitioners. Grammar in interaction will remain a fruitful topic bringing together linguists and researchers of talk-in-interaction. Last but not least, another research program is composed of workplace studies analyzing interactional practices, in particular technologically-intensive work environments. These studies continue the design-oriented tradition inspired by Lucy Suchman's work. Developments related to institutional interaction will be discussed thoroughly in subsequent chapters of this book, though here it might be useful to include a chronology of some of the main steps in the development of CA:

1964–1972 – Harvey Sacks lectures at UCLA, California
– idea of conversation analysis develops in conjunction with teaching and in collaboration between Harvey Sacks, Emanuel Schegloff, and Gail Jefferson

1970s – study of ordinary conversation as a research field is established

1973–77 – A series of classical articles are published: "*Opening Up Closings*" by E.A. Schegloff and Harvey Sacks (1973); "*A Simplest Systematics for the Organization of Turn-taking for Conversation*" by H. Sacks, E. Schegloff and G. Jefferson (1974); "*The Preference for Self-Correction in the Organization of Repair in Conversation*" by E.A. Schegloff, Gail Jefferson and Harvey Sacks. (1977)
– talk as a systematically organized, autonomous system

1979 "*Order in Court*" by J.M. Atkinson and P. Drew
– systematic analysis of institutional interaction drawing on a comparison between ordinary and institutional interaction

1980s – study of institutional interaction becomes an established research field

1984 "*Structures of Social Action: Studies in Conversation Analysis*" (eds.) J.M. Atkinson and J. Heritage
– research practice based on collections of cases becomes established via a collection of key essays

1987 "*Plans and Situated Action: The Problem of Human-Machine Communication*" by L. Suchman
– the idea of design-oriented conversational studies emerges

1990s – conversation analysis becomes diversified
– establishment of interactional linguistics studying grammar in interaction
– establishment of work place studies that carry out design-oriented studies in technological environments

1992 "*Lectures on Conversation*" by H. Sacks
– Sacks' lectures from 1964–1972 published

1992 "*Talk at Work*" (eds.) P. Drew and J. Heritage
– a key collection of institutional interaction studies

1996 "*Interaction and Grammar*" (eds.) E. Ochs, E. Schegloff and S. Thompson
– a key collection in interactional linguistics

2000 "*Technology in Action*" by C. Heath and P.Luff
– a systematic presentation of the idea of workplace studies

Figure 1.3 Milestones of Conversation Analysis

1.4 Studies on Institutional Interaction

A defining feature of CA is that it does not study talk in general, but rather specifies in detail naturally occurring interactional practices to illuminate the generic properties of talk and social action through which the constitutive nature of social reality is maintained. When it comes to the analysis of talk-in-interaction in institutional settings, the task is to disclose and specify the verbal practices and interactional arrangements through which the institutional practice is talked into being. The analysis of everyday talk tacitly assumes a cultural competence through which the activity types of the participants' interactional moves are recognized so that the inspection of the organization of talk-in-interaction can be carried out (Pomerantz and Fehr 1997). As best, CA's reverse engineering program, utilizing the context-free building blocks of talk-in-interaction to reveal the hidden rationalities of context-sensitive interactional practices, may open new fields for critical reflection. However, in institutionally distinct settings, the recognizability of parties' actions may not be pre-given, as the details of actions may be informed by expert knowledge or organizational specifics not known to outsiders. In any context, CA may disclose the sequential course of talk, but setting specific details may enlighten parties' orientation to their talk and "intentional strategies can be ascribed to the participants with substantial confidence" (Heritage 1990/91, 328).

In their seminal paper on turn-taking, Sacks, Schegloff, and Jefferson (1974, 729) originally proposed a comparative approach focusing on speech-exchange systems such as ceremonies, meetings and therapy sessions, which differ from the organization of turn-taking for everyday settings. They note that mundane conversational exchanges are based on the allocation of one turn at a time, whereas formal institutional occasions are based, to various degrees, on the preallocation of turns. In addition, these types of speech-exchange systems can be compared in terms of their functions, of which they name two (ibid. 729). The number of potential next speakers is maximized through allocation of one turn at a time, as in conversation. By contrast, the preallocation of turns allows the order of the contributions to be planned, permitting equalization (or hierarchization) of the distribution of turns. They do not, however, claim that these were the only functions of speech-exchange systems: on the contrary, "the functions which any system is design-relevant for may then be explored, and the various systems compared with respect to their consequences on any given function of interest" (ibid. 730).

Additionally, they notice that turn size also tends to be indexical to the type of speech-exchange system. The multiplication of sentence units in a turn characterizes preallocational systems, whereas increasing internal complexity within single (or minimized) sentence units is the central mode for local allocational systems (ibid. 730).[14]

Finally, they suggest that not all speech-exchange systems are on an equal footing (ibid. 730). The turn-taking system for ordinary conversation is both genealogically and functionally the most primordial. Therefore, all other speech-exchange systems that differ from ordinary conversation are conventional achievements, whose transformations away from the more primitive forms are the very method of constructing these functionally and institutionally distinct spheres of action. These early observations paved the way for the establishment of a specific area of research on institutional interaction (Atkinson and Drew 1979; Atkinson 1984; Maynard 1984; Heath 1986; Drew and Heritage 1992a).

Studies on institutional interaction explore patterns of interaction in order to show how they contribute to the praxis in question. The principle of reverse engineering leads to a comparative approach: the task is to analyze how institutional speech events differ from generic forms of mundane interaction, and moreover, to identify what resources and techniques help in accomplishing the departures from generic forms of interaction.

The comparative approach in studies of institutional interaction amounts to a strict methodological policy. The analyst's task is to demonstrate the relevance and the procedural consequentiality of the institutional context (Schegloff 1991). What this means is to take the relevance-to-the-parties as the warrant for relevance-for-the-analyst in order to specify how the orientation to a context has become consequential for the participants' conduct. The aim is to show in detail the procedural connection between the context and what happens in talk through the comparison of "sequences-of-that-sort" in the institutional and mundane contexts in order to find characteristic features of sequences of talk in each context. The analyst must thus single out aspects of the context, which the interacting parties themselves make relevant for the activity in question in its ongoing achievement. Further, it is not sufficient to show that the context is relevant for the parties, but one must specify and describe the way in which the context is consequential to the parties' actions and conduct in a given context. However, in most instances of institutional interaction the specificity lies not in the interactional patterns as such, but in their uses through which institutional tasks are accomplished. The analyst's task is the reverse engineering of the members' techniques, methods and procedures through which the context is reflexively constituted in the first place. In this fashion, studies of institutional interaction also concentrate on *doing*, on finding out how institutional realities are obtained and continuously updated (further discussion will follow in the next chapter).

We can briefly illustrate this by returning to the extract from the New Year's Eve call.

(2) [SPC:NYE:1964:1–2:Sacks Transcript]

```
1   Caller:  I can't call any of my friends or anybody cause they're just
2            gonna say oh that's silly or that's stupid I guess
3   Desk:    Uh huh
4   Caller:  I guess what you really want is someone to say yes I really
5            understand why you want to commit suicide I do believe you
```

```
  6            I would too
  7   Desk:   Uh huh. Well tell me about it
  8   Caller: Bou I a funny thing I know it's emotionally immature
  9            except that doesn't help
 10   Desk:   Uh huh
 11   Caller: I've got a date coming in a half hour and I ((sob))
 12   Desk:   I see
 13   Caller: I can't go through with it I can't go through with the
 14            evening I can't ((sniffle))
 15   Desk:   Uh huh
 16   Caller: You talk. I don't want to talk
 17   Desk:   Uh huh
 18→ Caller: ((laugh sob)) It sounds like a real professional uh huh uh
 19            huh uh huh ((sniffle))
 20   Desk:   Well perhaps you want to tell me uh why you feel like
 21            committing suicide
```

Here the very first turn of the extract (albeit not the first turn of the call) updates and displays for the recipient an aspect of the caller's understanding of the context of the call. The caller herself identifies the context of the call by stating: "*I can't call any of my friends or anybody*", thereby portraying the recipient as not belonging to the group of people she considers being her friends. Note also the generalized form of categorization "*any of my friends or anybody*", where the addition "*or anybody*" generalizes the target population, and shows that what she means is not friends in any strict sense of the term, but all people who are "friend-like," i.e., all intimates (Jefferson 1990). Further, this addition "*or anybody*" is an extreme case formulation (Pomerantz 1986), intensifying her complaint. The caller states that among her intimates there is nobody to turn to.[15] Thus, here the caller contributes toward achieving the context of the call as she herself sees it, by proposing that the recipient is a person who listens to her problems for reasons other than close intimacy. Naturally, this also contributes toward making the issue "doctorable", as the caller claims that she can not find help or even seek help among her friends and confidants, and therefore she has to turn to somebody beyond that circle (though we may imagine that the caller, since she brings up the category friend, is trying to invoke an imaginary frame in which this somebody, i.e., the call-taker, can act as a genuine friend).

Moreover, not only does the caller contribute toward establishing the context but also the recipient's actions promote the contextualization of the call. Namely, the agent's way of producing only minimal responses, lacking both evaluative components and news receipt tokens, provides an understanding of the contextualization invited by the caller. The caller in the first place displays her sense that she is calling somebody other than her friends, and for good reasons, because she thinks thåt her friends would see her problems as "silly" and "stupid". In that fashion the caller herself invites a possible understanding that she herself is making a plea for "professional cautiousness". Subsequently, the agent maintains this professional cautiousness and avoids any strongly evaluative responses. The agent's neutrality and professional cautiousness are further enhanced both by the absence of news receipt tokens such as "oh dear", "oh shit" or "oh good", which would not only mark the reception of new information but also the valence of the news (Heritage 1984b; Maynard 1996; 2003). Here the recipient abstains from evaluative contours, thereby displaying his understanding of the caller's contextualization of the call as a plea for professional cautiousness. Therefore, the achieved contextualization of the call, which has located it beyond the realm of mundane talk between acquaintances, has been a collaborative achievement by both the caller and the called (cf. Zimmerman 1992; Drew and Sorjonen 1997, 92–94).

Conversation analytical studies of institutional realities show that the context of interaction is not an external constraint manipulating interactants behind their backs, but rather contexts are made real and alive by the participants' own orientations to them. Here the fact that the call was made to a suicide prevention agency is not an external fact but an oriented-to feature talked into being by the parties of the interaction. This is not to say that there would not exist factual distributions of roles and power, but that these resources are made alive and consequential for the parties mainly through talk (Wilson 1991; Hutchby 1996a). Moreover, CA does not offer a consensualist reading of interaction (e.g., Fairclough 1989, 11–12; 1992, 17–20). CA's emphasis on the collaborative nature of conversation only means that a shared intersubjective orientation is a precondition for any interaction, be it conflictual or harmonious. For example, we noted in the call to the suicide hotline that there is some sort of misalignment between the caller and the agent (about which the caller made a complaint). But here it would also be too straightforward to disregard the actual interaction, and propose, for example, that a power struggle between the client and the professional is the cause of the misalignment. In this example, the caller herself invited a possible understanding that she was pleading for professional cautiousness (although it may well be that the original source of misalignment between the caller and the agent is exactly this). Nevertheless, the misalignment does not straightforwardly derive from the factual roles, but rather from the participants' understandings of their roles, as well as from their understandings of their understandings, as we have seen. Studies of institutional talk analyze precisely this: the ways in which talk-in-interaction in all its complexities and details is consequential for the parties in, and for, their attempt to reach their goals, focusing on institutional tasks in institutionally-provided settings.

This book takes seriously the assumption that institutional interaction always takes place at the crossroads of two institutions[16] (Peräkylä 1997a). The first of these is simply talk-in-interaction, a constitutive set of practices enabling all forms of institutional and noninstitutional interaction. However, we can also identify institutions, other than talk-in-interaction, which are somehow distinct from everyday life, such as medicine, law, bureaucracies, educational, therapeutic and military institutions, etc.[17] Furthermore, we tend to think that in these settings talk is organized to some degree differently than it is in ordinary, everyday, mundane talk-in-interaction. We can observe that objects formed in and for speech in courtrooms, classrooms, and therapeutic sessions are to a certain degree separate and different from those of ordinary conversation. To identify the difference and to encrypt the members' context-sensitive meaning-making and decoding of speech activities, the analyst must draw on the relevancies of both institutions.

In terms of their differences from mundane interaction, institutional interactions can be characterized as formal or informal. Formal institutional interactions are constitutively different from everyday talk so that the institutional event is created via the parties' orientations to pattern their interaction in a manner specific to the event, and to that event only. This allows us to study the ways in which the formal pattern of interaction is maintained and departures sanctioned. Informal institutional interactions may also differ from the regulative patterns of ordinary conversation, but the parties are allowed to depart from the institutional interactional format and resort to ordinary conversational forms. These quasiformal institutional interactions immediately pose a question about the procedural consequentiality of the context, i.e., the analyst's ability to determine how the context has become relevant for the parties in designing their talk in and for that context.

This distinction between formal and informal institutional interactions is undermined by the fact that the institution of talk-in-interaction is an enabling condition for both. That is, the formality of formal institutional interactions is only one aspect of these interactions, and a great spectrum of the generic assets of talk-in-interaction are also used. This observation broadens the scope of inquiry so that both in formal and informal institutional interactions the analyst explicates the ways in which the resources of talk-in-interaction are mobilized for the service of the institutional practice, so the analysis is not limited to a survey of institutional discourse in terms of potential differences from ordinary conversation. To give an example, Maynard (1989a; 1991b; 1992) has analyzed the way clinicians use perspective-display series to co-implicate the recipient's view. As Maynard has shown, the device itself is also prevalent in ordinary conversations but the focus of analysis is to demonstrate and respecify the characteristic use of such a device in an institutional environment.

1.5 Fields of Application

As I pointed out above, Sacks, Schegloff, and Jefferson's article on turn-taking (1974) also sparked comparative studies of different systems of turn-taking. Early on the studies aimed at specifying the very format through which the institutional practice is talked into being. Later studies on institutional interaction have the ways in which factors, such as turn-design, lexical choices, sequence organization etc., contribute to various institutional practices (ten Have 1999, 168).

In particular, much research has focused on medical/therapeutic and media interactions. Most studies of medical interaction have concentrated on doctor-patient interactions (e.g., Heath 1986, Maynard 1991a, Ruusuvuori 2000; Haakana 1999). These studies have amounted to a systematic description of a set of interactional practices constituting medical/therapeutic work in practice. As such, they contribute both to sociological disputes concerning the role of "power" in medical interaction and also to the practical understanding of medical work – detailing, complementing and correcting practicioners' theories of the interactional substratum of their work (Peräkylä and Vehviläinen 2003). In addition to doctor-patient interaction, recent studies have also scrutinized various other types of medical interactions, such as medical peer reviews (Boyd 1998), and multi-professional team work (Arminen and Perälä 2002). As with medical interactions, the focus in media studies has mainly been on the interviewer-interviewee relationship. Media interactions vary from more formal political interviews (Heritage and Greatbatch 1991; Clayman and Heritage 2002a) to more informal and openly confrontational media genres (Hutchby 1996b). Much of this work has concentrated on how journalists manage their professional roles in interaction with the interviewee(s) (Clayman 1992). Recently, historical changes in media interactions have also been studied (Clayman and Heritage 2002b).

Studies of institutional interaction have also examined the increasing role of technology in institutional settings. One of the earliest studies recognizing the role of technology was a longitudinal study of emergency dispatch centers (Whalen et al. 1988; Zimmerman 1992; Wakin and Zimmerman 1999). During the course of this study, computers and automation were introduced to operations. Instead of tiny dispatch operations based on passing paper notes – the sheriff over here, the local police department over there, the state police there – public safety answering points were established. The larger the dispatch centers became and the more the call volume increased, the more technology was introduced to manage the load, and to automate processes to increase efficiency. Computer-aided dispatch systems were introduced. For a call to the emergency centre to become official, it had to be documented, and this documentation was digitalized. The introduction of technology occurred simultaneously with and was tied to a shift in the organization of work. In large centers, a division of labor emerged between call-takers and radio-dispatchers. The people who took the calls were not the ones who worked the radios and decided whom to send and how to coordinate the response. The digitalization of documents also created problems. Initially, the paper forms were just transferred to computer screens. Instead of writing a note about the incident, the address, phone number, etc. and handing it to someone, the information was entered into a computer and transmitted electronically. The computer-based system amounted to a different organization of work than the paper-based. Furthermore, the computer interface itself became critical for managing the work and caller interaction. Some of the early digitalized documentation and information-sharing systems involved rigid features which made smooth co-operation with callers difficult (Frankel 1989; Whalen 1995; Whalen

1999; Whalen and Vinkhuyesen 2000). Significantly, similar observations have been made about the introduction of computers to the work of medical doctors (Heath and Luff 2000). Subsequently, workplace studies addressing the role of technology and the interactional accomplishment of work tasks have grown into a field of their own (Luff et al. 2000; Heath and Luff 2000; Arminen 2001a).

Survey interview interaction is another new area for CA research, and might have important implications for social scientific methodology (Houtkoop-Steenstra 2000; Maynard et al. 2002; ten Have 1999, 170–180; Hutchby and Wooffitt 1998, 173–178). Studies of survey interview interaction focus on the dilemma between standardization and local interactional requirements. This dilemma involves many troublesome facets. For example, the interviewee may display an inability to understand a question as phrased in the survey, thereby inviting the interviewer to depart from the standardized phrasing of the question. Or, the interviewee may depart from the scripted answering schemes and produce answers addressing new aspects, or provide more or less elaboration than the standardized options allow. In such cases, the interviewer may need to infer how to code the answers, or to negotiate with the interviewee. Further dilemmas might arise if an interviewee resists answering questions. Therefore, analyzing the interactional accomplishment of survey interviews will be a potentially relevant methodological field, and may be used to develop survey instruments. Hutchby and Wooffitt (1998, 178–197) also address the interactional nature of semistructured or unstructured interviews.

A third new area for CA is the communication problems of "deficient" speakers, such as aphasics (Klippi 1996; Laakso 1997; Goodwin et al. 2002; ten Have 1999, 189–192; Hutchby and Wooffitt 1998, 252–257). Since CA's general aim is to describe speakers' competencies, it may also help to define more exactly the types of communication problems that deficiencies create in actual communication. In conversations involving impaired speakers, verbal interaction is somehow hampered or obstructed. A disabled speaker confronts the problem of how to contribute to a conversation with limited resources. Consequently, different conversational and communicative practices evolve from "ordinary everyday conversation". In these cases, contextual features, and perhaps also non-verbal behavior, become increasingly significant. Enhanced understanding of such communication problems may open new therapeutic ways to help the client.

CA applications also extend to various other disciplines. One such new field is "discursive psychology", a version of discourse analysis (Edwards and Potter 1992; 2001; Hutchby and Wooffitt 1998, 202–228). This field addresses traditional cognitive and epistemological concerns but focuses on their interactional basis, questioning how the factuality of statements is interactionally designed or what techniques speakers use to preempt a recipient's scepticism.

Another new cross-section has developed between linguistics and CA (Ochs et al. 1996; Ford et al. 2002). A social scientist may find funny the suggestion that CA and linguistics intersect, since the whole CA enterprise may look rather linguistic. But as I have been trying to demonstrate, CA's perspective and set of methods may be applied in order to discern various dimensions of interaction, from social actions to syntax and prosody, and back. Studies focusing on linguistic questions analyze the intersection of grammar and interaction (Ochs et al. 1996; Tanaka 1999). It may address the ways in which grammar contributes to the organization of social interaction, and also the ways in which social interaction organizes grammar. We may think of it both ways: forms of social interaction have gained their grammatical representations, while grammar has also been shaped by interaction. Indeed, grammar is an inherent aspect of the organization of interaction, its mode. Finally, phonetics is also open to CA treatment. Prosody contextualizes and gives interpretative cues for identifying interactional moves, whereas the sequential order contextualizes prosody and generates tasks for parties to design the prosodic quality of their turn as being appropriate for the sequential position to which they are orienting (Selting and Couper-Kuhlen 2001).

1.6 Divisions

In contrast to many social scientific schools of thought, CA is a unified enterprise; its uniformity begins with its methodology and working principles. In CA, the objects of research are the instances of actual behavior that can be observed and recognized intersubjectively in contrast to ideal types, generalizations, and averages. The latter demand interpretative work that makes the relationship between the finding and the investigated state of affairs indeterminate. Consequently, most social scientific findings do not cumulate; they are fuzzy, thereby preventing elaboration of their exact felicity conditions (Heritage 1984a, 231–236). The working principles of CA are bound to its research object. CA analysis proceeds case-by-case and establishes observable patterns inductively, and the ways of doing analyses have lead to the establishment of an institutional form of cooperation, so-called "data sessions" (ten Have 1999, 102–104, 123–125). In a data session, a group of CA workers examine a stretch of material in an unmotivated way so that they might just notice something interesting. Then a line of focus is chosen on the basis of set of observations, and the major part of the work consists of the collaborative elaboration of the pattern noticed. Data sessions are an arena for educating prospective researchers, but are also brainstorming sessions for all. In this way, the uniformity of CA is maintained through its working style.

CA might at first seem especially distinctive and uniform, for very few accounts have emphasized its diversity. Nevertheless, for analytic purposes it is useful to stress the multidimensionality of CA's research object. As we already noticed, CA studies may focus on various layers of the architecture of intersubjectivity. More subtly, CA workers have individual styles and distinct methodological solutions. Of the recent overviews, ten Have's (1999) merits a distinction for its openness to methodological debates. Points of methodological bifurcation are worth considering more fully, as they single out fields needing further development, and thereby potentially make available new directions for research. Of the potentially disputable issues, CA's relation to ethnography and quantification are critical.

Generally, CA's findings are indifferent to ethnographic data. CA data exploration reconstitutes and specifies participants' ongoing orientation to interaction, thereby demonstrating their endogenous construction of the context. Through detailed inspection, the analyst reconstructs the sense of an ongoing social action, and no reference to external data sources is needed. For instance, in the introduction I was able to point out what was going on between E and M without any reference to ethnographic background knowledge. From an ethnomethodological point of view, the basis of social order is not hidden under the observable surface of the parties' conduct, but this very conduct, in its intersubjective availability, forms the methodical basis for parties to maintain and manage the understandability and orderliness of their actions. However, analysis of a sequential course of action presupposes the analyst's ability to recognize the activity types of the parties' turns of talk. As long as the analyst is a competent member of the culture studied, the ability to recognize social actions in interaction does not pose any practical problem, although we may dispute the role of commonsense knowledge in CA in analytic terms (Hutchby and Wooffitt 1998, 112–113). A lack of ethnographic understanding may turn into a hindrance if the analyst studies foreign cultures, isolated subcultures, or institutionally distinct settings. If the recognizability of participants' actions is not pregiven by shared cultural knowledge, ethnographic background knowledge may become indispensable. However, any ethnographic knowledge is always only a starting point for the discernment of parties' methodical design of their social actions. CA's aim is not to go beyond parties' actions to recategorize them, but to reverse engineer the parties' own machinery for doing social actions (ten Have 1999, 53–60).

The general line of argument as regards quantification proceeds in a parallel way. CA aims to establish a unique adequacy for its findings so that they reveal parties' orientation and methodical course of action in every singular instance. Consequently, coding and quantification are problematic since they may lead the analyst away from a sufficiently close analysis of the data (Hutchby and Wooffitt 1998, 115–119). However, there are some notable exceptions (ten Have 1999, 144–148). For instance, research may focus on a compound unit composed of several identifiable elements, the relationships of which may be too complex to be described comprehensively, but the aggregate level outcome of which may be an interesting phenomenon in its own right. Interestingly, CA's basic unit of analysis, a turn of talk, behaves much this way. A conversational interaction depends on the participants' ability to recognize the completion of a turn so that turn-taking can take place and the conversation proceed in an orchestrated manner. Ford and Thompson (1996) distinguish between syntactic, intonational, and pragmatic elements of talk, and study the interrelationship of these three elements statistically. They conclude that syntax alone does not project the end of a turn, but does when linked with intonation and pragmatics. Statistical analysis can improve our understanding of even the basic units of talk. However, Ford and Thompson worked case-by-case to achieve intersubjectively-valid coding, and used individual examples to demonstrate their findings. Finally, macroscopic entities can also be complex compound phenomena, whose individual contingencies may fall outside the interest of analysis. For example, a doctor's design of diagnosis delivery is related to several factors, such as the location of diagnosis in the encounter, the opacity of diagnostic information, the certainty of the diagnosis, and its controversiality (Peräkylä 1998). Together these factors amount to too many contingencies to be comprehensively described, but nevertheless it is possible to describe regular patterns in doctors' actions through individual case demonstrations and their statistical aggregation.

1.7 CA and Other Approaches

The question of CA's relationship to other approaches can easily be dealt with in a trivial way. For a trivial answer, you can just read what methodology books like this claim, summarize these claims, and define what each approach claims to be, that is, how they are presented for imagined readers. In this assessment, methodology books are given the role of informants, a role similar to natives in classical anthropological field stories. Quite another matter would be to investigate the sets of practices CA analysts and others use in the production of knowledge. Simply relying on informants' views treats their ability to give informed views as non-remarkable and uninteresting. CA largely evolved out of dissatisfaction with mundane research, which too readily accepted the informants' views as the basis of "scientific knowledge". For this reason, Sacks himself was very cautious to speak about other scientific approaches, as we can see in his response to a student's question about the relationship between his work and sociology:

"If you really want me to talk about what sociology ought to be about, or what relation any of these things has to what I do, I wouldn't want to do it in class, because that's like taking a position. These can't be handled seriously unless one takes them as the kind of issues they are; like take a line out of a book and try to see how that fellow came to write that." (Sacks 1992a, 31; see also Silverman 1998, 43–73)

Originally, Sacks's idea of the science of social life was that that it would reconstruct and analyze the practices that permit members of society to see and grasp things the way they do. The essential idea was to move beyond relying on what-everybody-knows. Instead the most basic details of interaction that allow parties to establish the ideas they have were to be scrutinized (Sacks 1992b, 26; Silverman 1998, 53–56). The aim was to develop an approach which can handle the actual details of actions, in order to be able to reverse engineer what this-and-that is made up of in society (Sacks 1992a, 27). The reproducibility of findings was the key for the scientific nature of the enterprise. Ideally, the reader would have as much information as the author so that the analysis could be reproduced (Sacks 1992a, 27; Silverman 1998, 53–56). In fact, Sacks states that his research is about conversations only in an incidental way, that conversation is something that one can get actual instances of on tape. Through the reproducibility of actual details of actual events the science of social life became possible (Sacks 1992b, 26).

In as much as Sacks strived for a strict, disciplined empirical science, his enterprise also traded on the analyst's intuition. The analysis of what this-and-that is made up of relies on the researcher's ability to recognize this-and-that to proceed toward its analysis.[18] Seen through Sacks' lenses, CA is a thoroughly ethnographic enterprise. For Sacks, ethnography was the only work worth criticism. Like ethnographers, Sacks was interested in what this-and-that is composed of, but through the reproducibility of analysis Sacks aimed at developing the science of social life further. Quintessentially, Sacks' work and the CA it spawned relies on the analyst's ability to "recognize x", and thus to proceed further toward its analysis. As already discussed, in institutional contexts in particular, the sensitivity and validity of the analysis may depend on the analyst's access to the particulars of context that may also be revealed through ethnography.

CA's relationship with quantitative (survey) analysis is different. I believe that the matter is not so much a question of a difference in methods (quantitative/qualitative) as some have suggested, but in the topic of research. While CA studies what this-and-that is composed of, quantitative (survey) analysis is about how this-and-that is distributed among the target population. In this way, CA and quantitative analysis do not mainly contradict each other; they simply address different orders of things. To borrow Garfinkel's phrase, they are asymmetrically alternate (Garfinkel 2002). In most cases, these types of studies are simply alien to each other.[19] It would not make sense to try to distributionalize elementary interactional practices, and ask, for instance, how adjacency pairs or questions are distributed in the population. However, on occasion distributional analysis can be added to the analysis of interactional practices. Many stylistic features are unevenly distributed among populations. The incidence of some patterns of speech can be quite narrow: age, gender, generation or situation specific. In these cases, variationist and interaction analysis can complement each other. In institutional contexts the incidence of interactional practices may vary and be of particular interest. It is also possible to combine the analysis of interactional patterns and the analysis of outcome interactions (see Heritage 1999; Heritage and Stivers 1999; Heritage et al. 2001). Also, the study of historical or cultural distribution of speech patterns is among the possibilities of combinatory studies (Clayman and Heritage 2002b). These issues I will return to in the final chapter.

Other kinds of approaches to interactional data offer a different set of questions. Quite clearly, the basic response of CA researchers is the methodological canon of procedural relevance (Schegloff 1991). The validation or procedural relevance for participants, as it could be phrased, is a sensible methodological policy which makes disciplined analysis possible, as I will show in next chapter. However, the principle of procedural relevance can be applied in different fashions. Moreover, it always trades on the analyst's competence in recognizing the relevance of actions. In this way the empirical validity of analysis is far from being settled for good. In any case, it is important to build ostensive proof from the details of the action analyzed, thereby preserving the rigorousness of the science of social life. Another matter is that different disciplines may also ask different questions, some of which may be more fruitful than others. Sellen and Harper (2001) point out that a massive number of laboratory studies have been done on reading on a screen versus on a paper. Most of these studies focused on ease or speed of reading, but did not pay any attention to how or why people read texts. Even if these studies were highly accurate in themselves, they do not address the salient properties of the alternative media, and as such are of only limited use for the design of technologies. Instead, analysis of the properties of reading as part of social practices opens a whole new array of issues, not necessarily contradicting earlier studies, but providing a view of the participants' set of alternative relevancies which thus offer completely different layers of findings.

1.8 Conclusion

Conversation Analysis is still a young enterprise, promising to develop a detailed and firm analysis of the intersubjective meanings of social actions. CA's internal complexity, however, is one of several obstacles which may hinder the fulfillment of its promise. Even though there are currently a number of useful introductions to CA which make the enterprise accessible to students and social scientists, these works also demonstrate what a tremendous effort is needed to learn the craft of CA. It is not easy to tackle seemingly trivial pieces of interaction and turn them into findings about the hidden rationalities and complexities of the procedural forms of human behavior that may revolutionize a reader's understanding of mundane matters. Harvey Sacks was very good at this. As a pioneer, Sacks also enjoyed a considerable degree of intellectual freedom. Currently, CA has developed into a tight discipline with its own methodological canons. Some amount of openness to CA's internal heterogeneity might help it to fulfill its promises to the human sciences, to both linguistics and the social sciences.

In terms of institutional interaction, CA's reverse engineering program aims at identifying the unique "fingerprint" of each institutional practice. Notably, this fingerprint is not the outcome of analysis but is its starting point, with the help of which the accomplishment of specific institutional tasks, identities, and inferential procedures are made available for research. Therefore, the analysis of institutional interaction ultimately aims at elaborating issues, such as the strategic aspects of interaction, the achievement of collaboration, or procedures whereby participants' differing perspectives are brought into alignment. In this respect, studies on institutional interaction are very close to Sacks' original idea to study members' methodical ways of accomplishing social tasks in interaction.

Recently, CA has also diversified internally. In terms of institutional interaction, it has developed more towards applied usages. Studies of technologically-mediated interactions are typical in this respect: these studies focus on the crossroads of the design assumptions of the machine and the user's assumptions. They may be informed by the practical concerns of either clarifying and solving problems in the user-machine interface, or explicating the properties of agent-client interaction for assessing and developing information systems vis-à-vis the participants' practical, situated concerns (Hutchby 2001; Hutchby and Wooffitt 1998, 245–252). Also more generally, studies of institutional interaction have become more sensitive of practicioners' knowledge. One potential way to address this question is to take into account the practicioners' "stocks of interactional knowledge" and interaction ideologies (Peräkylä and Vehviläinen 2003). Consequently, CA studies addressing the practicioners' knowledge also become involved in the field they study. They may try to falsify or correct assumptions that are part of professionals' understanding; or elaborate the picture of practices as seen by practicioners. CA may also add new dimensions to the understanding of practices described by practicioners' theory, or formulate new perspectives on practices that abstract descriptions have missed (Peräkylä and Vehviläinen 2003). These kinds of enterprises make CA a practical and relevant discipline, no longer merely a narrow field of scholarship.

Further Reading

– Currently there are two book-length introductions to CA (Hutchby and Wooffitt 1998; ten Have 1999). Ten Have's book is more academic, Hutchby and Wooffit are more oriented toward the analytic procedures as such. Both books are useful, and complement each other well.
- ten Have's web page also has a great deal of information on the field, including bibliographies.
http://www2.fmg.uva.nl/emca/
– Charles Antaki's web page has a guided introduction to CA.
http://www-staff.lboro.ac.uk/~ssca1/sitemenu.htm
– For background on CA, I would suggest Heritage (1984a), which introduces CA's ethnomethodological underpinnings. Silverman (1998) provides a succinct explication of some of Harvey Sacks' key ideas.
– Harvey Sacks' lectures (1992a and b) are in two volumes with almost 1400 pages, so they may be a bit too much for an introduction, but Sacks' science of social life will provide food for thought for almost everybody.
– Schegloff's home page is also worth visiting. Schegloff has generously posted many of his publications and voice samples of his materials are also downloadable.
http://www.sscnet.ucla.edu/soc/faculty/schegloff/
– For analyzing sequential order (including visual orientation), I would start with Charles Goodwin's work, some of which is downloadable.
http://www.sscnet.ucla.edu/clic/cgoodwin/
– For exercises, see
http://www.uta.fi/laitokset/sosio/project/ivty/english/sivut/exercises.html

Notes

1   I do not want to imply that there could not be complications to this basic procedure. An answer may not be given to a question, but that does not prove that a question would not have been posed. CA is strictly empirical, but not empiricist, in its orientation. For example, you can use deviant case analysis, discussed in Chapter 3, to deal with complications.

2   It is worth emphasizing that study of turn-design and turn-relations belong together in CA. One cannot be studied without the other.

3 Note that CA is neutral in terms of ontological presuppositions (cf, Woolgar and Pawluch 1985). It studies the maintenance of social and institutional *realities*. It does not claim that society and institutions could be reduced to "talk-in-interaction" even if realities are maintained by verbal and physical interaction.

4   A thorough analysis would demand access to the audio tape, which I do not have. According to Jefferson, who edited Sacks' lectures, the tape is missing (Sacks 1992b: 376, note 1). Here only the features available in the transcript are demonstrated. The analysis is always indexical to its constitutive practices (what kind of material is collected, how it is edited, etc.). This illustration is based on the transcript only, and, for instance, no attention is paid to potential variation in the "Uh huh" tokens (see Sacks 1992b: 376–415; Schegloff 1982; Jefferson 1984d; Gardner 1997). But I do not want to give a too dogmatic version of CA, also technically less than perfect materials should be used if the phenomena recorded are worthy.

5   Note that interaction is a real-time achievement. The whole sequence is not available for the interactants at any moment prior to its realization. Therefore, each turn of talk can only orient to what has already been said at that point, or to what the speaker can expect will be said, again on the basis of what already has been said.

6   I do not claim that my analysis of this sequence would be the only possible. Actually, this piece of data is inferentially rich, and seems to invite a slightly different interpretation from almost everybody. For instance, Membership Categorization Device (MCD) analysis would illuminate slightly different aspects of the sequence (see Jayyusi 1984). From a falsificationist point of view, no scientific statement is ever absolutely true. It may have just passed the test of having not been falsified yet. From a verificationist point of view, only those scientific statements that have been proven true can be accepted. However, satisfactory verification would be independent of any theory, which is notably difficult to achieve. If one accepts the falsificationist point of view, then imperfect scientific statements are acceptable as long as they have not been shown to be wrong. Actually, falsificationism holds a view that science advances by unjustified, exaggerated guesses followed by unstinting criticism (see Popper 1934/1977).

7   Again, it is also of pedagogical relevance to state how important the details of interaction are, and respectively, the accuracy of transcription. If there are details in an interaction that have not been transcribed, our sense of the interaction becomes respectively transposed. Here, for instance, we cannot be sure how exact this transcript is. If there had been pauses throughout the earlier course of interaction, this would considerably change our understanding of the exchange. If there have not been any pauses (as this transcript suggests), then the interaction seems to have proceeded "smoothly" until the caller starts making requests and complaints. Sacks (1992b: 387–389) makes use of this excerpt to show how the "undifferentiated" use of responses, like "uh huh", may give a speaker a reason to believe that she is not listened to very carefully.

8   The all-encompassing sequential implicativeness of interaction poses serious problems for interview studies. The interviewer may, for instance, attempt to give as open a floor as

30   *Institutional Interaction*

possible to the interviewee. The interviewer's attempt not to influence the interviewee is, however, itself consequential for the interviewee's responses. Inescapably, interview studies are locally accomplished achievements whose results are contingent and tied to their practical arrangements (for problems in experimental studies, see Schegloff 1991: 54–56).

9   A question invites an answer; a greeting invites a greeting, etc. This is the basic idea of the adjacency and adjacency pairs, like greetings (See Schegloff and Sacks 1973).

10 However, it is crucial to bear mind that this does not make the knowledge of the context of interaction useless for the analyst. The external knowledge is only to be used in a controlled way. Maynard (2003.) calls this position as a limited affinity between knowledges (to be discussed further in the next chapter).

11 This figure is partly based on Sanna Vehviläinen's lecture slides in a course we both taught in the early 1990s. I am grateful for permission to use her formulations.

12 Though traditional ethnomethodologists have sometimes been critical towards this idea (Hester and Francis 2001). Traditional ethnomethodologists want to study situated properties of action without any reference to contextual issues.

13 The critiques of the "normalization" of CA include, among others, Lynch (1993).

14 The observations concerning the relationship between the turn-allocational system and turn-size are probably open to empirical challenges. (As far as I know, not much work has been done in this area.) For example, preallocational systems can also be used to minimize the lengths of turns. An interviewer may ask panelists to answer straightforwardly to yes-or-no questions, and rounds of brief turns may be preallocated.

15 It is, though, noticeable that the utterance, "I can't call any of my friends (or anybody)", is not pragmatically completed even if it is a syntactically completed unit. This utterance works here as a preliminary to the telling of the actual issue (here, the problem). In ordinary conversations these preliminaries are routinely, although not always, responded to with acknowledgment tokens, such as "yeah", "mm hm", "uh huh" (Schegloff 1980). Again the analysis would benefit from the tape and a more detailed transcription.

16 This is a deliberate abstraction. I do not disagree with a reviewer who wrote that "institutions in fact involve a range of different activity types which seem to be more general than the institution in which they happen to be embedded, while still being different from the general procedures of talk-in-interaction. I have in mind activities like having a meeting, doing a diagnostic interview (whether done by a doctor or a car mechanic), inviting a perspective, telling bad news, etc." Indeed, that is the case.

17 Of course, participation in these institutions may also be part of everyday life, but a distinct part, so that such participation is realized through a set of specialized roles, a particular register of speech and constrained conduct. Normal, everyday life behaviour may be sanctionable in these institutions.

18 A conventional CA response would suggest that the researcher trades only on participants' validation, as the researcher only has to recognize the understanding of action the parties themselves originally (and for themselves primarily) have already displayed. For a particularly misleading notion, Seale (1999) discusses "self-validation of findings" as if the analyst's role could be completely bracketed. Note that this response still hangs on "recognizing x". This problem is particularly pertinent in institutional contexts, where parties may trade on special competences (see Chapter 2).

19 As already discussed, I do not want to imply that CA and survey studies could not benefit from each other. CA studies may analyze survey interaction. Survey studies and statistical analysis may shed light on distributions of interactional and related phenomena.

Chapter 2

Institutional Interaction

Society never exists in general, so that it would be a condition for particular phenomena, since interaction in general does not exist but only its particular forms. They are nor a cause or a consequence of the society, but they are the society themselves. Only the undifferentiated richness and abundance of each and every moment has given the general concept of society its appearance as an independent historical fact. Perhaps this presupposing of a bald abstraction is the grounds for fuzziness and uncertainty of this concept and general sociology this far – just as the concept of life did not allow any progress by looking at immediate reality as a unitary phenomenon. Only after studying specific processes within organisms, the sum of which life emerges, and only after finding out that life consists of interactions between organs and cells, the science of life did gain a firm footing.

(Simmel, 1908)

The study of institutional interaction poses specific challenges for conversation analysis, since analysis of institutional interaction differs from the analysis of interaction itself. In order to illuminate the institution's role in and for interaction in a given setting, the analyst needs to show the ways in which the context functions in a particular aspect or segment of an interaction, i.e. we need to examine the context's procedural relevance. In terms of methodology, this focus on procedural relevance provides criteria and a toolkit to avoid arbitrarily invoking a countless number of extrinsic, potential aspects of context. However, in order for the analyst to use procedural consequentiality as an analytical criterion, s/he must have sufficient knowledge of the context in question. Put simply, in order to analyze the endogenous construction of context, CA necessarily draws on a preliminary understanding of that context, just as in analyzing ordinary talk we draw on our everyday competence to recognize "what is going on". Normally, we routinely proceed from recognizing the activity type of talk to analytically explicating it, from "what is said" to "how it is said". In analyzing foreign cultures, isolated subcultures, or institutionally distinct settings, however, the analyst may not necessarily have sufficient cultural knowledge to recognize what the activities stand for to the parties themselves. In institutional settings an agent may orient to expert knowledge or organizational procedures taken for granted in the practice in question but not known to outsiders. If the analyst is unable to trace the relevant features the parties are orienting to in the setting, the analysis may remain superficial with regard to the institutional practice even if the sequential course of interaction could be accounted for. This reconstruction of the methodology for the study on institutional interaction also offers a potential point of contact between CA and other social scientific endeavours.

2.1 The Procedural Relevance of Institutional Context

The study of institutional interaction provides an arena in which the "larger" social order and situated interaction intersect. Consequently, the study of institutional interaction poses specific methodological questions insofar as the aim is to study talk and action in institutions as activities whose character derive from the ways parties orient to the institutional nature of their business. Briefly put, institutional interaction is a particular type of social interaction in which the participants (A and B) orient to an institutional context (C), such as medical, juridical or educational, in and for accomplishing their distinctive institutional actions (see Figure 2.1).

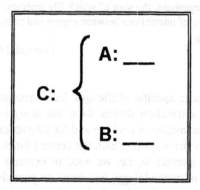

Figure 2.1 ABC for the Study of Institutional Interaction

The conversation analytical research enterprise particularly focuses on the situated process of parties' interaction. If the interacting parties (A and B) display an orientation to a context (C), they maintain and manage a particular meaning for the action achieved through their co-ordinated activities. In this way, CA adopts a strictly empirical focus that does not a priori speculate about the institutional meaning of action, but aims at characterizing it through a detailed examination of naturally-occurring activities. However, if the aim is to characterize the *institutionality*[1] of institutional interaction as opposed to analyzing talk-in-interaction per se, the researcher faces additional difficulties.

The first problem is the potential infinite richness of the context. For one, interactants may ascribe a wide array of attributes to each other, such as gender, ethnicity, age, and social status. Second, the institutional context itself is located in a society and composed of a number of potentially relevant aspects including the organizational mode, expert systems and beliefs. Therefore, the analyst does not face a crystal-clear image, such as Figure 2.1, according to which the analyst could invoke the context for the explanation of behavior. Instead the analyst encounters a murky reality, in which actors' behavior may be shaped by an infinite number of contextual features. The relationship between the observable action and the context is unclear, i.e. institutional reality consists of multiple layers of potentially relevant variables – such as gender, age, ethnicity, social status, institutional agenda, expert knowledge, the form of the organization.[2] All of these contribute to the context and power relationships between parties (see Figure 2.2).

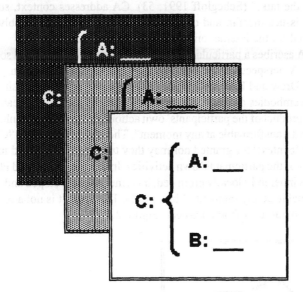

Figure 2.2 Infinitude of Institutional Contexts

CA has promoted a perhaps paradoxical solution to the problem of infinite contexts: it suspends the use of the context as an immediate explanatory resource. CA researchers are overtly critical of the so-called "bucket" theory of context, according to which context is treated as a pre-given framework which can be used to explain parties' actions (why such-and-such is done then) without scrutinizing the endogenous dynamics of interaction (Drew and Heritage 1992b, 19). Therefore, the focus is redirected from the relationship between the context and the interaction to the observable properties of the interaction itself. Technically, the notion of the "procedural relevance of the context" is the key for understanding the way CA deals with the relationship between interaction and the institution (Schegloff 1991; 1997;

1999). Through this methodology, CA becomes an evidence-based approach in which the participants' demonstrable orientations to the context or social structure form the bedrock of the analysis (and not the analyst's assumptions). The aim of the analysis is to show how the context or social structure "enters into the production and interpretation of determinate facets of conduct, and is thereby confirmed, reproduced, modulated, neutralized or incrementally transformed in that actual conduct to which it must finally be referred" (Schegloff 1991, 51). Further, the analysis is specified in light of this necessity to study the procedural consequentiality of context. The issue is not just to find and define the relevance of the structure, but to discuss and analyze the procedural "connection between the context so formulated and what actually happens in the talk." (Schegloff 1991, 53). CA addresses context, social structure and related issues insofar, and only insofar, as they are demonstrably relevant and consequential for the interaction in the context in question.

In all, CA ascribes a particular sense to the notions of context and social structure. From the CA perspective, the context is an achievement between participants in interaction. Drew and Heritage (1992b, 19) express this view very sharply: "the CA perspective embodies a dynamic approach in which 'context' is treated as both the project and product of the participants' own actions and therefore as inherently locally produced and transformable at any moment". They further state that "CA researchers cannot take 'context' for granted nor may they treat it as determined in advance and independent of the participants' own activities. Instead, 'context' and identity have to be treated as inherently locally produced, incrementally developed and, by extension, as transformable at any moment" (ibid. p. 21). The context is not a precondition for an interaction but its embodied aspect (Figure 2.3).

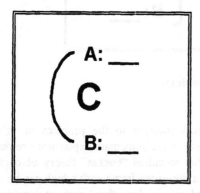

Figure 2.3 Interactional Achievement of Context

CA solves the problem of the infinitude of context by focusing on the demonstrably relevant and consequential aspects of context. For instance, if a participant's gender does not play a procedurally consequential role for the encounter analyzed, then it is considered irrelevant (though gender might not be irrelevant for the whole institution). CA is thus based on an analytic abstraction that restricts the scope of its inquiry to the local, situated sense of an activity. Such restrictions constitute a methodological policy enabling rigorous, cumulative findings. The findings thus gained have a demonstrable validity in terms of the participants' situated orientations and meaning making. Of course, if we now question the relationship between this local, situated, actual sense of the context, and a hypothetical, potential, virtual sense of the context, which may or may not have been actualized at a particular moment, we return to the bucket theory of context, and its related problem, the infinitude of context.

Finally, the problem of the infinitude of context is a version of the duality of social structure (e.g. Giddens 1984). Social structure can be seen both as a precondition for action but also as dependent on the action to be realized. On purely theoretical terms, this duality of structure is insurmountable. However, on an empirical level the issue comes back to the question of the adequacy of the analysis: is the analyst able to recognize, identify and analyze sufficiently the aspects of context that are relevant to the parties? In this sense, the key issue is not the external relationship between an interaction and its context but whether the analyst is sufficiently attuned to the context in and for a given interaction. This is a small, but nevertheless significant, reformulation of CA methodology for the study of institutional interaction, whereby the analyst's knowledge of the institutional context of a given interaction becomes an accountable part of the study. Moreover, researchers can and should enhance their sensitivity to the potential relevance of institutional contexts in order to improve the validity of their studies. Such a context-sensitive research procedure takes into account the role that the analyst's explicit or tacit understanding of the context plays in the study of contextualized interaction.

2.2 Respecifying the Relationship between Interaction and Context

In his discussion of the procedural relevance and consequentiality of context, Schegloff alerts readers to the "paradox of proximateness":

> If it is to be argued that some legal, organizational or social environment underlies the participants' organizing some occasion of talk-in-interaction in some particular way, then either one *can* show the *details in the talk* which that argument allows us to notice, and which in return supply the demonstrable warrant for the claim by showing the relevant presence of the sociolegal context in the talk; or one *cannot* point to such detail (1991, 64, emphasis in original) .

As such, Schegloff's formulation is incontrovertible and allows us to form a strict empirical policy for the study of interaction. However, his *claim trades on the analyst's taken-for-granted competence in presupposing an argument that formulates the context-relevant features of interaction to the object of scrutiny.* Schegloff assumes that an analyst is automatically competent to identify the context-relevant features of an interaction. According to Schegloff, it is the analyst's *argument,* which *allows us to notice* the relevance and consequentiality of context in the details of talk. Therefore, we may open this argument for examination, and pay attention to its relevance for the demonstrable visibility of context. If one *cannot* point to the *relevant presence of the sociolegal context* in the interaction, the problem may either be that the context is irrelevant for the accomplishment of that action or that the analyst's argument has been inadequate and has not allowed us to notice the relevance of context. Consequently, we may reformulate Schegloff's paradox of proximateness: if a sufficient argument informs the analyst about the role of sociolegal context for participants in organizing their conduct in some setting, then evidence for the pertinence of this context may be found, in so much as the context is procedurally consequential for conduct in the formulated context.

What, then, is an "argument" about the context-relevant features of interaction? CA works in an empirical and inductive way. Reverse engineering of institutional interaction is based on an explicit or implicit comparison with ordinary conversation (Drew and Heritage 1992b, 19). If interaction departs from the canonical patterns of everyday interaction in a systematic or invariant way, then we have a basis for the claim that parties orient to something which allows or forces them to depart from mundane interactional conduct. We may also distinguish a stronger and a weaker version of Schegloff's argument. According to the stronger form, only distinct patterns of speech and interaction represent institutionally-specific forms of interaction. Only if the sequential organization of interaction in an institutional setting is distinct to that setting only, can we claim that the institution itself is pertinent. In contrast, if sequences found in institutional interaction are part of the methodic practices for doing sequences of that sort in everyday interaction, then introducing social or institutional structures is not warranted (Schegloff 1991, 59). For instance, Schegloff criticized a study of emergency calls which connected the call-taker's recurrent use of insertion sequences, "interrogative series", to organizational and institutional contingencies supposedly dealt with in these calls. Schegloff (1991) claimed that a hasty conclusion about the institutional relevance of these sequences risked missing "the potentially general relevance of insertions to sequences of this type" (ibid.).

Schegloff himself notes that he is trying to increase understanding of talk-in-interaction (ibid. p. 65). Indeed this "strong" argument only makes sense if the sole purpose of the study is to analyze talk-in-interaction, and nothing else. Naturally, mundane forms of talk-in-interaction may take place in institutional settings, but from the perspective of talk-in-interaction only distinct new patterns that are not (yet) found anywhere else would be interesting. Schegloff (p. 65) further admits that "it is quite another to be addressed to understanding distributional or institutional or socio-structural features of social life, and to ask how talk-in-interaction figures in their production." He also notes that this branch of studies could be developed under the auspices of different methodological policy than the study of talk-in-interaction in its own right (ibid.).

Now, if we are to study institutional interaction in its own right we have to revise Schegloff's methodological policy. At this point, the weaker version of the argument concerning the relationship between interaction and context comes into play. According to this weaker version, any invariance, systematic pattern, or departure from canonical forms of everyday communication may be potentially relevant for accomplishing institutional tasks in a given setting. The weaker form of the argument also uses comparisons to everyday talk but does not assume that the distinctiveness of sequential forms is the ultimate criterion of procedural relevance. To return to the emergency call example, the call-taker's interrogative series is used to gather information directly relevant to his task of mobilizing an appropriate response to the emergency and in this way is clearly part of the institutional interaction in the strict sense of the term (Zimmerman 1992, 458). Here, the sequential form, the insertion sequence, is commonly used in ordinary talk but also has a particular use in institutional environments. In studying institutional interaction, then, the task is not only to identify and describe sequential patterns but to analyze and detail their use in the accomplishment of the institutional activity. Therefore, it is an empirical matter how fruitful and informative the comparison to the parallel activities in everyday settings turns out to be, and how detailed the comparison should be. As best, comparisons to parallel activities in mundane talk may allow the analyst to explicate particular forms of "doing sequences of that type" that stand for the particular institutional contingency. But there is no reason to believe that all forms of institutional interaction would entail unique sequential features.

When the task of the analysis is not only to describe sequential patterns of interaction, but to identify and explicate the ways in which interactional activities contribute to the accomplishment of institutional tasks, then the analyst's ability to connect the interactional patterns to the institutional activities becomes essential and makes relevant the analyst's context-sensitive understanding of the institutional tasks. As a whole, the weaker version of the argument concerning the relationship between interaction and context allows the emergence of a closer relationship between CA and other forms of human and social sciences on two levels. First, the focus on the uses of interactional patterns stresses the relevance of parties' understanding of their actions, and alerts us to the role of organizational policies and objectives and parties' understanding of these. Second, since there is no reason to rule out the possibility that invariances and regularities found in institutional settings might not be statistical, it becomes possible to combine CA findings with statistical aggregates. Thus, CA findings on the practices of talk-in-interaction can be complemented with questionnaire data on demographic or outcome variables, thereby offering us a new way to address the relationship between an activity's situated meanings and overall outcome. We will return to this issue in the final chapter.

2.3 Opening up the Notion of Context

As we have seen, study of institutional interaction presupposes a sufficient understanding of the context to build an argument sophisticated enough so that the relevant presence of context can be demonstrated. In this sense, Schegloff's paradox of proximateness can be complemented with a question about the analyst's competence: we can question not only the details of talk, but also how and under what conditions these details are seen as relevant.

Institutional activities are realized with the help of parties orienting to resources and constraints specific to the institution in question. The study of institutional interaction focuses on the ways in which these resources and constraints become observable and accountably relevant in an institution's naturally-occurring practices. Consequently, the analyst's knowledge of the institutional resources and constraints may help focus attention on those activities or practices informed by such professional knowledge, while it may also help to observe sets of practices departing or deviating from the sanctioned knowledge base of the profession or institutional practice.

What, then, are the basic dimensions of an institution which parties may orient to? To provide a minimalist account, we can distinguish two basic dimensions of institutions: knowledge and organization.

In everyday life, knowledge is a central resource that can be either tacit, taken-for-granted cultural knowledge or personal, biographical knowledge. Naturally, agents also have these resources in institutional settings, although institutions may also set limits on the invocation of people's resources. For example, in a courtroom or a scientific argument one should *not* trade on mundane assumptions or presuppositions. But institutions also have sets of specialized knowledge created for their particular purposes. Institutionalized expert knowledge is one of the resources helping to maintain distinct institutional activities (Drew 1991; Peräkylä 1995).

Institutional practices are partly realized through the parties' orientation to the special knowledge and beliefs necessary to accomplish their activities. Institutional interaction studies may focus on the ways in which these institutional resources become observable and procedurally consequential in actual institutional practices. To topicalize the relationship of interactional practices and an institutional body of knowledge, Peräkylä (1995) analyzed the ways in which HIV counseling was built upon the ideas of systemic family therapy. The study examined the therapists' ways of invoking ideas derived from this theory so that they could face and solve problems emerging in the encounter with the client. Mutual help in Alcoholics Anonymous meetings has similarly been studied as an institutional realm based upon its own set of beliefs (Arminen 1996; 1998). Occasionally, professions may also have theories of social interaction. These (quasi)theoretical and normative formulations concerning the preferable forms of interaction between professional and client have been called "interaction ideologies" or "stocks of professional knowledge" (Peräkylä and Vehviläinen 2003). In as much as the researcher is informed of these ideologies, comparison between actual interaction and professional beliefs becomes possible.

Consequently, a study may concretize, broaden, and detail the picture of interaction, but it may also correct the professional beliefs if the findings derived from actual interaction falsify the theoretical assumptions held by the professionals (ibid.).

The role of knowledge and beliefs in institutional practices can be summarized with the help of the following, simple figure (Figure 2.4). The invocation of expert knowledge and sets of beliefs (B) is used for building institutional interaction (I') distinct from mundane interaction (I).

Mundane Interaction	Institutional Interaction	
	B	Beliefs, Knowledge
	(ii)	(Interaction Ideology)
I	I'	Interaction

Figure 2.4 Beliefs and Institutional Interaction

However, knowledge and beliefs are not the only institutional resource. Institutions also have a regulated mode of organization that constraints and occasions the ways in which beliefs are invoked in and for the actual institutional practices. Thus, we in fact need a three-dimensional account of an institutional practice, as such practices consist of a set of knowledge, a mode of organization and the institutional interaction in which these practices are realized (see Figure 2.5).

Mundane Interaction	Types of Institutional Interaction		
	B	B'	Beliefs, Knowledge
	(ii)	(ii)	(interaction ideology)
I	I'	I''	Interaction
	(od)	(od)	(organizational discourse)
	O	O'	Mode of Organization

Figure 2.5 Beliefs, Interaction, and Organization of Institutional Interaction (BIO model)

A set of knowledge and beliefs (B), interaction (I), and mode of organization (O) are generic dimensions of any social action. In mundane interaction, beliefs and the mode of organization are pregiven, readily at hand, not distinctively ordered.[3] In institutional actions beliefs and modes of organization are conventionally produced (e.g., Maynard 1991a). Each dimension of social action has relative autonomy, so that neither of the dimensions can be reduced to the others (Mäkelä et al. 1996, 5-6). Interaction plays a specific role in the sense that these beliefs and organizational modes are maintained and renewed in interaction. If either the beliefs (B) or organization (O) are transformed, actual changes become observable and accountable for in the interaction (I). To conclude, by studying interaction we can scrutinize how the beliefs and mode of organization are made relevant and consequential for the actual practices of institutional interaction.

The relevance of this account of institutional interaction can be highlighted by comparing institutional practices which share one of the above three components of institutional practice. A case in point is the Alcoholics Anonymous fellowship and the professionalized forms of 12-step therapy. In terms of their set of beliefs, both draw on the twelve steps of Alcoholics Anonymous (see Anonymous 1952), and in that way depart from the mundane world as far as their set of beliefs are concerned. But they also differ from each other in terms of their mode of organization (see Mäkelä et al. 1996, 196–206). Interestingly, the central goal of both AA and 12-step treatment – the problem drinker's aim to sober up – is characterized in an opposite way in these two settings, as I will show with the help of data excerpts from both settings. In these cases the speakers characterize a third party's attempt to stay sober. Furthermore, these examples will demonstrate how the analyst's reading of interactional practice is embedded in his/her knowledge of the practice, and how that knowledge becomes relevant in the course of analysis.

Extract (1) comes from an Alcoholics Anonymous (AA) meeting; the speaker (Marja) gives an account of her phase of life when she was living with a partner who had had alcohol problems but at the time was abstaining from alcohol. The analysis will focus on a self-repair at line 3.

(1) (IA94Marja) (Arminen 1996; 2000)[4]

```
1   M:          And then on the side I was like (.) I was also (0.4)
2               also abstaining,=in a way this pe:rson kept me sober
3        →      cause he just couldn't- (1.0) didn't want to drink himself,
4               and didn't either approve of me drinkin. (.) And I
5               myself, I was so hor- horribly dependent on him, I
6               considered him as some sort of father figure °and° .hhh
```

In line 3, Marja produces a self-repair "he just couldn't- (1.0) didn't want to drink himself", which is clearly marked with a cut-off and a pause after the repairable, after which follows the replacement of the repairable. The repair distinguishes between "being unable to drink", and "being unwilling to drink". Even without further knowledge, we can note that "inability" and "unwillingness" characterize different reasons for abstaining. "Unwillingness" points towards a deliberate decision to not do something, whereas "inability" stands for actions that a person is not able to do, irrespective of that person's own deliberation. Thus, the repair replaces necessity with optionality, which specifically displays that the abstention was deliberately done. Through this repair, Marja has made relevant a distinction between being abstinent out of exterior compulsion, or out of voluntary choice. This portrayal of abstinence as potentially arising from a free choice has strong moral and ethical implications. By invoking a dimension of "deliberateness", the speaker performs moral work, constructing the action in moral terms that include the option of personal choice. We can thus note that here the speaker effectively uses a repair to build a description of abstinence which constitutes it as a moral object.

To further characterize the moral object here, we need to identify what it represents for a speaker informed by the kind of competence making the repair relevant. Here the self-repair does not convey an arbitrary or idiosyncratic distinction, but stands for the central tenets of AA starting from its third tradition:[5] "the only requirement of AA membership is a desire to stop drinking" (Anonymous 1952), which sets up the basis for AA's voluntaristic ethos. Through her repair, Marja ascribed an AA identity to her partner without saying so explicitly.[6] Consequently, the point of repair was not just to convey a moral distinction between two kinds of reasons to abstain (inability vs. voluntary choice), but to inform participants about a demarcation between AA members and other people through this distinction. The salience of the repair was connected to AA's set of beliefs, and informed those who could see the connection of what AA members are like. In this way, the analyst's ability to account for AA's "voluntary ethos" and its salience for the participants depends on her/his ability to draw on the underlying cultural matrix the participants make use of in the talk-in-interaction.

In extract (2), the organizational and activity context is saliently different from that of the AA. Here, the addiction therapist describes a patient's relationship to AA and to sobriety in a multi-professional team meeting at the 12-step treatment clinic. The aim of the meeting is to discuss and develop treatment recommendations for the patient. Notice how the addiction therapist's characterization of the patient is embedded in the activity context for making treatment recommendations. The therapist thus establishes a view on what the successful 12-step treatment would require of the patient. The focus will again be on the self-repair (lines 11 and 14).

(2) (MT 3, 17, 21-(18)10; T = female therapist) (Arminen and Perälä 2002)

01 T: I then asked if it would be so terribly shameful to go to AA?, (0.8) (like)
02   terr#ibly somehow?, # (0.3) difficult (0.3) almost felt like

03 saying that (.) (you knew) or I did say to her that (0.5) in this treatment
04 nothing happens like that?, (0.5) the greatest miracle that can
05 happen is that, (0.6) you become, like, committed to your own treatment
06 (0.8)
07 T: and she was somehow a bit surprised?, (0.6) >that< she has after all gone through
08 this in eighty five that:, (2.4) #it's funny (.) I don't know what the patients
09 expect that,# (0,6) no#ne of them#?, (0.4) or most of them do not
10 seem to understand that #the idea is that?,# (0.7) they should realise
11 → that they should care for themselves (.) but SOBER [SHE WANTS TO?, (0.6)]
12   [(((speaking in the background)))]
13 (0.7)
14 → T: wishes to be?, (0.3) she's got to be?, (1.3) it's not like she has any other choice,
15 is it?,

This extract crystallizes the key elements required of patients in 12-step treatment: going to AA (line 1), commitment to one's own treatment (lines 5 and 11), and sobriety (lines 11–15). The extract also reveals the most crucial difference between the 12-step treatment and AA despite their shared set of beliefs. In AA, the tenet that the alcoholic's own desire to stop drinking marks the starting point for recovery (Anonymous 1952) is molded into a voluntaristic practice. The idea that sobriety cannot be forced and that one's own wish to stay sober is the only basis for recovery also guides AA activities in practice (see Arminen 1996). In the 12-step model, AA's only requirement – the alcoholic's own desire to quit – is reformulated into a cornerstone of confrontation. Through confrontation the professionals aim at making clients accept their disease. Several crucial differences between AA and 12-step therapy thus emerge in the ways beliefs are translated into actions. For one, they differ with respect to time. In contrast to AA, which is not tied to any bureaucratic time schedules, in 12-step therapy professionals discuss time goals with patients, saying what they should do now in order to be better off in a half year (which would also be potential date for the outcome measurement of the therapy). In addition, the view of alcoholism as an illness is also expressed more distinctly in 12-step therapy. Patients are seen as victims of their disease: they "must" give up drinking. Thus, AA's voluntaristic practice gives way to a confrontational practice, legitimated by paternalistic assumptions privileging the professional's view of the patient's condition (for a history of the concept of confrontation, see Yalisove 1998). The therapist ends up replacing willingness and desire with obligation and lack of choice (14–15). As we can see, while AA and 12-step therapy are two institutional practices that seem to share the same ideology, in fact they are realized as critically different institutional orders, with diverse sets of beliefs.[7]

In brief, institutional interaction is a site in which the prevailing set of beliefs and mode of organization are made relevant and procedurally consequential for interactants. Moreover, all these components of institutional practice are reflexively linked to each other so that any change in one component is bound to have implications for other components. Even though professional 12-step therapy and AA seem to share the same set of beliefs, the adoption of these beliefs is occasioned and constrained by the organizational setting so that the very same set of beliefs is profoundly diversified according to the organizational context. Despite their common background, professional 12-step therapy and mutual help in AA differ from each other both in actual interactional practices as well as in ideology.

2.4 The Distinction between Mundane and Institutional Interaction

Analysis of the communicative texture of institutional interaction depends on making a distinction between ordinary talk and institutional occasions, so that we can single out the institutional relevancies in contrast to the expectancies prevailing in ordinary, everyday interaction. In this fashion, we aim at grasping the endogenously generated sense of each context in its own right, including on those occasions when the contextual relevancies depart from everyday concerns. This brings us back to the question of how an institutional interaction differs from a mundane interaction. There are two different methodical procedures for making this distinction: constitutive and regulative.

CA literature (see Billig's (1998) critique, and Schegloff's (1999) reply)[8] also acknowledges these two basic meanings for ordinary conversation, "constitutive" and "regulative". Both have operational value for studies of institutional discourse. By constitutive meaning, we mean the rules creating or defining the activity itself which have the conceptual form "doing X counts as Y" (Levinson 1983, 238; Rawls 1955; Garfinkel 1963). Let us now consider the methods of making this formal, constitutive distinction. According to this constitutive meaning, ordinary conversation (OC) is a speech exchange system in which turn size, order and content are not predetermined (Sacks, Schegloff and Jefferson 1974). In terms of institutional interaction, it allows us to distinguish between ordinary interaction and formally distinct, institutional speech events, such as interviews, chaired meetings, and ceremonies (ibid.). By regulative meaning, which will be discussed later, we mean the rules defining how things are done "normally" or "preferably". In CA literature, OC is commonly referred to as "trivial", "commonplace", "normal", "casual", and "ordinary" (Heritage 1984a, 238–240; 1989, 34; Drew and Heritage 1992b, 19). This allows us to distinguish institutional talk in terms of its observable contrast to "prototypical forms of everyday talk".

Sacks, Schegloff and Jefferson (1974) originally proposed the technical definition for OC, which I have called the constitutive meaning of OC. On the one hand, they identified the essential parameters for participation in interaction, while on the other hand, they conceptualized a mechanism for turn allocation that allows us to account for all the empirically observable patterns of turn-taking in all the instances of social interaction where turn-taking is not constrained by conventional arrangements. Their model for "ordinary conversation" is an empirical generalization based on various types of everyday interaction. As an empirical generalization it is open to complements, corrections, and specifications, should there be any empirical challenges. The model is constitutive in the sense that it formulates the fundamental dimensions whose "free variation" characterizes mundane interaction, i.e., if any of the parameters[9] (turn size, order and content)[10] is conventionally constrained, then the interaction in question is tilted in terms of participation rights which inevitably shows that some institutionally-constituted activity is taking place. Naturally, OC itself and its way of organizing turn allocation is sensitive to the local relevancies of social realities and identities so that any actual event may be contingently constrained and display some deviation from free variation. The fact that every turn creates a new context for the next makes it possible that a friendly chat at the dinner table may turn into a third-degree interrogation, or vice versa. The turn-taking mechanism itself is context-free, but its operation is context-sensitive to the finest detail. Despite these local contingencies, we speak about institutionalized interaction only when the parameters for participation are constrained not contingently but conventionally.

With formal settings, comparison to mundane interaction allows us to identify concentration of, and specialization and reductions in, the range of practices of particular procedures of talk-in-interaction (Heritage 1984a, 239–240; Drew and Heritage 1992b, 26). The formally distinct patterns of interaction are not only a unique "fingerprint" through which the analyst can recognize the type of interaction in question, but, first and foremost, are the members' way of organizing and structuring the accomplishment of practical institutional tasks. Consequently, it is not sufficient for the analyst simply to identify the patterns of interaction; rather, the analyst must demonstrate the working of interactional patterns in order to explicate how the institutional activities are managed. This pragmatic focus on usages of patterns also defends against the criticism that CA may invent "functions" for "apparently irrational procedures" (Silverman 1987, 2). The task is not only to find and characterize the defining features of each institutional practice, but also to show how they contribute to the praxis in question.

The participants orient to this defining feature of formal interaction, these formal restrictions on participation, thereby realizing the institutional activity in question. Departures from the format of interaction are accountable and sanctionable. The parties themselves display the normative character of the format for interaction so that the "formality" of an occasion is evidenced in the deviations from the "normal" course of the interaction, as we can see in the third extract, a news interview in which there are several interviewees [IE]. Here, the second IE wants to comment on an answer by the first IE although the interviewer [IR] has not addressed him. The second IE orients to his restricted participation rights, and requests permission to speak.

(3) (Heritage and Greatbatch 1991, 103)

```
1   LL:        ... and therefore I'm not going to accept the
2              criticism that I haven't tried to help victims=
```

```
3              =I've (.) been trying to help them (0.2) off and
4              on for twenty-five years.=
5   ( ):       =.hhhh=
6   MW: →      =Can I- can I say something abou[t this.]
7   IR:                                        [Yes in]deed.
8              (0.5)
9              e:r (0.7) As (0.5) frank (.) Longford knows so
10             well .hh er my views ... ((continues))
```

We can see that the formal speech exchange system is maintained even on those occasions when the parties depart from the conventions of the format, i.e., the parties themselves acknowledge the normative, sanctionable status of the format, thereby maintaining it. In formal institutional interaction the participants' orientation to "tilted participation rights" maintains the distinct institutional reality.

The scope of the formal, "constitutive" distinction between institutional and mundane interactions is limited in two respects. First, only some institutional realms are organized as being "formally" different from everyday interactions (typically, courts and classrooms), and most institutional practices are not "formally" different from mundane interactions in terms of the "constitutive" dimensions of talk-in-interaction.[11] Second, the "formality" of formal institutional interactions is only their aspect: the description of the formal characteristics of any interaction is only a minimal account of the basic rules concerning the type of interaction which does not take into account participants' maintenance of intersubjective understanding or their regulative concerns about how they should talk and interact within their formal framework (Atkinson and Drew 1979, 68). The participants realize their intersubjective understanding and regulative concerns through applying talk-in-interaction in a context-sensitive manner.

Also, in institutional contexts, talk-in-interaction is an "enabling institution" which coordinates the behavior of all participants by allocating differentially at any moment differing opportunities for differing types of participation (Schegloff 1987, 208). It is through this institutionalized organization of talk-in-interaction whereby all other institutions are talked into being (Heritage 1984a, 290; 1989). In this respect studies of institutional interaction also examine the "institution" of talk-in-interaction. The systematic, normatively implemented, orderly organization of talk enables the sequential orchestration of activities whereby institutional contexts are also managed. This enabling character of talk-in-interaction is pervasively present in all institutional realities as long as orchestration of participation is tied to any form of interaction between persons.

Further, talk-in-interaction is not a threshold to an institutional reality, but a continuously updated basis for an intersubjective working consensus for the accomplishment of any task. It does not only enable activities but also constrains the participants. The parties have to ceaselessly maintain an intersubjective understanding to sustain the basis for the orchestration of activities. Any, even momentary, loss of intersubjective understanding is always potentially repairable, thereby overstepping the accomplishment of the actual institutional tasks. This primordial role of talk-in-interaction can be shown with the help of the fourth extract, which is taken from a political news interview after the French national elections in 1995. The interviewee [R] is Mr Rocard, a French minister, who speaks with an audible accent.

(4) (IAYork0595)

```
 1  R:          .hhhhhh (0.4) <he failed because (.) ↑the↓::: (1.5)
 2               left-wing: (0.4) after the: two mandates of-f Francois
 3               Mitterand is not in a good state. .hhhh >but
 4               be carefu:l< eu:: i-in ↑a:ll of our countries: (.)
 5               the:re: i:s (.) a:: (0.3) public unsatisfaction about
 6               unemployment, .hhhhhhh public worri: about
 7               delinquency:: about (.) the extension of dr-
 8               drug=consumption .hhhh eu::h a::nd
 9      →        da:n' de:' u::rba::n .nfh >disagregation=
10    Q→         =if=I=may=say=s[o<
11  I:   →                      [°yes.°=
12  R:           =.hh and this is not o:nly: french ↓diagnosis,
13               .hhhhh so you have a move of protest against
14               a-anyone who governs in a way↑:: we have not
15               yet=f::fo↑u:nd a:::[: sufficient remedy >for all this<
16  I:                             [(a')
```

In the middle of his answer (question not shown) Mr Rocard interrupts his answer to provide a ritualistic apology "**if I may say so**" (marked with Q) after an audible language problem "**eu::h a::nd da:n' de:' u::rba::n .nfh >disagregation**". The interviewer notably orients to the apology with the help of a quiet response token "**yes.**". During this unmarked, small exchange the parties have shifted away from the institutional frame to a more primordial frame of talk-in-interaction in order to check and to confirm the existence of intersubjective understanding. Even if this exchange was occasioned by a language problem of a second-language speaker, we should not fail to grasp its generic relevance. Institutional interactions are always embedded in talk-in-interaction, which forms the precondition for the accomplishment of any institutional duty. Therefore an orientation to the problems of maintaining intersubjectivity may always momentarily replace an orientation to institutional goals. Intersubjective understanding is always a necessary (but not sufficient) precondition for institutional interaction.

From these examples we can draw two conclusions. As Drew and Heritage (1992b, 21) have pointed out, "a hard and fast distinction" cannot be made between institutional and everyday interaction. In all instances of interactional events the work of talk-in-interaction permeates each particular institutional practice. Second, even if we can at times draw a distinction between institutional and mundane interactions according to their formal characteristics, this "formality" is only one aspect of formal institutional interactions. All institutional interactions, both formal and quasi-formal, utilize a vast array of generic properties of talk-in-interaction. Therefore, the analyst must show the relevance of the institutional context insofar as the aim is to shed light on the institutional interaction. At this point, the regulative distinction between ordinary and institutional talk steps in, and the procedural relevance of context becomes a crucial methodological principle, not least for quasi-formal institutional interactions.

2.5 Rereading the Procedural Relevance of Context

The canon of procedural relevance draws its power from a comparative approach and relies on the regulative ideal. The aim is to show in detail the procedural connection between the context and what actually happens in talk through comparing "sequences-of-that-sort" in the institutional and mundane contexts in order to identify characteristic features of such sequences each context. Notice that we are not comparing institutional talk and ordinary talk where turn order, content, and size are not constrained, but actual instances of talk in different contexts (Schegloff 1991, 59–61; 1997, 172–183; Button 1992, 216–217). Here the regulative principle comes into play.

To flesh this out, let us examine what the procedural relevance of context means in practice. Extract (5) is taken from Button's (1992) study of job interviews. Again, the institutional activity is managed with question-answer pairs. Here, the interesting aspect relates to the way the panelists [P] treat the candidate's [C] answers.

(5) (Button 1992, 215–216)

```
1   P:            ... thank you Madam Chairman (.) Huhrm (.) What sort of
2                 sty::le do you see (.) yourself as- as a le::ader of- of (.)
3                 a- a team of teachers.
4        →        (0.5)
5   C:   →        D'you mean how w'd I get other people to do it.
6        →        (1.5)
7   C:   →        Well er:: (0.5) .mpt I think there are two ways of
8        →        approaching tea::m teaching (0.5) .hh it can either
9                 be a school based philosophy
```

The teacher candidate (C) displays observable difficulty in understanding the question by initiating a repair (at line 5), which itself follows a delay (4) after the original question. The recipient, interviewer (P), however, withholds from making the correction that would be due after the repair initiation, and a one and a half second pause (6) is opened. This pause marks that the recipient was withdrawing accountably from the relevant action. After the pause the interviewee answers the original question, which is still troublesome for him as his delays and hesitations indicate (7–8). This would have also offered the recipient an appropriate place for correction, which is not produced.

In order to understand this occasion of talk, Button (1992, 216–219) uses regulative ideals of everyday conversation to point out the specificity of the institutional occasion by referring to the routine, normal ways of how problems of understanding may be dealt with in ordinary conversation. Normally, the recipient's understanding difficulties that have occasioned a repair initiation are corrected so that the recipient's understanding of the question is not an issue. In this manner, the comparative focus on institutional talk allows us to appreciate the institutional relevancies that allow parties to depart from regulative patterns of everyday talk.

Before drawing any conclusions, however, we need to explore how distinctive this occasion is; in other words, we need to specify our understanding of the procedural consequentiality of the context. I have shown that the procedural consequentiality of the context trades on the regulative patterns of everyday talk. To proceed further, we may note that digressions from regulative patterns also take place in ordinary conversation. In terms of institutional discourse, this means we must specify the distinctiveness of these digressions from regulative patterns of everyday talk in institutional occasions.

The enabling character of talk-in-interaction means that parties may draw inferences from each others' turns to reflexively shape their understanding of the ongoing social action. Consequently, parties are not mechanically tied to expectancies at any point, but they may also depart from the expected, regulative course of actions to renew the definition of a situation (Heritage 1984a, 242). For example, the refusal to produce a projected action, such as a correction after a repair initiation, is a generic interactional resource (see, Jefferson 1993). Let us examine an instance from an ordinary telephone call (extract [6,] see also Drew 1997) to get a better sense of this phenomenon. A mother [Mum] and a daughter [Lesley] are discussing one of the mother's friends (referred to as "she") who has been successful in arranging to have somebody take her back home from the evening church service. Subsequently, however, the daughter's stance to the mother's telling takes the mother's breath away.

(6) (Holt:SO88(II):2:8:7–8)

```
1    Mum:      … c'z she gets someone'take her homeyou see so,
2              she's alright
3 Lesley:      Oh sh- so she still comes t' chu:rch does she
4              in the eve[nings?
```

5	Mum:	[Oh yes c'z someone takes her h-all
6		the way ho:me.
7	Lesley:	.hhh hOh:.
8	Mum:	So:, hhm:, h[m so she's alright,
9	Lesley:	[.hh
10 →	Lesley:	That's a bit'v'n imposition though isn'it?
11 →		(0.3)
12 →	Mum:	What dear?
13 →	Lesley:	.hhhh
14		(.)
15 →	Mum:	Well they don't seem t'mind, hm
16		(.)
17	Lesley:	.tch uh Don' take you home though do they.
18	Mum:	eh heh huh
19		(.)
20	Mum:	We-:ll?
21	Lesley:	.t.hhhhhh
22	Mum:	They would if I: p-if I:-: pre[ssed for it?
23	Lesley:	[.hhhhhhhhhh
24	Lesley:	Ye:s.
25	Mum:	B't I do:n't huh hm:.

Here, as in the previous extract, the speaker (Mum) displays an understanding difficulty by initiating a repair (12) following a delay (11) after Lesley's assessment that was uttered as a question (10). Lesley orients to this understanding difficulty as indicated by the inbreath (13). But she withholds initiating a turn, a correction that would be due, and after a brief gap (14) Mum responds to Lesley's assessment (15). Lesley uses the interactional resource to withhold from the third position action (correction), thereby putting her mother under pressure to respond independently without assistance. Here, the use of an interactional resource to withhold from a third position activity was occasioned by an orientation to disagreement. Lesley, who still after her mother's response was maintaining her disagreement by pointing to the fact that the mother's friends do not take the mother home (17), did not let her mother off the hook, but pursued her response with the help of her own refusal to clarify her first turn.

We can conclude that digressions from the regulative patterns of ordinary conversation, such as a refusal to engage in third position activity, are generic resources both in institutional and mundane contexts. Consequently, the relevance of Button's study is not in the identification of institutionally particular patterns of speech, but in the explication of a characteristic use of a generic pattern in and for a specific context.[12] That is, studies of institutional interaction, except for formally orchestrated interactions, do not reveal interactional practices that would be "specific", "particular" or "unique" as such, but display a party's (or parties') orientation to the institutional relevancies at hand and how they may accomplish an institutional activity through the interactional practice. In a job interview, the interviewer may not only refuse third position activities, but may also attribute the mis-communication, thus constituted, to the interviewee. The digression from regulative ideals of ordinary conversation, a refusal to produce a correction due, gains a specific institutional relevance. The interactional orchestration of the interview format here becomes interesting as we connect it to our implicit background knowledge of what job interviews are about. In this fashion, we may appreciate the interactional pattern as a demonstration of a mechanism of how job interviewers use their institutional power (see also Hutchby 1996a and b). In this context, the interviewer displays his institutional power to make the interviewee accountable for all the answers irrespective of the actual role the questioner may have had. Any speaker, like Lesley, can occasionally withdraw from the third position activities in ordinary conversation. But Lesley, or anybody in a mundane context, does not have any particular institutional power to make the other party responsible and accountable for the behavior that has been interactionally constituted. Therefore, even if there are similar kinds of interactional practices both in mundane and institutional settings, these "similar" practices do gain distinct meanings through their reflexive tie to the context and the institutional identities it makes relevant. The methodological implication is that interactional patterns should not be studied as if they were completely free from external reality; rather, the aim is to analyze the reflexive relationship between the interactional pattern and its context. The meaning of any "sequential object" (turn, pair of turns, sequential course of interaction) is understood in its context, which is itself maintained with the help of interactional practices in, and for, the context in question.

Insofar as we want to study institutions through their interactions, the organization of interaction in institutional contexts is not interesting just because it is interactionally constituted, but because of what this constitution reveals about the institutional resources used in performing institutional tasks. Button's study, for example, identified a strategic use of power in interaction. The interviewer forces the interviewee to be the only utterer of an answer by withholding from the third position action, so that the interviewee became the only accountable source of an answer. In terms of the analysis of institutional forms, identifying the interviewer's digression from the regulative conversational pattern allows us to understand the interactional management of the institutional task of conducting a job interview.

A salient feature of informal institutional interactions is that they are carried out to a great degree with conversational forms common to ordinary conversation. In institutional settings, however, conversational items and practices at home in ordinary conversation may gain an institutionally distinct meaning, as we can see in this striking well-known example (Heritage and Sefi 1992; Heritage and Drew 1992b). A health visitor [HV] who is visiting the home of a newborn baby makes a comment evidently referring to some sucking or "mouthing" behavior of the baby. The baby's father [F] and mother [M] respond to the comment in somewhat different ways.

(7) (Heritage and Sefi 1992: 367)

```
1    HV:       He's enjoying that [isn't he.
2    F:                          [°Yes he certainly is=°
3    M:        =He's not hungry 'cus (h)he's ju(h)st (h)had
4              'iz bo:ttle .hhh
```

The father aligns with the health visitor, displaying an overt agreement with the health visitor's remark. In contrast, the mother replies defensively, thereby rebutting the implications of the health visitor's remark as she has heard them. The remark *"he's enjoying that, isn't he"* carries an implication of blame for the mother. According to the mother, as her response shows, the health visitor did not express innocent delight, but conveys concern about the baby's well-being. The health visitor's remark made the mother self-conscious about her role as the caretaker who is accountable for the child's welfare. Consequently, the mother defends herself against the health visitor's complaint, as she has heard the remark.

The parties of this small speech exchange do not speak in any institutionally distinct way. However, the design of responses shows their orientation and understanding of the broader context with the help of which they select and assign a function to the utterance (Drew and Heritage 1992b, 33). The mother's defensive response to the health visitor's remark (which could be understood innocuously, as the father's response displays) makes publicly available her understanding of the context, thereby also contributing to the sense of this context. For the mother, the health visitor is an authority who evaluates and controls her conduct. Therefore, the mother's response reveals the institutionality of the occasion, and we may add, makes the institutional expectancies procedurally relevant for her conduct. Of course, the family institution is also made relevant here, so the parents build their role in relation to the health visitor according to their division of labor (ibid.). The mother constructs herself as a client, and the father as a co-conversationalist in relation to the health visitor. Although the mother's response displays institutional relevancies of the occasion, the type of her response is not unique or distinct to institutional contexts. Anybody who has ever lived in an intimate relationship knows that on occasion innocuous remarks may be challenged. What makes the mother's response interesting is its reliance on institutionally-specific relevancies. Consequently, the analyst must draw on the implicit or explicit understanding of the institution in question to explicate the way in which context has become relevant for the design of her turn. Eventually, the study proceeds in a hermeneutic manner so that interactional details are interpreted vis-à-vis their context, the sense of which will be clarified by reference to the actual interaction.

Professional-client encounters as a context also have at least one common feature. It is not a coincidence that in the job interview it is the interviewee who is held accountable (and not the interviewer), and respectively in the health visit it is the mother who feels controlled (and not the health visitor). The distribution of speech activities follows the antecedent distribution of "factual" roles between the parties in "real life" though the actual distribution is an empirical question and always open to local contingencies (Wilson 1991, 37–39). A professional-client role distribution is presumably a constitutive feature of these interactions.

Finally, we may return to the notion of "procedural consequentiality". Schegloff, who coined the term (1991), has been adamant in claiming that to demonstrate the procedural consequentiality of a context it is not sufficient to show that the context is relevant for the parties, but that it is necessary to specify and describe the ways in which the context is consequential to the parties' conduct in a context. As such, the principle of procedural consequentiality is a reasonable methodological rule, which should inform not only conversation analysis but any research on social action, i.e., the analyst should be able to prove the consequential relevance of the contextual features invoked for analyzing the social action in the first place. The key question concerns the distinction between the generic versus the institutional relevance of sequential patterns. Schegloff (1991, 61) claims that we first have to address the generic relevance of sequences and only subsequently try to seek what is institutionally distinctive about them. Accordingly, if an interactional pattern is an endemic "part of the methodic practices of doing *sequences of that sort*, then there is no warrant for introducing *social structures of that sort* into the account" (ibid. 59). In other words, Schegloff warns against making "an ecological misjudgement" in which a phenomenon found in a given context is taken as characteristic of that context without inquiring about its potential generic relevance. If a "factual" institutional context is invoked to account talk through its function in the context, it may distract one from studying of how conversations are accomplished by naturalizing the talk. Instead, the task would be to explicate the conversational construction of activities so that, for instance, the specificity of the design of a complaint to the police could be discerned.

Notably, Schegloff's inquiry aims at understanding talk-in-interaction, and only secondarily the institutional features of talk (ibid. 65). However, insofar as the task is to explicate the relevance of talk for institutional activities, the methodological canon of procedural relevance becomes a criterion of how to take the context into account without falling into overinterpretation. The aim is not so much to spell out the distinctive interactional forms, but to reverse-engineer the constituents of the relevant institutional activities, irrespective of their potential commonality with the interactional forms used. Consequently, the analyst should not bracket the context completely out of the analysis but direct the use of contextual knowledge so as to be able to show in detail how the talk is oriented to the context. Further, if the aim of the study is not just to understand talk-in-interaction but to discuss how the talk in its context contributes to the institutional practice, the analyst may need to refer to institutional tasks or goals so as to explicate the ways in which interactional patterns have gained distinct meanings in that context. As we saw in the job interview and health visitor data, the specificity of these instances may not lie in the formal distinctiveness of their interactional patterns, but in their uses of interactional activities through which institutional tasks were oriented to and carried out.

To conclude, the methodological canon of procedural relevance does not bracket the analyst's understanding of the institutional context but directs the use of this knowledge so that the relevance of the institution for the details of talk can be singled out and specified. If we follow Schegloff's primary line of investigation and aim at specifying the interactional distinctiveness of institutional communication, we have to draw on the institutional practice to explicate the local, situated meaning of the conversational construction of the activity. If we study the relevance of conversational interaction for institutional reality we address the perceived relevance of talk for the institutional praxis.

2.6 Dimensions of Institutionality in Interaction

In an empirical analysis, the researcher's task is to seek demonstrable features of institutionality in interaction. As Heritage (1997, 164) has pointed out, the task is both easy and difficult, because institutional features can be found anywhere in interaction. Nevertheless, Drew and Heritage (1992b) have reconstructed a helpful scheme that may guide the study of institutional interaction (see also Heritage 1997; ten Have 1999). According to Drew and Heritage (1992b), there are six partly overlapping dimensions to probe the institutional nature of interaction.

---

1. Turn-taking organization

2. Overall structural organization of the interaction

3. Sequential organization

4. Turn design

5. Lexical choice

6. Interactional asymmetries

Figure 2.6 Dimensions of Institutionality in Interaction

Just to show the usefulness of this list (which is an empirical taxonomy, open to revision and additions), I will briefly comment on some features of the data extracts presented in this chapter. These dimensions have been discussed more thoroughly in Drew and Heritage (1992b) and Heritage (1997).

As we saw above, the organization of turn-taking is a fundamental dimension of talk-in-interaction. In institutional interaction, specific arrangements for turn-taking organization may be one of the elementary ways to adapt the interaction to the institutional tasks at hand. Significantly, both extracts 1 and 2 are extended turns (from AA and the 12-step therapy). On both occasions the special arrangements for turn-taking are part of the members' practices for constituting the sense of these activities (mutual help/professional therapy, see Arminen 1998; Arminen and Perälä 2002). As for multi-professional team work (as in extract 2), I do not know of any systematic studies of turn-taking organization, but this would certainly merit a closer look, and might prove to be a fruitful approach. In extract 3, the parties display their orientation to the specific system of turn-taking in political news interviews. Extract 4, however, shows that also in formal institutional interactions, like political news interviews, the parties may momentarily skip the formal turn-taking if the maintenance of intersubjectivity requires it. Also in job interviews (extract 5), the parties' orientation (albeit asymmetric) to specific constraints in turn-taking is the starting point for the institutional tasks.

In this chapter, I have not really discussed the overall structural organization of interactions, salient as the theme is, although the point about the different activity contexts of extended turns in AA and the 12-step treatment alludes to the overall structural organization of these interactions. Interactions are organized in different forms in AA and 12-step therapy, which could also be addressed through describing the overall structural organization of these interactions. In this way, description of the overall structural organization of interaction can provide a mediating level between the detailed analysis of individual sequences of interaction and more general organizational concerns. For instance, in doctor/patient interactions this is one of the permanent issues (ten Have 1991; Heritage and Maynard forthcoming). I will return to this issue in Chapter 7, on strategic interaction, where I will deal with the organization of job interviews in a way which allows candidates to be assessed. In job interviews, the interviewers may withhold information from the candidate to obtain the candidates' sincere views which are uncontaminated by the interviewers' views (Komter 1991). This strategic nature of the job interview is also observable in extract 5. In political news interviews, the role of the analysis of the overall structural organization of interactions may seem less clear, but it might bear on the differences between program types and journalists (Hutchby 1996b).

A focus on the sequential organization[13] brings the analysis back to the level of details. The power of sequence organization gets the sharpest expression in extract 7, in which the mother and the father respond quite differently to the health visitor's query. Through their responses, parties create different sequential courses of action. This sequence organization also bears directly on the participants' identities, which are invoked through engagement in sequential activities. AA and 12-step treatment are similar in terms of turn-taking, so that in both contexts extended turns prevail. In terms of sequences, the extended turns in AA and 12-step treatment realize different actions: autobiographical storytelling in AA, while in the multi-professional team meetings extended turns are used to evaluate patients. Also, the details of talk gain particular meanings through their belonging to sequences that are part of larger courses of actions.

Turn design intertwines closely with sequence organization. In extract 7, the alternate ways the father and the mother respond to the health visitor's question become observable through their turn design. The father's response is designed to be responsive to an innocuous remark, whereas the mother's response is directed to a complaint. In this way, the analysis of turn design opens up the participants' sequential meaning making. This meaning making is consequential for the nature and course of action, and for the related emerging social identities. In a similar fashion, the object of analysis in the AA and 12-step data extracts was a particular kind, a self-repair. Through self-repairs parties show their orientation and preference for a particular turn design, rather than the repaired one. In both cases, parties repair their turns to create and to maintain implications appropriate to the sense of the action they seem to be oriented to.

Lexical choices are really an elementary level for the analysis of interaction. They are related to turn design, as turn design is to sequence organization. For example, I originally became interested in self-repairs in AA when I noticed that they seem to be involved in a social practice whereby AA members amend the implications of what they had said. AA members seem to be sensitive about not criticizing other AA members or the AA program in public. Essentially, these types of self-repairs consist of the speaker's orientation to her/his lexical choices so that through the repair the troublesome lexical item is replaced or modified with a less troublesome item. Consequently, a relatively small detail, such as the substitution of "could not drink" with "did not want to drink" (in Finnish, *ei voinu- halunnu*) turns out to be a valuable interactional practice in itself, and also an elementary level for the social practices of mutual help (Arminen 1996; 1998). When analyzing the 12-step treatment, I also first became interested in some lexical items, namely the ways in which the staff members refer to patients' talk. This also involves systematic lexical practices, for instance framing of the patient's view with phrases, such as "according to X", "N said she had done/been" or "Y thinks that ...". Through these lexicalized practices staff members seem to distance themselves from the patients, and legitimate their own interventions and confrontations as in extract 2. Also on a lexical level, AA provided me with an implicit point of comparison to the 12-step treatment, as I had earlier studied the ways in which AA members refer to each other's experiences. The way the treatment professionals referred to the patients' experiences could be contrasted with AA practices, starting from the lexical choices made when constructing these descriptions.

The study of interactional asymmetries allows us to return to general issues of institutional realms. Various dimensions of interactional asymmetries prevail to a greater or lesser extent in institutional interactions, as we have seen in the examples used in this chapter. In political news interviews, parties maintain the sense of ongoing action through their explicit orientation to (and acceptance of) asymmetric participation rights in interaction. The job interview extract reveals the asymmetric power distribution among participants. In a health visit, the family/gender roles and institutional agenda of health visiting are interwoven, exposing asymmetry between the clients (mother and father). In the 12-step treatment, much of the work of the multi-professional team is devoted to legitimating treatment recommendations through privileging staff views over client views. AA is largely an exception in that much of the interactional arrangements between participants are organized so as to maintain egalitarian relationships between parties. This makes AA an exceptional, though not unique, type of institutional interaction.

2.7 Conclusion

The procedural consequentiality of context is a central methodological canon in the analysis of institutional interaction. The analyst's task is to show in detail the way in which parties build their activities as allowable and appropriate for their context. The principle of procedural consequentiality need not be interpreted in a narrow way, according to which only exclusively specific patterns of institutional interaction bear the imprint of procedural consequentiality. In this case, the analyst's task would be to find patterns of interaction specific to that context, and to that context only. As we have shown, there is no warrant for a claim that only interactionally distinct patterns would be relevant for institutional practices. Some exclusively distinct patterns may be found in formal types of institutional interaction, but all institutional interactions utilize generic patterns of talk-in-interaction. These generic interactional patterns nevertheless may have characterizable uses in the institutional setting. The analyst's task is to reverse-engineer the members' techniques, methods and procedures through which the institutional reality is reflexively constituted in the first place.

Essentially, the principle of procedural consequentiality offers a comparative approach. The analysis focuses on the difference between what goes on canonically in ordinary talk and what happens on some particular institutional occasion. This comparative analysis does not preclude the analyst from using knowledge of the context but directs its use so that the particular institutional relevancies of the interaction may be revealed. The comparison of mundane and institutional interaction makes relevant the parties' resources that are particular to institutional occasions, such as institutional identities (Zimmerman 1998) and the exercise of institutional power (Hutchby 1996a and b). In this manner, an analysis of institutional interaction that seeks to explicate the role institutional constituents play in the actual interaction addresses general sociological themes, such as the exercise of power. This also provides a point of contact between conversation analysis and the social sciences. CA may seek to explicate the manner in which power, institutional identities, theories informing practices, or interaction ideologies – such as student as self-directed learner, dialogic doctor/patient model (see Peräkylä and Vehviläinen 2003) – become evident at the surface of the interaction (if they even do). CA practitioners who study institutional interaction might benefit from paying closer attention to background knowledges and sets of beliefs that may be the relevant sources informing the ways subjects apparently, but perhaps not obviously, design their actions.

To conclude, I have reconstructed the methodology of conversation analytical studies on institutional practices, and have also discussed linkages with other scientific enterprises. I have suggested that CA's attempt to reverse-engineer the endogenous sense of interaction would benefit from opening the supposed context. The minimalist model for context takes into account the set of beliefs and the mode of organization of institutional practice. Consequently, social scientific knowledge of the set of beliefs and the modes of organization becomes relevant for conversation analytical work. CA, for its part, may increase our understanding of institutional interaction by respecifying the interactional substratum of institutional practices. CA may concretize, broaden, detail, and even correct our grasp of the situated meaning-making of institutional practices.

Further Reading

– There are at least two major collections of worthy articles on institutional interaction (Drew and Heritage 1992a; Boden and Zimmerman 1991).

– The issues related to context have been thoroughly discussed in Duranti and Goodwin (1992) and in a special number of *Research on Language and Social Interaction* 31(1), introduced by Pomerantz (1998).

– Doug Maynard (2003) has an interesting line on the relationship between ethnography and CA, with his notion of "limited affinity".

– For exercises, see http://www.uta.fi/laitokset/sosio/project/ivty/english/sivut/exercises.html

Notes

1 Some ethnomethodologists, like Hester and Francis 2001, have been critical toward the idea of the generic "institutionality" of institutional interactions. Nevertheless, the failure to account a characteristic "institutionality" of an institutional interaction is a serious flaw.
2 Of course, this list of variables is mixed. The modern institutions involving specific organizational contexts, and traditional anthropological institutions, such as gender and age,

would benefit from separate methodological discussions. Of the latter, gender has recently been studied in detail, for instance, Stokoe and Smithson 2001; MacIlvenny 2002; for age in interaction, see Nikander 2002. A further question would concern the relationship between modern institutions and basic anthropological institutions. Just an elementary outline of these issues will be provided in this chapter.

3   Strictly speaking, beliefs and modes of organization are historically shaped and culturally specific (cf. Moerman 1988; Ochs, 1988). For most practical purposes, studies of interaction can be realized in relation to "folk knowledge" without setting this relationship as the focus of research (cf. Wagner 1998).

4   The original language is Finnish, but the translation is sufficient for our purposes here (for the original transcript, see Arminen 1996).

5   AA's recovery program consists of 12 steps that are suggestions for individual members on how to recover from addiction and 12 traditions that are suggestions for AA groups how to organize AA activities (see Anonymouus 1952).

6   Alternatively, the repair could be heard as avoiding "labeling", i.e., Marja says that her partner abstained "just for fun" and not out of necessity. This hearing would be possible if the parties were not AA members. Marja's story as a whole seems to suggest that she orients toward AA and that her talk should be understood respectively. This alternative hearing is interesting as it may display how a person who does not know anything from AA might hear Marja's talk. This raises the issue of the relevance of contextual knowledge for the analyst. If the analyst lacks contextual understanding of the activities, the inferences drawn from the materials may contradict sharply the parties' own understanding. This lack of contextual sensitivity is something CA is heavily criticized at times. A further issue would be the distribution of different hearings among participants. Of course, also participants may have different knowledges and respectively understand each other in different ways.

7   Notably, I have mainly discussed "lexical choices"; there would also be other differences in the other layers of the organization of the interaction between these institutional practices. I will briefly discuss these at the end of the chapter.

8   Additionally, the author is indebted to the discussants on the ethno hotline. The exchange initiated by John Wheatley, Sally Jacoby, and Tom Wilson (October–November 1995) was most illuminating and raised many of these issues. In particularly, Tom Wilson's conceptual clarifications were invaluable.

9   Originally, Sacks et al. (1974) listed a total of fourteen items. They included items such as recurring speaker change, brief but common overlaps, use of turn allocation techniques, repair mechanisms, etc. Some of the items are logically connected to each other; some items are not characteristic of ordinary conversation but are common to all possible systems of talk-in-interaction, including various institutional interactions. In particular, turn size, order and content are crucial for the distinction between ordinary and institutional talk.

10   In addition we might name the length of interaction, or number of parties. On some institutional occasions the length of interaction is severely restricted, but note that court proceedings, for instance, may last years, whereas calls to institutional agencies may take only seconds. Therefore, the length of interaction may have relevant constraints in some institutional contexts. The number of parties is also restricted on some institutional occasions. But we may also note that the telephone conventionally limits the number of interactants to two. Since the turn-taking mechanism allocates only two turns at a time (the current and the next) this technical

constraint does not obstruct the working of turn taking even if it affects it. For practical reasons, questions concerning the number of parties will not be discussed here.

11 Douglas Maynard commented that only a small minority of institutional interactions may be formally organized, whereas a large majority of them are quasi-formal. For instance, according to Maynard only about 5% of US legal cases end up being dealt with in a courtroom (under formal restrictions), whereas most cases are settled informally and behind the scenes. It may be that there prevails a general preference for informality. The broader consequences of this preference (or its empirical demonstration) have to be discussed elsewhere.

12 Actually, Button (1992) claims that the job interview he studied was formally organized. Whether the interview was formally organized throughout is not relevant here, but the crucial point is what the parties accomplished through the digression from the regulative patterns of mundane talk, i.e., through the maintenance of "interview orthodoxy".

13 As mentioned in the introduction, we can distinguish sequential organization and sequence organization. The former is a broader term that concerns ordering and positioning of any actions and utterances. Sequence organization concerns courses of action that have been realized through talk. In actual analysis this distinction is very difficult to hold; it is more useful analytically than practically.

Chapter 3
Analytic Procedures

If all mankind minus one, were of one opinion, and only one person were of the contrary opinion, mankind would be no more justified in silencing that one person, than he, if he had the power, would be justified in silencing mankind.

(John Stuart Mill, 1843–83)

This chapter tells a story of scientific discovery based on my studies on addiction therapy. The analytic strategy applied in much conversation analytical work resembles that of analytic induction (Mill 1843–83; Lindesmith 1947). I will discuss the principles of analytic induction and show how they are used in practice. This will be demonstrated on a grass-root level with a set of materials from an ongoing research project. The aim is to describe a path to discovery, making it accessible for outsiders to CA as well. The narrative will disclose in detail the path from an amorphic mass of data to the polished, publishable and potentially applicable finding. Some analytic procedures have already been mentioned in the previous chapters, but here they will be introduced in practice. In addition, the reliability and validity of findings will be discussed. Specific emphasis will be put on the fact that science audiences have diversified and results have to be reported in recipient-friendly ways to serve the needs of different audiences.

I will start by describing the complete research process. The data transcription conventions that are essential for CA work will then be presented. Before moving to data analysis, I will consider the reliability, validity and relevance of findings. Essentially, the chapter focuses on the data analysis. The general principles of analytic induction guide the data analysis. Here the principles are adopted for the analysis of interactional, transcribed data. With modifications, these principles could also be applied to other data types. The analytic process is divided into five stages: identifying the phenomena, grouping the cases, outlining the dynamics of the phenomenon, blueprinting the manuscript, and writing up. Each stage of the analysis will be discussed with the help of references to empirical data. The chapter closes with a discussion about the applicability of findings.

3.1 Research Process

The research process as a whole is worth addressing, if for no other reason than to keep in mind that research involves more than just telling clever stories. As a whole, the CA research process is not that different from any other empirical research. You need to begin by designing the study carefully, including data collection and the study's relevance; indeed study design is an important but often neglected aspect of research. As with any research, data analysis is another key component; you can only write up the findings after you have thoroughly analyzed the data. In addition, before writing you need to carefully consider your audience: presenting your findings is a recipient-oriented process, and by thus focusing on your audience you can also more easily address questions concerning the applicability of your findings. In all, the research process consists of five phases.

1. Study design

2. Plan for data collection and consolidation of theoretical framework

3. Data collection and analysis

4. Reporting of findings

5. Applying findings

Figure 3.1 Research Process

In most CA literature issues concerning study design have been ignored. Study design nails together the research topic, theoretical framework and the plan for data collection. As a research paradigm, CA does not present ready-made solutions to study design, assuming only that the researcher is committed to addressing naturally occurring social processes through the sequential analysis of recorded data. Research design should address at least the following questions: which social processes are addressed, from whose point of view, and for whom, i.e., whose interests are being served? The collection and analysis of data is always based on a selection. Of all the possible interactive practices in the world, you choose one or some to study. Also, from a strategic point of view, the researcher should be able to give a compelling answer to why certain data is worth collecting. This answer may be self-evident to the researcher but not at all clear to the audience and reviewers of the study. When answering the question "why that data" you will also need to consider what the data analysis will consist of, how the data will be addressed, for whose interests, etc. Institutional encounters often consist of a professional and a client, and the researcher should keep in mind that the different parties may have different goals and define the situation differently. For instance, in medical doctor-patient interactions, doctors may at times turn towards their computer; from the patient's point of view it might seem like the doctor is turning away from the patient, while from the doctor's point of view using the computer during a consultation may be part of the necessary record-keeping routine, and thus unaccountable. One's perspective of an action or practice may influence one's interpretation of it (cf. Ruusuvuori 2000; Heath and Luff 2000). Thus, in CA as in other methodologies, the researcher should have the necessary background knowledge not to miss significant details or to pursue their meaning too one-sidedly. A study design taking into account the acquisition of sufficient background understanding also improves the quality of data analysis, so that the researcher learns to be open to any features found in the data, an empirical maxim of CA.

A detailed data collection plan addresses the questions of when, where and how much data should be collected. It is important to make a detailed and careful plan, because the researcher cannot often fill data gaps after the fact, since materials are time-bound and the researcher may not have unlimited access to the field. A general rule for the amount of data is saturation (Alasuutari 1996). That is, after a certain point new data does not reveal anything quintessential that would not repeat or be parallel to existing findings. Saturation, however, is a theoretical concept. Schegloff has often said that one is a number, i.e., one case may be enough to show and explicate an interactional pattern, a social fact. A completely different matter is the distribution of a pattern: when, where and how often we can expect to find the observed pattern. Generally, CA studies are descriptively strong in detailing phenomena, but weak in a variationist analysis which would elaborate the distribution of patterns. A limited number of cases may be sufficient for finding systematic patterns, though a comparative analysis attempting to elaborate differences between selected groups of cases or to study the distribution of patterns in target groups requires much larger amounts of data. In this sense, how much data you need depends upon the research questions you are trying to answer.

In analyzing interactional data, the researcher may have been committed to a certain theoretical framework in advance. In such a case, the researcher needs to convince the audience that the approach is fruitful and better than potential alternatives. To be compelling, you need to have a sociological imagination. You need to make the object of the study alien, unknown to the audience, and show that this study may solve the puzzle. In other words, you have to be able to extract an unknown aspect of a common subject, and then build a compelling case that you will be able to teach us something invaluable about this subject by scrutinizing this unknown aspect. Howard Becker calls the first part of this strategy "the Wittgenstein trick" (Becker 1998, 138).

Wittgenstein writes "Let us not forget this: when 'I raise my arm', my arm goes up. And the problem arises: what is left over if I subtract the fact that my arm goes up from the fact that I raise my arm?" (Wittgenstein 1958, § 621). With the help of the Wittgenstein trick you can formulate an unknown aspect of the known fact. When you have found a puzzle, you can establish systematic ways to solve it. But if you do not have a puzzle, you do not know where to start.

Data analysis and the transcription of data, the central part of the conversation analytic work process, will be discussed below, but first a few words about reporting your findings.

When you report your findings, communication is the dominant maxim, both for oral and written presentations of your work. In both contexts, it is useful to imagine how you would describe your findings to somebody face-to-face. Scientific conferences are useful in that they provide actual occasions where researchers can tell about their findings to colleagues from other places. At best, a 15–20 minute presentation can indeed be an informative package opening a new perspective on a phenomenon. However, in such a limited presentation, you must practice strict self-discipline, as in this amount of time you cannot convey much more than one idea. If you prepare your presentation carefully, however, you can provide the necessary background, your research question, and an empirical demonstration of your thesis. Such a presentation is subsequently a potential publication with minor modifications. If you do not have the chance to give an oral presentation, you should nevertheless imagine such an occasion in order to best determine what common ground you share with your audience. Indeed, one of the most common errors in scientific texts is to take too much for granted: theoretical notions are unexplained; the author's key ideas are not explicitly stated; practical and discursive aspects of data are not articulated; data extracts are presented as if they could "speak" for themselves, as if the reader had been there and could immediately grasp what was going on. Only rarely are scientific texts overburdened with metacommentary. In most cases texts would be improved by clearly stating the thesis, the purpose for writing, and by showing how the researcher set up their study and arrived at their conclusions.

Until recently, science was largely done for its own sake. Currently, however, funding for science is meeting increasingly utilitarian pressures. But this emphasis on utility is not wholly negative: many amazing discoveries have actually been made in very practical contexts, for instance, the principles of Gibson's (1979) ecological psychology, or the invention of "Turing's machine" (Turing 1950). Conversation analytic studies can reverse engineer how social practices are composed, and thus enable us to see potential alternative ways of performing them. This is possible both in social contexts involving persons interacting with persons and in technological contexts where person-to-person interactions are supported by technical artifacts. Conversation analytical findings can both correct and complement the understanding of social interaction provided by professional interaction ideologies (Peräkylä and Vehviläinen 2003). In this sense, they potentially open up new perspectives on professional interaction by allowing us to rethink its practices. Technologically-enhanced forms of social interaction and communication present a new challenge. In this context, CA can address communicative affordances of technologies, their possibilities for action (Dourish 2001; Hutchby 2001) by opening up both the potential and the limitations of technology through its focus on how technology is actually used. CA can thus provide resources for, or even participate in, design processes.

3.2 Transcription of Data

In CA, the initial stage of data analysis, after its collection, is data transcription, and we can hardly overemphasize its importance. Since it has been discussed many times (e.g., ten Have 1999, 75–98; Hutchby and Wooffitt 1998, 73–92; see also Atkinson and Heritage 1984, IX–XVI), I urge readers to consult these more thorough presentations of the transcription process; here I will just recapitulate some of the key points. Appendix 1 provides a key for transcription conventions.

First, the primary purpose of transcription is pragmatic: to render a conversation or other type of social interaction meaningful to the recipients. Further, a good transcript is an analytic exposition of an interactional practice so that it highlights and foregrounds its salient aspects. For instance, the next transcript makes visible a familiar, recognizable interactional pattern.

(1) (NB:52:2:66; Davidson 1984; Hutchby and Wooffitt 1998, 82)

```
1     P:      Oh I mean uh: you wanna go to the store er anything
2             over at the Market [Basket  er   anything? ]
3 →   E:                        [.hhhhhhhhhhhhhhhhhhh]h Well honey //
```

Here the transcript seems to make transparent the kind of activity going on between P and E (even without any further knowledge of the situation). Note that E overlaps with P, though P holds his turn and continues despite E's prolonged inbreathe. This kind of detailed transcript tells us that P seems to have continued to keep the floor even after the recipient E had indicated through her inbreathe her orientation toward the transition relevance of the turn. The transcript shows that P persists in doing something, and that E orients to P's persistence. When we read the verbal content of the transcript, we notice that P keeps on making proposals to E, while E orients towards declining P's proposals, as can be seen in how she initiates her turn. The transcript makes visible the parties' ongoing construction and monitoring of their relationship. The sequential timing of E's prolonged inbreathe reveals her orientation to P's action.

We may now ask whether we have any evidence for characterizing P's and E's actions the way we did. If E starts her inbreathe in overlap with P's proposal, it is noteworthy that P continues his proposal, and does not allow E to answer. It seems that P anticipated a rejection of his proposal at that point. Now, how was P able to anticipate rejection? There must have been some recognizable feature in E's conduct which allowed him to anticipate her rejection. The timing of E's inbreathe seems a candidate, for E initiated her inbreathe outside a possible transition point. E had chosen not to give affirmative responses at earlier possible completion points (there are two possible completion points in the first line). Instead, the initiation of the word "basket" was not a possible completion point. At that point P's activity was not completion relevant. (If it had been completion relevant, P could have given away his turn immediately; for further evidence of this pattern, see Arminen 1998.) P's turn seems to have been unfinished both syntactically and pragmatically at the point where E came in. P's activity was pragmatically incomplete, as he could not monitor an affirming response at this point. In other words, E initiated her response at a point which did not indicate an initiation of acceptance, thereby giving P good grounds for continuing his proposal.

Transcripts tell us stories, they give us material to reconstruct social activities, and give us evidence to draw conclusions about observable details of conduct. However, transcripts are rarely sufficient in themselves. For instance, in the excerpt above, we could have argued that E actually oriented to the possible completion of P's turn at the point where she came in. In this respect, the transcript lacks sufficient detail. According to the transcript, P's prosody at the point "Market" does not signal closure. However, nor are there any markings of rushing through, i.e., that P had oriented keeping the turn over the possible completion and resisting the possible turn transition. It is possible that the stress on M in "Market" is a pre-closing pitch peak, which indicates a designated possible completion at the next grammatically suitable point (Schegloff 1996a, 83–88). But again, careful analysis would demand listening to the interaction, as the transcript is not sufficient; indeed, it is not reasonable to expect the transcript to be excessively detailed at all points. Furthermore, transcription conventions are also relevant here. In "Market Basket" the initials are capitalized, as if to indicate a proper name, which would of course unanimously delay the first possible completion until the end of "basket". Capitals in CA transcripts generally stand for loudness but that does not seem to be the case here. Indeed, it may be useful for the sake of clarity to mark known proper names and concepts with capitals, but in this case that convention should be mentioned.

As a whole, transcripts are devices that make the analysis easier and help to communicate findings to the audience. The analysis itself should be based on recordings, so that the accuracy of the transcript can be checked and the salient details added to the original transcript (and in some cases extra details not relevant to the analysis deleted to avoid unnecessarily complex transcripts). Transcripts can never be perfect. Good transcripts illuminate the dynamics of turn-taking and the essential characteristics of speech delivery. Turn-taking involves details about the turn initiations (do they involve para-linguistic elements, such as inbreathe, pitches, hesitations, re-cyclings, etc), turn closings (are they marked with prosody? do they happen at the first possible point? are there excrements, rush-throughs, etc?), overlaps (do speakers speak simultaneously, from where to where), gaps and pauses (for how long in tenths of seconds). The characteristics of speech delivery involve noticeable features of stress, pitch, loudness, speed, and recognizable prosodic patterns.

As no transcript is ever perfect, a reasonable strategy is to start from the elementary features, and add details to the degree that they become relevant for the analysis. Gail Jefferson's transcripts (as the one above) provide a good standard that is still sufficient for most purposes. For a novice, it is wise to start from the features of turn-taking and to advance to characteristics of speech delivery after transcribing the elementary features of talk.

Visual data pose further complications for data transcription. Video recordings are preferable records of face-to-face interactions so that non-verbal activities, gazes, gestures and postures can be included. Multi-modal interaction processes cannot be analyzed without access to these visual materials. For instance, interactions can be partly or completely computer-mediated and not analyzable without access to visual data. In social interactions it is reasonable to start the transcription from the primary interactional media, in most cases speech, and add visual information to the degree required (see Heath 1986; Goodwin 1981). In computer-mediated interactions the visual data link may be the primary interactional mode. In these cases, speech provides additional information about the users' understanding of the situation (see Chapter 8 in this book; Suchman 1987; Heath and Luff 2000). The problem with visual data is the excessive amount of information, and transcripts can also become very complicated to read. A possible solution is to use frame grabs taken from the video tape (Chapter 8 in this book; Goodwin 1994; Goodwin and Goodwin 1996; Heath and Luff 2000). This practice enables the researcher to communicate the findings more effectively, and to some extent makes the excessive transcription process easier.

The other possible further complication is the use of data from scientific minority languages (languages other than English). In these cases, it is sensible to distinguish between the data analysis and the presentation of findings: the data analysis is based on the original materials in the original language, and is assisted with the transcription of data. The findings may be communicated in languages other than the original. Paul ten Have (1999, 93–94) discusses the various ways translations of data are presented in publications. In some cases only translations are used, but methodologically the most rigorous way to present data translations involves three lines:

1. a line in the original language

2. a morpheme-by-morpheme gloss of the line in the target language,

3. an "idiomatic/free" translation in the target language.

Below is an example of this rigorous way of presenting data translations (also, more grammatical information could be included in the gloss line, see Sorjonen 1996).

(2) [V2Peitsi1089] (Arminen 1998, 128–9)

3   mä olen pystynyt ↓ samaistumaan, (0.4)
               I   have been-able-to identify-with
               I've been able to ↓identify with others, (0.4)

4 →   .hhh Mä en   ↑tiedä? mul-= >jotenkin tuli< tossa
               I   do-not know I-(have) somehow came there
               .hhh I don't ↑know? I've-=>somehow I got< an idea

5 →   ku mä ajattelin   niin, (.) onkohan?, (.)   vuodenajalla
               when I was-thinking so   has+(intens.)   time-of-the-year
               when I was thinkin erm, (.) if=you-know?, (.)   the time of

This kind of three-line presentation is the most accurate way to present data translations, though many journals do not want three-line data excerpts. Therefore, in practice it is not always possible to use this system. Also, specialist journals, such as *Research on Language and Social Interaction*, suggest that three-line translations should be used only if necessary for the data analysis. Three-line data translations are necessary, for example, if the analysis focuses on the syntactic features of talk-in-interaction that are shaped differently in the original language and target language (the language of publication). If the researcher discusses features that do not depend on the syntactic variation between languages, findings can just as well be presented in translations only (though the originals should be available if requested).

3.3 Reliability and Validity

At best, reliability and validity should not be seen as mere "icing on the cake", but should inform the whole research process and enable the generation of findings that are both trustworthy and newsworthy. Following Peräkylä (1997b), reliability can be defined as the potential repeatability of findings so that they are not accidental and idiosyncratic. Validity can be defined as the accuracy of findings in terms of the avowed topic of research. These issues can be divided into four broad themes: external and internal reliability, the validity of the analysis of single cases and extracts, and the validity of generalized findings. The key issues have been summarized in Figure 3.2.

External reliability:
  - temporal, ambulatory and organizational inclusiveness
  - theoretical sampling of recordings
  - complementary ethnography and document usage

Internal reliability:
  - technical quality of recordings
  - adequacy of transcripts

Single case validity:
  - ostensive demonstration (transparency of claims)
  - validation by next turn (next turn proof procedure)
  - participants' validation (the procedural relevance)

Validity of generalizations:
  - constant comparisons
  - comprehensive data treatment
  - refutability principle
  - deviant case analysis
  - quantification of findings

Figure 3.2 Reliability and Validity in Conversation Analysis

As discussed, a condition for CA was the possibility of making recordings of natural situations. Sacks did not start studying conversations out of a theoretical interest or for their own sake, but because recordings afforded him an intersubjectively available source of data. "... I started with tape-recorded conversations ... because I could get my hands on it and I could study it again and again, and also, consequentially, because others could look at what I had studied and make of it what they could, if, for example, they wanted to be able to disagree with me."[1] (Sacks 1984, 26; originally lecture, intro, Fall 1967, reprinted Sacks 1992a). In this way, recordings offer a methodical basis for an enterprise whose findings are publicly criticizable and refutable, thereby opening a possibility for a strict empirical discipline. The potential availability of materials for scientific publicity does not itself solve all the issues of reliability and validity. In the field of institutional interaction, in particular, further questions stem from the use of recordings as the basis of the analysis. The key question concerning the external reliability of studies using recorded materials is whether they are indeed representative of the social practice the researcher claims they are. Peräkylä (1997b) has addressed this issue in terms of the inclusiveness of recordings, focusing on the ambulatory and temporary aspects of events.

Individual interactions are often part of a longer trajectory. For instance, many psychotherapies are long-lasting, and therapy sessions may vary according to their stage in the therapy process. Family therapies are often composed of a pre-determined set of meetings, each of which has a pre-defined agenda. This does not mean that we cannot analyze individual moments of interaction for themselves, but the researcher should be sensitive about making claims about the practice if the analysis is based on materials covering only some part of the institutional process. Of course, the researcher may try to be inclusive in the data collection, aiming to collect materials from the relevant stages of the institutional process. Alternatively, ethnography may be used to complement missing parts of the practice analyzed, and also to provide sufficient background understanding for the analysis. Work processes are also often complex, involving multiple interactions and ambulatory aspects. For instance, a traditional air traffic control unit composed of three persons (radar controller, the so-called "flight strip man", and assistant controller). Analysis of air traffic control operations cannot sensibly be limited to the interactions of any single person, but should cover the complete unit. These types of questions are best dealt with in the workplace study tradition (Luff et. al 2000; Heath and Luff 2000). CA studies have also been criticized for neglecting the organization of workplaces. Sarangi and Roberts (1999) claim that CA studies have one-sidedly analyzed the front regions of the workplaces, and neglected the backstages. There is no real reason why this should be so,[2] except that there are practical limits on what kinds of materials can be collected and how much can be analyzed. Therefore, data collection is not a neutral and purely technical operation, but a critical step in the overall research process. A reflexive study design involves creating a data collection plan which takes into account the study's overall aims. In this respect, of course, data collection in CA does not differ from that of any other (qualitative) study (for study design, see Silverman 2000).

The internal validity of a study concerns the quality of its data. Recordings are always only recordings, so things that are inaudible, or invisible, remain so for good. The recording arrangements should therefore be carried out carefully to minimize data loss. Sometimes a researcher may need to balance between getting a good recording and minimizing interference to the studied setting. No ultimate solutions exist (for a thorough discussion of these issues, see Goodwin 1994b; for a more recent discussion, see ten Have 1999; and ten Have's web site http://www2.fmg.uva.nl/emca/). The adequacy of transcripts is salient both for the analysis and for the presentation of findings and will be discussed next. (for data transcription, see Atkinson and Heritage 1984; Hutchby and Wooffitt 1998; ten Have 1999).

CA work starts with actual instances of data, not from averages, ideal types, or generalizations. Consequently, the validity of CA research can be demonstrated on the level of individual exhibits of interaction. This opens a possibility for the ostensive demonstration of claims, or what Peräkylä (1997b) calls the transparency of analytic claims. A CA researcher should always be able to pin down the analysis to a demonstratable detail of talk and action. As we saw above, validation by the next turn is the elementary technique of CA analysis. This has been discussed most elegantly in

Heritage 1984a. In more general terms, CA trusts the participants' validation (Seale 1999). This does not mean that the researcher would ask the participants what they were thinking or had intended (as some reseach methodologies would advise), but that s/he would pay attention to the features of talk-in-interaction oriented to by the participants, and account for them in a manner compatible with the way participants themselves treat them. CA thus utilizes the participants' own work to achieve an intersubjectively available course of action, the resource upon which the analysis is based. In their early texts both Sacks and Schegloff meditated upon this practice on several occasions:

> We have proceeded under the assumption (an assumption born out by our research) that in so far as the materials we worked with exhibited orderliness, they did so not only to us, indeed not in the first place for us, but for the co-participants who had produced them. If the materials (records of natural conversation) were orderly, they were so because they had been methodically produced by members of the society for one another, and it was a feature of the conversations we treated as data that they were produced so as to allow the display by the co-participants to each other of their orderliness, and to allow the participants to display to each other their analysis, appreciation and use of that orderliness. Accordingly, our analysis has sought to explicate the ways in which the materials are produced by members in orderly ways that exhibit their orderliness and have their orderliness appreciated and used, and have that appreciation displayed and treated as the basis for subsequent action. (Schegloff and Sacks 1973, 290; see also Heritage 1984a)

The same principle of the participants' validation gains a specific meaning in the context of institutional interaction, where it is transformed into the principle of procedural relevance, as discussed.

CA researchers, however, are rarely satisfied with simply stating how an individual instance of data works (though they are sometimes criticized for only describing individual pieces of data). Rather, through the analysis of instances of data, analysts try to identify generalizable invariances. In the analysis of ordinary talk and action, this means the generic features of interaction, while for institutional interaction, the task becomes to identify the generic building blocks of institutional practice. However, this search for generalizable findings poses generic problems on the validity of a scientific argument. CA methodology closely resembles that of analytic induction (see Seale 1999, 83–84; for underlying philosophical notions, see Llobera 1998; Lindesmith 1947). Constant comparisons are carried out on several levels. Individual instances and sequences are compared to each other to note parallel features, which are potentially a recurrent phenomenon. Instances of an identified phenomenon are compared in different settings to observe their setting-specific features. Parallel instances are compared in ordinary conversation and institutional settings. The ultimate aim is comprehensive data treatment in which all instances of a phenomenon are surveyed, and deviations from the originally-stated phenomenon are sought. Deviant cases are used for strengthening the analysis, either by modifying the original account so that deviant features can be included in the modified account, or by accounting for deviant cases, thus preserving the original analysis. Finally, tabulations can be used for a quantified account of the phenomenon.

3.4 Data Analysis

In particular, Charles Ragin (1987; 1994) has shown that most types of social research can be broken down into varying combinations of elementary logical operations. In a more accessible way, Howard Becker (1998) demonstrates how the logic of truth tables underlies many research strategies. Truth tables can also be usefully applied to describe the logic of CA data analysis, even if truth tables are rarely explicitly presented in CA studies. The types of logical operations used in CA resemble analytic induction, as has been discussed (Mehan 1979; Maynard 1984; ten Have 1999).

Truth table logic simply means that an object is described with a matrix of possible features. For example, let us examine P's and E's interactional pattern in extract 1 with the help of a truth table. The analysis will particularize an analyzable phenomenon, breaking it down into its constituent parts by examining its identifying details. For instance, P and E are involved in producing a special kind of overlap: it is both lengthy (passing the first possible place where the floor could have been changed) and also non-competitive (lacking features characteristic of competitions for turns). As a truth table, a lengthy, non-competitive overlap is the following.

Feature (present in the specimen)	Truth condition	yes	no
Overlap		x	
The length of overlap: brief			x
The length of overlap: long (over the first transition relevance place)		x	
Competitive overlap (Signs of competition: raised voice, rushing, etc.)			x

Figure 3.3 The Truth Table Analysis of Interactional Patterns

The analysis can next detail the individual case and include new, parallel cases so that the account may be developed through comparisons to a collection of cases. A collection of cases sharing similar characteristics to those shown in the truth table thus form the material for analyzing the phenomenon in question. By analyzing collections of cases, we are able to redefine and specify the original phenomenon. For instance, we would most certainly notice that in addition to the characteristics mentioned, the overlap between P and E is produced non-verbally, through inbreathe. This raises issues concerning how we define the whole phenomenon of overlap, i.e., what kind of parallel activities should be called overlaps. For the sake of clarity, we can call this a non-verbal overlap, which then leads to the question of whether there are other types of non-verbal overlaps than inbreathe. The truth table could then be developed as follows:

Feature (present in the specimen)	Truth condition	yes	no
Overlap		x	
Overlap – non-verbal		x	
Heavy inbreathe in overlap with the prior speaker		x	

Figure 3.4 (continuation of Figure 3.3) The Truth Table Analysis of Interactional Patterns

In this manner, the targeted phenomenon is refined in the course of the analysis. We started with the category of overlap, but have ended up speaking about a heavy, prolonged inbreathe produced in overlap with a prior speaker. Now, we might have found a potential phenomenon, i.e., an interactional practice which carries an intersubjective meaning. If we are correct, then we have noticed an identifiable and characterizable social resource that parties in interaction are able to produce, orient towards, and make use of. In terms of the ways such interactional pattern are used, if we have been able to find a reasonable number of parallel cases, we would most likely notice that the cases cumulate in certain activity contexts, and that there exist slightly variant patterns in various activity contexts. Here, the heavy, prolonged inbreathe was produced in overlap with a proposal. Might accusations be met with the same device? Would there be any noticeable difference in interactional sequences in these activity contexts? The analysis proceeds towards identifying social practices, whose interactional architecture is then opened up.

A characteristic feature of analytic induction is comprehensive data treatment (Lindesmith 1947; Becker 1998), so that all cases are carefully scrutinized. The analysis checks to what degree the cases sharing similar elementary features (in the truth table) resemble each other in other relevant respects. If modifications are found, the hypothesized underlying pattern is revised accordingly. New conditions are added to the truth table until a systematic, coherent pattern is revealed. Cases that do not obey the rule as formulated are called deviant cases (Schegloff 1968; Clayman and Maynard 1995). Three different accounts may be given of the deviant cases. The analyst can first check whether the parties themselves orient toward the deviancy of their departure from the canonical pattern. For example, in Chapter 2 (extract 3) I showed how an interviewee oriented toward his discursive role, and asked permission to ask a question in an interview. Orientations to deviant behavior demonstrate the party's understanding of the underlying normative framework, and thus reveal the overwhelming relevance of the basic pattern. Secondly, the analyst may reformulate and generalize the basic pattern so that the "deviant case" eventually falls under the same general rule. This strategy is actually quite common, since most analyses start from a provisional understanding that is increased and sharpened through the evidence gathered through case-by-case analysis. However, only rarely are reformulations of hypothesized regularities written up. The most famous case is Schegloff's (1968) analysis of landline telephone call openings. In all but one of 500 telephone call openings the answerer spoke first. But by considering the deviant case, Schegloff was able to reformulate his regularity from "the answerer speaks first" to a "summons-answer sequence". That is, the answerer does not just speak first, but answers a summons. In a deviant case, when the answerer failed to answer, the caller repeated the summons by saying "Hello" and thus solicited an answer. In this way, the originally formulated regularity was rephrased in a stronger form, which also included the deviant case. Finally, genuinely deviant cases in which parties do not display any orientation to deviancy and which cannot be accounted for with a reformulation of the regularity need separate analysis explaining why they emerge. The analyst seeks local contingencies to account for the departure from the pattern, so s/he can show that only contingent factors caused the deviancy. For example, in my AA meeting study I showed that in the meetings AA speakers systematically referred to earlier speakers to display their solidarity (Arminen 1998). Speakers could, however, withhold from referring to prior speakers without overtly orienting to avoiding referring them. A contingent fact was a quarrel between them. On occasion, it could be shown that speakers withhold from referring to prior speakers due to their quarrel, thereby actually orienting toward maintaining solidarity by avoiding causing a public strife.

As a whole, CA aims to treat data comprehensively, and also to extend the analysis to each case. Consequently, the findings should apply to all cases in the corpus including deviant cases, which are accounted for as explicated above. The generalities found through CA analysis are thus rigorous, and should apply to the whole corpus analyzed. The generalizability of findings beyond the corpus, however, is an open empirical question. A careful analyst discusses both deviant cases and borderline cases to sharpen the analysis and to specify the phenomenon in question (Schegloff 1992b;

1996b). An elaborate analysis seeks universal structures of talk-in-interaction but is receptive to the context-sensitivity of interactional patterns.

In the next sections, I will go through the analytic procedure briefly introduced above. Although I do not have the space here to reproduce a complete analysis, I will select parts of a study to demonstrate how it was worked out. In Appendix 2 there is a handout of this study (the set of data extracts).

Identifying the Phenomenon

To start an analysis you have to choose a phenomenon. In most CA studies of ordinary conversation, the topic is a particular kind of sequential pattern. Famous examples include Pomerantz (1984; 1980) on second assessments and on fishing, Davidson (1984) on subsequent versions of invitations etc., Heritage (1984b) on change of state tokens, and Schegloff (1992b; 1996b) on confirming allusions and on repairs after next turn. In institutional environments in particular, studies may focus on a theme, topic or process that is relevant for the business at hand, e.g., contesting evidence in court (Drew 1992); advice giving in health visits (Heritage and Sefi 1992), giving and receiving a reason for a visit to a doctor (Ruusuvuori 2000), and discretion in medical/therapeutic interaction (Silverman and Peräkylä 1990; Bergmann 1992). Actually, in institutional environments many studies also combine these approaches and address the use (or avoidance) of particular sequential patterns in a goal-oriented environment, for instance, perspective display sequences in medical interactions (Maynard 1991b; 1992) and in counseling interaction (Vehviläinen 1999), repairs in class rooms (Mchoul 1990), laughter in medical interaction (Haakana 1999), and the sequential organization of the ownership of experience in group therapy (Peräkylä 1995; Arminen 1998). Of course, there may not be a clear-cut distinction between studies focusing on sequential patterns or on institutional practices, as all CA studies address the way activities come off sequentially.

Let me give you an example of how I once moved from an observation to an identification of a phenomenon and its analyses. When I was doing a research project studying interactions in 12-step addiction treatment, I was struck by what was going on in some of the data. The following extract comes from a peer group interaction (i.e. a group of patients having a session together without the therapist). They had been asked to think about what their lives would be like half a year after the treatment period. The extract starts with T's answer (Tiina, one of the patients, N1 = unidentified female patient, M2 = the senior member of the group who acts as a secretary, writing down answers for the therapist to read, P = another patient).

(3) (VR 2 28:3–10)

1 T: £Mää vastaan et emmä tie°d(h)ä°, hhhe hy hy (.) .vhhh
           £I'll answer that I don't kno°(h)w°, hhhe he he (.).vhhh
2   (0.4)

3 T: →   Ehkä raittiina?, (0.6) Ehkä en e°lossakaa°. hh
    Perhaps sober?, (0.6) Maybe not even a°live°. hh
4   (0.6)
5 N1:   [(--)
6 M2:→ [(Panenksä mä tähän et) ↑TOIvottavas[ti °raittiina°,
    [(Shall I put here that)   ↑HOPefull [y °sober°,
7 T: [N:: en tie̲dä?,
                                       [e:: I don kno̲w?,
8   Toi[vottavasti raittiina vois< (.) sanoo?, h
         Hop[efully sober I guess (.) one cd say?, h
9 P: [YHH
10   (0.5)

There is a striking discrepancy between Tiina's answer (lines 1–3) and what the
senior member volunteers to write down (6). Tiina's nihilistic answer reveals her
sincere understanding of her situation (as a middle-aged addict, the odds start to be
against her: it is not easy to quit a habit since that is pretty much all she has left). The
senior member (M2), by contrast, says what he seems to think the therapist would
want them to say. In all, at least on some occasions there is a deep gap between the
officially prescribed or desired state of affairs by the treatment clinic and the patients'
individual views. This is something we could call an observation. It is nowhere near
an identification of a phenomenon, but it provides a possible starting point. If you
are interested in what is going on at an addiction treatment center, you might then
try to pay attention to such a gap between official goals and the patients' individual
views. But to move toward an analysis you have to narrow down your interest, and
find ways to articulate manageable aspects of this more general structural feature.
Actually, during the course of the research project, I became involved with a series
of investigations all handling details of this structure. We studied the professionals'
ways of confronting patients who expressed undesired views (Arminen and Leppo
2001; Arminen and Halonen forthcoming), the ways the multi-professional meeting
constructed an institutional view over the patients' own view (Arminen and Perälä
2002), and the ways the patients talked about the group therapy rules in the peer
group (Arminen 2004).

In sum, the analytic procedure first identifies a generic structural feature, and then
breaks it down into a set of observable and identifiable practices which themselves
consist of enumerable interactional patterns. For instance, I initially noticed that the
peer group explained the rules of group therapy to every new incoming patient, and
that there seemed to be something systematic in the way these rules were discussed
in the peer group. Consequently, my first step in analyzing this potential phenomenon
was to collect and describe in a preliminary way all the instances in which therapy
rules were discussed. Figure 3.5 is an authentic summary of that work process, and

as you can see the cases are grouped and labeled somewhat impressionistically. The codes under the labels, like VR4, s.8, r.7 (Peer Group session 4, transcript page 8, line 7), stand for individual instances of the phenomenon,[3] and you can find some examples of the data in Appendix 2. Group number five, "interpreting rules through reformulation", includes the most cases, and also the widest variety of subtypes. So, at least the numerical evidence speaks for the salience of this group of cases. However, as discussed, even unique cases can be analytically and practically relevant regardless their lower frequency. However, if no other criteria prevail, you can use the number of occurrences to help you identify recurring features, which are worth scrutinizing in more detail. I chose this track.

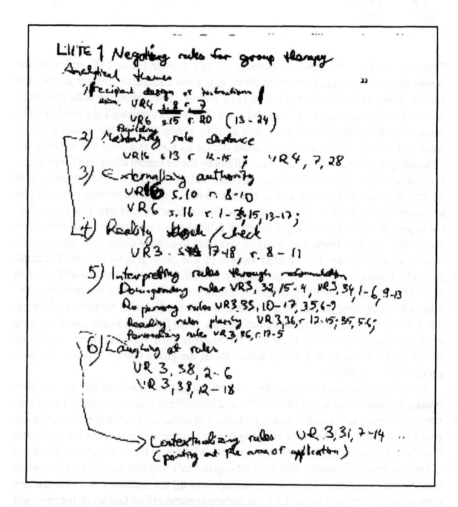

Figure 3.5 Identifying the Phenomenon

Grouping the Cases

After you have identified a potential phenomenon, you have to decide on strict criteria to define which cases belong to your corpus. The inclusion criteria must be explicit and articulated so that they can be presented as a truth table (Figure 3.3). In my study of how patients discussed the rules of group therapy, I decided to include only cases in which a particular rule was mentioned, and I excluded general talk about rules that seemed to be too open-ended. Whatever you choose to study – advice sequences, proposals in negotiation, or laughter – you have to be able to explicitly articulate what you will count as the analyzable phenomenon and which sequences you will include in the analysis. In this way, you can define the exact corpus and select the instances of data which meet your criteria. However, the inclusion criteria have to be formal so that even possible variations within the phenomenon are scrutinized, i.e., the inclusion of cases should not be so selective that you only choose cases that meet your expectations concerning the nature of the pattern. For instance, if you are studying the openings of mobile phone calls, you would need to study all the openings in your corpus, not just those that meet your intuition of what mobile phone call openings are like.

By refining your analysis, you can then investigate variation within the pattern. When you define the exclusion and inclusion criteria for the corpus, you can also group your cases into types. If you have a uniform pattern, then you will just have instances of one type and you have to prove that no variation exists. Most studies concern patterns that involve some amount of permutation, however. In my study on the rules for group therapy, I ended up finding six distinct types of how rules were brought up in the peer group (see Appendix 2). In terms of simplicity, the first class is "reading rules plainly" without any additions. Other ways of treating rules include "rephrasing of rules", i.e., stating them in other words, but without any systematic valence. Further types included "contextualization of rules", in which rules were enriched and explained with details of local knowledge and context. "Downgrading of rules" meant that the rule was rephrased in a weaker form so that its force was decreased. The two last types were relatively uncommon. The first was the "personalization of rules" in which some personal significance was attached to the rules. "Laughing at rules" involved non-serious references to rules that invoked audible bursts of laughter.[4] After you formulate the typology, you can start selecting the clearest and the most representative cases for the write-up of your findings.

Outlining the Dynamics of the Phenomenon

When you have found a pattern or invariance in your data, you have reached the first step of making a finding. However, to communicate your finding you have to articulate its relevance. The relevance may involve the newness of a finding, how it compares with prior knowledge: does it bring up something yet unsaid; the accumulation of knowledge, how the finding relates to prior studies: does it detail, elaborate or challenge earlier views; the cultural and social location of the finding: does it concern a particular social practice or institution, does it take a fresh look at some social or cultural object; and finally, on the practical side: does the finding involve a direct or indirect practical benefit, does it allow us to rethink or elaborate some institutional practice? Once you are able to articulate the relevance of your finding, you can discuss and outline its dynamics from that perspective.

When you want to communicate a finding that makes a contribution to your chosen field, one strategy is to compose a narrative. By pointing out and explicating an interactional practice, you can discuss a practice in a social world that stands for a socially constituted meaning. As Becker pointed out in his discussion of Wittgenstein's trick, you can first pose a problem concerning the social practice, and then present a solution. To return to my own analysis of how rules were used in the addiction treatment clinic, my generic observation was that the clinic's rules were treated as accountable, i.e., only rarely (in deviant cases) were the rules taken at face value. This observation allowed me to link the study to the debate on rule use (see Lynch 1993), and question what people were doing with rules if they were not following them blindly. In general, ethnomethodology has replaced the rule-following model with the model of accountable action: "According to that theorem actors may, or may not, act in accordance with the normatively organized constraints which bear upon them – subject only to the condition that 'deviant' actions may ultimately be recognizable, accountable and sanctionable as such" (Heritage 1984a, 291–292).

I concluded that the manner in which rules are applied in a particular setting tells us not only about rules but also about the ways in which they contribute toward making the setting what it is. A setting is constituted through the parties' conduct, and this conduct is oriented to rules, though not in a mechanical but in an accountable way. The sequences of rule explication exhibit this reflexive relationship between rules, their application and the setting.

From this perspective I outlined a draft displaying the sense of the dynamics of the phenomenon (Figure 3.6). I started from the general notion that since rules are tied to their articulation they are also context-sensitive and therefore negotiable. In this respect, rules and instructions are like other recipient-designed activities. The analysis proper starts with introducing the ways rules are presented in contextualized ways in the addiction treatment clinic. Subsequent discussion concerns the ways rules are rephrased in interaction. The most typical pattern in the addiction treatment clinic is the downgrading of rules. Then the discussion concerns deviant cases, which include both the personalized presentations of rules and the plain reading of rules. The discussion is closed with cases in which the participants' ambivalence toward rules surfaces through laughter.

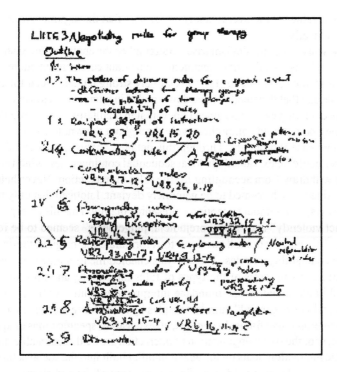

Figure 3.6 Outlining the Manuscript

Drafting the Manuscript

After outlining the dynamics of the phenomenon, you can start drafting the manuscript. First, you select a reasonable number of data instances so that you can demonstrate your points with reference to data extracts. Optimally, each claim is proved through data extracts. In practice, most articles also include hypothetical arguments that are not empirically tested, but from the CA point of view only empirically demonstrated points are valid in the final instance. In most cases, you must limit the amount of data due to space restrictions. Moreover, it does not make sense just to present data; you must reserve space for a convincing analysis of it. Therefore, you must present a sufficient amount of data to support your arguments, but steer clear of presenting any data that is not immediately relevant to your analysis. Also, avoid unnecessarily lengthy data extracts.[5]

After you have selected your data extracts, you have to decide upon the best order to present them in the manuscript. For each section place the clearest and strongest example first, with any subsequent extracts adding onto and elaborating the canonical pattern demonstrated through the first example.[6] Each data extract should provide some added value for the overall analysis. Be sure that the argument is coherent and proceeds logically.

Finally, you can use the deviant cases to strengthen the analysis. For example, in my analysis of rule use in addiction treatment, the deviant cases turned out to be crucial. Initially, it seemed possible to show a relatively strong tendency that the rules were accountable and that they tended to be downgraded in interaction. However, given that there were deviating cases, and since I knew that in qualitative studies regularities are weak if they do not hold comprehensively throughout the whole corpus, I examined each deviant case thoroughly. Through this detailed analysis, I observed that some of the cases could be explained via local sequential contingencies, which enabled the parties to withdraw from accounting for the rules in interaction. Nevertheless, a few cases remained which seemed to be genuinely deviant. I noticed that only three rules were – always, and without exception – presented plainly. The rules "respect others", "do not act violently" and "avoid prejudicial judgements" seemed to be resistant to accounts. This observation allowed me to reformulate the original thesis about the general accountability of rules. The analysis enabled me to notice that social actors make distinctions in terms of the types of rules they apply, and thus all rule use is embedded in the social actors' mundane interpretative frame. That is, parties orient to the generality of "general" moral principles by not holding them accountable in an everyday interpretative frame. In contrast, all extensions, specifications or applications of tacit rules for the social organization of interaction are held accountable. In this way, therapeutic interaction floats on the accountability built into the social actors' cultural competence (see Appendix 2 for the final manuscript of the addiction clinic study).

Writing Up

Writing up is the final stage of the analysis, during which the explication of findings is rethought and finalized. When writing up the analysis of excerpts, you can elaborate on your points and also alter the basic organization if necessary (which you might need to do if midway through the analysis you end up reformulating your original thesis, as I did in the example above). Also, at this stage you can check to see that you have included the right amount of data. Once you have a written draft, you can solicit feedback from your teachers and/or peers; their comments are invaluable in editing the final version for publication.

At best, a scientific text enables us to understand the relationship between the general and specific. Becker (1998, 126) urges writers to develop their conceptual skills and discuss individual cases without using any of the identifying characteristics of the actual case, such as discussing schoolwork without using words like "teacher", "pupil", "classroom", etc. At the same time, the details of actual cases are the living cells that give readers a grasp of the lived reality. Ideally, studies of interaction always tie together abstract generality and concrete details, but do not get stuck in either dimension.

Writing up is also your final opportunity to recipient-design your work. If you are targeting a specialist journal on interactional studies, you must focus on a detailed explication of interactional patterns and address the relevance of findings vis-à-vis prior studies in the field (see articles in *Research on Language and Social Interaction* or *Discourse Studies*, for example). If you are targeting another type of specialist journal, you have to show that you are making a contribution to that respective field; be aware that a focus on interactional details for their own sake is most likely to be met with criticism (for articles designed for specialist audiences, see Heritage and Stivers 1999; Arminen and Perälä 2002; Arminen 2002a). Generalist journals sometimes also accept CA analyses, but in these cases you have to carefully link the contribution to ongoing debates in the field, and show the relevance of your findings in terms of the general discipline (Maynard 1991a; Schegloff 1992b; 1996b; Peräkylä 1998).

To serve addiction studies, the study of peer group practices in an addiction clinic argues a general point about the natural limits of therapeutic practices and treatment efforts due to their accountability to clients, a point I make by showing details of interaction. I demonstrate that clients used their everyday cultural competence, interlinked with tacit mundane moral standards, to solve the contingencies of using the rules and managing the therapeutic interaction. Thus, the details of the interaction revealed that clinical efforts to influence the clients' conduct were constrained by their accountability to mundane moral standards that set the outer limits for what is regarded as appropriate therapeutic practice. Identification of these constraints served treatment studies to be applied to the clinical practice.

3.5 Applying the Findings

CA studies can have practical relevance on at least at three levels. Their value can be heuristic, critical, or innovative. Heuristic value simply means that studies can address some social or institutional practice and so generate reflection on that practice. During the study on addiction treatment, we occasionally organized sessions for the clinic staff to watch and discuss segments of videotape we had selected to be of interest to them. My impression is that the staff sincerely enjoyed these sessions, and that the tapes and the transcripts allowed them to reflect on their work practices. A more elaborate way is to collect instances of a particular practice, and select cases in which a "similar" practice is carried out with different means or with differing outcomes. For the addiction treatment clinic, I collected a sample of cases in which professionals confronted patients (see Arminen and Leppo 2001). By comparing these cases, the professionals were able to contemplate their ways of encountering patients. Many times the professionals had sharp views about these scenes, and their expert analyses of them were thought-provoking for me, too. Still, there are limits to these kinds of heuristic uses of CA: they do offer participants a chance to view and reflect upon their practices from the outside, but they do not go much beyond that.

CA studies can also be used critically, though CA is not commonly thought of in these terms. For example, CA studies can be used for evaluating professional practices: if the researcher commits her/himself to a position, practices seen as problematic from that position may be criticized. In our study of multi-professional teams in the addiction treatment clinic, Riikka Perälä and I pointed out that information concerning clients was used in a tendentious and one-sided way in those meetings. We also explicitly stated that, from our point of view, their neglect of aspects of client information was problematic and might be harmful. At that point we had stepped on thin ice. First, we jeopardized co-operation with the clinic from which we got our materials and whose support we might still need (for a discussion of this, see Forsythe 2001). Second, by taking a stand we opened ourselves to criticism. Despite our scientific work and access to ethnographic materials etc., we did not have any means to prove that the practice we had criticized really was harmful to the clinic the way we claimed. If no outcome measurements or other similar data is collected, CA studies can rarely if ever prove any claims about the outcomes of practices.[7] Nevertheless, CA researchers are as able as any other concerned citizens to make educated guesses. Ultimately, the question of whether to take a stand is an ethical choice (see Jayyusi 1991).

Furthermore, not all criticism is negative, and CA might provide some opportunities to provide "positive" criticism instead. For example, during a study on the use of mobile internet connected devices (initially WAP phones), I videotaped device use and observed occasions of "usability" problems (to be discussed in Chapter 8). These usability studies were critical of WAP (which indeed turned out to be a giant failure). Interestingly, despite the generally negative findings concerning the usability of WAP and the user experiences, the study could also make a positive contribution to mobile technology development. Experienced users of mobile devices in particular oriented toward potential features of applications that were not (yet) available: i.e., users tried to do things with their mobile phones that could be done in principle but which did not yet exist in practice. Such observations (positive criticism) reveal the innovative potential of CA studies.

CA studies also have innovative potential in that they can open our eyes to details in the social environment we have not known existed. To notice an oriented-to feature of a communicative device or a potential use of a pattern of speech in a certain context has potential for social innovation. Also, elaboration of an existing pattern may allow us to become conscious of some pattern we have not noticed earlier. J.M. Atkinson's (1984) study of how to generate applause in political conventions is a good example of this category. His scrutiny of politicians' methodical ways of making the audience applaud enabled not only speechwriters to consciously use these gimmicks but also enabled enlightened members of the audience to recognize attempts to invoke applause. To my knowledge, J.M. Atkinson achieved some success as a consultant in this area. Stivers and Heritage's work on doctors' online commentaries is another example of work that concerns strategic moments of some professional practice, thereby involving innovative potential (Heritage and Stivers 1999).

Systematic applied CA research poses questions of its own. Systematic application of CA research would demand implementing CA work inside larger research and development programs. Within the field of the research and development of communication technologies, Paul Dourish and Graham Button have coined the idea of "technomethodology", in which the ethnomethodological backdrop would be implemented inside the whole perspective of the research and development process (Dourish 2001). Another systematic applied practice could combine CA with outcome measurements. This type of combined study could potentially answer questions concerning the relevance of interactional patterns on the outcome of institutional practice (see Heritage 1999; Heritage et al. 2001). I will return to these issues in the final chapter.

3.6 Conclusion

CA studies are distinctively empirical. This distinctive empirical quality starts with the minute transcription of data, following guidelines originally set up by Gail Jefferson and subsequently modified according to various research questions. The elementary analytical logic of CA closely resembles that of analytic induction (Lindesmith 1947). The whole corpus is analyzed to find invariances applying to all the instances of a respective type. Cases that do not seem to follow the pattern are called deviant cases, whose analysis is an important part of the research process. The deviant cases are analyzed so that it can be shown that they either 1) indirectly display the orientation to the basic pattern, 2) that there are local contingencies that explain them, or 3) that the basic pattern can be modified so that either 1 or 2 applies. Initially, CA studies concern sequential patterns, but they may also address the specificity of institutional practices, or the particular realization of sequential patterns in institutional environments. The aim is to break generic phenomena into clearly identifiable practices consisting of analyzed interactional patterns. Written findings should be recipient-designed to address the intended audience.

On the whole, however, the CA research process is not that different from other empirical human sciences. It is critical to have a good research design, which creates a meaningful unity of research topic, theoretical framework and data collection plan. You can also consider the applicability of your studies, which might have heuristical, critical and/or innovative value. CA studies may be positively critical or innovative if they amount to findings that enable recipients to notice or become conscious of features of the social environment they have not been aware of.

Further Reading

– Pomerantz and Fehr (1997) provide a brief but useful introduction to data analysis.

– Peräkylä (1997b) discusses reliability and validity carefully.

– Silverman (2000) considers many generic issues on study design in a practical way.

– For further issues in the logic of social studies, I would suggest you go beyond CA. Becker's (1998) and Ragin's (1987; 1994) books also discuss the principles of analytic induction.

– For exercises, see http://www.uta.fi/laitokset/sosio/project/ivty/english/sivut/exercises.html

Notes

1   At least initially, CA has truly been a falsificationist enterprise.
2   Actually, Maynard's book on plea bargaining (1984) is essentially about the backstage of the juridical process, and currently there are many CA studies that also concern back regions.
3   If the materials are in digital form, the references could be on the exact timing of the instance (and only secondarily to the transcript). Still, transcripts can be handier in building a collection. This and many other details depend on your individual working style.
4   The title "laughing at rules" is not exactly accurate, since without detailed analysis is not possible to say reliably what the persons are laughing at. Notice how difficult it is to label types. For instance, "non-serious references" could be considered an alternative label for the type. However, it is much more vague, as it is hard to pin down any demonstrable criteria for (non)seriousness apart from audible laughter (excluding nervous bursts of laughter). A more technical label might be "sequences in which explaining the rules is met with laughter". As a whole, I have always avoided technical jargon when possible, even at the expense of some technical accuracy.
5   Novice analysts seems to believe that the "data speaks for itself". Consequently, long stretches of data are supposed to give a reader "see-it-yourself" understanding of the practice without any deeper analytic exposure. Unfortunately, I think this solution is too easy. Data does not speak for itself; at least it does not speak in any unanimous way. Therefore long data extracts without careful analysis are seldom a useful device to make any systematic point. Only carefully analysed instances of data should be presented.
6   Sometimes researchers have a heroic tendency to want to tackle the most complicated case first as if to prove their analytic skill. Analytic skills could preferably be demonstrated by providing an analysis that is elegant in its clarity.
7   This may also be the very reason why CA studies will never become the mainstream of applied studies.

Chapter 4

Encountering a Client

Psychologists commonly speak as if the abstractions of relationship ("dependency", "hostility", "love", etc.) were real things which are to be described or "expressed" by messages. This is epistemology backwards: in truth, the messages constitute the relationship, and words like "dependency" are verbally coded descriptions of patterns immanent in the combination of exchanged messages.

(Bateson, 1969)

An institutional encounter takes place at the crossroads of the client's and the professional's perspectives. A key dimension of institutional interaction is how they manage this disparity in their perspectives, for it imposes communicative tasks on both the client and the professional. The client needs to present or formulate an appropriate reason for the encounter. For example, in doctor-patient encounters patients must display the "doctorability" of their problems, i.e., patients orients to describing their problems as being appropriate for medical care (Ruusuvuori 2000; Heritage forthcoming). In business negotiations, parties may pay considerable attention to how they present their trustworthiness and reliability to the opposite side.

In institutional encounters, however, the question is not only self-presentation but also how to relate to the other's perspective. The professional needs to elicit the client's perspective in order to deliver her professional view on the matter. The professional's ability to invoke the client's experience and knowledge becomes particularly crucial in therapeutic, medical and counseling interactions. Furthermore, the fact that each person has unique and exclusive access to his own experiences, in effect owns their own experiences, is significant in the institutional setting, as professionals have to find ways to tackle this ownership of experience. Later in this chapter I will discuss a particular solution to this problem using a perspective display series, which means that a professional takes the client's perspective into account by first eliciting it.

The other side of an institutional encounter is the professional's maintenance of a professional distance from the client. This can take various forms in different contexts, involving issues such as neutrality, sensitivity and avoidance of argument. Institutional encounters thus set somewhat contradictory requirements on the professional, who may both need to display understanding and sensitivity towards the client's concern but also maintain sufficient disengagement not to react personally in a way which might be considered inappropriate.

Institutional encounters create specific expectations in both clients and professionals. Furthermore, both clients and professionals share a common goal to establish an intersubjective, mutual orientation to the institutionality of the occasion. In this chapter I will first view the generic social structure of institutional interaction. I will then discuss the disparity of the professional's and the client's perspectives, and ways of dealing with this disparity. Finally, I will deal with the issue of the maintenance of professionality. As a whole, this chapter provides an introduction to the empirical scrutiny of institutional interaction.

4.1 Accountable Actions

Accountable actions form the basis of institutional interaction. Drawing on ethnomethodology, we can say that any social action is accountable.[1] In social life any action can be recognized, reported and sanctioned. As Heritage (1984a) has said, such accountability is the key principle upon which the social organization of actions rests; it is the micro-foundation for societal life. In institutional settings accountable actions serve as a foundation to build up a relationship between parties so that the state of affairs can be subjected for action. In any institutional occasion parties use the accountability of actions to portray the issue at hand so as to hold it reportable and manageable in terms of the possibilities and constraints set by the institution. This contextually-appropriated accountability provides the generic social structure of institutional interaction. The study of institutional interaction, then, analyzes the means, techniques and structures of interaction through which actions are organized so as to be appropriate to the practices they themselves realize.

The accountability of actions pervades all institutional interaction, though it takes various forms in different settings and appears on different levels. In doctor-patient encounters, the task-specific form of accountability is the doctorability of the patient's problem, in calls to emergence services it may be the reportability and helpability of the caller's concern, in juridical settings it is the fit with legal procedurality, etc. Following Sacks's early discussion on accountability, we can outline some generic dimensions of institutional interaction using some of his examples of calls to or from a suicide helpline (for recent discussions of service encounters, see Wakin and Zimmerman 1999; Baker et al. 2001).

(1) (Sacks 1992a, 72)

1   A: Hello. This is Mr Smith.
2   B: Hello. I was referred to your office by Mr Jones from
3   the Conciliation Court, and I felt perhaps someone

4		there would make an appointment for somebody there

4   there would make an appointment for somebody there
5   to talk to me. I don't know what I want to say to you
6   except I'm confused and the trouble –
7   Ask the questions. I can answer them …

(2) (Sacks 1992a, 72–73)

1   B: Hello.
2   A: Mrs Gray?
3   B: Yes.
4   A: This is Mr Smith of the Emergency Psychiatric Clinic.
5   B: Yes.
6   A: I spoke to your daughter who was quite concerned about
7   you and I wanted to talk with you and see if we could
8   help in some way.

(3) (Sacks 1992a, 73)

1   A: Hello this is Mr Smith
2   B: Say, my husband is suicidal and, I mean, he's
3   attempted it about a half a dozen times …

These call openings display some of the basic features of institutional interaction. First, institutional replace mundane reasons for social exchange. The account of the reason for the call is placed at the first possible place after the communicative availability of the recipient is achieved. The openings of these calls are thus systematically truncated and reduced from "ordinary telephone call openings" (cf. Schegloff 1986; Houtkoop-Steenstra 1991). Not only is the exchange of "how are yous" dropped, but also reciprocal greetings and identifications are only partial or missing. The reduction of these openings further underscores the accountable action as the only linkage between parties.

An account of the problem also establishes a functional asymmetry between parties: the description of the problem[2] ascribes discursive identities of helper and help-seeker to the parties. In this way the interaction is given a practical frame and direction. The presented trouble implies a need for action, or at least an assessment. Further, troubles-talk implies seeking a solution that is not available to the help seeker alone. The goal-rational character of institutional practice also amounts to a normative standard allowing assessment of the success of institutional interaction in terms of its implied task.

The ways in which accounts are constructed also embodies and builds the institutional character of the encounter. Parties orient to giving a source or a basis for the existence of a trouble (Pomerantz 1991/91). In extract (1), a conciliation court is the referring authority, in 2 the daughter is the source of information, and in 3 suicide attempts are mentioned as evidence. In giving evidence of the trouble the parties move towards constructing a "case". Information and knowledge about the trouble is not presented as such, but in a recipient-designed manner (Arminen and Perälä 2002). In this way the information is fitted to the institutional procedures, and the case is built as manageable in and as designed for the institutional framework. If the case is fitted to the institutional framework, it becomes manageable – in medical settings, doctorable. Constructing the doctorability of a problem is already part of the treatment. Orientation to doctorability carries the parties beyond their individual perspectives: the patient is not just stating his unease but moves towards another's perspective through his account of the problem. In giving evidence that I am feeling bad, or giving evidence about how I know that you/he/she feels bad, the party acknowledges the perspectual limitations of this knowledge. The accountability of a problem also allows a move towards analysis of how the problem has emerged, and scrutiny of a new perspective from which the trouble might begin to vanish.

The accountability of action provides the generic social structure of institutional interaction. In institutional encounters the relationship between parties is constructed through an accounted state of affairs so that it can be dealt with and managed in the institutional framework. Thus, the study of institutional interaction concerns the tools, devices, techniques and the structural organization of interaction through which the parties aim to achieve their institutional goals.

4.2 Orienting to the Client's Perspective

In dealing with the institutional task at hand a key question is how to take into account the other's perspective. In this section I will discuss how this surfaces in interaction, and some of the techniques to deal with our limited access to another's perspective. I will also show how everyday interactional procedures are also a resource in institutional settings. I will first introduce three techniques – fishing, candidate answers, formulations – which are also commonly used in ordinary conversations to overcome the limited access to the other's perspective or experiences. My discussion begins with indirect ways of inviting the other's perspective to more overt expressions through which the other's inner states are invoked. In each case, I will elaborate some specific applications of these techniques in institutional contexts. Afterwards I will address the perspective display series: sequentially, these are a more extended way to address another's experiences, and to manage the disparity of perspectives.

Fishing

A common context in which the limited access to the other's viewpoint comes to the surface is telephone conversations. Telephones are a form of technology affording social exchange at a distance (Hutchby 2001). But since telephones do not afford visual access to the other's situation, they enhance the parties' perspective-boundedness in a conversation. The management of the parties' limited access to the other's viewpoint is a routine precondition for a successful telephone interaction. The disfluencies caused by failing to recognize the other's perspectual limitations can be striking. For instance, a 3–4 year old child whose speech may otherwise be fluent lacks still a theory of mind (Mitchell 1977), and is thus unable to take into account another's limited access to her own situation. A child tends to refer to all the properties of his current situation, like visible toys and tv-programs, as if the recipient on line would also have immediate access to them. Culturally competent members have learned to take into account the other's limited access to one's own experiences. One of the ways to handle the other's ownership of experiences has been called "fishing" (Pomerantz 1980).

Fishing can be formulated as a rule. When a party expresses limited knowledge of a matter to which the other party has privileged access, the other party becomes accountable for her/his knowledge (Mäkelä 1997). Telephone conversations are a forum in which fishing commonly takes place.

(4) Pomerantz 1980 (NB:II:–1) [Peräkylä 1995, 134]

```
1       B:  Hello::.
2       A:  HI::::.
3       B:  Oh:hi:: 'ow are you Agne::s,
4   →   A:  Fi:ne. Yer line's been busy.
5       B:  Yeuh my fu (hh)- .hh my father's wife called me .hh
6           So when she calls me::, .hh I can always talk fer a
7           long time. Cuz she c'n afford it'n I can't. hhhh
8           heh .ehhhhhh
```

The social distribution of knowledge and the consequent limitation on access to the other's knowledge is a profound social fact. Fishing also stands for the moral character of social interaction. It relies on and displays an underlying principle of co-operation so that the recipient orients to the other's limited access to her own knowledge as a request to provide a fuller, authorized account of the matter (lines 4–7). Providing an account of one's past inaccess to social interaction portrays a person's principled co-operation on further occasions, whereas declining to provide such an account of inaccess might turn out to be socially sanctionable. The consequences of this orientation to social reciprocity are manifold, not least in maintaining normative pressure for group cohesion. In the age of mobile phones, teenagers consider it accountable if somebody keeps her/his phone turned off for any lengthy period. Consequently, group pressure generates a new communicative etiquette implying, among others, a necessity to possess certain devices and to be interactionally available at any time. This is the social dynamics of how "a must" is engendered.

The social distribution of knowledge is a crucial dimension for any institutional interaction, but it is particularly significant when dealing with experiential knowledge. In therapeutic encounters, for example, it is critical to overcome the client's potential unwillingness to discuss difficult intimate issues. Fishing and other tactics that might transform the ownership of experiences from a hindrance to a resource are therefore invaluable for therapeutic process. HIV counseling sessions based on the Milan School Family Systems theory provide an example. Peräkylä has shown that a permutation of fishing, called "circular questioning", is used to pre-empt the patient's potential reluctance to discuss dreaded issues. A family member who was present was first asked to present her or his view of the matter concerning the patient's inner experiences. After the family member had produced a description of the patient's feelings or fears, the patient systematically oriented to sharing his own version of his experiences. In this manner, the ownership of experiences was transformed from a potential obstacle to a fruitful resource for therapeutic practice. The standard pattern can be laid out as follows.

Chart 4.1 The Standard Pattern of HIV Counseling (Peräkylä 1995, 112–113)

(1) Co:	Invites Client 1 to produce a description of something related to Client 2's inner experience	
(2) Cl.1:	Produces the requested description	
(3) Co:	Invites Client 2 to respond to the description given by Client 1.	
(4) Cl.2:	Produces the response.	

Peräkylä notes that in HIV counseling circular questioning "constitutes a most powerful device to elicit clients' discussion of matters that they may initially be reluctant to talk about" (Peräkylä 1995, 141). He gives an example of the therapist's asking the client several unsuccessful direct questions before successfully eliciting the client's talk about the proposed topic via circular questioning (ibid. 139–141).

Permutations of this interactional dynamic can be traced in other therapeutic settings also. One such therapeutic practice is sharing rounds (Wootton 1976). In sharing rounds parties use extended turns one after another to describe their personal experiences. At the outset it may look that no interaction is taking place during these extended monologic turns. If the sharing turns are monologues, these sharing sessions seem to offer a social paradox: why do people come together in fellowships like Alcoholics Anonymous week after week to tell individual monologues? On a closer look, however, we may note that experiences are co-constructed during individual turns. Conventionalized expressions, such as "I identified with X" or "just like X said", show that members lean on each others' tellings in constructing their own experiences. Sharing is built upon participants' orientation to listen to each others' stories to be reminded of their own experiences that have become relevant vis-a-vis what has already been said. In this manner, prior turns provide a search procedure to find something relevant to say here and now that is relevant not just for oneself but relevant also for those who have experienced something similar (Sacks 1992b, 3–16). In sharing, prior turns are treated as prompts that have made relevant personal experience as being shareable in relation to what has been said. The interactional orchestration of sharing becomes underlined when a speaker has difficulty finding the words to go on. On these occasions prior turns may provide the resource to proceed.

In extract 5, the speaker in an AA meeting, Peitsi, is first telling how he got into AA with the help of "medicine" (alcohol). Then he makes several attempts to open a new topic, before he succeeds via a reference to what Kultsi has said.

(5) Arminen 1998, 128–9 [V2Peitsi1089]

```
1      P:    .hhh Mut sen   lääkkeen kautta  mä oon  päässyt
                   But that medicine through I    have got
             .hhh  But with the help of that medicine I've got

2            tähän   je:ngiinki. (1.0) .mth Ja  täällä jengissä
             into this ga:ng too. (1.0) .mth And here in this gang

3            mä olen pystynyt      ↑samaistumaan, (0.4)
             I    have been-able-to identify-with
             I've been able to ↑identify with others, (0.4)

4  →         .hhh Mä en    ↑tiedä? mul-= >jotenkin   tuli< tossa
                  I do-not know  I-(have) somehow came there
             .hhh I don't ↑know? I've-=>somehow I got< an idea

5 →          ku  mä ajattelin     niin, (.) onkohan?, (.)  vuodenajalla
             when I  was-thinking so      has-the+(intens.) time-of-the-year
             when I was thinkin erm, (.) if=you-know?, (.) the time of

6 →          jotain     osuutta asiaan      että:,
             something part    in-the-matter that
             the year has somethin' to do with the fact tha:t,

7 →      .    .hhh mullakin on ollut vähän semmosii=
             .hhh I've also had     a bit of such things=

8 →          =Kultsi puhui jotai      tos=
             [name] talked something there
             =Kultsi spoke about over there=
```

9 →   =semmosii?, (0.5) p̲i̲nna   ollu tiukalla ka̲:ks ↓viikkoo:
               such   nerves(sl.) been on-edge for-two weeks
               such things?, (0.5) my n̲e̲rves've been on edge for two̲:

10   ↓nytten °et°, .hhh
               now   that
               ↓wee:ks ↓now"°uh°, .hhh

The multiple attempts to open a topic provide us with a sense of the speaker's
difficulty in finding words (lines 4–7). Eventually, Peitsi uses an earlier speaker's talk
as a resource (7–9), with whose help he finds a way to formulate his own experience
as talkable (9–10). Reference to the others' experiences is invoked as an invitation to
proceed with sharing one's own experience. In sharing, speakers use each others' talk
as a resource when expressing their own sentiments, and reformulate and reevaluate
their own experiences with the assistance of this new understanding.

The social distribution of knowledge is the interactional backbone of sharing. In
sharing, turns are made reciprocally relevant by designing subsequent turns as being
occasioned by prior ones, and a methodical basis for finding that "I am not alone with
my problems" is established (Arminen 1998).

Candidate Answers

Though the social distribution of knowledge does not allow anybody direct access
to what others know or intend, we can infer others' experiences and intentions
through common sense. We routinely make educated guesses about items in
others' knowledge domains; such educated guesses are called "candidate" answers
(Pomerantz 1988). Offerings of candidate answers are extremely common both in
everyday life and in institutional surroundings (Bergmann 1992). They can also
be used for various purposes, though as an information-seeking strategy they have
some core features and some recognizable implications for interactions. In her study
of candidate answers Pomerantz offers a list of cases including examples from both
mundane and institutional contexts.

(6) Examples of candidate answer offerings (Pomerantz 1988, 360)

1.   "And have you been treated all right by the police?"
2.   "Is that in any way related to the police, that bruise?"
3.   "Was Tom home from school ill today?"
4.   "Did you just see me pull up?"
5.   "Did you step out for a few minutes?"
6.   "Are you going to be here for awhile?"
7.   "Is that Temple?"
8.   "Should I just go ahead and pick that up and put in a couple of tiles to build it up?"
9.   "Do you have a sign-in today?"

Offering a candidate answer creates a balance between the questioner's and the recipient's knowledge domains. First, as a query it attributes authority to the recipient and displays orientation to the recipient as the source of knowledge. But, in offering a candidate answer, the questioner also guides the recipient to respond in a certain way. The recipient is not only given sense of what the recipient considers relevant but also what the anticipated answer might be. Pomerantz (1988) concludes that offering a candidate answer is useful whenever the speaker has a reason to guide the recipient towards giving particular information. Candidate answers are thus an accountable part of purposeful actions. Consequently, parties may build an intersubjective understanding of the action they are participating in with the help of candidate answers. The questioner displays the relevancies of the situation through the query, which in turn becomes a source of inferences for the recipient. Pomerantz (1988) pays attention to this inferential work in her field notes, in which she analyzes the inferences she drew from a candidate query.

(7) Pomerantz 1988, 361 [Field note]

> I parked my car and was walking to my office at Temple University. A block away from the building, a truck pulled over and the passenger pointed up the street and asked, "Is that Temple?" I confirmed that it was. The man asking for the information did not offer a reason for seeking the information. Yet I saw the request in terms of his attempt to get to Temple University. His publicly available circumstance was that he was in a car going somewhere. As a member of this culture, I knew that drivers typically have destinations and that drivers sometimes go to unfamiliar destinations. I assumed that his seeking information about the location of Temple University was responsive to his concern (as I inferred it) to arrive there.

Candidate answer offerings are part of communication dealing with purposeful actions in everyday and institutional settings. In institutional settings, candidate answer queries are linked to the strategic purposes of action. An institutional agent may try to get the other party to produce descriptions suitable for the institutional framework. The activity context may also narrow the range of possible answers, for instance, in survey interviews. Candidate answer queries are also commonly used in juridical settings, where the aim is to establish and confirm the existing evidence, as I will discuss in Chapter 6. The properties of interrogative talk are also present in child sexual abuse investigations. These investigations may be particularly difficult, as children may be unwilling and incompetent to talk about sexually abusive incidents. Therefore, professionals argue that they must assist children in revealing the abuse. According to Lloyd (1992), one such technique to help children talk about abuse is candidate answer queries. In using candidate responses, the interviewer helps the child determine a suitable answer in cases where the interviewer anticipated that answering the question would be difficult.

(8) Lloyd 1992, 113 (Q2) ((Jason and an adult are animating the Jason doll.))

> 1 → A: … Was Jason standing up or laying down or what?
> 2   ((Jason stands up the Jason doll))
> 3 → A: Standing up?
> 4   C: Sort of like this, kneeling. ((Jason makes the Jason
> 5   doll kneel, then lets it fall face down.))

In interrogations, candidate answer queries strengthen the chance to establish evidence as they allow minimal responses as confirmations. Open questions that may not have been answered can therefore be rephrased as candidate answer complements, allowing minimalist responses which are more easily obtainable. Nonetheless, the recipient is still held as the accountable source of the answer. The candidate answer query only assists the recipient in making the answer simpler.

(9) Lloyd 1992, 114 (Q3)

> 1 → A: … You can show me who he touched. Did he touch
> 2 →   Kristin?
> 3   C: Um hmm.

Candidate answer queries can be used to guide the recipient to confirm the anticipated state of affairs; they utilize a generic preference for agreement that prevails in most conversational interaction (see Sacks 1987). In child sexual abuse investigations, interviewers do not seem to orient to a neutral investigation, but rather seek to confirm the alleged abuse. Candidate answer queries are functional in guiding the recipient towards the oriented outcome and they are commonly used in variable environments – ranging from courtrooms to discussions with non-native language speakers – where parties may have difficulties to answer. This constructive side of candidate answer inquiries, however, can endanger the reliability of the information gained.

Formulations

Antagonistic constellations between parties provide a further contingency in institutional settings. The parties may not only be reluctant to talk about their inner states or reveal their knowledge, but may be oriented to preventing the opposite side from gaining knowledge. In negotiations, a skillful negotiator never lets the other side know anything beyond what is absolutely necessary. For instance, the final offer is best kept secret or the other side would exploit this knowledge to maximize its gains, even beyond the original final offer. Inasmuch as knowledge is a strategic resource in an institutional encounter, the parties' talk-in-interaction reflects this strategic constellation in their selection of interactional devices. In antagonistic settings parties may not rely on verbal practices, such as fishing or candidate queries, which are based upon an underlying assumption of co-operation. Instead parties must mobilize coercive devices that force the other side to show their position, or at least, to express their assessment of the position they are claimed to have. One such device forcing the other side to assess its position is a formulation. Formulations are interpretations of what has been said or meant and in this sense resemble candidate queries. In both cases, the speaker offers a candidate understanding, but designed in different ways. In formulations the act of attributing a specific interpretation is done explicitly, e.g., "so you are saying/meaning x" whereas in candidate queries the inferential quality of the query may remain implicit. In conflict situations, the formulations of what the other party may have meant put the targeted party into a position to reject or accept the alleged interpretation. In addition, irrespective of whether the formulation is confirmed, the formulation opens a chance for a reformulation. Therefore in resolution-oriented conflicts, such as negotiations, formulations enable the parties to test their positions to move towards the resolution of the conflict.

Walker (1995) has studied the work of formulations in union/management negotiations. She shows that formulations are used to "test the water" to reduce chances that the prospective offer would be turned down. Formulations are thus central in negotiations via their resolution-implicative capacity. Walker also shows that the design of a formulation has crucial implications for its reception, whether it is accepted or rejected. A blunt, unequivocal version of what the other party has said invites rejections and subsequent reformulations in which the meaning of what has been said is spelled out; the trajectory goes from what you said to what I meant.

(10) Walker 1995, 127 (Management: Andy (A), and Bill (B); union: Pete (P))

```
15  P:  can I put that into a (0.8) bit more straightforward manner ( ) (0.9)
16      you're saying that 'til it's agreed nationally ((co. name))
17      [won't have it=
18  A:  [no
19  A:  =no [we're not saying that at all]
20  B:      [no we're not saying that ]
21  P:  ( )
22      (0.2)
23  B:  let's say it another way
24      (1.7)
25      if it costs a thousand pounds to build a (0.5) ((product name)) twenty
26      five right now (0.7) then in a shorter working week it's not (gotta)
27      cost us any more. (0.4)
```

A blunt attribution of what a party has said (lines 15–17) invites a rejection (18–19) and a reformulation that opens the gist of what has been meant (23–27). Here the strong intersubjective orientation is displayed by the choral response (19–20). In contrast, formulations that are mitigated and more open may be confirmed.

(11) Walker 1995, 127 (Lines 1–13)

```
 1   P:    you're not actually saying that you DON'T want a shorter working
 2         week if I'm right. (0.6) [you're just saying that you can't afford=
 3   (?)   [((cough))
 4   P:    =one at this: (0.6) particular time.
 5         (0.3)
 6   B:    .t .hh [can I- ]
 7   A:           [we are] realistic enough to appreciate (0.3) that (0.7) factors
 8         (0.3) impinging on us from outside (0.8) MAY WELL ONE day result
 9         in us having to: (0.5) to e- oo- (0.6) ach[ieve a thirty seven=
10   B:                                              [bu-
11   A:    =hour working week. but the [circumstances withIN must be (0.6)
12   B:                                [bu-
13   A:    suitable (0.7) to enable us to do it.
```

Here the negation "you are not saying" (1–2) frames the formulation more openly than a straightforward attribution of what the other party has said. Therefore, a concessively designed formulation creates a chance for it to be accepted. Note, however, that both accepted and rejected formulations invite reformulations that keep the negotiations going on, and allow the parties to test their positions to find a possible resolution. In his ongoing work, Drew (2003) has compared the work formulations do in various settings, and has pointed out, as Walker (1995), that design features of formulations are crucial for the work they accomplish in the activity they contribute to.

Perspective Display Series

In everyday life bad news tends to be told in patterned ways. Messengers tend to avoid breaking the news directly, instead giving clues and hints about bad tidings, thereby inviting the recipient to infer or guess the news. If the recipient guesses right, the messenger can simply confirm what the recipient says. In this manner the messenger and the recipient co-construct the news delivery distributing responsibility for news-telling more equally. Hence, the news bearer also reduces the chances of becoming blamed for the bad news. Further, after the recipient has broken the news, the original news bearer is back in the position to complement or assess the news as it has already been told.

This same interactional dynamics may be put to institutional uses. For example, Maynard (1989b; 1991b; 1992) has studied the "perspective display series" in pediatric work where clinicians have to inform parents about bad test results concerning developmental problems. In this setting, clinicians seem to organize the interaction systematically so that the recipient's perspective is co-implicated in the presentation of the diagnosis.

(12) Maynard 1991b, 164 (8.013, simplified version)

```
1   Dr. E:   What do you see as his difficulty.
2   Mrs C:   Mainly his uhm- the fact that he doesn't understand
3            everything and also the fact that his speech is very
4            hard to understand what he's saying lots of time.
5   Dr. E:   Right ... I think we basically in some ways agree
6            with you, insofar as we think that David's main
7            problem you know does involve you know language
```

In telling bad news, clinicians tend to use a perspective display series that is minimally composed of three turns. First, the clinician asks or invites the recipient's perspective. After the client has responded or given the assessment, the clinician may produce the second assessment. The perspective display series is an interactional resource that allows the perspective questioner to take the second position, i.e., to assess the other's turn after it. We will notice that this "going second" or "speaking second" is a strategic resource (Sacks 1992b, 340–344).

Depending on the parties' relationship, a perspective display series may serve different functions. When parties are aligned the perspective display series allows the clinician to confirm and elaborate the lay view, as we can see in this more detailed and extended transcript (13) of the case we just examined above.

(13) Maynard 1992, 337–338 (8.01,3)

```
1    Dr:  What do you see? as- as his (0.5) difficulty.
2         (1.2)
3         Mo: Mainly his uhm: (1.2) the fact that he
4         doesn't understand everything (0.6) and
5         also the fact that his speech (0.7) is very
6         hard to understand what he's saying (0.3)
7         lot [s of ti ] me
8    Dr:  [ right ]
9         (0.2)
10   Dr:  Do you have any ideas wh:y it is? are you:
11        d [o yo ] u? h
```

```
12    Mo:  [ No ]
13          (2.1)
14    Dr:  .h okay I (0.2) you know I think we basically
15          (.) in some ways agree with you: (0.6) .hh
16          insofar as we think that (0.3) Dan's main
17          problem (0.4) .h you know does: involve you
18          know language.
19          (0.4)
20    Mo:  Mm hmm
21          (0.3)
22    Dr:  you know both (0.2) you know his- (0.4) being
23          able to understand you know what is said to
24          him (0.4) .h and also certainly also to be
25          able to express:: (1.3) you know his uh his
26          thoughts
27          (1.1)
28    Dr:  .hh uh:m (0.6) .hhh in general his
29          development ....
```

The doctor first asks the mother's view of her son's problem (line 1). After mother has told her view, the doctor is in a position to elaborate on that view. First, the doctor checks the mother's level of knowledge (10–11), and after the response, he proceeds to offer a more "technical" and "detailed" version of the child's problem (14–29). Notice that the doctor produces this medical version only after he has expressed agreement with the child's mother (14–15). In this fashion, the medical diagnosis is presented as being co-authored by both parties and the potential for resistance is precluded.

When parties are weakly aligned, perspective displays assume a new function. After eliciting the client's view, the clinician may proceed to upgrade the lay view. In the next extract, the clinician has asked the mother's view on how she feels about her daughter's progress at school. The mother has responded that she is not at the same level as her peers, that she is kind of slow.

(14) Maynard 1992, 341 [3.047]

```
1    Mo:  ... and I have seen no progress, from
2          September to June. For her learning
3          ability, she is slow.
4          (0.6)
5    Dr:  That's what we uh:: also found on- on
6          psychological testing. .hhhh That she was.
7          per- not performing like a normal (0.2) uh:::
```

```
8          six and a half year old uh (0.4) should.
9    Mo:   mm hmm
10   Dr:   And that she was performing more uh (0.3)
11         .hhh what we call as a borderline (0.4)
12         rate of retardation .hhh uh:::m
13         (2.2)
14   Dr:   For a normal (0.4) kind of might use a
15         number .hhhh it's usually about hundred
16         (0.2) or more. (0.6) and anywhere between
17         uh:: (0.3) eighty two and (1.2) uh::::: (0.4)
18         ninety is kind of uh:: (0.4) borderline
19         (0.6) kind of uh:: (0.2) .hhh functioning.
```

Again, the doctor starts with an explicit agreement (lines 5–6), but then he reformulates the mother's view from slowness of development to abnormality (6–8). At this point the mother still produces a response token that displays her recipiency at line 9. Subsequently, the mother withholds from producing response tokens (note the two second silence at line 13). This may indicate potential resistance or difficulty in accepting the diagnosis. Here the perspective display series has allowed the clinician to anticipate the client's stance so that he can offer the diagnosis in a recipient-designed way that would allow the maintenance of working consensus as far as it could go. The clinician may lean on the provisory alignment and present the diagnostic view not as a challenge but as an upgrade of the lay view.

When the professional and the client do not just have some disagreement, but stand miles apart, perspective displays may be used to reduce the disparity between perspectives. In extract 15 the clinician has elicited the client's perspective through a set of questions. The parties' positions as they have surfaced can be summarized as follows.

Chart 4.2 Semantic Content of the Participants' Claims (Maynard 1992, 344)

Parent's perspective	Clinician's perspective
the basic condition is hyperactivity	hyperactivity is one condition among several
the problem is temporary	the problems are not temporary
there is no brain damage	there is brain damage, which is the basic condition

In this case the disparate views might let us foresee an argument and conflict. In extract 15 the clinician finally reveals her diagnosis. But the diagnosis is built upon several concession/reformulation moves in which the clinician first comes towards the client before introducing reformulations that again move away from the client's stance. The final moves are presented in the next extract.

(15) Maynard 1992, 348–349 (30.186)

```
1    Dr:  Now when you say: uh you know, the ter:m
2         something wrong with the brain, is very
3         vague, we don't like it (.) you
4         don ['t like it.    ]
5    Mo:       [ Yeah right. ]
6    Dr:  But .hhhhh when we have to descri:be Barry's
7         problems, we would have to say that there is
8         something, that [ is not ] working right
9    Mo:                  [ Yeah ]
10   Dr:  in the brain
11   Mo:  Mm
12   Dr:  that's causing these things. It's causing
13        the hyperactivity, .hhhh [ it's:  ] causing him
14   Mo:                           [Yeah ]
15   Dr:  ta see the wor::ld, in a different way, from
16        other children,
17   Mo:  Mm yeah
18   Dr:  It's causing him to be:- his (.) thoughts to
19        be maybe a little disorganized, when he
20        tries ta order the world,
21   Mo:  Mm::
22   Dr:  in his mind. And .hhhh if you know, we had
23        ta say, uh if we had ta give a diagnosis
24        (0.2) .hh you know when you write away to
25        schools:: or ta other doctors, you have to
26        write something down as a diagnosis. I feel
27        that hyperactivity, just alone, wouldn't be
28        enough.
29        (0.2)
30   Mo:  Mm [ hmm ]
31   Dr:     [ .hhh] and that we would have ta say
32        something like brain damage.
33   Mo:  Mm hmm
34   Dr:  in terms of (0.2) of Barry's problems
35   Mo:  Mmm.
```

```
36    Dr:   Because it's a kind of thing that's- it's
37          not jus:t hyperactivity that's gonna be
38          helped with a little medicine. .hhhh He- he
39          is going to nee:d, (0.5) a s- special
40          education: (.) all the way through.
41    Mo:   Uh ha. ·
42    Dr:   We feel.
43    Mo:   Yeah.
```

In commenting on the client's view, the doctor orients to bridging the gulf between perspectives. She manages to find a point of contact between her and the client's view in that they both dislike the vagueness of talk about brain problems (lines 1–5). The client's perspective, thus, is used as a resource to construct alignment in ancillary issues despite massive disagreement on pivotal issues. This strategic alignment serves to maintain a working consensus between parties (cf. Jefferson 1984). In presenting her diagnosis, the doctor takes into consideration her knowledge of the client's view and orients to conflict potential. Finally, the diagnosis is presented in the most cautious way. First, the doctor frames it as hypothetical, not actual (22–23). In selecting a hypothetical description, the speaker widens the recipient's interpretative possibilities. The truth-value of a hypothetical description may be bracketed. If the parent chooses, she might say that no diagnosis was given, that there was just some "hypothetical talk". In a similar manner, were the doctor's diagnosis challenged, she could retreat behind the wall of hypotheticality, and say that it was just hypothetical.

The doctor also appeals to her institutional accountability in presenting the diagnosis, saying it her duty to make a diagnosis (24–26). In representing herself as an accountable party in interaction, the doctor works towards a discursive coalition with the client. She distances herself from her medical authority by ascribing the necessity of making a diagnosis to external parties. Further, these distancing moves also delay the talk about potentially controversial issues, like "brain damage" (32) or "need" for "a special education"[3] (39–40). Therefore at least a momentary identification between the doctor and the client becomes possible.

Also, when parties have exactly opposite views, the knowledge of this contradiction may be valuable. In the face of opposite views, perspective displays may be used to anticipate and control the conflict. For example, in extract 16, we see a parent's response to a perspective display query.

(16) Maynard 1991b, 182 (22.049)

```
1     Dr N:   Mister Smith are there any things about
2             Charlie that worry you?
3     Mr G:   Not a thing.
4     Dr N:   Nothing?
5     Mr G:   Nothing.
```

After this query the doctor knows of the wide gulf between their perspectives, and can then use her knowledge to minimize and control the outburst of conflict. The doctor has still made an attempt to invoke the client's view on the child's problem, but when these are unsuccessful, she moves on to present her diagnostic evaluation (extract 17).

(17) Maynard 1991b, 183 (22.125)

```
 1     Dr N:  Well (1.8) there's (0.3) a disagreement on
 2            exactly (0.2) whether there is a problem or
 3            not. (0.5) I think rather than belabor the
 4            point of whether we- (0.3) whether there is a
 5            problem or not? (0.1) I think we should give you
 6            what (0.5) we found (0.4) which is a[fter      ] all
 7     Mrs G:                                    [ Mm hmm]
 8     Dr N:  what you came here for.
 9            (0.3)
10     Mrs G: Mm hmm
11            (1.9)
12     Dr N:  F::rom (0.5) straightforward pediatric [ point ] of =
13     Mrs G:                                        [ Yeah ]
14     Dr N:  = view,
15            (0.2)
16     Dr N:  His general health, a:fter he got over that hundred
17            and three [ poin ] t eight temperature (.hhh) i:s-
18     Mrs G:           [Yeah ]
19     Dr N:  has not been the problem.
20            (0.2)
21     Mrs G: Yes
22            (0.4)
23     Dr N:  Uhhh (0.3) But a general evaluation. (1.7) it
24            was very noticeable some of what you described.
25            (0.2)
26     Mrs G: (mm hmm)
27     Dr N:  Charlie has a problem with language.
28            (0.4)
29     Mrs G: (mm hmm)
```

First, the doctor orients to the existence of a potential conflict, and suggests that they not get stuck in an attempt to arrive at an agreement (lines 1–5). Here, too, the diagnostic assessment starts with an expression of agreement. The doctor notes that the child's general health is unproblematic (16–18). In moving from good news to bad news, the doctor makes a reference to what the child's mother has said (23–24).

After these precautious, preliminary moves, the doctor goes into initiating talk about the child's problem (27). In the face of conflicting views, the use of perspective display queries may produce knowledge to anticipate the misalignment, thus allowing controversial issues to be brought up with extra care, and avoiding or softening an outburst of conflict.

The perspective display query is an interactional device which helps a news bearer solicit the recipient's view before launching the news. It may be used to strengthen the alignment between parties, or soften and disarm a foreseeable conflict. Vehviläinen (2001) has pointed out that perspective display queries may have other functions in other settings. In her study of career counseling courses for the unemployed, she has explored the argumentative uses of perspective display series. The counselor may aim at inviting the student's perspective in order to confront ideas she considers implausible. The perspective display series then functions as part of a reflective process whose goal is to invigorate the student's self directed learning. Perspective display queries, like most interactional devices, assume functions in a context-sensitive manner so that goals specific to that setting can be accomplished.

The value of perspective display series can also be seen in the problems which may arise when the recipient's perspective is neglected. In contrast with the diagnoses proffered via perspective display series, Maynard (1989b) has also studied cases where the recipient's perspective is neglected. In extract 18, the doctor expresses her admiration to the parents' efforts (lines 2–4) and builds a linkage to the parents by speaking as a parent (4–6), but subsequently gives her diagnosis more or less straightforwardly.

(18) Maynard 1989b, 64 [Roberts]

```
01    Dr. D:   I think- you know I'm sure you're anxious about today and I
02             know this has been a really hard year for you. And I think
03             you've really done an extraordinary job in dealing with some
04             thing that's very hard for any human being or any parent- and
05             you know Mrs. Roberts and I can talk as parents as well as
06    Mrs. R:  True
07    Dr. D:   uh my being a professional. Its HARD when there's something
08             not all right with a child, very hard. And I admire both of
09             you really and, and as hard as it is seeing that there IS
10             something that IS the matter with Donald
11             (0.4)
12    Dr. D:   He's NOT like other kids
13             (0.4)
14    Dr. D:   He is slow
15             (0.4)
16    Dr. D:   He is retarded
```

17	Mrs. R:	HE IS NOT RETARDED!
18	Mr. R:	Ellen
19	Mrs.R:	HE IS NOT RETARDED!
20	Mr. R:	Ellen, please
21	Mrs.R:	No!
22	Mr. R:	May- look-its their way of- I don't know
23	Mrs. R:	HE IS NOT RETARDED ((sobbing))
24	Dr. D:	He can learn and is learning
25	Mr. R:	Yes he is learning
26	Dr. D:	And he's making good progress, and he will continue to make
27		good progress

The doctor characterizes the child in lines 12 and 14 without getting any response from the child's parents. Subsequently, she launches her diagnosis (line 16) which occasions an agitated opposition (17–23). Faced with a straightforward diagnosis, the son's mother protests and refuses to accept what she hears. After the outburst, the doctor resorts to good news trying to establish a new working consensus before returning to delicate issues. The neglect of the recipient's perspective may lead to troubles and even shut down communication between parties. This same interactional dynamics has also been found in addiction therapy where the aim is to confront the patients (Arminen and Halonen forthcoming). If the addiction therapist pushes the patient too far, he may risk losing the working consensus if the conflict becomes unmanageable. If confrontations are not carefully and sensitively recipient-designed, they may function counterproductively to block the situation or occasion an open controversy.

With the help of perspective display series news or advice may be tailored to the client. However, in some professional practices, smooth and efficacious interaction may best be achieved by withholding the relevance of the client's view. Some professional tasks may be presented as impersonal routines that are to be passed through quickly, without further discussion or debate. When the aim is a fast routine, then the client's perspective is best to be kept aside. Silverman has studied pre-test counseling of HIV, in which the counselor's task is to give advice on safe sexual practices in brief sessions. In this setting the advice is not tailored according to a client but is presented as information to anybody. Advice as impersonal information is interactionally a less delicate activity than personalized advice. The avoidance of personalization allows a neutral encounter and a quick pace of advice giving.

(19) Silverman 1997, 172 [US2]

1	C:	THE RECMMENdation is: (0.2) uh: fo:r people: (0.8)
2		who have been been at risk <u>any time</u>=

```
3     P:  =mmhmm=
4     C:  =regardless of: (0.4) uh::m (0.6) their (1.2) sexual
5         ac[tividy]       whether it being- going from you know=
6     P:    [mmhmmm]
7     C:  =z:ero to very active .hhh ah the recommendation is
8         still that everyone be retested once a yea:r=
9     P:  =yeah
10        (0.4)
11    C:  until there is actually a test for the virus itself=
12    P:  =right
13        (1.6)
14    P:  (tch)okay=
15    C:  =okay? (.) any other questions?=
```

Advice as information requires only a minimal uptake from the recipient, and is a tightly-packed interaction sequence that may be used as a routine procedure. Parallel with Silverman's findings, Peyrot (1987) has paid attention to how addiction therapists may also use "oblique references", like "people" in extract 18 or the generic "you", in giving recommendations to their patients. The indefiniteness plays down potential conflict, and may smooth the interaction. The ambiguity of the target of advice shifts responsibility for receiving the advice to the recipient only. Consequently, potential resistance is ruled out, but this also means that recipients do not need to show their uptake of advice and their inclination to follow the advice is not brought up in the encounter.

4.3 The Maintenance of Professionality

Thus far I have discussed how the professional and client may relate to their perspectives. Another key dimension involves the management of participant roles. As discussed, the client may need to present her reason for the institutional encounter as serviceable (e.g. doctorable etc.) and in so doing the client also orients to her client role. For her part, the professional needs to manage her role as a professional. Parties may have role expectations that constrain the conduct and the range of activities that are considered appropriate for the professional. Institutions may also have rules, regulations and ideals that guide professional behavior. I will briefly discuss three basic strategies to maintain a professional role. The professional may align with institutional authority, subordinate to the institutional authority, or display neutrality towards clients and the issues dealt with.

Aligning with Institutional Authority

In institutional settings the professional may present himself as a representative of
an organization. Self-presentation as an institutional agent may invoke institutional
authority which provides grounds for the proposed course of activity. Pronoun
choices are a simple, common, and powerful discursive technique through which the
participant roles may be managed. The professional may use the institutional "we"
to display the production framework of talk or a footing in which the speaker only
speaks on behalf of the authoritative source (Levinson 1988; Goffman 1981). The
use of the institutional "we" is very common in medical settings (see extracts 13–14,
17). The doctor may, for instance, present herself as the one who reflects (thinks),
and attribute agency to "we", who is presented as the agent "doing" the things.

    (20) Silverman 1987, 57 [117:5]

    1   D: What I think we should do is that we first need to confirm that
    2   that is the diagnosis and that there is nothing else wrong with
    3   the heart itself. And to do that we do a special test called
    4   a heart catheterization …

The doctor does not ascribe medical authority to himself only. Rather, self-presentation
through the institutional "we" invokes the medical authority through a linkage to a
larger unspecified entity. The medical "we" may also work as a persuasive device.
The doctor avoids taking the responsibility alone and attributes it to a source that is
beyond the current situation. The medical "we" as an authority that is absent from
the ongoing situation sanctions the decisions, as their basis is not situated. The
doctor may shift from "I" to "we" thereby invoking a larger authority to legitimate
treatment proposals.

    (21) Silverman 1987, 58 [117:5]

    1   Dr: Hm (2.0) the the reason for doing the test
    2 →   is, I mean I'm 99 per cent certain that all
    3 she's got is a ductus
    4   F: Hm hm.
    5   M: I see
    6 →   Dr: However the time to find out that we're
    7   wrong is not when she's on the operating table.

Here the doctor also avoids the possibility that he would be accused of clinical error.
The pronouns as such are omnipresent devices that may be used in role ascription

in any setting (see Drew and Heritage 1992b, 30–31; Neville 2001). The choice of pronoun stands for the discursive position thereby being a part of the arrangements through which participation roles are distributed in any ongoing moment.

Subordination to Authority

The professional may not always need to align with the institutional authority, but the agent may present herself as being subordinated to the rules, regulations or schemes of action that oblige her to perform the tasks at hand. In particular, in a setting in which resistance or controversy can be anticipated, the professional may distance himself from authority and present himself as one who is being subordinated to carry out the predetermined tasks. The professional's self-presentation as a subordinated agent may orient to an anticipated controversy that may be precluded or softened if both parties can be aligned through their subordinated positions (e.g. extract 15). The institutional agent as well as the client can both be represented as being in a position where they have to follow a predetermined course of action whether they like it or not. In HIV pre-test counseling, the counselors (the institutional "we") remind the clients that this is what they have to do with anybody.

(22) Silverman 1997, 154–155 [UK1]

```
1      C:  we also need to go over with you what happens (.)
2          when someone gets a positive test result,
3      P:  Yes.
4      C:  but plea:se remember we have to do this with .h
5          everyone who's tested .hh[h and we're not saying=
6      P:                          [Ri:ght.
7      C:  =that we think you know you're in (.) any greater
8          ris[k (of uhm of a) positive result. .hhhhhh=
9      P:     [No (           )
```

Through subordination to an external authority, the counselor may manage to ascribe subordinated identities to both parties who just have to follow the given course of action. The professional's subordination to authority may thus reduce the gulf between the institutional agent and the client who are presented as standing on the same side. This self-presentation may also have a factual background. The professional may be accountable for carrying out the predetermined courses of action. The self-presentation may thus reveal institutional or organizational power relationships, but whether this is the case is an empirical question. In any case, through subordination to authority the institutional agent invokes a production format where the speaker is just a relayer of words whose authoritative power resides elsewhere (in an unspecified location, cf. Maynard 1984). The production format in which both parties are submitted to an external authority also depersonalizes the interaction as the interactants are not speaking as themselves, but as representing something else. This depersonalization may also extend to the client who is not addressed as an individual but as the subject of a predetermined institutional routine.

(23) Silverman 1997, 155 [UK1]

```
1       C:  er: I have to ask you this have you ever injected
2           drugs.
3       P:  No.
4       C:  Because they're the sort of highest ris:k (.)
```

Note that the impersonal production format of the interaction is a collaborative achievement that may be functional for both parties. The high degree of depersonalization may save face for both sides. The impersonality of institutional interaction may thus not need to be criticized on every occasion, for such impersonality may also function as a practical shield which allows discussion of delicate issues without a fear of getting hurt. Subordination to authority as a strategy may thus not reflect only the agents' subordinate positions in settings, such as social work and addiction therapy, but also the parties' sensitivity to potential face threats in dealing with fragile identities (Rostila 1995).

Displaying Neutrality

Neutrality towards the persons involved or issues dealt with is a characteristic norm for professionals in certain institutional settings. Of course, neutrality does not apply to all encounters, such as antagonistic settings where agents represent opposing parties, as in a courtroom. Nevertheless, neutrality is a central disposition in settings where the professional has to maintain equality between clients, or avoid taking a stance with respect to clients. Neutrality is a theoretically prescribed norm for professional conduct. Sacks was thrilled at Freida Fromm-Reichman's advice on how to be a good psychiatrist: "to be able to listen, and to gather information from another person, in this person's own right, without reacting along the lines of one's own problems or experiences" (Sacks 1992a, 768; 1992b, 259). Fromm-Reichman prescribed neutrality and objectivity as a norm for a therapist doing intensive psychotherapy – this, of course, was anathema for Sacks who did not see neutrality and objectivity as being possible in a good psychiatric practice. In any case, neutrality as an ideal permeates variable professional settings. Neutrality is also ideologically prescribed for quality journalism in Western countries. Concern about neutrality is particularly pressing in political news interviews. The neutralistic stance can again be expressed with the help of footing or the production format, like subordination to authority (see Goffman 1981; Levinson 1988; Clayman 1992). Through the choice of footing, journalists may distance themselves from the opinions or views expressed, and attribute them to some source. In presenting themselves as a mere animator of words reflecting some other person's position, journalists manage to stay "neutral" whatever opinions are expressed. In extract 24, the journalist frames his question by attributing the inbuilt supposition to a third party (lines 1–3). Later, he renews his neutral footing when using a morally attuned descriptor, "collaborator" (line 8).

(24) Clayman 1992, 170–171[Nightline 7/22/85: 17]
((Discussing violence among blacks in South Africa))

```
 1 1→  IR:  Reverend Boesak lemme a- pick up a point uh
 2           the Ambassador made.
 3           What- what assurances can you give u:s .hh
 4           that (.) talks between moderates in that
 5           country will take pla:ce when it see:ms thet
 6           any black leader who is willing to talk to
 7           thuh government is branded
 8 2→        as the Ambassador said a collaborator
 9           and is then punished.=
10     AB:  =Eh theh- thuh- thuh Ambassador has it wrong.
11           It's not thuh people who want to talk with
12           thuh government that are branded collaborators
```

With the help of the animator's role, the journalist stays clear and distances himself from opinions that are potentially politically explosive. The neutralistic footing also brackets, at least formally, the journalist's personality away from the discursive realm of the news interview so that the journalist's opinions and views should not be addressed. The neutralistic stance is an active achievement that can also be seen from the repair work the journalist may need to accomplish if he has relapsed away from the footing. In extract 25, the journalist seems to be about to pose a follow-up question from the first person stance, but then reinitiates the question by attributing the assertion to a third party (lines 11–13).

(25) Clayman 1992, 170–171 [MacNeil/Lehrer 6/10/85a:CT:4]
((Discussing the U.S. decision to continue to honor the SALT II arms control treaty with a Reagan administration official.))

```
1    IR:  How d'you sum up thuh me:ssage. that this
2          decision is sending to thuh Soviets?
3    KA:  .hhh Well as I started- to say:: it is ay- one
4          of: warning an' opportunity. Thuh warning
```

5		is (.) you'd better comply: to arms control::
6		agreements if arms control is going to have
7		any chance of succeeding in thuh future.
8		Unilateral compliance by thuh United States
9		just not in thuh works ...
10		((Four lines omitted))
11	→ IR:	But isn't this- uh::: critics uh on thuh
12		conservative- side of thuh political argument
13		have argued thet this is:. abiding by thuh
14		treaty is:. unilateral (.) observance. (.)
15		uh:: or compliance. (.) by thuh United States.

Here the repair work discloses the journalist's active involvement in the maintenance of the neutral stance. The lapse away from the neutral stance (line 11) allows the recipients to infer the journalist's position on the matter. This also shows what a precarious achievement the footing is, and how skillfully the journalist must manage the neutral stance.

4.4 Conclusion

In this chapter I have begun the analysis of institutional encounters on three basic dimensions. Institutional interaction is always based on an accountable state of affairs that offers a reason for the encounter. This accountable state of affairs is further treated so as to make it manageable in terms of the institution in question. In addition to formulating a case, which can be handled in an institution, the parties ascribe each other with institutionally-attuned identities. Consequently, managing the parties' perspectives and their possible disparities becomes a key dimension of interaction. I have also discussed the basic techniques to evoke the other's perspective or inner states. Fishing, candidate queries, formulations and perspective display queries are interactional resources through which the other's perspective may be made relevant. Perspective display series were discussed as a strategy through which the disparities between perspectives are anticipated, managed and mitigated. I also examined three strategies of how a professional can meet clients' expectations. Alignment with authority allows professionals to present themselves as a representative of the organization, and may also work as a persuasive device that legitimizes the course of action chosen by the professional. In subordinating to authority the professional may seek alliance with the client as they are both then presented as being subordinate to power. Finally, the professional's maintenance of a neutral position towards persons and issues involved serves to maintain institutional objectivity.

Further Reading

– Doctor-patient interaction involves many of the dimensions of the client-professional relationship discussed in this chapter. For further studies in this field, see Heritage and Maynard (forthcoming).

– Emergency calls are another prominent area that concerns client-professional relationship (Whalen et al. forthcoming).

– Help-desks are an increasingly salient form of customer-business relationships, though there have not yet been many studies on these yet (Baker, Firthand Emmison 2001).

– For exercises, see http://www.uta.fi/laitokset/sosio/project/ivty/english/sivut/exercises.html

Notes

1   Accountability is one of the key concepts of ethnomethodology (see e.g. Heritage 1980; Lynch 1993). Accountablity refers to the descriptions and explanations people offer in order to understand/explain what is going on. The account explains the actions people engage in to themselves but also makes them accountable to others and provides a basis for social order. In Garfinkel's (1967, 11) words: "Ethnomethodological studies analyze every-day activites as members' methods for making those same activities visibly-rational-and-reportable-for-all-practical-purposes, i.e., accountable as organizations of commonplace everyday activities." Accountability is also a problematic concept due to its polyphonic character. It gains different meanings in different contexts.

2   I do not want to imply that institutional interaction concerns only "problems", though often it does. Further, the problem language game can be applied to most institutional interactions: The salesperson's "problem" is to get the product sold, etc.

3   Originally, I mistook the word choice "special education" to stand for a fine example of a circumvent description, because "special education" sounds almost like what all good parents would want for their own children, albeit we know that this was not exactly what was meant here. Doug Maynard pointed out to me that "special education" is an institutional term deriving from a federal law that guarantees public education for children with physical and mental disabilities. Therefore this phrase raised the problem of stigma, and it was by no means a "skillfully circumvent description" as I originally thought. My misunderstanding is a good example of the analyst's need to have sufficient background understanding so that inappropriate referents and meanings are avoided.

Chapter 5

Classrooms and the Transmission of Knowledge and Expertise

> Soon common people will learn to read, but it is another thing to understand. To understand, you have to be able to read between the lines.
>
> (Queen Lovisa Ulrika 1720–1782)

The transmission of knowledge and skills is the task of pedagogic institutions, but skills need to be passed on inside any expert system. In classrooms, pedagogic exchange has been going on for hundreds of years so that robust patterns, such as the teaching cycle and exam questions, have survived. Their survival despite sometimes fierce debates on pedagogic forms and styles suggests that these elementary patterns may serve some tacit interactional tasks at the heart of pedagogic institutions. In classrooms, these basic patterns allow both the transfer of knowledge and the assessment of students. In this chapter, I will discuss five basic patterns of classroom talk including lecturing, the pedagogic cycle, repairs, correctional activities, and the organization of extra curricular activities. At the end of the chapter, I will also briefly introduce some alternative practices that are particularly important in adult education.

For practical reasons, I have limited this chapter mainly to classroom talk. Classrooms are not only a rich source of data on a sociologically-important type of institutional activity of which almost all of us have some personal experience, but they also illuminate properties of the transmission of knowledge as it is applicable in and for modern societies. I will first introduce five basic patterns of classroom talk, and then discuss their contribution to classrooms and learning, before addressing how these patterns are linked together to form classrooms as a particular discursive formation. I will then show that the significance of classroom interaction lies in the way it helps establish a depersonalized goal-rationality, which ultimately allows the emergence of a self-disciplined epistemic relationship to the external world. In this sense, I not only discuss classroom interactional patterns in detail, but also deliberately allow some interpretative work concerning the constitutive role of classroom practices in molding modern subjectivity. Even if conversation analysis allows the scrutiny of minute details, the findings are always open to inferences beyond empirical detail. In other words, conversation analytical studies can have a bearing on debates about values and moral judgements (Jayyusi 1991). It may therefore be useful to differentiate between discussions about empirical findings, and the inferences and conclusions drawn from these findings.

5.1 Basic Patterns of Classroom Talk

Even if pedagogic ideals have swung back and forth throughout the history of education, and its aims have been rethought several times from Kant to Foucault, from Rousseau's critique of civilization to Adorno's reconsideration of education after Auschwitz, changes in classroom interactional practices have been much slower. Though the role of rote learning has diminished, and physical punishment has become widely unacceptable, nevertheless many elementary interactional patterns have survived. Classroom interactions still involve activities that can be characterized as "lecturing", "pedagogic cycles", "repair sequences", "correctional activities", and "organized extra-curricular activities". Not only do these interactional patterns exist in contemporary schools throughout the world, but these patterns are also tied to each other, forming a quintessential pedagogic discourse, which may still survive new school reforms.

Lecturing Format

Alec McHoul notes that teachers speak over 80 per cent of the time during high school lessons, and much of this speech is monologic (McHoul 1978, 208). Teaching via extended multi-unit turns that we may call "lecturing" has been, and still is, a central pedagogic activity in classrooms, and as such takes up a considerable share of the given time. Naturally, as McHoul readily admits, there is no point in arguing about the exact share of "lecturing" in classrooms. The proportion of time spent on lecturing varies depending on the grade, subject, topic etc. In any case, lecturing is a constitutive pedagogic activity, with undisputed importance for classroom pedagogy. This said, if lecturing is a monologic activity, what can we say about it through conversation analysis? Against conventional wisdom, I want to propose that lecturing, and many other monologic forms of talk, are not unidirectional processes. Lecturing is based, or should be based, on a two-directional process. An interactional substratum is an enabling condition for lecturing. If interaction vanishes, only then does lecturing become monologic in a pejorative sense.[1] However, before entering into an empirical analysis, I will introduce first the rest of the basic patterns of classroom discourse.

Pedagogic Cycle

A phenomenon called "the pedagogic cycle" is probably the best-known interactional form of pedagogy. Using slightly different terms, it has also been discussed in a number of studies (see Bellack et al. 1966; Sinclair and Coulthard 1975; Mehan 1979). It is a simple, clear and distinct three-part structure. In Mehan's (1979) terms, it is composed of initiation, reply and evaluation. Classroom researchers have documented it throughout the world (e.g. Schieffelin's (1996) study of the missionary school in Bosavi, Papua, New Guinea). The next data extract by Muller comes from South Africa.

(1) Muller 1989, 317 [C1]

```
1    T:  Brownian motion. What is Brownian motion? If you still
2        remember. Anybody, who can remember? ....
3    S:  Is the haphazard movement of particles.
4    T:  Haphazard movement of particles (writes on board) ...
5        you said this is Brownian motion ...
```

Like many sequences, such as the perspective display series we examined in the previous chapter, the pedagogic cycle is again a three-position structure. The teacher asks or otherwise initiates a student's response, whose adequacy the teacher then evaluates. The fundamental feature of the pedagogic cycle is that the teacher's evaluative turn may take different forms depending on the student's answer. The teacher may confirm the student's answer either through plain acceptance, repetition (as in extract 1 above), or through positive assessment. The teacher may also reformulate the answer (as may be starting on at line 5), or reject the answer. The teacher may also withhold from using the third position, and instead initiate a new activity. Minimally, the teacher can assess the rightfulness of the answer, the answerer and the way of delivery of the answer (you have to raise your hand before answering, etc.). The flexibility of the pedagogic cycle makes it an important interactional resource, whose functions for pedagogic discourse I will return to later.

Repair Sequences

Repairs have a natural place in classroom interaction. One such location is the third position in the pedagogic cycle, i.e., the teacher may initiate/perform a repair as an assessment of the student's response. In this case, the repair can be seen as a variant of the pedagogic cycle. Extract 2 offers a case in point. Through lines 1–6 the teacher formulates a question, at line 8 selects the student to answer, and after the initiation of the answer, the teacher takes the floor back, correcting the student at line 11.

(2) McHoul 1990, 353

```
1    T:  ... c'd anyone
2        (1.2)
```

```
3        T:    see – a concentric – zone pattern developing for their
4              particular
5                  (0.2)
6        T:    Portsville model?
7                  (3.0)
8        T:    Ye::::s
9                  (0.4)
10  →    X:    We've got our – manufacturing industry
11  →    T:    *No* residential we're int'[rested 'n]
1   →    X:                           [ O  h  ]=
13  →    X:    =yeh well we got our (basic) residential – just
14             outside the CBD …
```

Here the teacher performs both the initiation of the repair and the correction of the student's talk. Note that the correction concerns the presupposition of the student's answer: after the student has displayed his surprise through the change of state token "oh", the student self-selects and continues his answer with the help of the corrected presupposition. Actually, McHoul points out that these kinds of other-initiated-other-repairs are relatively rare in comparison to other types of repairs in classrooms. The multitude of repair types in classrooms also reveals that they are multifunctional, a point I will return to later.

Correctional Activities

Though much less discussed in the scientific literature than the pedagogic cycle, correctional activities are well known in lay knowledge of classroom behavior. Correctional activities belong to the less desirable features in the classroom, and their forms have likely undergone major changes in the history of pedagogy. However, some kinds of correctional activities seem to belong to the essential features of classroom interaction. In extract 3, the teacher interrupts the giving of an assignment (line 5), and uses her gaze and naming of a student (lines 5–77) to sanction improper classroom conduct (lines 4 and 6).

(3) Macbeth 1994, 141 [sc3:5a]

```
         ((T. is reading aloud an assignment.))
1        T:    Okay so, lem- keep goin' with this. = Include plenny' uv
2              dialogue,
3              an' be shure ta' use quotation marks properly. =
4        S:    = (              :) =
5   →    T:    =Make ssh[ure Kathy, ((T. holds gaze through line 7))
6       (S):            (            )
```

7 →   (1.5)
8 →   T: Make sshure you hava title on yer work. (thissus) vury
           important ...

Correctional activities are embedded in classroom discourse in many different ways. They assist the realization of other classroom activities, or they are a vehicle for maintaining order, a precondition for pedagogic activities. In another sense, formal turn-taking and the teacher's privileged access to the floor occasion the maintenance of the students' shared attention as a practical problem (McHoul 1978). Correctional activities remedy the loss of free turn-taking in which anybody at any transition-relevant point could be addressed as the next speaker, thereby providing a partial solution to the problem of shared attention in the classroom. Thus correctional activities are doubly contextually-bound to classroom discourse, so that they are occasioned by other forms of classroom interaction and they also maintain order, a prerequisite for classroom discourse.

Extra Curricular Activities

As a category "extra-curricular activities" may sound somewhat clumsy. However, activities organized outside of the regular curriculum seem to form a systematic and recurrent activity type in classrooms. Furthermore, these extra-curricular activities have not emerged accidentally, but offer a complement to curriculum activities. Neither are extra-curricular activities pedagogically empty, but are intricately tied to the pedagogic agenda. Activities such as sharing rounds or collaborative storytelling differ from traditional teacher-centered pedagogic activities but nevertheless make relevant the pedagogic agenda. The formal difference from other activities coupled with their strong tie to the overall goals of school work make extra-curricular activities an intriguing topic.

5.2 Making Sense of Pedagogic Interaction

To make sense of pedagogic interaction, I pose two questions: what is accomplished with classroom activities, and what is the relationship between different activities? If classroom interaction is at least largely composed of the five forms described above, how do these activities contribute to what is going on in schoolwork? Or, we could pose the question: do we know what is learned in school? Presumably, learning not only covers "facts", but also ways of organizing knowledge, learning to learn (for the second degree of learning, see Bateson 1972). In a broader sense, formal education entails learning ways of participating in the activities of a complex society. The school system is essential for a modern society so that its members acquire the taken-for-granted skills to learn how to learn to participate in the complexities of modern life. In this respect, formal education is a process of forming subjects. In terms of its organization, a school acts as a basic model for a goal-rational organization, such as a bureaucracy or corporation. Through school a student learns how to act as a subject of a complex bureaucracy or a corporation. In terms of subject formation, school as a format is more profound than various educational discourses. As a whole, school allows a student to develop a self-disciplined epistemic relationship with the external world, the disciplined bureaucratic ear.[2]

However, in order to understand school discourse, an empirical analysis must address both the individual forms of interaction in classroom, and how these different activities are connected to each other. Conversation analysis is of course an inductivistic approach, starting the analysis from individual cases and proceeding toward individual classes of action. But by understanding a sequential activity, we can also shed light on the connection between that activity and its wider context. In other words, understanding an activity means seeing it in context. Consequently, I will begin by analyzing individual actions, but then proceed by analyzing relationships between activities in an effort to construct a comprehensive account of classroom discourse.

5.3 Approaching the Lecturing Format

It is still a matter of some dispute whether "monologic forms of talk" can be analyzed through CA techniques. We can start with the point that any format of interaction is an achievement: monologues do not just go off randomly, but they have to be occasioned if recipients are to be taken onboard. There is a difference between somebody speaking to herself for an extended period and somebody delivering a monologue to other(s). If we notice somebody speaking to himself in a bus or subway, we may wonder whether the person is mentally challenged and has lost touch with reality, or indeed these days we may try to see whether the person is wearing a hands-free telephone, and is in fact speaking to somebody. Of course, nuances may be added: a person speaking on a hands-free may have deliberately chosen the situation to show off with the help of the technical device, and may indeed be giving signs off through his talk to co-present others. In any case, we can distinguish between deliberate monologues to targeted recipients (co-present or distant) from extended turns that passers-by or eavesdroppers may hear (cf. Goffman 1981).

The achievement of monologicality is always analyzable: we can examine how, to whom, and with what consequences the monologue is achieved. For example, in my study of interaction in Alcoholics Anonymous (AA) meetings, I examined the role of opening rituals, such as the moment of silence, in the achievement of shared attention to ratify the individual speakers' use of extended turns. By declaring the moment of silence, unanimous attention can be directed to the person taking the floor after the silence, and if the participants accept such floor-taking the meeting organization has gained ritual ratification (Arminen 1998). Similarly, the teachers' techniques for gaining or attempting to gain students' unanimous attention and maintaining the floor might be studied.

In analyzing the interactional properties of monologues themselves, we can focus on at least three aspects: the ways they are situated and recipient designed; the ways they are sequentially organized, and what they imply about the role distribution between parties. The following data extract from a geography lesson introduces these issues:

(4) McHoul 1978, 209 [5B7–125/H: 230–40]

```
 1     T:  So we have a concentration
 2         (0.2)
 3     T:  of commercial activities
 4         (0.2)
 5     T:  n the heart of the city
 6         (0.2)
 7     T:  then of course we must have smaller regional
 8         (0.4)
 9     T:  er shopping centres or shops
10         (0.4)
11     T:  e::r satisfying customers
12         (0.2)
13     T:  on the outskirts of town
14         (0.3)
15     T:  Right well that finishes our discussion for Portsville
16         eighdeen eighdy to eighdeen ninedy
17         (0.3)
18     T:  Now I did ask you f' homework to read Portsville
19         eighdeen ninedy to ninedeen hun'red
20         (1.2)
```

First, we can notice a clear rhythmic pattern. The lecturing monologue is split into small chunks. In fact, the units are even smaller than turn construction units (or TCUs, Schegloff 1996; Ford et al. 1996). A TCU can be defined as the smallest possibly complete turn at which point a transition to a next speaker becomes possible and relevant, but not necessarily actual (e.g., classroom talk). Here the talk is divided into units shorter than TCU so that there are recognizable pauses before the completion of TCUs after which new increments are added. In Carolyn Baker's phrase, the subject is presented through "baby steps". Baker has noticed that a skillful computer help desk worker can orient to the client's state of knowledge so that advice can be attuned according to the client's competence. If a caller sounds knowledgeable in terms of her computer trouble, the advice may be presented in larger entities and in a less detailed manner. If the caller appears to lack knowledge, the help desk worker may design her assistance to be composed of small bits of information that are as concrete and as detailed as possible. Here, the teacher's lecture is also divided into small units that are attuned to the teacher's understanding of the students' ability to receive information. In this sense, even a monologue is a recipient-designed activity, maybe even a recipient-driven activity. Although without a video-tape of the parties' visual orientation we cannot closely examine the speaker's attunement to the recipients, we can expect that in institutional settings as well conduct is based on ongoing real-time monitoring of the recipients' activities. At least at times, the teacher may try to orient to students' note taking so that the lecture's progress and the pacing of speech follows students' reception of talk. As long as students are busy writing up what has been shown or said, the next bit of information will be delayed. Ideally, the delivery of new information is adjusted to the ongoing reception of information so that the recipients are neither drowned with information nor are bored by a lack of stimulus. However, the monitoring of recipients' actions does not occur automatically; the lecturer may also forget the audience and become immersed in his own train of thought (which from the recipient's point of view may be spontaneous and thrilling, or messy, self-absorbed, and opaque). Nevertheless, in the above data, the teacher delivers information in units that seem to be designed to be accessible to the recipients.

Further, the grammatical construction of the lecture's units seems quite complex. The sentences are lengthy multi-part units more resembling written than oral language. In this way, the teacher acts as an animator of the written text so that the source and authority of the speech are absent. In dividing the text into small chunks the teacher allows students to take notes for remembering key notions and ideas in the original text. In this sense, modern education is no different from medieval grammar schools, since both focus on preserving the sense of alien texts. In all, the rhythmic sequencing of talk bears on the recipient design of talk. In his analysis of courtroom talk, Drew (1992) notes that the interrogator may use silences to design slots for audience appreciation. That is, the interrogator may pause after a witness response he considers particularly relevant or revealing so that the listening audience (including judge and maybe jury) have time to digest the point. In a similar manner, a teacher may use pauses to try to capture the students' attention. Moreover, the timing of pauses is essential, as in courtrooms; the pauses may be used for highlighting key terms and notions so that a pause after (or before) an item inside a turn construction unit may mark the item to be preserved.

On a more global scale, classroom talk is also organized with the help of topical frames. In the extract above, the topic is closed explicitly (lines 15–16), and a new topic is subsequently initiated (lines 18–19). Topical frames constitute the global structure of lessons. In all, quite a lot can be said about the interactional orchestration of lecturing. Indeed, this sketchy analysis opens many questions for further studies that would be highly relevant in a didactic sense as well.

The students' role as recipients at first seems clear and unquestionable. The teacher talks and is the active party; students remain silent, listen to the talk and are passive. However, things are not always as they appear. Strictly speaking, the students' role is not passive, consisting instead of two active activities: remaining silent and listening. Both these activities are necessary conditions for felicitous classroom interaction. Remaining silent is not something that just happens but is an active achievement (consider how challenging this is even for university students).

To examine this challenge further, let us compare the role of information recipiency in classroom interaction to information delivery and reception sequences in ordinary conversation. Three main points can be made about news delivery sequences in mundane interaction: the news recipient displays active recipiency, news is received according to its valence, and personal closeness is a key dimension for the relevance of news (Maynard 2003). For practical reasons, I will use extracts from talk among adults, though I believe that the central points would also hold for children as news recipients. First, we can point out that the recipient is an active party in the news telling. In extract 5 V tells news about Jani to J.

(5) Heritage 1984b, 303 [Rah:I:8]

```
1      V:  Oh I met Jani :e, eh: : :m yesterday an' she'd
2           had a fo:rm from the Age Concern about that
3           jo:b.h=
4 →    J:  =Oh she has?
```

J, the news recipient, receives the news with the change of state token "oh" (Heritage 1984b). In this way, the news recipient makes available to the news bearer what, if anything, has been news to her. Active recipiency also allows the recipient to take part in agenda setting, by topicalizing aspects of the news for further discussion. Consequently, the recipient may participate in news telling by guiding the news bearer to take up relevant aspects of the news and by closing down irrelevant aspects or news that turns out be "no news" to the recipient. News telling is thus a collaborative process in ordinary conversation.

Second, news is received according to its valence, whether good or bad. In (6), news with a strong valence is told, but note that the evaluation is done from a strictly situated point of view.

(6) Maynard 1996 [NB:1–2]

```
1      A:  So, Elizabeth'n Willy were s'poze tuh come down las'
2           night but there was a death i'n the fam'ly so they
3           couldn' come so Guy's asked Dan tuh play with the
4           comp'ny deal so I guess he c'n play with 'im So,
5      B:  Oh good.
```

Note that B does not treat the information about Elizabeth and Willy as news. By withholding acknowledgement of these facts the recipient effectively puts them into the background, whereas the fact that Dan can play with Guy is foregrounded via its active reception and valence. In this small exchange A and B display their constitution of social matrix in this context, in which the facts are valued according to their relevance for their game. The fact that Elizabeth and Willy are not coming or the death in their family is not news is that they do not bear any relevance for the game. Also, things related to the game are evaluated for their impact on the game. In this way, the valence of the news is relevant, and is judged according to the situated relevancies at hand.

Third, in everyday life the relevancies at hand tend to be personal. In extract 7, Emma and Nancy, who are on the phone, watch on TV how the assassinated President Kennedy's coffin is moved to an airplane.

(7) Maynard 1996 [NB:II:2:3]

```
1        Emma:  Hey that was the same spot we took off for
2               Honolulu. (0.4) Where they put him on, (1) at that
3               chartered place,
4  →     Nancy: Oh really?
5        Emma:  y::Yea::h.
6        Nancy: Oh:? For heaven sakes.
```

Kennedy's assassination was an event that shook large parts of the world. Emma will remember that Kennedy's coffin was put into the plane on the same spot she thinks she once took off for Honolulu. Note that Nancy immediately grasps the salience of Emma's view, and far from seeing it as marginal participates in upgrading its relevance. Here we see the way the mind works: the salience of events emerges thorough their connection to biographical knowledge and personally formed preferences. Naturally, this organization of relevancies has its limits. Quite likely Emma knows that the validity of her personal sets of relevancies is delimited. She knows that the salience of her piece of information about the spot in which Kennedy's coffin was put onto a plane can be shared only among those with sufficient background knowledge, that is within her circle of friends, whereas for others it is just as unimportant as the fact that Elizabeth and Willy were not showing up or the death in their family is for A and B. Only within the limits of mutual biographical knowledge can Emma share her personal viewpoint as a benchmark for meaning, whereas in other circumstances more impersonal sets of criteria for relevance prevail. This brings us back to school.

Classroom interaction is a central institutional practice whose agenda is to teach participants to receive and manage information for its own sake without reacting to it personally. The ability to handle information in a disengaged and neutral fashion is indeed essential for various modern institutional practices. For example, John Heritage (1985) has examined the relevance of journalists' missing news markers in political news interviews. In broadcast interviews, journalists avoid conversational response tokens, such as "oh" or "really", with whose help they would treat the interviewee's talk as new and informative. In this way, journalists manage both to maintain neutrality vis-à-vis the interviewee's speech and to display that the primary target of the program is the listening audience and not the journalists themselves. As we saw in the previous chapter, Sacks (1992) was also pleased to notice that psychiatrists were taught to collect information from their patient for the patient's sake and to avoid reacting to the patient's talk along personal lines. Such neutrality to information, as we have just seen, is learned in school.

The ideal of managing information impersonally also permeates extra-curricular activities in school. In primary schools, teachers commonly organize sharing time in which pupils are prompted to share their personal experiences about their lives out of school. Sharing time sounds as informal as school can get, but it also allows children to develop their linguistic skills through storytelling. Additionally, the teacher's evaluation of stories connects the sharing time to the school agenda in multiple ways. In extract 8, the teacher has asked children to tell stories of what has happened to them; this is Deena's story.

(8) Cazden 1988, 13 [Deena's Day]

Deena's Day

```
 1  Deena:  I went to the beach Sunday /
 2          and / to McDonalds / and to the park /
 3          and I got this for my / birthday / / [holds up purse]
 4          my mother bought it for me /
 5          and I had two dollars for my birthday /
 6          and I put it in here /
 7          and I went to where my friend / named Gigi /
 8          I went over to my grandmother's house with her /
 9          and she was on my back /
10          and I / and we was walking around / by my house /
11          and she was HEAVY / /
12          she [was in the sixth or seventh grade / /
13  → T:        [OK I'm going to stop you / / I want you to talk about
14  →       things that are really really very important / / that's
15  →       important to you but can you tell us things that are
16  →       sort of different / / can you do that? / /...
```

At line 13, the teacher interrupts Deena's sharing, and requests that she describe "important things" and not just ordinary events. In this way, the teacher points out the specific set of criteria of what is considered relevant at school. An adequate story is specific in that it is not just about regular life or personal matters, but surpasses the relevance given by individual biographical experience. Extra-curricular activities are also part of the school agenda according to which students are supposed to learn to process information on a super-individual level. This information is not supposed to be managed solely through personal preferences or opinions. Cazden's (1988) analysis also shows that teachers prefer topic-centered narratives that convey information in well-formed packages to oral chat about separate remembrances as above. Both in terms of topic and format these extra-curricular activities contribute to a cognitive model that we may call a bureaucratic relationship to the world. Information is to be processed for its own sake without reacting to it according to one's personal experiences or opinions, and without evaluating information through one's personal preferences.

This bureaucratic maxim permeating schoolwork is the primary foundation for the uneasiness experienced in classroom pedagogic situations. Students have to learn to distance themselves from their own experiences but still remain active in the classroom. Students are placed in a constrained position: they must disengage from their own feelings; they are not allowed to become enthusiastically involved (they may not yell or share aloud their immediate thoughts); but neither may they become indifferent and stop listening to what is said. The ultimate achievement of schoolwork is the bureaucratic ear that students must adopt.

At this point, we can begin to make connections between the various types of classroom interaction. The precondition for felicitous information delivery is that the recipients remain receptive to information; they need to construct relevance for the distributed information. In ordinary conversation, the recipient's active role and the respective mutual shaping of news telling contributes to the intersubjective basis for information delivery. In schools, the relevance for information is constructed through the accountability of the students' performance: information is made personally relevant by the fact that students are assessed, and their success in school depends on these measurements. During lessons, the pedagogic cycle – the questioning – remains the central device for measuring information reception and for building personalized relevance for information. Correctional activities, for their part, are a response to the problems in maintaining students' receptiveness. Extra-curricular activities are an attempt to counterbalance the one-sided criteria for the relevance of information, criteria based solely on measurement.

5.4 Pedagogic Cycle

Since the pedagogic cycle is one of the best-known interaction formats in education, it may not come as a surprise that it is rooted in ordinary conversation. The three-part structure consisting of an initiative action, a reply and a response forms the basic module for the maintenance of intersubjective understanding (Heritage 1984). Through a three-part sequence the parties in interaction can form and check their mutual understanding of the ongoing action. The pedagogic cycle is a particular application of this generic interactional sequence in and for pedagogic purposes. Cazden (1988) has laid out a comparison between question-answer-response sequences in ordinary talk and in the classroom.

(9) Cazden 1988, 30 ((an invented example))

Conversation	Classroom Talk
1 What time is it, Sarah?	1 What time is it, Sarah?
2 Half-past two.	2 Half-past two.
3 Thanks.	3 Right.

The first obvious difference between mundane and pedagogic questioning lies in the third turn of the sequence, which reviews the preceding action in quite different ways and as such constitutes these as different activities. In pedagogic questioning the third position response is characteristically an evaluation that establishes a pedagogic frame for the sequence. Through the third turn the speaker displays her understanding of the prior turn and also publicly manifests the relevant dimension of the prior turn. "Right" as the third position response selects correctness as the relevant quality of the prior turn. In contrast, "thanks" portrays the prior turn in terms of its helpfulness. Furthermore, the evaluative third position manifests the asymmetric role distribution between parties. Through evaluation, the teacher (or anybody taking that position) displays herself as a knowledgeable recipient who has the ability and authority to assess the value of the prior contribution. In this way, the pedagogic cycle is based upon exam questions rather than sincere questions.

The asymmetry between parties and correctness as the relevance criterion for contributions are key dimensions of the pedagogic cycle, but not the only ones. Levinson (1992) has used the notions of "language game" and "activity type" to try to capture the specificity of distinct types of activities, such as classroom interaction. Broadly speaking, Levinson proposes that there are underlying tacit dimensions that characterize what kinds of speech activities are regarded as acceptable and preferable in a given type of activity. Consequently, the analysis may aim to open up these tacit dimensions of the activity type so as to describe and specify its fundamental parameters. Let us examine the properties of the pedagogic cycle with the help of a few examples. Levinson himself uses an invented example that is a caricature of classroom interaction.

(10) Levinson 1992, 87 ((invented example))

1	T:	What are the names of some trees?
2	Cl:	There are oaks.
3	C2:	Apples!
4	T:	Apple-trees, yes.
5	C3:	Yews.
6	T:	Well done Johnny!
7 →	C4	Oak trees!
8 →	T	No Sally, Willy's already said that.

Notice that not all "right" answers are valid: even if Sally's answer was right in terms of its truth value, it was not a legitimate answer as it repeated what had already been said. Note, too, that the rules of the game are not explicitly stated; they are a tacit property of the activity. It is not specified under which conditions repetition is forbidden, or why it is forbidden. Is the classroom interaction merely repeating a common sense cultural norm that unnecessary repetition should be avoided? Or does the classroom interaction ascribe some immaterial property rights to contributions so that Sally was not allowed to break Willy's copyright? Levinson's point is that a quintessential part of what is learned at school is language games. Furthermore, as the rules of the language game are tacit, they are indexical to the events of playing the game and can be learned only by playing it. The indexical rules of the pedagogic language game can, however, be analyzed through the data of the interaction itself. In extract 11, we can notice that a specified participation framework prevails in the classroom.

(11) Baker 1992, 11 ((Grade 1 Reading Lesson))

1	T:	It could well be just like last week's story
2		couldn't it? What was our story last week?
3 →	S:	One Cold Wet=
4 →	T:	=Oh, someone put (up) their hand up. They
5	S:	Uhh!

```
 6  →  T:  They might've even had the right answer.
 7         Helen.
 8  →  H:  One Cold Wet Night.
 9      T:  One Cold Wet Night. (From) the look of the outside
10         I think it might be a cold wet day. (2.5) And perhaps
11         a cold wet night. Alright well our story this week is
12         Yes Ma'am. Yes Ma'am. ...
```

Again, a seemingly right answer is not treated as a legitimate answer. Students are taught not only to provide a uniquely adequate answer but to orient to the allocation of turns so that the right answer should be given during a proper turn. In 11, the teacher did not hear the answer in line 3, or pretended not to have heard it, or was oriented not to hear the answer unless it was produced according to her allocation of turns. In any case, the teacher is oriented to not only teaching the content of the subject but also the participation framework that the pupils are to follow.

Finally, there is a situated organization of relevancies determining which of the right answers are to be treated as valid.

(12) Baker 1992, 11 ((Seventh-Grade Humanities Lesson))

```
 1      T:  ... Remember we did two diagrams to show the
 2          difference between the middle ages and the
 3          contemporary times. Which diagram did we
 4          draw for the middle ages. Robyn?
 5      R:  A triangle?
 6  →  T:  Good, a triangle. Who was up the top, Rob?
 7      R:  Pardon?
 8      T:  Who was at the top?
 9  →  R:  The man?
10      T:  Pardon?
11      R:  The man?
12  →  T:  The man was. He was. What was the man's
13          name?
14  →  R:  The king
15  →  T:  Right. The king. Good girl. Right. So the
16          king's up here. Who was down the bottom.
17          Poor old fellow.
```

At line 9, Robyn, a student, gives an answer that subsequently is treated as insufficient by the teacher at line 12. After the teacher's prompt (line 12), Robyn produces the answer that the teacher treats as sufficient (line 15). As the king is by definition a man, why was "the man" not considered the right answer? Of course, there is a difference in the level of abstraction. Not all men are kings (even if some would want to think so). But in another lesson on a higher level of abstraction, "the man" could be an adequate answer instead of "the king". Besides truthfulness, sequential position and participation framework, there are even more subtle aspects to the relevance of answers. The language game of the lesson that sets the criteria for appropriateness of answers also defines the appropriate level of abstraction.

Eventually, this example shows how the validity of an answer is tied to the topic of the lesson, which itself is realized through the situated construction of the sets of criteria for the validity of answers. In any case, students not only learn a fixed set of knowledge, but also identify the context-sensitivity of the knowledge, i.e., that each discourse has its own sets of criteria defining the validity of contributions. These discourse types underlie the explicit agenda of the classroom, and are seldom brought to the surface of classroom talk. However, students' success at school greatly depends on their skill at learning these underlying largely taken-for-granted and subtle distinctions which nevertheless provide the foundation for the rest of schoolwork.

The teacher may also give cues or mark which items or parts of the text are to be saved. These cues may be rhythmic and prosodic, such as the pauses in the data extract on lecturing (extract 4). The teacher may not only mark some items to be saved but may also guide students to particular aspects of the teaching materials. Of course, any material may be approached from several angles, and various aspects of the content could be topicalized (Sacks 1963). Therefore, the teacher has to guide the recipients to attune to the relevant dimension of the subject. For instance, in teaching languages the focus may be on the lexical, grammatical or prosodic aspects of the language. The teacher may thus focus on some aspect, and mark the aspect in her speech, as we can see in extract 13, a Swedish lesson in a Finnish high school. For the sake of simplicity, I have translated both the Swedish and Finnish into English. The Finnish parts of the speech are **in bold**. I have used a glossary line where the syntax of the translation departs crucially from the original talk. During this part of the lesson, the teacher was reading from the course book and then posing questions about the materials. In her use of the pedagogic cycle, the teacher points out in various ways which aspects of the material are to be preserved.

(13) SV 1993, 2[3]

1   T: och norr i norr   plågades löparna AV <MYggsvärmar>
          and north in north were-tormented joggers by swarms-of-mosquitoes
          and north- in the north joggers were tormented BY <SWarms of mosquitoes>

2   (.) vad betyder de plågades   av myggsvärmar (.)
          what means it were-tormented by swarms-of-mosquitoes
          (.) what does it mean were tormented by swarms of mosquitoes (.)

3   löparna (.) vad är det på finska (.) Niina
         joggers (.) what is it in Finnish (.) Niina

4   N: **hyttysparvia**
         swarms-of-mosquitoes ((as an object))
         swarms-of-mosquitoes

5   T: ju   plågades   av myggsvärmar (.)   hur ska ni översätta
         yeah were tormented by swarms of mosquitoes (.) how will you translate

6   sat- hela satsen   **hyttysparvet-** (.)
         sen- the whole sentence **swarms of mosquitoes-** (.)

7   S: **kiduttivat   juoksijaa**
         were tormenting a jogger

8   T: **nii (.) elikkä s-passiivilla agentilla ilmastuna**
         [c.p.] that-is s-passive   via-agent expressed
         yeah (.) that's expressed via s-passive and an agent

9   **niinku usein** (–) (.) och så   har vi verbet …
         like   often   and then have we the-verb
         like often (–) (.) and then we have the verb…

At line 1, the teacher reads a sentence from the textbook. In formulating a question about the sentence she picks up a relevant part of the material, here a grammatical structure (line 2). Note that in taking up the grammatical structure the teacher transforms the syntax of the original sentence by taking away the object, "the joggers", and introducing only the verb and its agent, "were tormented by swarms of mosquitoes". Only after presenting the key aspect of the material, does the teacher restore the object of the sentence, "the joggers", at line 3. The teacher also reformulates her question from "what does it mean" to "what is it in Finnish" (2 and 3). Presumably she has reformulated the question after monitoring the students' lack of willingness to respond. The reformulation also makes explicit that students may answer in Finnish, but note that the original question "what does it mean?" points out that the exercise is not just a translation for the sake of translation. After the student's answer, the teacher says the answer and repeats the relevant aspect of the text (5), and then again reformulates her question. As an increment to her question, the teacher initiates the answer by producing its first item in the correct grammatical form (5 and 6) in contrast to the faulty form in the student's response (4). In this way, the teacher performs an embedded correction (Jefferson 1987) but avoids sanctioning the student who had been active in taking the floor to answer. However, after initiating an acceptable answer, the teacher allocates the floor to another student

(S), who then completes the answer (7). For the closing of the pedagogic cycle, the teacher still explains (in Finnish) which grammatical form was the preservable item in the exercise (8–9).

As a whole, the pedagogic cycle is part of the classroom language game, in which the task is to save the relevant items and aspects of the source material but also to maintain a particular participation framework connected to the participation roles and their sequential accomplishment. Schoolwork thus concerns learning not only separate topics but also learning the classroom language game which forms the tacit, taken-for-granted basis for education, and more generally, for participation in complex organizational settings. In other words, schoolwork does not simply consist of learning separate subjects, but also of learning sets of criteria for what to learn, recognizing situated cues about the relevance of items taught and making distinctions between various aspects of knowledge. The pedagogic cycle is salient in that it allows the participants to maintain intersubjective understanding of the action through which the sets of relevance criteria for making the distinction between preservable and disposable elements of classroom talk are brought to the surface.

5.5 Repairs

Repairs are a generic conversational practice through which all types of interactional troubles can be managed and repairables corrected (Schegloff et al. 1977). Repairs cover any kinds of problems in talk in interaction: semantic, syntactic, prosodic, pragmatic, etc (Arminen 1996). Further, repairs are a reflexive practice so that the repair itself points out an item to be repaired irrespective of whether the repairable item is "faulty" in any abstract non-contextual sense. In classrooms, repairs are put to specific pedagogic use. The third position of the pedagogic cycle offers a natural place for initiation of a repair. Instead reformulating the answer, the teacher may use a repair initiation to mark the insufficiency of the answer, allocate the turn back to the student, and also to guide the student towards a satisfactory answer. The reflexive quality of repairs allows them to be used to address any aspect of talk, which makes them a useful resource for maintaining a classroom language game where the relevance criteria are partly tacit. Through repairs the teacher may focus on the particular aspect of talk thereby informing recipients about the ongoing criteria of relevance. Repairs can also be used recursively so that they form long, extended sequences in which the teacher and student collaboratively produce an acceptable answer as we can see in extract 14, again from a Swedish lesson in a Finnish high school. At line 5, the student answers the teacher's question, occasioning a lengthy repair sequence. The correction is finally completed at line 13, and confirmed by the teacher at line 14. I have marked with (a) the trouble source, (b) repair initiation, (c) correction, and (d) the confirmation of the repair.

(14) IA 1993, 5 (9)

1   T: mmh-m (.) när man kom längre söderut (.) och
            mmh-hm (.) as one came further south (.) and

2   längre alltså av vilket adverb är (ännu) de där
            further so   of which adverb is (still) that

3   formen längre söderut- va är längre söderut på
            form   further south-   what is further south in

4   finska (.) Hanna
            Finnish (.) Hanna

5 a,b→ H: **etelään   tai etelään päin**
            to south or south bound

6 b→ T: va
            what

7 a→ H: etelään
            to south

8 b→ T: n<u>ii</u>
            [c.p.]
            ye<u>ah</u>

9 a,b→H: **<u>ete</u>lään suuntaan tai jotain**
            south   direction or something
            <u>so</u>uth bound or something

10 b→ T: längre
            further

11 b→ H: **niinku=**
            erm like=

12 b→ T: =långt läng-=
            =far furth-=

13 c→ H: **=pitemmälle**
            =further

14 c,d→T: **niijust   pitemmälle kauemmas§etelään (.)**
            that's right further   farther away south (.)

15   *((clears throat))*   vad betyder de **upp**för mig
                                   what means that struck me
                                   what does it mean it struck me

The teacher's repair initiations follow a systematic trajectory. The teacher starts with an open repair initiation at line 6 which is occasioned by a hearing or understanding difficulty (Drew 1997). Subsequently, at line 8 the teacher indicates with her response token that the student's answer is incomplete thereby returning it back (Sorjonen 1996). Since the student still has difficulties finding an acceptable answer, the teacher takes up and utters the trouble source "längre" [further] at line 10. The student is nevertheless still unable to answer, and produces a search expression "niinku" [erm like] which also works as a repair initiation. At line 12, the teacher facilitates the repair by providing the basic form of the trouble term "längre" [further], and as the teacher is uttering the trouble source, the student provides an adequate translation. At line 14, the teacher confirms the repair and repeats the adequate answer, also providing two translations of the term that had proved troublesome, thereby marking and pointing it out. As a whole, the teacher's use of repair initiations helps the student to produce the correction, i.e., display learning in practice. The teacher designs the repair according to the recipient so that new cues are provided to allow the student to gain understanding. The teacher thus builds up a zone of proximal development (Vygotsky 1978), in which the student is given a chance to gain insight via the teacher's assistance.

5.6 Special Pedagogic Formats: The Reflexive Relationship between the Goal and the Format of Interaction

In adult education in particular, there are many other pedagogic formats besides classical classroom interaction. The differences in format also reflect partly differing educational goals. The officially prescribed goals for adult education involve issues such as empowering students, facilitating self-reflection, building motivation for change, etc. (Vehviläinen 1999; Miller and Rollnick 1991). A good example of an alternative learning practice is the "sharing round" commonly used in various therapies (Wootton 1976; Arminen 1998). Harvey Sacks (1992b, 260) even suggested that the power of AA (Alcoholics Anonymous) resides in the series of stories.

> A collection of people get together and tell a series of stories, one alike to the next, i.e., places like AA involve a series of stories where we come to see that we're all in the same boat, and people figure that they're understood and that they're not alone – where among the problems present in therapy is that for all you know, given that the therapist doesn't respond with telling you he had the same experience, nobody had the same experience as you.

In AA, learning takes place through co-construction and transvaluation of experiences with the help of a series of stories. In mutual help groups such as AA speakers build functional narratives that help them to learn to cope with their problems. In AA, speakers display a double perspective on their problems and testify that their worst experiences have become their most valuable experiences that have paved the way for recovery. i.e., they aim at transvaluating their experiences through storytelling. This transvaluative co-construction of experiences proceeds implicitly and indirectly as members help others by analyzing their own experiences in ways that make these relevant for others as well. Mutual help in AA is a methodical achievement in which recipients can learn to meditate upon their own experiences when speakers share their experiences in a mutually relevant way.

It is not mere coincidence that storytelling is the basic form of activity in mutual help groups. In meetings members can relate series of stories to display their understanding and appreciation of each other's experiences. Second stories are a key aspect of members' work to build the sense that "we are all in the same boat". The interpersonal communication through series of stories constitutes the bedrock for mutual aid in mutual help meetings. Indeed, storytelling is not only a method for problem solving but also a vehicle to build and manage relationships between members. During their extended turns, AA members also construct and display the degree of alignment and affinity they have with other meeting participants. Alignment markers and *as X said* devices are used to build reciprocal and intimate relations between speakers. The intimate meeting atmosphere is an artful achievement as members publicly and intersubjectively display the identification and affinity they feel with one another.

The format of interaction is also reflexively related to the nature of the institutional practice, contributing to the particular nature of the activity in question. For instance, in terms of its format, mutual help differs from professional counseling and various types of therapies (as mentioned in Chapter 2). Firstly, in contrast to psychoanalysis and psychodynamic approaches, AA interaction is based upon reciprocal personal revelations: there is no professional disengagement. Secondly, in contrast to professional counseling, brief therapy, and systemic family therapy, mutual help is a highly discreet approach insofar as AA members avoid explicit advice giving in meetings (but not necessarily outside them), but instead focus on their own experiences that only indirectly offer others new ways to understand their own experiences (cf. Silverman 1997, 109–181). To conclude, various types of professional therapies and mutual help involve particular constraints on what will be regarded as allowable contributions. These constraints vary according to the type of therapy so that each therapy is an achievement that relies on participants' orientation to the constraints characteristic of that type. In mutual help, reciprocal personal revelations are prompted and disengaged advice is discouraged. These features together form the nature of mutual help in which personal relationships are built through reciprocal revelations, and the hierarchical relationships between participants in a meeting are played down through discouraging advice giving.

As a whole, mutual help contributes toward transvaluating the participants' experiences. This goal is linked to its specific interactional arrangements, which distance it from professional forms of counseling or therapy. In a similar way, the formats of educational interaction are reflexively linked to their goals. The organization of an AA meeting into a sequence of stories also makes it possible to build a figurative worldview in which specific instances or events are constructed as being part of a larger whole that can be used for making sense of each other's experiences. The meaning of a singular episode may become generalized so that it can be used for making sense not just of identical experiences but of all experiences that bear a symbolic resemblance to the original story. This gives a specific symbolic quality to AA as a pedagogic event. The question is no longer about the similarity of experiences but about a way of looking at experiences to configure them as an AA member's narrative. In AA, second stories are contributions to mutual help in which participants help each other by helping themselves through organizing their own experiences (Arminen 1998). Mutual help, thus, is an art of interpersonal exchange where relationships between participants are strongly reciprocal. The format of interaction also maintains this specific type of institutional action.

5.7 Conclusion

Despite sometimes fierce debates on pedagogic ideals, basic patterns of classroom interaction have survived for centuries. Classroom interaction is still largely composed of "lecturing", "pedagogic cycles", "repair sequences", "correctional activities", and "organized extra-curricular activities".

This chapter not only analyzed these basic patterns, but also tried to discuss the relationship between these different activities. In schools, the relevance for information is constructed through the accountability of the students' performance. The assessment of the students' performance in schools builds relevance for the information delivered at school. During lessons, the pedagogic cycle is the central interactional tool for measuring information reception and for designing personalized relevance for information. Correctional activities are the teacher's response to the problems of maintaining the students' receptiveness. Extra-curricular activities offer a solution to balance the otherwise one-sided criteria for the relevance of information. As a whole, the chapter demonstrates that there exists a reflexive relationship between the goal and the format of interaction in pedagogic settings as well. The individual forms of activity are not completely random and separate but compose a web of action that configures the nature of the activity. Consequently, the goals of adult education, for example, are served with forms of interaction that differ from traditional classrooms. Activating students and their reflective skills is a major challenge in adult education as well as therapeutic settings, and makes relevant new kinds of pedagogic forms. For instance, the dissemination of personal views and model learning may be organized through a series of perspective displays (sharing). It is a procedure to elicit views symmetrically from all participants and in this way differs significantly from interactions based on a client-professional relationship, such as the traditional forms of education.

Further Reading

– Hester and Francis (2000) have compiled a good collection of texts on educational matters.

– There are also a number of salient individual articles written by C.Baker, A. McHoul, D. Macbeth (see references). You can find further references to their work in the bibliographies on ten Have's web page: http://www2.fmg.uva.nl/emca/

– Vehviläinen (1999; 2001) discusses adult pedagogy, counselling and alternatives to traditional classroom interaction.

– For exercises, see http://www.uta.fi/laitokset/sosio/project/ivty/english/sivut/exercises.html

Notes

1   It seems that some of the problems of web teaching, particularly in talking-head lectures, may derive from this lack of the possibility for recipient design. Videotaped or otherwise technically-mediated lectures may suffer badly from the lack of two-directionality.
2   The bureaucratic ear is a metaphoric expression dating back to Kafka. It stands for impersonal, purely goal-rational but devoted information retrieval from the external world.
3   The analysis of the extract is based on Sanna Vehviläinen's exercise on the teaching cycle in Jan Anward's course on classroom interaction at the University of Helsinki, 1993.

Chapter 6

Strategic Interaction

There might actually occur a case where we should say: "This man *believes* he is pretending".

(Wittgenstein, 1951)

Harvey Sacks paid much attention to the strategic aspects of interaction. A characteristic of strategic interaction is that an actor may aim at getting somebody do something without appearing to do so. For instance, you can avoid giving help without refusing to do so if you treat the request as a joke. The strategic aspect of interaction is interwoven in all types of encounters, and is based in everyday talk and interaction. In institutional settings, the strategic nature of interaction is most significant in legal settings, particularly in cross-examinations. It is also a feature of media encounters, such as when avoiding an interviewer's questions. Of the various resources for strategic interaction, I will discuss describing as an activity, counter moves for avoiding negative implications, the placement of activities, the design of question series, and the use of the second position. In many of these actions, the speaker exploits the prior speaker's turn to meet his/her own aims. During the course of this chapter I will address a variety of institutional settings, but first I want to briefly consider the question: what is strategic interaction?

6.1 Definition

In order to define strategic interaction, we need to go as far back as Sacks' discovery of CA (see Schegloff 1992a), when "a wild thought" occurred to him while he was analyzing the call to the suicide prevention center we examined in Chapter 2.

(1) Sacks 1992a, 6

```
1    A:  This is Mr. Smith, may I help you?
2    B:  I can't hear you.
3    A:  This is Mr. Smith.
4    B:  Smith.
```

In extract 1, the caller reports a "hearing problem". He appears not to properly hear the answerer's name. When the hearing problem is repaired (line 3), the caller confirms his hearing by saying the name (line 4), after which the turn returns to the answerer. Consequently, the call progresses so that a place in which the caller could reciprocate the answerer by telling his name is not established at its canonical place at the beginning of the call. Additionally, it may be assumed that the agent has to display his orientation to the delicacy of the situation and avoid asking the caller's name directly. Therefore, the name never gets spelled out (see Sacks 1992a, 3–11, 72–80).

At this point a wild possibility hit Sacks. Was this an orderly phenomenon of the sequential nature of speech? Before Sacks, few people had analyzed the sequential properties of actual speech. For instance, content analysis aims at abstracting the topical content of talk, but does not question how topics are brought up, or how talk is organized. Sacks kept on asking questions such as whether talk is organized in an orderly fashion. Could talk be analyzed as a set of methods and procedures for doing things? Were these methods and procedures a basis for the orderly organization of talk and its understanding? Was the caller avoiding giving his name without refusing to give his name through a "strategic" hearing problem? Starting in 1964, Sacks began to make a series of discoveries about social life, such as how to get someone's name without asking it (give yours), how to get a chance to talk again (ask a question), or how to deprive a certain group of their rights without doing it overtly (describe the group as imitators, i.e., blacks were described as imitating whites in 19th century literature). As a whole, Sacks proposed that talk (and other social actions) are *methodic* (and strategic) ways of *doing* things (see Schegloff 1992a; Silverman 1999; Hutchby and Wooffitt 1998; ten Have 1999).

A partial definition of strategic interaction[1] is that it is an attempt to get another party to do Y by doing X; this X does not request Y directly, but implies that it is the next relevant thing to do without saying so directly. A strategic action thus always involves an implicit, covert goal that is not at the surface of the action. Multiple forms of strategic actions exist. In deceptive actions, activities are designed to mislead the other party to act in a desired way. Television police shows, for example, have taught us a lot about the ways in which police officers may pretend to know more than they do in order to lead the suspect to believe that confessing is his only alternative. Strategic actions also vary according to their goals: they can be collaborative, or as we more often think, competitive, etc. (for various types of strategic interaction, see Goffman 1969).

Mundane interaction is the bedrock for strategic interaction. On average, by the age of three a child learns that the design of requests may have an impact on their success. The ability to choose between alternative ways of doing an action to increase its chance of success is a condition for strategic action. Further requirements include the ability to take into account the other's perspective (for a theory of the mind, see Mitchell 1977). Only when A and B can reason about each other's intentions and states of knowledge, can they act strategically (when A knows that B knows that A knows B knows that A intends to get Y, A may reason that she improves her chances of getting Y by doing X, to which B may offer a counter move).

A profound conceptual difficulty with respect to a strategic interaction concerns the relationship between intentionality and the form of action. Generally, we ascribe intentionality to the strategic action, i.e., A wants (has an intention) to get B to do Y by doing X. However, our knowledge of intentions is based on observable actions, i.e., that A has done X, from which we have inferred that A has intended to do X. Unless we have an independent source of knowledge, our inferences about underlying intentions and motivations are based solely on observable actions, which do not provide any first hand data on the underlying cognitive states. The very definition that the strategic action works for a covert purpose presupposes a hidden aspect that can only be inferred and not observed. Furthermore, intention is always embedded in its activity context: only a recognizable social action or goal makes it possible to blueprint the act according to the requirements of the action or goal, as originally noted by Wittgenstein: "An intention is embedded in its situation, in human customs and its institutions. If the technique of the game of chess did not exist, I could not intend to play a game of chess. In so far as I do intend the construction of a sentence in advance, that is made possible by the fact that I can speak the language in question" (Wittgenstein 1958,108, see also Duranti 1997).

At times, it is also possible to distinguish between strategic and non-strategic actions on the basis of their form. With this in mind, we can still address Sacks' example of the hearing problem. Do we know that the caller *pretended* to have a hearing problem (intentional, strategic action), or was the hearing problem sincere, or was the unwillingness to say one's name a primary state that led to an inability to hear (in which case the strategic form of action that emerged by fiat)? Based on our current knowledge of repair practices, we can say that "I can't hear you" is a very rare repair initiation at the emergence of a hearing problem in comparison to "what?", "huh?" or "sorry?" (see Drew 1997). Therefore, we can give a qualified answer: the case does not *look* like a sincere hearing problem; it does not seem to belong to the paradigm of people's ordinary practices for initiating repairs. For the same reason we can also reject the third possible explanation. Naturally, we do not know the underlying causes of hearing problems, but we do know how people ordinarily repair hearing problems regardless of the cause. This is where we better leave this issue.

In addition, there is a fine line between a strategic action and a conventionalized indirection. Fishing, such as "your line's been busy", is marginally a kind of strategic action, yet it is also very close to a conventionalized indirection such as "it's hot here" meaning "open the window"; (for a discussion, see Pomerantz 1990/91; Heritage 1990/91). It is uncertain whether children learn to be strategic deliberately, or whether they only afterwards realize the strategic significance of the forms of actions they are learning. A child may not learn to lie, but may notice that she has said something that has not been the case and still gotten away with it. The realization that you are able to get away with untruths is a path-breaking moment, after which the distinction between true and false becomes potentially strategically relevant. Thus, actions that may subsequently be called strategic may have emerged by fiat and not by conscious design. This means, simply, that the difference between strategic and non-strategic action may at times be relative. Indeed, it may turn out to be as difficult to find purely non-strategic actions as actions which have been strategically designed down to their finest detail. But having said this, there are nevertheless clear prototypical forms of strategic actions.

Socratic dialogues offer a literary archetype of strategic interaction (see Plato 1977). In these dialogues, Socrates uses several strategies to undermine the opposite position. First of all, Socrates plays ignorant and asks the other party to teach him something. Subsequently, Socrates' talk shows that he has in fact asked an "exam" question whose answer he knows only too well. Through his skillful use of the second position he eventually undermines the other party's argument. As a key device, Socrates uses candidate answer inquiries, thereby leading the other party to admit views which in the end contradict the original position the party was trying to defend. Socrates' dialogues also reveal the multidimensionality of interaction. Each question is always part of a larger activity, an aspect of a wider argumentative sequence. As a whole, Socrates' dialogues are adept representations of the strategic aspects of ordinary conversation. These dialogues condense, represent, and rhetorically embellish the interactional patterns of strategic design of talk deployed in everyday life and in institutional settings.

6.2 Basic Forms of Strategic Interaction

In strategic interaction A tries to get B to do Y by doing X that somehow impinges on B. Although such interaction is based in mundane encounters, some institutional environments are reduced to and specialized in the strategic dimension of interaction. Typical environments include courtrooms, media interviews and job interviews, whose goals are related to manipulating the participants' images: demonstrating/ contesting guilt (courtroom), creation/violation of positive self-image (politicians in media; job seekers in job interview). Negotiations are a particular form of strategic interaction, and will be dealt with separately in the next chapter.

I will start by examining lexical choices, and demonstrate how descriptions themselves can have strategic value. Then I will show that strategic actions are always open to counter moves; in media interactions, for example, interviewees may try to avoid questions, in which case their skill is manifested in their success in avoiding answering hostile questions without refusing to do so. I will also discuss deceptive interactions, focusing on fabricated alignments, what Goffman (1969) also calls seduction. In a deceptive seduction, the victim is led to believe that the other party is on her side so that she would relax and provide the information sought. Strategic actions are often composed of extended sequences, of which I will discuss the strategic question series. Finally, I will address the use of the second position, in which the speaker designs her actions so as to avoid taking a stance until the other party has revealed his position, which then can be exploited for the tasks at hand.

6.3 Lexical Choices, Strategic Nature of Descriptions

On March 3, 1991 in Los Angeles, Rodney King, an African-American motorist, was stopped for speeding and subsequently beaten by four white police officers. The case became widely known and caused public outrage when an amateur video photographer's tape of the incident was broadcast on television. The police officers involved were put on trial for excessive use of force. Given the blatant use of force on the tape, many TV viewers were certain that the officers would be convicted. When the jury found the police officers innocent, an uprising took place, and crowds of outraged people destroyed considerable areas of the city. A year later, at a federal trial, two of the four police officers were convicted of violating King's civil rights and two were acquitted.

The Rodney King case provides excellent, albeit terrifying, material on the strategic nature of descriptions. In a careful and lively analysis of the first trial, Charles Goodwin (1994b) shows how the defense was able to code, highlight and use graphic representations of the tape to build up an account of the case such that the jury acquitted the defendants. After the trial, some of the jury members said that eventually they could not be certain about guilt beyond a reasonable doubt. At the first trial, the prosecution played the tape of Mr. King's violent arrest as a main piece of evidence, and believed that the tape would speak for itself, convincing anybody about the defendants' guilt. By contrast, the defense used an expert witness who had carefully analyzed the tape to build an alternative vision contesting this lay understanding. As Goodwin (1994b) puts it, it became a politically charged theater rehearsing contested visions. The video tape's murky pixels were used to construct incommensurate versions of the same event: "a brutal, savage beating of a man lying helpless on the ground versus careful police response to a dangerous 'PCP-crazed giant' who was argued to be in control of the situation" (Goodwin 1994b, 606). The prosecution claimed that excessive force had been used against Mr. King, while the defense claimed that Mr. King had been the aggressor and the police were just responding to Mr. King's actions to protect themselves. Following Goodwin (1994b), let us examine the courtroom interaction, seeing how the defense built up an expert version of the self-evident appearing piece of evidence to contest the taken-for-granted mundane view of the course of events.

To contest the likely lay perception that the police were arbitrarily beating a helpless victim, Sergeant Charles Duke, the expert witness, built up a coding scheme to describe the course of action from the police's point of view. The expert first proposed that the beating should be analyzed as being composed of distinct uses of force rather than as a singular entity. Instead of speaking about "beating" or "blows", he rephrased the event using technical terminology, where the key terms were "use of force", "assessment", and "escalation and de-escalation of the use of force".

(2) Goodwin 1994b, 617

```
1  Expert:   There were,
2            ten distinct (1.0) uses of force.
3            rather than one single use of force.
4            ...
5            In each of those, uses of force
6            there was an escalation and a de-escalation, (0.8)
7            an assessment period, (1.5)
8            and then an escalation and a de-escalation again. (0.7)
9            And another assessment period.
```

In his testimony, the expert was careful not to use mundane terms, so that "beating" and "blows" became "the assessment and the escalation and the de-escalation of the use of force". The expert testimony thus shifted away from the mundane framework to the professional realm. Accordingly, a matter that might have appeared to belong to the sphere of mundane moral judgment was transformed into an exclusive, expert realm, where distinct professional knowledge was necessary to understand the events. From the defense point of view, the objective of the expert testimony was just this: to place the incident beyond mundane competence so that the jury had to rely on experts to decide how to perceive what they saw.

To convince the judge and jury, an expert coding scheme was applied to the entire incident, moment by moment, so that the whole sequence of events was seen from the expert frame of reference. The visible images on the tape were singled out, highlighted, and translated into expert language to neutralize their mundane meanings. In extract 3, the defense builds up an instructed way of seeing violence from the expert frame of reference vis-à-vis the videotape shown simultaneously.

(3) Goodwin 1994b, 617 ((defense dialog))

```
1  Defense:  Four oh five, oh one.
```

> We see a blow being delivered.

=Is that correct.

```
2  Expert:   That's correct.
```

> The- force has been again escalated (0.3)
> to the level it had been previously, (0.4)
> and the de-escalation has ceased.

...

3 Defense: And at-
At this point which is,
for the record four thirteen twenty nine, (0.4)

> We see a blow being struck and thus the end of
> the period of, de-escalation?

Is that correct Captain.

4 Expert: That's correct.
Force has now been elevated to the previous level, (0.6)
after this period of de-escalation.

Note that the defense lawyer first uses ordinary terms in referring to the visible activities on the tape and in that way invites the recipients to see the scene using their default vocabulary. After the recipients have been invited to see the image, the expert substitutes the mundane with the technical description, so that "a blow" is transformed into a "cease of de-escalation". The defense lawyer thus works as an intermediary between the mundane and professional worlds, thereby facilitating translation from a lay view to an expert vision. This defense teamwork contributes toward codifying the supremacy of the expert vision through presenting it as an outcome of a translation process. Further, the use of both the lay and the expert frames of reference forestalls simple counter translations, since the recipients have already been instructed to see the mundane details and to translate them into a technical account.

The translation from a lay view to a professional vision does not only require a complete rescripting of the sequential course of action moment by moment; it also depends on reforming the relationship between the figure and the ground. In selecting particular images to be highlighted and articulated verbally it also sets the rest of the visual content in the background, thereby establishing a constraint angle on the sequence of events. In extract 4, the expert witness selects details to be highlighted in order to preserve a particular angle on the chain of events (see also Figure 6.1).

(4) Goodwin 1994b, 619 (lines 1–13 and figure 6 Goodwin 1994b)

1 Prosecutor: So uh would you,
2   again consider this to be:
3   a nonagressive, movement by Mr. King?
4 Sgt. Duke: At this time no I wouldn't. (1.1)
5 Prosecutor: It is aggressive.
6 Sgt. Duke: Yes. It's starting to be. (0.9)
7   This foot, is laying flat, (0.8)
8   There's starting to be a *bend.* in uh (0.6)
9   this leg (0.4)
10   in his butt (0.4)
11   The buttocks area has started to rise. (0.7)
12   which would put us,
13   at the beginning of our *spec*trum again.

**Figure 6.1 Sergeant Duke Analyzes the Rodney King Videotape. A Drawing
Based on a Still of the Rodney King Trial.**

First, the foregrounding can be noticed. As the prosecutor presents a candidate answer
inquiry and proposes that some of Mr. King's movements were non-aggressive, the
expert witness, after refuting the candidate answer, starts to detail Mr. King's barely
visible body movements to provide a focused view of a minute aspect of the visible
material. In this fashion, the expert foregrounds Mr. King's activities setting into the
background the fact that four standing police men had surrounded Mr. King laying
on the ground. Through foregrounding and selective description the expert manages

to bring Mr. King's subtle body movements to the center of a sequence of events he is recounting. Further, the extensive use of phrases "it's starting to" and "has started to" (lines 6, 8, 11) suggests that in a minutiae movement there is an imaginable seed for a forceful course of action. In effect, the expert offers a narrativized account of the piece of data inviting the recipients to see in any of Mr. King's minor movements a potential for aggression to a degree more than what is actually visible at any point. The interplay between the visible evidence and the verbal testimony expands upon and strengthens each.

Through verbal testimony and associated discursive practices the domain of scrutiny (the video tape) is transformed into an object of knowledge that is constituted from a particular angle. The argumentation is not produced as a statement consisting of independent propositions, but as a demonstration in which verbal descriptions refer in a certain way to the visible images on tape, inviting particular interpretations of these images that are reinforced through the talk at work in the testimony. In this vein, a hermeneutic circle is established so that a particular view invites certain objects to be foregrounded, thereby providing evidence for the proposed vision in the first place so that further evidence will not need to be taken into account. Not least, the demonstration is a real-time sequential achievement, in which the expert witness's talk, gestures, and ostensive actions are coordinated vis-à-vis a piece of evidence whose meaning is articulated simultaneously.

In the final extract for this section the force of the foregrounding is shown. Through his questions the prosecutor again tries to downplay Mr. King's role and emphasize the police officers' role in the incident.

Figure 6.2 Foregrounding an Activity. A Drawing Based on a Still.

Goodwin 1994b: 625

> *After demonstrating by playing the videotape*
> *that Mr. King appears to be moving his right hand,*
> *behind his back with the palm up.*

1	Prosecutor:	That would be the position you'd want him in.
2		=Is that correct. (0.6)
3	Sgt. Duke:	Not, (0.2) Not with uh:, (0.2) the way he is. (0.6)
4		His uh:, (0.4) His leg is uh
5		Is bent in this area. (0.6)
6		Uh:, (0.2) Had he moved in this hand here being uh:
7		(0.4) straight up and down.
8		That causes me concern (0.7)

9	Prosecutor:	Uh does it also cause you concern that
10		someone's *step*ped on the back of his neck.
11	Sgt. Duke:	(0.6) No it does not.

By way of answer, the expert witness again focuses on Mr. King's minor movements to show evidence of his aggression (lines 3–8). At lines 9–11, the prosecutor aims at building a contrast and maintaining an alternative line on the incident via his question concerning the fact that one police officer was stepping on Mr. King's neck. From the frame of reference chosen by the expert witness that fact is insignificant to his account of the course of events.

In his conclusion, Goodwin stresses that we should not be misguided to think that Mr. King's trial is an isolated incident: similar discursive practices are also used elsewhere. Descriptions are perspective bound and potentially salient morally and politically. As Sacks (1963) would have been ready to admit, a description is never perfect and complete but is always selective and purposeful, however innocent description as an activity may look and is often falsely thought to be. In its selectivity a description always highlights the object from a certain point of view and hides other aspects. Consequently, in everyday life and in institutional environments descriptions do matter, as they make certain qualities of objects available affording courses of actions related to those aspects (Pomerantz 1987). In particular, in morally charged environments, such as rape trials, selecting descriptions is a delicate and most consequential activity (Drew 1992; Matoesian 1993). For example, in the late 1990s, the term "gentleman rapist" was used in a police internal training session to describe a certain type of rapist in Finland. When the term somehow became public, a fierce debate broke out whether such a term could be allowable under any circumstances.

Even a single term or word may have flaming potential. However, descriptions are mostly taken for granted, as if their meaning were natural and as if describing were not a socially relevant activity. Studies of interaction may provide useful insights into the discursive practices of describing, thereby revealing the tacit basis of societal life.

6.4 Avoiding Questions Without Refusing to Answer Them

I have already touched upon the strategic relevance of answers in challenging the implications of questions. In this section I will discuss Steve Clayman's work on how politicians and public figures avoid questions in news interviews. In journalistic interviews, interviewees, politicians in particular, may have to face adversarial questions, which are potentially damaging to their public image. Historically, the interview context may also be changing and becoming more overtly adversarial (Clayman and Heritage 2002b). Faced with incriminating and hostile questions, interviewees somehow have to stand the pressure and counter their harmful implications so as to avoid damaging to their public reputation. Interactional skills can really make the difference, such that some interviewees appear to maintain moral strength at the point where someone else may lose face completely. On the other hand, an ability to detect the interviewee's covert evasive moves helps the audience to tell the difference between honesty and slippery evasion.

Mostly, an interviewee may not refute questions or avoid them overtly. Only an extremely popular figure may simply try to refuse a hostile question, and hope that it will be taken as a sign of courage in the face of an unjustified question. But a refusal to answer or an overt evasion may also launch a snowball if the ulterior motives for evasion become targeted repeatedly. Tactless refusals or noticeable evasions may thus become news themselves, generating media attention leading potentially to a scandal (for scandals, see Lull and Hinerman 1997). Therefore, the interviewee's main option is to try to avoid questions without seeming to do so. Reformulating the question is one such counter practice that allows the interviewee not to answer the question without refusing to do so. Extract 6 presents a clear, overt case of the reformulation of a question as a practice for trying to manage the damaging implications inbuilt into the original question.

(6) Clayman 1993, 168 [The Best of Nightline 1990 0:8:45] ((GH is Gary Hart.))

```
1 JRN:   Uh- (0.5) I told you::. (0.4) some days ago when we
2        spo:ke, and I told our audience this evening that I
3        would ask you both questions. I will ask you thuh
4        first now: just before we tak a brea:k because I
5        think I know what your answer's gonna be.=
```

```
6  1→      =Did you have an affair with Miss Rice?
7  2→GH:   .hhhh Mister Koppel (1.1) if thuh question: (.) is
8          in thuh twenty nine y:ear:s of my marriage, including
9          two public separations have I been absolutely and
10         totally faithful: to my wife .hhh
11 3→      I regret to say the: answer is no:. ...
```

An answer given through an overt reformulation begins with a paraphrase that changes the implications of the original question. Here the interviewee substitutes the question about an affair with a question concerning his fidelity during his twenty-nine years of marital life. The subsequent talk then answers the reformulated question and not the original one. An answer via a reformulation entails negative and positive dimensions. Negatively, the reformulation enables the interviewee to leave some aspect of the original question unanswered. Here Gary Hart avoids answering whether he had an affair with Miss Rice. Positively, the reformulation allows the interviewee to move beyond the frame of reference of the original question and to topicalize new issues leading to new layers of meaning. The interviewee opens up a topic concerning virtues, such as his fidelity and humility in as much as he admits and regrets his shortcomings. In all, the reformulated question appears to bear less damaging implications to the interviewee and additionally allow him to open up topics that might improve his public image. Of course, an overt reformulation like this may be subjected to a counter move so that the journalist could repeat or rephrase his question that had not been answered. Here the journalist's preface to his question (lines 1–5) may also have been relevant for the design of the answer. The fact that the question will be the first of two (line 3), that it will be presented just before a break (line 4), and that the journalist thinks he already knows the answer to the question (line 5) inform the interviewee in crafting his answer. However, without further knowledge of this particular context (the amount of time left, etc.) it is difficult to know the inferences the participants may have drawn from these clues. However, the journalist's remark on his knowledge may show that he was not expecting anything dramatic, and that he was going to let the interviewee get away with that.

Reformulations may also be less overt. The interviewee may only answer part of the question, or some aspect of the question. The answer may also start through addressing or questioning the presuppositions conveyed by the question.

(7) Clayman 2001; 1993, 182–183 [US 22 July 1985 PBS MacNeil/Lehrer: South Africa] ((FW is U.S: Ambassador to South Africa.))

```
1    JW:   But isn't this (.) d- declaration of thuh state of
2          emergency:: ( ) an admission that the eh South African
3          government's policies have not worked, an' in fact that
4          the um- United States ( ) administration's policy of
```

5		constructive eng<u>age</u>ment ( ) has not worked.
6	→ FW:	I do <u>not</u> agree with you .hhhh that the approach <u>we</u> have
7	→	taken (.) toward South Africa is- ay- is an incorrect
8		appr<u>oa</u>ch. .hhhhh <u>We</u> want ( ) tuh s<u>ee</u> that s- system
9		cha<u>nge</u>. We wantuh s<u>ee</u> South Africa <u>end</u> apartheid.
10		We wanta s<u>ee</u> basic rights established for <u>all</u> South
11		Africans. .hhhh We wanta see p<u>ea</u>ce and sta<u>bili</u>ty in that
12		country. .hhh An' that's a PERfectly respectable g<u>oa</u>l.
13		S<u>e</u>cond. (.) Thuh w<u>a</u>y we have purs<u>ue</u>d <u>i</u>t .hhh I <u>a</u>lso
14		believe .hhh is thuh most SENsible way ( ) in dealing with
15		a dangerous situation. .hhh U:Sing our <u>influe</u>nce. .hh to
16		cha<u>nge</u> government's th<u>i</u>nking…

The interviewee begins his answer by asserting his disagreement with the interviewer. In this way, he characterizes the question as being based on the interviewer's opinion, and thereby controversial. The overtly stated disagreement thus works as a counter move in itself as it accuses the interviewer of having stretched beyond his role as a journalist who should ask questions and not profess his opinions. Subsequently, the interviewee reformulates the question about the failure of the policy to a question about the correctness of the political approach. In that vein, the interviewee avoids answering the question about the failure and instead argues about the correctness of the political approach in terms of its goals. Here the overtly stated disagreement may presumably also work against the journalist for repeating the question that has already been framed as controversial (unless the journalist were able to argue that the question had not been answered at all).

Finally, skillful answers may exploit all the properties of questions. For instance, any ambiguity or inadequacy of the question may be useable property for designing an answer.

(8) Clayman 2001; Clayman and Heritage 2002a, 243 [UK: BBC Today: June 1993: Social Security Cuts] ((IR: John Humphrys; IE: David Howell))

1	IR:	… Mister Howell what are the attractions as you see
2		them: uh- of this workfare idea?
3	RH:	.hh Well (.) hh it seems to me to be ludicrous that we
4		are spending according to the government more than
5		eight billion pounds: in support of the unemploy:ed
6		on condition that they do nothing whatsoever .hhh to
7		(r) help society. .hh And I believe the time has come
8		when- when we've got to recognize: that (.) par::ing
9		down benefits is not the an:swer. That isn't how
10		savings can be made.

11   .hhh Savings ku- <u>huge</u> savings could be made: if ahm
12   (.) <u>one</u> the unemployed people were offered the right
13   to work and given an opportunity to work ....

Here the interviewee appears to answer in a roundabout manner. Instead of explaining the advantages of the workfare idea, he attacks the disadvantages of the current situation, stating the amount of billions that are spent keeping people idle. But note that the design of this answer exploits the vagueness of the question. A way to make an idea attractive is to tell what is wrong in the current situation. This is simply to say that if you ask a roundabout question, you may expect to get what you asked. For an interviewee the interviewer's mistake is a double fortune, first in that it may be exploited fully, and second in that it may be done safely as the journalist is very unlikely to countermeasure problems caused by his own mistake. The design of the question is always crucial for the answerer who may also use the question's properties for strategic purposes.

Given the importance of media performances, conversation analysis can be used as a resource for understanding the media critically. After all, interviews depend heavily on basic conversational structures, and a sequential view is essential for analyzing media interactions. It allows the scrutiny of adjacent actions, such as questions and answers, so that meaning in its discursive context may be explored. For instance, an answer may be excellent, but not to the question. In order to offer principled criticism of the media, we need to be sensitive to the details of media interaction in order to analyze its seamless ongoing construction of meaning.

6.5 Fabricated Alignments

Fabricated alignments are important resources when co-operation is needed to gain access to information that only another person possess. Goffman (1969) uses the term "seduction" to refer to situations in which a party falsely pretends an alliance to exploit the emerging relationship for her own purposes. Also, in antagonistic institutional settings forms of fabricated alignments may be used. "Brainwashing" is an ultimate example. In brainwashing the victim is put under such extended pressure that when given a helping hand the person is ready accept it under any conditions, even to alter the mind set completely and adopt a new identity (for brainwashing, see Sargant 1961; Winn 1983). Within shorter time spans, other types of fabricated alignment may be used. In interrogations, a "good cop"/"bad cop" role-play may acted, as we have often seen on TV. The bad cop threatens the suspect and acts uncivilly so as to induce the suspect to turn toward the good cop, who then may harvest the goods. In any case, interrogations involve getting the witness/suspect to tell all the relevant information, even if that would be harmful to the person himself. At this point you might be thinking that given the power imbalance between the parties, the task is simply to coerce the subject to confess. However, that account does not seem to hold. Goffman (1969, 41) notes that during the Inquisition in Europe, persons accused of witchcraft often knew what they were expected to say to stop the inquiry. As early as the eighteenth century, judges decided that confessions extracted through torture were not valid. Subsequently, the task has been to induce the suspect to co-operate and offer testimony that would be appropriate in terms of the law. Having to rely on the suspect's co-operation demands that police find a suitable mode of interaction with the suspect to induce her/him to co-operate. Consequently, as meager as the suspect's position may seem, it contains some leverage to bargain about the conditions under which co-operation may take place (see also Sacks 1992b, 391–393). As a corollary, interrogators may go to considerable effort to set the scene such that the suspect would co-operate. One such strategy is a fabricated alignment with the suspect. The following data extracts come from a police interrogation of a suspect whom the police think they "know" has killed two persons, and who seems to "know" that the police "know" it. The task is to elicit a proper confession that would stand up in court. In this case, the power imbalance is transparent, but note the technique the police officer uses for inducing the suspect's co-operation.

(9) Watson 1990, 291 [Statement of Stuart Riley] ((a pseudonym))

```
1  → Officer:  W'l then yer: telling me now thetcher a man'v honor.
2                right?
3                (0.3)
4     Riley:     Yeh ah'm a man'v honor.
5                (0.8)
6     Officer:   Awright?
7                (1.5)
8  → Officer:    Ah you honorable enough:? (0.7) et this ti:me tuh tell
9                me:, (0.8) what (.) motivatedju?
10               (0.7)
11    Riley:     Ah: tol' y-you ah don' ha:ve'm gonna have t'think about
12               da:t. Dass wah ah wanna talk t'Mistuh ↑Gordon.
13    Officer:   Awri:ght.
```

The officer uses a brief lead (lines 1–2) to his question proper (lines 8–9). As a lead to a question the officer offers some social acceptance of the suspect. Given the gravity of the suspect's situation, the offer may sound more tempting than what it might appear under other conditions. That is, the suspect may be led to think that through accepting the officer's offer he may still save his integrity and face, although almost all the rest might have already gone. After the suspect's acceptance (line 4), the officer formulates his question so that it uses the suspect's acceptance of the prior question as a part of its design. The officer suggests that the ascribed identity the suspect has accepted is conditionally relevant for his next action, i.e., the suspect may show that he is the man of honor (as he just said) by telling what motivated him to do what he did. Although the suspect does not immediately perform the action requested, he admits his accountability and states his readiness to talk at another time (lines 11–12).

Note that this practice seems to be used recurrently, at least in the next interrogation. In extract 10, the officer attributes to the suspect the fact that he appears to be a smart fellow.

(10) Watson 1990, 289 [Statement of Stuart Riley]

```
 1  → Officer:   I don'know you seem like a pretty smart fella t'me.
 2  →            (3.4)
 3  → Officer:   Are you smart enough tuh reali:ze thet the:: (2.0)
 4              police he:re in the homicide bureau'v uh (.) build
 5              u(.)p uh:: (0.6) case against you: tih the point, (1.4)
 6              where we feel yu- we gotcha::: (0.6) nailed t'the wal,
 7     Riley:   Couldn' say nothing about dat (boh),
 8              (0.4)
 9     Officer: Pard'n,
10     Riley:   t Ah couldn' say noth'n about dat.
11              (0.3)
12     Officer: Well,
13              (6.0)
14              We work very hard et ar ↓ job, (0.9) mghhm. (3.4)
15              We've taken statements::,
16              (1.0)
```

As in the previous extract, the officer first ascribes a positive identity to the interviewee. Here the suspect does not accept the offer, but note the lengthy pause of more than three seconds (line 2). The officer orients to the chance that the party might take the turn and delays his reinitiation of talk until a lengthy pause has appeared. That is, the officer has allowed the sequential implications of the question to bear on the suspect for a considerable time, audible as the suspect's pause. After no response, the officer again uses the identity ascribed to the suspect as part of the design of further talk. But note that no request or answerable question is posed to the suspect, possibly reflecting the suspect's refusal to co-operate at this point. Nevertheless, a systematic practice seems to be at work in the interrogations. Some concession is offered to the suspect, such as a chance to save self-respect or integrity. Subsequently, the next action is introduced as a condition for the concession provisionally given. This sequence seems a kind of a game in which a reward has been promised in the provision that a subsequent move will also be accepted.

In all, these examples show that even in a firmly asymmetrical interaction, both parties have a certain amount of self-determination, or power, if one wishes to put it that way. The professional seeks and needs the suspect's co-operation or manifest consent that ultimately leads to testimony or a confession. This reveals a generic feature of interaction, in that antagonistic interaction also requires some co-operative consensus. Part of strategic interaction entails defining the nature of the game: the parties may seek to define the game as being suitable for their purposes in terms of how competitive or co-operative it should be.

6.6 Strategic Uses of Questions and Question Series

Many forms of strategic interaction are established through extended and multi-layered sequences. In this section, I will deal with three types of extended sequences. First, I will return to the issue of the selection of game type, and show how competitiveness/cooperativeness can be achieved through the timing and pacing of actions. Subsequently, I will address confrontations in settings as different as therapy and job interviews. Finally, related to confrontations, I will consider the building of contrastive versions.

Strategic Focus and Timing of Questions

In the United States, involuntary commitment hearings are organized for persons whose putative mental instability has gotten them into serious enough trouble. After an initial shorter detention, involving evaluation and treatment, a formal judicial hearing is mandatory if extended commitment is proposed against the person's will. In the commitment hearings, a representative of the public defender's (PD) office counsels persons seeking their own release. A representative of the district attorney's (DA) office serves as a prosecutor in the proceedings. In all, these hearings are enacted displays of the competence or incompetence of the person in question. The role constellation in these hearings follows a predetermined routine. The public defender tries to save clients from involuntary commitment, aiming to demonstrate their social and interactional competence as evidence of their harmlessness and ability to take care of themselves. In contrast, the district attorney tries to make the putative mental patient display her/his incompetence or dangerousness to others. In this manner the hearings are organized around opposite games played by the PD and DA with the interviewee. As Holstein (1993) shows, however, these opposite games display interesting interactional dynamics: PDs may engage in what may seem like hostile behavior to help their clients, whereas DAs may use "friendly" conduct to convict the defendants. In selecting the focus and timing of their questions, PDs and DAs invoke a co-operative/competitive game in order to demonstrate the competence/incompetence of the interviewee.

To keep their client out of trouble, PDs attempt to make their interrogations simple and straightforward in order to facilitate as coherent an image of their clients as possible. The design and timing of the PDs talk is crucial for the display of the client's competence. For instance, a PD may choose to use yes/no questions, which should pose as minimal a challenge to the client as possible. A PD may also choose to take a turn after audibly incomplete or incoherent answers, to save the client from getting into more serious trouble. Ultimately, the PD may even interrupt clients who appear to be talking in a manner which might damage themselves. The following two extracts are taken from Holstein's (1993) field notes; these are not as detailed as transcripts, but may still offer a glimpse of the phenomenon.

Holstein 1993, 98 ((Field Note: Metropolitan Court; J1, DA3, PD1, Drl3, Fred Smitz; // signs are for marking the initiation of overlap))

```
1      PD1:   Where would you live?
2      FS:    I think I'd go to a new board and care home not
3  →          populated by rapists // and Iranian agents.
4  → PD1:     ((breaking in)) Fine, Mister Smitz now would
5             you take your medication?
6  → FS:      I would if it didn't pass//through the hands of too many Russians.
7  → PD1:     ((breaking in)) Do you get an SSI check Mister Smitz?
```

At lines 4 and 7, the PD breaks in when the client begins to talk in a way harmful to his case, allowing others think he is delusional. Even though an exact analysis of field notes is impossible since the notes lack sufficient detail, the challenge of the PD's task is easily observable. To avoid letting the interviewee get into trouble, the PD should time his incomings exactly. For example, the PD could and should have come in earlier at line 4, as the answer would have been complete and suitable after "I think I'd go to a new board and care home". But the client may have at that point marked his turn as being incomplete, thereby signaling the recipient to refrain from taking the turn. Thus, the PD should have bracketed his conventional preferences for the timing of turn-taking and taken the turn *before* the client arrived at a transition relevant place in terms of its syntactic, prosodic and pragmatic completeness, but that kind of early timing might itself be audible as a sign of trouble. Further, to keep the client out of trouble the PD should also have anticipated trouble before there were any signs of it. Worse still, the client's second answer is even more difficult from the PD's point of view because the first sentence in the conditional is not sufficient in itself, but projects a continuation (Lerner 1991). In addition, the conditional makes the favorable answer only conditional. Nevertheless, it is important to appreciate that "interruptions", conventionally held to be hostile movements (see e.g. Beattie 1981), might also be used as a quintessential part of a co-operative game. Activities such as interruptions do not possess a unified meaning, but achieve meaning through the context.

In these commitment hearings, DAs adopt exactly the opposite tactic in managing interaction with the interviewee. As we will see in the next extract, they often use a tactic called "letting them hang themselves": the DAs just let the interviewees talk and believe that psychotic symptoms will come up if they are allowed to speak without constraint. Pay attention to the DA's response at line 22.

Holstein 1993: 104–105 ((Field note, Metropolitan Court; Jl, DA2, PD2, Dr12, Lisa Sellers))

1	DA2:	How do you like summer out here, Lisa?
2	LS:	It's OK.
3	DA2:	How long have you lived here?
4	LS:	Since I moved from Houston.
5		((silence, approximately second or more[J.H.]))
6	LS:	About three years ago.
7	DA2:	Tell me about why you came here.
8	LS:	I just came.
9		((silence))
10	LS:	You know, I wanted to see the stars, Hollywood.
11		((silence))
12	DA2:	Uh huh.
13	LS:	I didn't have no money.
14		((silence))
15	LS:	I'd like to get a good place to live.
16		((silence five seconds))
17	DA2:	Go on. ((spoken simultaneously with onset of next utterance))
18	LS:	There was some nice things I brought.
19		((silence))
20	DA2:	Uh huh.
21	LS:	Brought them from the rocketship.
22 →	DA2:	Oh really?
23 →	LS:	They was just some things I had.
24 →	DA2:	From the rocketship?
25	LS:	Right.
26	DA2:	Were you on it?
27	LS:	Yeah.
28	DA2:	Tell me about this rocketship, Lisa.

At line 22, the DA displays an interest in the interviewee's talk with "oh really?" in contrast to the previous neutral recipiency tokens, like "uh huh" (lines 12 and 20). This also reveals the strategic design of the DA's performance. He appears innocent, but he works toward guiding the interviewee to reveal herself in a manner that would degrade her credibility. The "cosy" character of "oh really" is remarkable in two respects. First, it does not treat the previous turn as repairable; the DA does not display any overt suspicion about the interviewee's visit to a rocketship. Indeed, "oh really" treats the previous turn as a piece of news, and requests the news bearer to go on. In this manner, the DA normalizes an unexpected object, thereby helping the interviewee hang herself. Secondly, as discussed in the previous chapter, change of state tokens, like "oh", are rare in many institutional contexts, including courtrooms. "Oh really" departs from the prevailing formal style in the courtroom. For the listeners, like the judge, this deviation from the norms governing self-presentation may give a further clue that something unusual and accountable is taking place. As a whole, the DA's performance is deceptive: he uses forms of talk that are normally associated with co-operation. He lets the other party talk freely and displays interest in her talk. Again, as with the PD's talk, the meaning of the forms of talk seems to be directly opposite to their canonical meaning in ordinary talk. The interviewees, who lack the ability to reflect on the meaning of linguistic forms in context, are thus in even deeper trouble than they think they are.

Confrontation

Confrontation is a verbal practice in which the confronter challenges the other party by leading that party to produce a version which contradicts or implies a contradiction to what the person has already said, thus contesting the earlier version. Confrontations are practiced in some types of therapy, e.g., in addiction therapy (so-called confrontational therapy, see Arminen and Halonen forthcoming), but parallel practices can also be found in other contexts, such as job interviews. Confrontations can also be compared with perspective display series, in which the recipient's perspective is first asked or made relevant prior to the presentation of one's own view. As we saw in Chapter 4, perspective display series are mainly used for building alignment and avoiding controversy, but I also pointed out that they can be used argumentatively (Vehviläinen 1999; 2001). In contrast to perspective display series, confrontations are adversarial in that the confronter aims to influence or exploit the discrepancy in perspective.

The first two examples are from Bleiberg and Churchill's study on confrontations in a psychotherapy session between a middle-aged therapist and a young patient, who expresses her wish to live without the interference of her parents.

(13) Bleiberg and Churchill 1975, 274

```
1     Pt.:   I don't want them (my parents) to have anything to do with my life,
2            except ((pause))//security(?)
3 →   Dr.:   You live at home?
4     Pt.:   Yes.
5 →   Dr.:   They pay your bills?
```

6   Pt.:   Yeah.
7 → Dr.:   How could they not have anything to do with your life?

In extract 13, the psychiatrist challenges the patient's view through two questions that imply an alternate vision. To do so, the psychiatrist uses candidate inquiries that guide the patient to admit facts that imply a contradiction to what she has said. The use of candidate inquiries also reveals the psychiatrist's strategic design of talk. The candidate answers he purports impose a contradicting view on what the patient has said, but as inquiries they make relevant the recipient's consent thereby inviting the patient to collaborate in a joint production of the confrontation. In this way, the confronter manages to turn the patient's own talk against herself. Maximally, the confrontation may amount to a double sanction as the confronted person may not only notice a contradiction in her mindset but also notice that she appears incoherent, providing further impetus to change her mindset or its verbalizations so as to at least appear consistent.

In extract 14, the psychiatrist carries out a reduction *ad absurdum* through which he challenges the patient's claim.

(14) Bleiberg and Churchill 1975, 274

1   Pt.:   I don't=have much=faith=in therapy or anything anymore.
2 → Dr.:   You don't have any faith in anything?
3   Pt.:   No.
4 → Dr.:   You want to live? Or you want to die?
5   Pt.:   I don't want to die; I'd be dead (very low voice)
6 → Dr.:   O.K., so there's obviously some evidence that you want
7   to live. Is that right?

The patient initially complains about her therapy process, or professes disbelief in therapy. As an increment to her claim, she then adds an extreme case formulation, saying she does not believe in anything anymore (on extreme case formulations, see Pomerantz 1996). Effectively, the psychiatrist tackles only the latter, generalized complaint, and not the prior one. (A more detailed transcript would allow us to assess whether the psychiatrist himself participated in the production of the latter claim by delaying his taking of a turn with any pause longer than a beat between the first and second claim.) Consequently, the psychiatrist uses candidate inquiries to induce the patient to contradict her generalized complaint, but noticeably does not deal with the patient's more substantial dissatisfaction.

In general, the confronter may use specialized expert knowledge or cultural common sense (as in the extracts above) to build up an alternate vision challenging the other party's perspective. The alternate vision may also bear on the situated specifics of the claim and activate a perspective shift to something contesting the proposed vision, as we can see in the next example. This data comes from a group therapy session in a Finnish addiction treatment clinic. One of the patients, Hans, has been telling about a visit to an AA group that he considered a failure. After the round of patients' experiences the therapist starts to ask questions, and turns towards Hans.

(15) Arminen and Halonen forthcoming ((Tm= Male therapist, H= Hans, male patient, S=Sari, female patient, M=unidentified male patient, F=unidentified female patient; translated from Finnish))

```
 1    Tm:   What? #uh# what then Hans (mister) was so, (0.8)
 2          negative then. (0.8) in your experiences in the
 3          gr[oup.
 4    H:       [I $d(h)on,t$ know somehow I [imagined that,? (0.5)
 5    M:                                     [kröhöm ((coughing))
 6    H:    one guy stared at me there? or surely he ↑ loo:ked at me
 7          all the time when he talked about his things,
 8          (0.8)
 9    Tm:   yeah,?
10          (0.5)
11    H:    he sort of like hit me erm he (0.3) somehow like
12          disapproved of my talk (there).
13          (1.8)
14    Tm:   °I see.°
15          (0.6)
16 →  Tm:   Were there plenty of people.
17          (0.3)
18    H:    There's like about °thirty.°
19          (0.3)
20    Tm:   .yeah
21          (0.8)
22 →  Tm:   h- how about the other,? (0.5) twenty ↑ nine guys
23          what did they,=
24 →  H:    =y'know they just looked at $that one.$ [heh heh heh
25 →  All:                                           [heh heh heh
26 →  All:  HEH HEH HEH [HEH ((all laugh together))
27    S:                [he looked at you and you at him
28          (0.5)
29    H:    yeah yeah=
30    F:    he he .hh=
31    M:    =heh heh heh hch
32          (3.0)
33    ((The therapist turns to another patient))
```

First, the therapist asks Hans to tell more about his negative group experience (lines 1–3). After Hans's account, the therapist makes a candidate answer inquiry (16) that serves as grounds for building an alternate vision. The therapist's initial request to Hans can also be seen as preparation for a confrontation. As an unsatisfactory AA group experience potentially jeopardizes the addiction therapy process, the therapist must address it. The therapist's initial question thus sets up an information gathering with whose help a potentially harmful incident may be opened for further discussion. Here the therapist picks up on the fact that only one person's behavior had been the basis for Hans's assessment of his group experience. The therapist also takes Hans's description that there were "about thirty people" (18) there literally, and asks "how about the other twenty nine guys" (22). By attributing hyper-exactness to Hans's description, the therapist invokes a comical frame and also portrays Hans's concern as having been overdone in the face of what seems to have happened. Here the confrontation has a tease-like quality (for teasing, see Drew 1987), which may also soften and mitigate the activity. Consequently, Hans collaborates in the production of the perspective shift, and some laughter starts to appear in his voice while he utters "$that one$" (24), after which the laughter bursts open immediately. The placement of the first laughter quality in Hans's voice suggests that there – at that point – he is recognizing that it is the guy who was staring him at the meeting (and not he himself) who had been the comical figure. The fact that all others instantly join in laughter with Hans (25) suggests that the transgressive reading proposed by the therapist caught its recipients. In this case, the confronted person and recipients acknowledge and accept the confrontation and the problem gets laughed off by laughing together.

Often, however, confrontations are not overtly acknowledged as in extract 15, where the confronted person laughs first and then invites others to join in demonstrating his acceptance of the confrontation and its confirmation by the therapy group. It is less certain whether the previous confrontations (extracts 13 and 14) were successful in inviting the confronted person to reflect on her mindset or whether they just blocked the therapy process at that point. As a whole, confrontation is a delicate activity. Unsuccessful attempts at confrontation, which invite open opposition or silent resistance without any acknowledgement, may block the therapy process until a working consensus between parties is rebuilt again (Arminen and Leppo 2001; Arminen and Halonen forthcoming).

Interactional practices appearing in job interviews can also be recognized as confrontations. It may well be, however, that only rarely does the punch line of the confrontation get spelled out in this context. The institutional task of job interviews, to gather an impression of job seekers and test their suitability for the position, makes them a likely scene for strategic moves. Inasmuch as the task is to collect pure, intact information from the applicant in order to prepare as reliable an assessment as possible, interviewers are cautious not to allow any of the applicants to gain new information which would help one of them improve his appearance in situ. To put it bluntly, interviewers want to know the applicants' sincere motivations and level of skills concerning the position. For these reasons, job interviews tend to be conducted in a certain way so that the questions are ordered according to the goal of the practice.

The following data extracts come from Komter's (1991) study on Dutch job interviews. I won't provide a further introduction to the next two extracts because I want you to consider whether they exhibit some recognizable systematic features or pattern. The key is the order in which the questions are posed.

(16) Komter 1991, 160 ((translated from Dutch))

```
1    I:  Why did you really uh (.) want to become a secretary ?
2        The kind of company is not so important?
3    A:  No that doesn't matter [ I'm interested in the work.
4    I:                         [ doesn't matter.
5    A:  I've never done it and it looks all right to me so uh
6 →  I:  What do you imagine it to be actually.
```

(17) Komter 1991, 160–161 ((translated from Dutch))

```
1     I:  what I'm actually very curious about, that is uh (.)
2         what uh (.) is exactly the: motivation for you, to
3         apply for this very function right, of coordinator.
4     A:  ... and I also think uh I have really for myself the
5         idea uh (.) well I can do something with it. And I
6         also have some feeling for it, and uh I also think
7         uh I just enjoy it.
8  →  I:  In what respect uh do you expect that uh in this
9         function you'll have direct uh contact with uh
10        children, [and parents?
11    A:            [hm.
```

In these sequences, the interviewers move systematically from "sincere", information-seeking questions to exam questions, or questions in which they show that their knowledge would be relevant. The interviewers first ask questions addressing the *applicant's* information territory, i.e., the applicant's motivations and motives, prior to questions concerning matters belonging to the *interviewer's* information territory, i.e., the job's requirements and profile. Why are the questions posed in this order? Or, what is accomplished by asking questions in this order and in not any other order? As Komter (1991, 161) puts it, the interviewers lead the applicants "to 'show their hands' in a situation where the interviewers know their cards."

By asking the interviewee's motivation first, and giving the grounds for assessment only afterwards, the interviewers withhold their strategic knowledge so that applicants are not allowed to tailor and recipient-design their answers with the help of the interviewer's detailed knowledge of the vacancy. Interviewers thus gain a picture of the applicant's uninformed motivations prior to detailing the job requirements, and applicants are not allowed to offer a version of what they think the interviewers want to hear based on the knowledge revealed about the job requirements. This order of questions also allows interviewers to use the applicant's motivations when assessing his or her appropriateness for the vacancy. Part of the evaluative task of job interviews is already observable in the latter questions in extracts 16 and 17, where the interviewers display that they hold the job seeker accountable through their knowledge of the specifics of the vacancy that are not known to the applicant. In this fashion, the interviewers may assess the applicant with the help of a set of criteria that has not been available to the interviewee at the time when the assessing has been done. On rare occasions, an offshoot of the assessment is given to an applicant in the course of an interview. If the outcome is negative, a kind of confrontation will be realized.

In extract 18, the applicant has answered questions concerning his wishes regarding the job and reasons for applying for it, after which it turned out that the vacancy is very different from what the candidate had thought. The applicant nevertheless stated that – all the same – he would still be very motivated to get the position even if it is different from his original expectations. Here, the interviewer gives his assessment of the candidate.

(18) Komter 1991, 162 ((translated from Dutch))

```
1    I:   So you have clearly come for a different function, uh
2         (.) still you can motivate reasonably well why you
3         also want to be considered for the function as we have
4         just explained to you, it doesn't alter the fact that I
5         personally have doubts, (.) if you are a the right man
6         for this function, b if the motivation for this specific
7         function, can be reached in so short uh a time ... I
8         don't think that you are motivated for this specific
9         function, for that the time is too short.
10   A:   Yes.
11   I:   And so it doesn't seem right for me to say well okay
12        this occupation attracts you too, well okay.
```

As in extracts 13–15, the person is led to contradict his previous mindset. Here the job seeker is led to display his uninformed motivations, and then his informed motivations vis-à-vis the requirements of the job. The contradiction between these two sets of motivations is then seen as a lack of integrity and consistency that as such would offer sufficient grounds for rejecting the candidate. It is likely that such direct negative evaluations are fairly rare in job interviews. However, the confrontational practice described above may still be a regular procedural tool of job interviews, even though its offshoot may not be spelled out very often.

Various games can also be combined. At times, job interviews may also use deception, so that instead of withholding information the applicant may be misguided through misleading information. For instance, certain research and development positions may be advertised emphasizing the academic aspects of the work so as to increase their attractiveness, but in practice candidates lured by the academic side of work are turned down as the meant but not stated aim was to find persons willing to do "real work".

Building Contrastive Versions

In adversarial situations, parties orient to building versions of events that support the credibility of their claim and discredit opposing claims, as we saw in the context of Rodney King's trial as well as in involuntary commitment hearings. In cross-examinations, when parties who are equally competent in interaction pursue their arguments, the competitive versions may stack into long question-answer pair sequences. The organization of courtrooms gives the cross-examiner the power to set the agenda through questions, while the witness may try to rebut the cross-examiner's version by the design of her answers. Eventually, the cross-examiner tries to juxtapose the facts via the design of questions that would imply a contradiction in a witness's testimony and damage its credibility. Building contrastive versions is related to confrontations, but here the contrast is between items that have "just been said" and "said earlier" or known through prior knowledge. Further, the aim is not to try to influence the recipient but to challenge his public credibility. That is, the talk is designed as if the other party were an equally skilled strategic player who due to his position conveys only certain information and is unlikely to confirm damaging details regardless of whether they are true or false.

In rape trials, for instance, the defense attorney treats the alleged victim's talk as if it were a strategically designed, selective version of what has happened. Through series of questions the attorney aims at establishing what has happened that the witness has not told and may have reasons not to tell. In extract 19, the attorney asks questions concerning the evening the witness had spent in company which included the defendant.

(19) Drew 1992, 479, 506 [Da:Ou:2:1]

1   A: Well y<u>ou</u> kne:w. at that ti:me. that the defendant
2   was. <u>in</u>:terested (.) in <u>y</u>ou (.) did'n you?

```
 3  →      (1.3)
 4  → W:  He: asked me how I'(d) bin: en
 5  →      (1.1)
 6  → W:  J- just stuff like that
 7  → A:  Just asked yuh how (0.5) yud bi:n (0.3) but
 8  →      he kissed yuh goodnigh:t. (0.5) izzat righ:t.=
 9    W:  =Yeah=he asked me if he could?
10         (1.4)
11    A:  He asked if he could?
12         (0.4)
13    W:  Uh hmm=
14    A:  =Kiss you goodnigh:t
15         (1.0)
16    A:  An you said: (.) oh kay (0.6) izzat right?
17    W:  Uh hmm
18         (2.0)
19    A:  An' is it your testimony he only kissed yuh
20         ('t) once?
21         (0.4)
22    W:  Uh hmm
23         (6.5)
24    A:  Now (.) subsequent to this...
```

The witness and the attorney are here pursuing competitive versions of the same course of events. The attorney maximizes the contrast between versions through his turn at lines 7–8, where he first attributes a position to the witness and then contrasts it with another fact that seems to be incompatible. The position attributed to the witness may appear to be taken directly from the witness' previous turn, but in fact it is in a subtle way distinct from the witness' original position. In his version, the attorney transforms the witness' position by shifting "just" from modifying "stuff like that" in the latter part of her turn to modifying "how she'd been" at the beginning of the turn. That is, whereas the witness claims that the suspect had only asked how she had been and engaged in other talk that had been just as inconsequential as asking "how are you", the attorney instead claims that the witness has said that the suspect had just asked how she had been. As minute as this shift of the placement of "just" may seem, it allows the attorney to build a powerful contrast between what he claims the witness had said and what he claims otherwise knowing about the case. Here, as elsewhere, scalar adverbs and particles, like "just" are a potent discursive device (for extreme case formulations see Pomerantz 1986). Furthermore, the attorney manages to fabricate a version of events which departs from what the witness actually said, and still attribute this new version as being hers. Of course, this kind of manipulation of evidence violates the rules of judicial conduct, but given its subtlety the audience, including the judge and jury, overlooked it. There are also further reasons why the attorney's manipulation of evidence was overlooked at this particular point: the witness' answer to the previous question at lines 4–6 appears to have been evasive, which seems to have made it a possible target at that very moment. First, the witness did not straightforwardly reject the attorney's suggestion that she had known about the suspect's interest in her, but initiated her answer by telling the fact that he had asked how she had been. However, at that point the witness does not treat her answer as having been sufficient and projects a continuation through her prosody and the particle "and" (line 4). Subsequently the witness does not immediately produce the continuation projected, and a pause of more than a second opens line 5, after which the turn is completed with a generalization "just stuff like that". The delayed production of the latter part of her turn and its designed unspecificity allow it to be heard as evading something more to be told. The attorney seems to have heard it that way and suggests through his contrast that the witness would have had more to tell than she chose to reveal (for further analysis of this sequence, see Drew 1992).

These sorts of contrast devices seem to be used systematically in cross-examinations. Here is another from the same trial.

(20) Drew 1992, 510 [Da:Ou:45/2B:1]

```
 1      A:  Now (.) subsequent to this: uh (0.6) uh you
 2  →       say you received uh (0.8) a number of
 3  →       phone ca:lls?
 4          (0.7)
 5      W:  Yei:s
 6          (0.4)
 7      A:  From the defendant?
 8          (1.2)
 9      W:  Yeis
10          (0.8)
11  →   A:  And isn't it a fa:ct (t)uh (.) Miss ((name))
12  →       that you have an unlisted telephone number?
13          (0.3)
14      W:  Yeis
15          (1.2)
16  →   A:  An' you ga::ve the defendant your telephone
17  →       number didn't you?
18      W:  No: I didn't
19          (0.3)
20      A:  You did't give it to [him
21      W:                       [No:.
22          (10.2)
23      A   Dur:ing the:se uh, ...
```

Here the attorney sums up separate facts that the witness has told in different stages of her testimony to build up a contrast between what these facts together seem to imply and what the witness has stated directly. The fact that the suspect has called the witness even though she has an unlisted number opens a puzzle. How has the suspect got the number, if the witness had not herself given it to him? The puzzle is open for a solution that implies a much closer relationship between the witness and the suspect than what she has admitted. Although the witness rejects the attorney's candidate inquiry whether she had given her number herself, the implied assumption has brought up an alternative way for seeing the relationship between the witness and the suspect that casts a possible doubt on the witness's version.

The building of contrastive versions is a salient strategic activity in adversarial contexts, trading on the various resources available. First, information from different sources is selectively summed up to construct an alternate vision that establishes a contest between versions. This construction may also rely on the use of common sense assumptions, such as the fact that an unlisted telephone number is accessible only to a class of people to whom it is given. Finally, building of contrastive versions utilizes sequential properties of talk so that it may be occasioned by features of talk that are vulnerable to unfavorable hearings, such as evasiveness in extract 19.

6.7 Second Position

Confrontations and contrastive versions both utilize the second position. In both activities the speaker's own claims are turned against himself. In the second position, the speaker's talk is employed as a strategic resource so that the person is not only allowed to speak first but also encouraged or forced to state her claims or arguments first to expose their potential weaknesses. The party who adopts the second position waits or even induces the other party to go first and not until the argument has been rendered challenges it. Commonly, the power position in interaction is associated with an ability to initiate the action trajectory for the occasion and to set its agenda (e.g., Frankel 1984; 1990). More complete interactional control, however, may be achieved only if the initiator also engages in evaluative actions concerning the other party's contributions, as in pedagogic cycles in the classroom, where the teacher asks the questions and then assesses the answers (Chapter 5). Socratic dialogues are also an archetypical example of this combination of initiative actions and subsequent deployment of the second position[2] (see Plato 1977). But even when the agenda is free, the utilization of the option to go second may offer a powerful strategic resource. Hosts of argumentative call-in radio programs are often skilled in deploying the second position to maintain control on the air. In these programs, the callers usually first go through an initial screening, after which a caller may be let on the program. The host then introduces the caller and after an exchange of greetings the floor is open. Generally, the callers go straight to their topic and start to pursue their argument.

(21) Hutchby 1996b, 62 [H:26.1.89:2] ((Caller is female))

```
 1   Caller:  .hh E:rm, uw- u-women've been fighting for
 2            equalitie:s (.) e::r fo::r, u-yihknow many yea:rs,
 3            .hhh an:d i-it seems to me that erm, they- want
 4            their cake and eat it.
 5            (0.5 )
 6   Caller:  Er:m.
 7            (0.3)
 8  →Host:   m-d- You s- You say you sa:y "the:y" but I mean:
 9  →         .hh er your voice seems to give awa:y thee erm,
10            .p fact that you're a woman too.
```

One of the properties of the second position is that it allows you to argue without engaging in an argument. That is, the person who goes second does not need to expose a claim but can concentrate on scrutinizing the other's argument. One such dimension through which an argument may be challenged concerns the relationship between the speaker and the alleged principal of the argument. In extract 21, the host claims to see a discrepancy in the fact that a female speaker criticizes women, in general, for their excessive demands for equality. Notably, the host does not take any stance regarding the argument, but contests the caller on logical grounds (without saying that in so many words, i.e., that the caller herself is a member of the group that she criticizes so that in effect she criticizes herself or, at least, opens her argument for such a logical contradiction). The ability to engage in an argument without revealing one's own stance is one of the benefits of the second position.

(22) Hutchby 1996b, 63 [G:3.2.89:4]

```
 1   Caller:  Ni::nety per cent of people, (.) disagreed with the
 2            new propo:sals for thee N.H.S:. in the White Paper.
 3            (0.8)
 4    Host:   You're- you're quite sure about that
 5  →         You say ni:nety per cent of the people disapprove
 6  →         uh- .h as if you have carried out your own market
 7            rese:arch on this.
```

In extract 22, the host again manages to engage in the argument with the caller without displaying his personal stance. Here, the host challenges the caller's epistemological position; the host seems to assume that it is not generally known how people think about the issue in question, so how can the caller claim to have such knowledge. In so doing the host also treats the caller as an average citizen who is not supposed to have any expert knowledge. In effect, the caller is sanctioned for being out of line in producing an argument whose validity an average competent member of society cannot assess. Consequently, the host manages to turn the tables, and sanctions the caller for either pretending to claim more than what he can actually know or for relying on arguments that are out of line for this type of show. The second position, thus, may also be utilized to balance the lack of expert knowledge. Undoubtedly, this also invokes a special tenor for the program. Finally, since the second position allows the party to distance himself from the argument, it also enables him to open alternative perspectives on the issue in question, as we can see in extract 23.

(23) Hutchby 1996b, 61–62 [H:30.11.88:2:1]

```
 1  Caller:  I think we should (.) er reform the la:w on
 2            Sundays here, (0.3) w- I think people should have
 3            the choice if they want to do shopping on a Sunday,
 4            (0.4) also, that (.) i-if shops want to open on a
 5            Sunday th- th- they should be given the choice to
 6            do so.
 7  Host:    Well as I understand it thee: (.) the la:w (.)
 8            a:s they're discussing it at the moment would allow
 9            shops to open .h for six hou:rs, .hh[ e:r ] on a=
10  Caller:                                       [Yes.]
11  Host:    =Sunday,
12  Caller:  That's righ[t.
13  Host:               [From:, midda:y.
14  Caller:  Y [es,
15  Host:      [They.wouldn't be allowed to open befo:re that.
16            .hh Erm and you talk about erm, (.) the rights of
17            people to: make a choice as to whether they
18            shop or not, [o:n ] a Sunday,=what about .hh the=
19  Caller:               [Yes,]
20  Host:    =people who may not have a choice a:s to whether
21            they would work on a Sunday.
```

Here the host shifts from the perspective of shoppers to that of those who work in the shops. Note that at lines 16–17 the host topicalizes the caller to have spoken about "the rights of people" even though, in fact, the caller has not quite placed his point in that disursive realm. By invoking the notion "the rights of people", the host seems to tacitly appeal to the maxim that all people should have equal rights. In this fashion, his perspective shift to include shop employees in the category of people also appears as an ethically grounded position. Again, a subtle shift in the position attributed contributes toward undermining the argument.

In all, the second position may be employed in various contexts and institutional environments. I recall that the then-presidential candidate Tarja Halonen, who in 2000 became Finland's first female president, was often careful not to speak before her main rivals had spoken in multi-candidate interviews. In this way, she managed to be in a position to assess and respond to her main competitors' turns. Additionally, in multi-candidate interviews where turn-taking was organized in rounds allowing each candidate only one turn per question, the person speaking afterwards could no longer be challenged. The application of the second position may even amount to a presidential tenor in performance.[3]

6.8 Conclusion

The starting point of this chapter was to establish the relevance of Sacks' initial discovery for the analysis of strategic interaction. Sacks proposed a technique to reverse-engineer action into its constitutive steps, which are thus observable patterns of social actions. Following Sacks, social actions can be subject to empirical scrutiny, which breaks them down into their constitutive methodic procedures as analyzable trajectories. Sacks' initial observation is relevant for a wide array of strategic actions that can be shown to consist of chains of practices whereby A aims to get B to do X without overtly doing so. As for the constitutive parts of strategic action, describing is a salient but often neglected social action. The salience of descriptions derives from their seen-but-unnoticed properties that guide the recipient to see the object of description from a certain angle and in a certain light. In their selectivity, descriptions are consequential in that they imply and even project possible courses of action in the domain activated by the description. The fact that people tend to take descriptions for granted, without considering them to be serious actions but rather merely reports of observations that just somehow "innocently and subconsciously" emerge, only increases their relevance for strategic action. A naive recipient who supposes that a description stands for the object in a pure and unmitigated way not only opens himself to being deceived or misguided, but also misses any chance to trace the misinformation or to counter it. Studies of interaction are potentially important in revealing the profound semiotic work descriptions do in various settings. Finally, I have emphasized that the opponent's actions are a crucial resource for the design of talk and other moves in a strategic interaction. The second position – allowing the other party to go first – can be utilized strategically in various settings. Among others, it allows the party to engage in an argument without revealing her own stance, thereby allowing her to limit herself to explicating the weaknesses of the argument that is put forward first. Analysis of the second position shows how salient it is to take into account the sequential orchestration of activities that is critical for the composition of social actions.

Further Reading

– There are a number of monographs on juridical interaction, but one collection includes many of the most basic readings (see Travers and Manzo 1997).

– Clayman and Heritage (2002a) and Hutchby (1996a and b) have dealt the strategic aspects of media interaction.

– As I stressed, Sacks (1992a and b) was also a devoted analyst of the strategic aspects of interaction, see in particular his early lectures in 1964.

– A master analyst of strategic interaction is Erving Goffman (1969), though he never went very far into the details of interaction.

– For exercises, see http://www.uta.fi/laitokset/sosio/project/ivty/english/sivut/exercises.html

Notes

1   The relationship between properties of action and interaction may also be confusing at times. It may seem that "strategic character" is a property of "action" rather than "interaction". However, also strategic "actions" are recipient-designed, and their strategic nature depends on their interactive design. For instance, a letter, e-mail or a proposal may be a strategically designed action, but it is a strategically designed action only due to its recipient-designed properties, i.e., relationship to the recipient(s). Hence, not to complicate matter further, it may be sufficient to use the term "strategic interaction" as it may be difficult to find strategic actions in vacuum.
2   Sometimes the distinction between the third and the second position may seem tricky. A: "What's the time?" B: "Eight pm." The third position response "thanks" is said vis-à-vis the question in the first position. The second position response might go "You are now talking about Greenwich time?". The second position does not display the speaker's orientation to the position of the turn the speaker is oriented to. Note that if this were not the case, the 177th turn in a conversation would occupy the 177th position.
3   Though, as mentioned, I do not intend to claim that the second position is the power position in interaction. The first position, for example, has the advantage in agenda setting. Given that interactions are thoroughly strategic, any sequential position is open for strategic uses, and none is essentially strategically more powerful than others.

Chapter 7

Negotiation

And if it's such things as the fact that occasionally in a household, if there's a dispute as to when it is that one should go to sleep, or what kind of car one should buy, or the like, discussion can resolve it, you're getting a rather fantastic extension. But then, discussion is something that everybody knows about, and agreeing is something that everybody knows about, and perhaps it is, then, a kind of institution which can appeal by virtue of its familiarity, in the sense that Christ appealed with love as something that everybody ought to know about, and hoped also to change the world.

(Sacks, 1966)

Negotiations are a form of strategic interaction in which a deliberate goal is to reach an agreement or a compromise between parties' interests. A quintessential part of a negotiation is a bargaining sequence in which a party formulates a position and a recipient aligns or misaligns with it. These bargaining sequences are indeed the focus point of negotiations. However, in practice most of the work in negotiations precedes or follows bargaining sequences. Although parties share a common goal, their opposing interests separate them. Consequently, negotiations amount to extended problem-solving activities whose components can be scrutinized through CA. Negotiators must pay special attention to entries to and exits from proposals in which new dimensions of relevance are brought up: entries must prepare a common ground between opposing parties in order to establish a degree of alignment to launch the bargaining process, while in the post-proposal stage negotiators may need to reconsider their positions to keep the negotiation process working. Negotiations differ from ordinary, mundane interactions in various ways; for example, some negotiations are organized formally so as to avoid the emergence of arguments, etc.

In a formal sense, the term "negotiation" refers to a particular class of activities, such as business negotiations, wage agreement negotiations, diplomatic negotiations, etc. Many people probably have some experience with negotiations concerning property transactions, such as cars or real estate. If we take these as an example, we realize how significant negotiation practices can be. Negotiations concern valued objects, and so are highly consequential in terms of societal organization. In this chapter, I will focus on negotiation as a class of institutionally distinct activities and their related practices, as well as on some related practices, such as mediation and plea bargain. However, it is worth noting that the term negotiation is also widely used in a metaphoric sense.

In particular, constructivist literature often uses the term "negotiation" to refer to various types of social activities in which some kind of semiotic work takes place so that meanings are transformed, i.e., "negotiated", but I am not here concerned with these metaphorical uses.

7.1 The Mundane Basis for Negotiation

Although negotiations concern a distinct class of activities, it is useful to begin by considering some mundane practices that are utilized in institutionalized negotiations. Invitations, offers, proposals and requests all project a parallel sequential course, in which the next activity in sequence is either their acceptance or rejection (Davidson 1984; 1990). Let us call this recognizable sequential course a proposal sequence, which, for instance, can be distinguished from an argument (cf. Coulter 1990; Dersley and Wootton 2000; 2001). In contrast to arguments, proposals involve a goal, which transforms the interaction into a project that becomes accountable in terms of its success. On the contrary, arguments are not necessarily connected to any external goal, which may also account for their durability. Proposal sequences and institutional negotiations are always part of a project directed towards some end. When parties share a common goal, it directs them to orient to maintaining their working consensus so as to achieve their goal. If parties lose their orientation to a common goal, the arena is open for argument. In this vein, there are some primary activity types used in mundane practices, which are also used in distinctly institutionalized negotiation. Furthermore, these mundane practices offer a training field for the analyst to develop sensitivity toward the various permutations and complications to which negotiations are subject.

In mundane life, a canonical proposal sequence runs as in the following simple case.

(1) Schegloff 1972, 107; Heritage 1984a, 254–255 [SBL:10:12]

```
1    A:   Why don't you come and see me some [times
2    B:                                       [I would like to
3    A:   I would like you to
```

Here A makes a proposal, B accepts it, and A confirms the acceptance. Significantly, B's acceptance of the proposal is done in the first possible place. Actually, it overlaps the last item of A's turn at the point when the completion of A's proposal could be anticipated.[1] A's confirmation then sanctions the outcome of interaction sealing its intersubjective meaning. Thus the canonical proposal sequence in ordinary conversation is again a triadic structure: proposal – acceptance – confirmation.

In *negotiations*, by contrast, the prevalence of this canonical sequence is almost nil. If you have any doubt about this, check any data set on negotiations to see how many similar cases you find. Bearing this in mind, we can try to open up the sociological conditions for the existence of this canonical proposal sequence. As a whole, it presupposes that A and B share a common world in which A's proposal opens an opportunity for a chain of events that is from B's viewpoint 1) realizable, 2) possible in terms of participation, 3) desirable (on further preconditions for a shared activity, see Goffman 1983b). In negotiations these preconditions are rarely met at once. Indeed, if parties define a situation in the same way, there is no need for negotiation. On the contrary, in negotiations, A and B differ in terms of their beliefs of what would be 1) realizable, 2) possible in terms of participation, and 3) desirable, or even minimally acceptable. Thus, negotiations are largely an activity type in which parties aim to mold their shared understanding concerning the proposal, and/or reshape the proposal so that it would fit with the parties' understanding and definition of the situation.

Moreover, negotiations are a form of strategic interaction in which parties reflexively shape their actions in terms of their expectations concerning the activity type. That is, even if the preconditions for a successful outcome were satisfied, the parties may nevertheless continue to exploit the possibilities for gaining further benefits that negotiation as a practice offers them. A golden rule repeated in various negotiation tactics guides is that you should never accept the first offer (e.g. Camp 2002). In real life, if you bid on an apartment or a car and your offer is straightforwardly accepted, you may initially be relieved and happy, but afterwards you might have second thoughts, and wonder whether you did something wrong. As an institutionalized form of activity, negotiations are a powerful machine that shapes the negotiators' conduct, thereby maintaining negotiation as a distinct class of strategic action.

In everyday life, the acceptance of invitations, offers, proposals and requests is subject to infinite numbers of complications. Consequently, "negotiating practices" have their home base in mundane social interaction. A scrutiny of interactional work through which proposals or their understandings are shaped and reformed also helps us appreciate negotiation practices in institutionalized environments. Further, this preliminary view of mundane practices allows us to identify, locate and differentiate in distinct activity contexts negotiation practices that do not prevail in daily life and may thus be specific to the activities in question.

To proceed systematically, complications to the basic proposal sequence can be located in three sequential positions:

1. post-proposal,

2. pre-proposal

3. co-construction of proposal.

I will briefly address the different types of complications that occur in different locations, considering various things that complicate proposal sequences. I will later use these findings to analyze institutionalized negotiations.

Post-Proposal

The most typical post-proposal complications fall into four categories. The recipient may a) make an inquiry that opens up new dimensions of relevance concerning the proposal, b) the recipient may set conditions on the acceptance of the proposal, c) the recipient may delay the answer, or d) the recipient may reject the offer.

a) *Further information or dimensions* of an issue are made relevant before a response to the original inquiry is offered. The answer is made on condition of these further dimensions or aspects of the issue.

(2) Schegloff 1972, 79 ((invented example))

1	*	A:	Are you coming tonight?	Qb			
2		B:	Can I bring a guest?		Q1		
3		A:	Male or female?			Q2	
4		B:	What difference does that make?				Q3
5		A:	An issue of balance.				A3
6		B:	Female.			A2	
7		A:	Sure.		A1		
8		B:	I'll be there.	Ab			

Rather than straightforwardly accepting the proposal, the recipient may give a conditional answer that opens a new dimension of relevance. An inserted sequence is opened before the response to an original action (proposal) becomes relevant (Schegloff 1972). As in the case above, each insertion is open to further expansions. Consequently, a multidimensional position structure emerges. Importantly, each new dimension of relevance has to be dealt with first prior to returning to the previous dimension which leads back to the original action. The position structure – levels which create a kind of "stairway" – is nicely illustrated with the help of this invented example. Working with real data, the analyst may face severe difficulties in locating the dimension of relevance the parties are tackling at any given moment. You must have an adequate grasp of the position structure of the sequence before you can analyze it. In natural data, inserted sequences are extremely common. Apart from negotiations, emergency and service calls provide another instance in which inserted inquiry sequences are routinely used prior to answering the original request (Wakin and Zimmerman 1999).

b) *The acceptance of the proposal* is made dependent on some conditions. In extract 3, Ilene and Charlie have already made some arrangement about a trip to Syracuse. However, Charlie calls Ilene back after some complications have come up.

(3) Drew 1984, 130 [Trip to Syracuse:2]

1	C:	So tha: [:t
2	I:	[k-khhh

```
 3 →   C:  Yihknow I really don't have a place tuh sta:y.
 4      I:  .hh Oh:::::.hh
 5          (0.2)
 6 →   I:  .hhh So yih not g'nna go up this weeken?
 7          (0.2)
 8      C:  Nu::h I don't think so.
 9      I:  How about the following weekend.
10          (0.8)
11 →   C:  .hh Dat's the vacation isn't it?
12 →   I:  .hhhhh Oh:. .hh ALright so:- no ha:ssle, (.)
13          s [o
14      C:     [Ye:h,
15      I:  Yihkno:w::
16     ( ):  .hhh
17      I:  So we'll make it fer another ti:me then.
```

Here, the complications do not immediately follow the proposal or offer, but emerge only afterwards. Nevertheless, the complications which have emerged activate the conditional relevancies set up by the original action. The parties open up the issue that had been temporarily sealed. These kinds of delayed complications are more often the rule than the exception in negotiations. At line 9, Ilene modifies her proposal in the face of the problem, but also her modified proposal is rejected on the basis of conditions that are not met, i.e., that the trip should not be done during vacation (line 11). At line 17, Ilene situates the plan in an unspecified future. Such designed, purposeful vagueness allows parties to retreat from an unsuccessful action without further damage and leave the issue open for a more suitable occasion without sanctioning them to pursue the matter further in any accountable way. This social exit device is also used a great deal in negotiations.

c) *The answer to the proposal is delayed*; the proposer uses the delay to modify the proposal.

(4) Davidson 1984, 106 [NB:38, 92]

```
1      A:  C'mon down he:re,=it's oka:y,
2 →        (0.2)
3 →   A:  I got lotta stuff, I got be:er en stuff 'n,
4 →   B:  Mm hheh heh heh "beer [ 'n stuff" huh
```

The recipient need neither accept nor reject a proposal, but may also simply delay the answer. In a real-time interaction, any audible delay, here 0.2 seconds, can be heard to project a dispreferred response, i.e., rejection of the proposal (Pomerantz 1984a). Here the proposer monitors the recipient's delay and anticipates a rejection, thereby launching a new offer at line 3. Through his modified offer, the proposer succeeds in eliciting a response that comments on the modified offer – but without explicitly showing the recipient's stance on the offer. In negotiations, in which turn-taking is not formally constrained, response timings and possible delays can be a critical resource for deciphering involuntarily-given signs of the party's stance (see also Schegloff 1988).

d) *The proposal is rejected*; the proposer reformulates the proposal. Here a rejection is followed by a series of offers.

(5) Davidson 1990, 150–151 [NB 52, 266]

```
 1  Offer      P:   Don'tchu want me tuh come down'n getchu
 2                  t'morrow en take yih down: duh the beauty parlor
 3                  (0.3)
 4  Rejection A:   What ↓ for.=I jus' did my hair it looks like pruh
 5                  uh pruhfessional.
 6                  (0.4)
 7  Offer      P:   Oh I mean uh: you wanna go t'the store er anything
 8                  over et the Market [ Basket er anything?      ]
 9             A:                      [.hhhhhhhhhhhhhhhhhhhhhh ] h=
10             A:   =Well ho [ ney (l-)]
11             P:            [ Or R i ] chard's?
12                  (0.2)
13  Rejection A:   I've bou:ght ev'rythai:ng,
```

The rejection of the proposal does not necessarily close the proposal sequence, but may also invite a new proposal or series of proposals, as above. Each new proposal is iteratively open for the same complications as the prior one.

Pre-Proposal

Proposals are generally not made out of the blue, but rather a favorable environment may be sought or built with interactional work (Bilmes 1995). The recipient's availability for the proposed course of action is a primary condition for a proposal. The party may also seek to take into account the recipient's perspective to prepare a suitable ground for the proposal, which may then be tailored according to views solicited from the recipient.

(6) Drew 1984, 133 [JGII(b):8:14aff]

```
 1   J:  So who'r the boyfriends for the week.
 2       (0.2)
 3   M:  .k.hhhhh- Oh: go::d e-yih this one'n that one yihknow,
 4       I jist, yihknow keep busy en go out when I wanna go
```

```
5           out John it's nothing .hhh I don'have anybody
6           serious on the string,
7     J:    So in other words you'd go out if I:: askedche out
8           one a' these times.
9     M:    Yeah! Why not.
```

Prior to asking M out, J inquires about M's boyfriends for the week in a non-serious frame. M gives first her non-serious response, maintaining the mode the inquiry had adopted. Her subsequent answer, after the non-serious preliminary, displays her availability for the action J subsequently asks her to engage in.

In ordinary conversations, there is a class of conventionalized actions, such as "can I ask you a question?" which can be utilized to prepare the ground for a delicate or otherwise complicated action. These "pre-pre's" open up a possible trajectory in which an account may be offered before launching the delicate action.

    (7) Schegloff 1980, 132

```
 1    Pam:    H'llo::,
 2    Vicky:  Hi:. Vicky.
 3            (0.4)
 4    Vicky:  You ra:ng?
 5    Pam:    Oh hello there yes I di::d.
 6  →         .hh um I nee:d tuh ask you a
 7  →         questio:n?
 8            (0. 4)
 9  →Pam:     en you musn't (0.7) uh take
10  →         it personally or kill me.
11            (0.7)
12    Pam:    I wan to kno:w, (0.7)
13            whether you: will(b) would
14            be free: , (.) to work o:n um
15            tomorrow night.
16            (0.4)
```

At lines 6–7, Pam states that she needs to ask a question. However, before asking the question, she informs the recipient about the nature of the prospective issue by saying that she should not take it personally or kill her. As Schegloff (1980) has shown, this trajectory is conventional. Items like "can I ask you a question?" or "can you do me a favor?" are systematically used to allow the speaker to insert some further talk so as to instruct the recipient how to hear the forthcoming question. The party aims to attune the recipient favorably towards the proposal prior to presenting it, by giving it a particular sense or setting up a specific frame in which the proposal should be heard.

Co-Construction of Proposal

The parties may also seek to distribute responsibility concerning prospective courses of action. That is, the proposal may be presented so that its design allocates some amount of responsibility to all the parties involved. The proposal can be split in parts, so that each party is allowed to contribute to the emerging proposal. A kind of participation framework may be built up such that no unequivocal asymmetry between a proposer and a recipient is established. Through co-construction of proposals the parties achieve a distributed responsibility concerning the prospective courses of action (Jacoby and Ochs 1995). In extract 8, A's question about what time B wants to leave not only sets off a possible trajectory for an action in which B would be a co-party with A, but also invites B to participate in the construction of the proposed course of action by inciting B to offer a timing for the action.

(8) Davidson 1984, 102 [Bike Ride]

```
1    A:   What time you wanna lea:ve.
2         (0.3)
3    B:   ((smack)) Uh: : sick clo:ck?
4         (0.5)
5    A:   Six (uh) clo:ck? hh=
6    B:   =Is that good.
```

7.2 Bargaining Sequence

The bargaining sequence is the nucleus of institutionalized negotiation practices, where the parties display their positions so that agreement can be reached, or the negotiation has to be continued to reconcile incompatible positions prior to launching a new bargaining sequence. A formal negotiation may thus consist of a series of bargaining sequences; in between these sequences parties may seek to ground their own position and reason about the opponent's position to create suitable conditions for generating proposals. The bargaining sequence, like its elementary forms in ordinary conversation, is a three-part structure: proposal/offer, response, and confirmation/acknowledgement. Let us take an instance of plea bargaining as an example. The plea bargain is a common pre-trial procedure in the US, in which the defense attorney and district attorney try to find a mutually acceptable outcome for (petty) criminal cases without a trial. Plea bargains always involve a bargain sequence. In extract 9, the sequence is the second bargaining sequence in this case, and is linked with the first one in various ways (for the transcript of the complete case, see Maynard 1984, 211–213). In the first sequence, the public defender (PD) has proposed a twenty-five dollar fine, which the district attorney (DA) does not accept and a side sequence develops before their return to bargaining. Here the judge

(J) summarizes the fact that the defendant has already served some time, i.e., he has been locked in for more than ten hours, after which he occasions a new bargaining sequence.

(9) Maynard 1984, 213 ((The Frank Bryan case))

```
1      J:   Well we know he spent ten hours and uh maybe (        )
2           some more. And what do you think would be reasonable,
3           Jeffrey
4      (6.0)      ((DA looks through files))
5      DA:  Seventy five dollar fine
6      PD:  Why don't we compromise and make it fifty
7      DA:  It's done
8      PD:  Arright
```

At line 5, the district attorney makes his proposal. At the next turn the public defender does not straightforwardly accept the offer, but makes a counter proposal that is immediately accepted by the district attorney. The outcome is confirmed by the public defender's "arright" at line 8. The counter proposal at line 6 is presented without a delay or a hesitation displaying an orientation to plea bargaining as an institutional activity.[2] Although the counter proposal performs a rejection of the proposal, it is not produced as a dispreferred activity as in mundane social interaction. Instead, the parties' orientation to the existence of contrasting positions as a manageable aspect of their talk becomes manifest. Also, the judge works for the achievement of compromise. First, he summarizes their knowledge of the case (i.e., that defendant has already received some punishment) making relevant a concession from the party who had rejected the previous proposal. Second, he designs his question to the district attorney not to elicit a new proposal but a position report. The judge's question invites the addressed party to display his position (Maynard, 1984: 81–84). That is, the judge acknowledges the disparity between the parties' perspectives by not asking for a proposal but a report of what the DA would *think* is appropriate. In recognizing the perspective dependence of the proposal solicited from the DA, the judge opens a chance for the mitigation concerning the forthcoming proposal. In this way, the PD's counter proposal at line 6 is in line with the judge's effort to make the parties' acknowledge the perspective boundedness of their positions. The overall structure of the plea bargaining consists in this case of a proposal (not shown above), and two counter proposals, i.e., the PD made the first proposal which the DA rejected, subsequently the judge (above) solicited a counter proposal from the DA, which the PD responded to with a counter proposal, which the DA accepted. In all, these bargaining sequences are the key moments of negotiations, and are themselves open to various types of expansions.

Like proposal sequences in ordinary conversation, bargaining sequences are prone to various modifications and extensions. In extract 10, an instance of a bargaining sequence is taken from a negotiation of commodity traders who are arguing about the terms and conditions of the sale of milk products. The original offer has been previously made in writing, while revisions and the possible acceptance of the revised offer will be done by phone. H is the seller, G the prospective buyer.

(10) Firth 1995a, 209–210

```
 1   G:   =yeah
 2   H:   but listen the:- the [very best-]
 3   G:                        [ but uh   ] these uh- these
 4        u:h shipping per- uh company they are charging
 5        I think same
 6        (1.2)
 7        same as before
 8        (0.7)
 9   H:   it's probably the same (.) let's see a:h: (1.0) ah-ah-
10        wha:t I can do now for the:: shipment from uh dubai to
11        uh dohah is around (.) u:h forty dollar per:: per tonne.
12        (1.0)
13   G:   uh hu(hh:)h:
14        (3.5)
15 → H:   .hh but listen, the- the very best I can do for the sixteen
16 →      kilo feta now is one thousand six hundred an' sixty
17        (3.8)
18   G:   dubai? (0.3) or dohah?
19   H:   dohah
20        (2.0)
21   G:   no we will take dubai one thousand six hundred
22        (1.0)
23   H:   u:h that's (.) you know uh that's- that's not imposs-
24        eller not possible for me because you know there
25        .hhh is the problem with thee u:h (.) minimum prices
26        (.) I had to uh follow the minimums prices. (0.7) .hh
27        an' that i:s (.) one thousand six hundred an' fifty (.)
28        see en eff ((CNF: Cost and Freight)) uh (.) dubai
```

At line 2, H volunteers to make an offer, but is interrupted by G who continues providing information about the shipping arrangements that are an aspect of the prospective contract. H returns to his offer at line 15. G responds to the offer with a clarification request (line 18), and after the answer makes a counter proposal (line 21). H rejects the counter proposal and provides an account that opens up a new dimension of relevance, the minimum prices. The bargaining sequence works as a knot point of the negotiation upon which the multidimensional position structure of the negotiation process will be assembled. The negotiators orient to proposals in building entries to proposals, and exits from the rejected proposal so that a fabric of associated dimensions of relevance will be weaved to allow parties to elaborate on the offers to create the possibility of compromise.

7.3 Preliminaries to Proposal

In negotiations, the preliminary work preceding the submission of a proposal may be a massive, long-lasting effort. For instance, an Israeli peace negotiator mentioned that the negotiation process in Oslo in the 1990s had cost him more than a thousand sleepless nights, caused him to drink thousands of cups of coffee, lost him twenty pounds in weight and undermined his marriage. Moreover, each time a proposal is rejected there may begin a new lengthy preparation process before a suitable moment for a new proposal is reached. Also, the nature and complexity of the negotiation directly bear on the preproposal tactics.

A plea bargain is said to consist of at least two pre-proposal tasks: finding a common perspective on the case (agreeing on the facts) and making a common evaluation of the defendant's character (resolving what the moral character is) (Maynard 1984, 107–108). Not until the pre-proposal stage is successfully managed and a sufficient intersubjective agreement on the nature of the case is reached can the negotiation proper be launched. Decisions concerning what charge and sentence are appropriate (i.e., the negotiation proper) are tied to the parties' understanding of the "facts" and "the character of the defendant". The pre-proposal stage thus has a direct bearing on the outcome of the negotiation. Plea bargains are made more complex by the fact that the negotiation may also include "negotiation" on what will be considered relevant for the case. This reflexivity of negotiation makes available a potential infinitude of perspectives that can be applied to the case in question. The reflexive reworking of the dimensions of relevance is a local, situated outcome of talk at work that can not be predetermined from some neutral, external perspective. That is, the negotiators themselves may lack a definite idea of the limits of the relevance for the case. In extract 11, the public defender brings up the issue of the defendant's looks; the judge first dismisses this issue, but then the PD explains why the defendant's looks are relevant in this particular case.

(11) Maynard 1984, 135 [Drunk Driving]

```
1     PD2:   Now this is a case which oughta be- which is eminently
2            disposable. Uh Lynn Heater is a uh, a young lady,
3            beautiful by the way, absolutely beautiful
4     J1:    Mm
5     PD2:   She looks like Kim Novak right down to the toes. She
6            works as a waitress for Bill's new place called- out
```

7		in the shopping center
8	J1:	Okay let's get to the case heh=
9	J1:	[h a h h a h h a h .hhhhhhh]
10	PD2:	[Well this is all very important because] this is part
11		of the defense [ya] see, uh as a witness, the jury won't
12	J1:	[Ha]
13	PD2:	hear [a word] she says, they'll be too busy looking at
14	J1:	[Ha ha]
15	PD2:	her. In any event, but …

Here the PD suggests that the defendant's looks are a relevant aspect of the case, since her stunning good looks would derail any neutral, ordinary trial. Part of the negotiator's skill is the ability to activate dimensions, which could possibly support her own position, even if these dimensions at first seem marginal and distant. An unanticipated shift of perspective may suddenly strengthen this position.

In more complex negotiations, there are also multiple pre-proposal tactics. For example, real estate agents do not just try to convince a prospective buyer of the value of the property, but may also try to lead the person to believe that rival offers are about to come in (the ghost rival strategy). In the ultimate case, a real estate agent may ask a colleague to call during the negotiation and pretend that he was receiving a call from another prospective buyer. Also, false expectations can be created. A real estate agent may lead a prospective seller of the property to believe that an unrealistically high price would be gained from the property so as to induce the decision to sell the property. This also demonstrates the multilayered embeddedness of negotiation practices. In the real estate business, for example, sales arrangements have to be negotiated first, before the agent can go ahead and try to sell the property.

The major complexity in many negotiations is the fact that their agendas have to be agreed upon prior to the negotiation proper. Negotiations are preceded by negotiations over what they should be about. These prenegotiations involve issues such as the agenda, schedule, and the relationship between items on the agenda. Such prenegotiations are a crucial part of the negotiation process, because it is here that parties construct a view of what the negotiable issues are: this is highly consequential for the subsequent process. At the outset, parties may have disparate views and interests. This disparity in perspectives emphasizes the need for interactional tools and devices which would allow them to access each other's perspectives, and thus be able to reformulate their own positions. As discussed in Chapter 5, formulations can be used to force the other side to display its position, or minimally to assess its alleged position. Interestingly, Walker (1995) pointed out that both positive and negative formulations play a strategic role in negotiations. Positive formulations are designed to be confirmed, and through them mutually acceptable concessions can be made. On the other hand, negative formulations, which invite rejections, are also useful in negotiations, as they occasion reformulations that may keep the negotiation process moving. Extract 12a is from an annual union/management wage agreement

negotiation at which the parties are discussing the agenda of the forthcoming talks.
The union representative, Pete, has suggested that re-evaluation of the sick payment
scheme should be part of the agenda, but management puts forward an alternative
suggestion that they are ready for a discussion as long as it does not cost anything and
that it will be postponed and dealt with separately, and additionally that it should also
take into account the abuse of sick payment benefits. At lines 27–31, Pete formulates
what he sees as the management's position.

(12a) Walker 1995, 115–116 [WGE:2:A:235] ((Management: Kev (K), Andy (A)
       and Bill (B); union: Pete (P).))

```
 1    A:   I mean I think (0.9) that we have (0.6) quite accepted (0.5) a
 2         discussion on the subject but we have certainly (0.5) all we've
 3         said is that sorry we can't offer you anything on them. they
 4         have to stay as they are,
 5         (2.4)
 6    K:   and even if it was a favourable time what I'm saying is
 7         that we- (0.4) we would have to be talking (0.9) fairly
 8         toughly (0.3) about it and n- and (0.4) about this say
 9         we (0.8) that it was seen that we could well afford (0.7)
10         a pro rata increase in sick payments. (0.8) then we
11         would have to talk about .hhhhhhhh the interpretation of:
12         =er:: (.) certain people's absences and so on and so
13         forth and do and do and implementing the procedures
14         I mean that's the sort of area I don't want to get in:to
15         that (0.9) in these sort of negotiations.
16         (0.6)
17    P:   I se [ e what you mean. ]
18    K:        [ where there's mon] ey on the ta:ble. (0.8) er::
19         (0.6) there there is:: (.) there's quite (0.7) we're not
20         talking about (0.4) anybody genuine it's the- (.) it's
22         the very small minority (1.1) er- who (0.6) seem
23         seem to be, (.) might be wrong. (0.8) I would never
24         ( ) if (they) hadn't seemed to be spoiling it for the
25         majority.
26         (1.1)
27 →  P:   so what you would do is an in depth analys (.)
28         analysing
29         [of it  ] (0.4) [and you would like] to do it away from=
30    K:   [that's] what [ we would do        ]
31    P:   = a (0.3) wage negotiation.
32         (0.5)
33    K:   .t (.) e- ye- ye- but I will talk about it now but that's
```

```
34        the sort of scene I(w) I would like to set up for
35        doing this and I think that would be[ a good thing, ]
36   A:                                      [ and that's off ]
37        the record is it?
38        (.)
39   K:   Y:ES all this is off the record there's nothing being
40        recorded. that's (0.4) .hh and I think it's fair that you
41        know how we're thinking.
42        (0.5)
```

Pete's formulation (lines 27–29 and 31) is cautiously designed so as to maintain the union side tendentiously, but also to allow concessions to management. Pete selects an acceptable aspect of the preceding management's position he can agree with, but refrains from taking up Andy's point about management's unwillingness to offer any increases in sick benefits and Kev's view that evaluation of the sickness benefits scheme should be connected with "tough talks" on the abuse of sickness benefits. Instead, Pete restores the fact that re-evaluation of the sick payment scheme could be distinct from the wage agreement and formulates it as an in-depth analysis (line 27). There is a shift from "tough talks" (lines 7–8) to "in-depth analysis" (line 27). The choice of term is highly consequential here. The term "in-depth analysis" is concessionary in that it does not project any demand or a specific time constraint, nor follow the "tough talk" line. In presenting a version of the management's position he could agree with, Pete contributes towards defining a common ground between the opposing sides. Also, Pete's receipt of Kev's preceding turn at line 17 is revealing in terms of the parties' positions. He acknowledges Kev's allusion to the abuse of the sickness benefits but does not display any attempt to topicalize and discuss that matter further. Pete thus co-operates with Kev in curtailing further talk on a potentially divisive issue. In this fashion, negotiators discuss item by item what issues will be brought up on the agenda of the negotiation proper, and also consider connections between items on the agenda. The parties may also agree with each other for completely different and conflicting reasons. Here, management seems unwilling to tie the evaluation of sickness benefits to the wage agreement negotiations due to the potential costs, while the union seems to accept disconnecting evaluation of these benefits from the wage agreement negotiations to avoid talk about the abuse of sick benefits. This is the way negotiation works: distant, conflicting issues are brought together so that opposing parties may both gain something (or avoid losing something), and thus make a compromise between conflicting interests.

At lines 30 and 33–41, management displays their qualified agreement with the position Pete had attributed to them. As a qualification, management stresses that everything that has been said is off the record. After their response Pete makes a new formulation, which this time is more negative in its design (see extract 12b).

(12b) Walker 1995, 115–116 [WGE:2:A:235] ((continuation of 12a))

```
43 →  P:   so you would like the shop stewards to take it on
44         faith that (they) would (.) be discussing this (0.8)
45         a:t (a) different ti:me.
46         (1.1)
47    B:   ( [ )
48    P:   [in dep [th:
49    K:            [no no not this year.
50         (0.3)
51    B:   no
52    P:   no: [I never said this year.
53    K:       [not thi-
54         (0.4)
55    K:   but we WILL (0.3) YES definitely. (0.4) we will
56         this is something we could look at (0.3) and this
57         is an area .hhhhh
58         [I could say  ] in principle ] .hhh [a-
59    P:   [(there's always) n]ext y e a r. ]
60    A:   [ (       )   ]              [but it is
61         quite possibly something which (0.4) could result
62         in a:=er (1.4) fundamental change? (0.3) which may
63         not be:? (0.7) in your view (ve-) beneficial.
```

At lines 43–45, Pete projects a sceptical reception of the management's offer that the shop stewards should just trust that management will keep its word. The formulation does not receive any immediate response, but a pause is opened at line 46. Pete's continuation of his formulation does not mitigate his turn by downgrading it (cf. extract 4) and displays that he is not offering any further concessions. At line 49, Kev may have oriented to Pete's initiation of his continuation "in de…" as projecting a time description, and he rejects Pete's turn in overlap with it, denying that management has any inclination to engage in talks during the ongoing year. In selecting the timing of talks as his topic of response, Kev manages to disengage from the pivotal aspects of Pete's talk (see also Jefferson 1984b). At lines 55–58, Kev clarifies management's position by stating their interests in talks "in principle" at some unspecified future moment. The restated management position invites Pete's frustrated complaint, "there's always next year", after which Andy warns that the outcome of talks might not be beneficial for employees. At this point the negotiators' positions seem to be locked. Management representatives do not want to tie themselves to any substantial promise about re-evaluating the sick payment scheme, so instead they search for new arguments for why the union should give up their demand for further talks on the issue. In contrast, the union representative pursues more substantive promises on talks about the sick benefit scheme and does not take any stance on the management's counter arguments. Without a concession from either party, the negotiation remains blocked. In the worst case scenario, maintaining your own position becomes a task in itself, in which case the negotiation ends in a dead end. On the other hand, a negotiator should never be too easy, one who always concedes first. Negotiators must work hard to strike a balance between blocking the negotiation completely, and being too quick to make concessions, leading to a weak outcome.

7.4 Post-Proposal Expansions

Each rejection of a proposal returns the interaction to the situation preceding the proposal. Subsequently, the negotiators have to find out how far from re-entry to bargaining they are. If a proposal is met with a counter proposal it displays a party's understanding that they are close enough to an agreement that they may continue bargaining. A straightforward rejection, on the other hand, demonstrates that the other party does not yet see a chance for bargaining; in this case, the parties have to rework their ideas concerning the case, and settle the facts and relevancies prior to re-entry to a proposal. Also, the way the proposal is rejected is informative and consequential for the subsequent negotiation process. In extract 13, we return to the plea bargain of Frank Bryan (see extract 9), and examine how re-entry to a new proposal (lines 43–49) is managed after the first proposal had failed at lines 6–11.

(13) Maynard 1984, 212–213 (The Frank Bryan case)

1	J:	He's been here uh now for uh, six hours
2	DA:	So've I your honor
3	PD:	I- I belie(h)ve heh heh
4	J:	We'll give you credit for time served
5	DA:	Yes heh heh heh
6	PD:	Okay uh, twenty five dollar fine does that sound
7		justice- uh justiciable
8	DA:	Well um um uh
9		(0.8)
10	PD:	I made it up, I'm sorry I didn't look at the
11		(dictionary), I (made it up)
12	J:	He's gonna dismiss the one four eight[3]
13	PD:	Okay
14	J:	'n you plead to the six four seven ef[4]
15	PD:	Yeah
16	J:	And what would you realistically-
17	PD:	Well what are you asking for, lemme- I mean I
18		always usually go along with whatever Jeffrey
19		((DA3)) says

```
20    J:   How long was he in jail
21   DA:   He bailed out uh, I can't tell from my note here,
22         other than the fact that uh, does your honor
23         indicate the time that (    )
24    J:   We never know, how long they were down there
25   PD:   Well let me ask him, I assume his momma bailed
26         him out after she called the co(h)ps on him heh
27         fin(h)d out wha(h)t was all about, finally
           ((PD leaves room and returns 45 seconds later))
28   PD:   It sounds to me like between ten to twelve hours
29         in jail
30   DA:   He has uh one prior conviction in this jurisdiction
31         with the um sheriff's office of, interestingly enough,
32         uh striking a public officer and uh disturbing
33         the peace
34   PD:   Will you knock it off, you wanna make a federal
35         case out of this
36   DA:   No, I- I just think that it's not uh this uh happy go
37         lucky chap's uh first encounter with uh (the law)
38   PD:   Statistically if you got black skin you are highly
39         likely to contact the police, uh substantially more
40         likely than if you're white, now c'mon, what do you
41         want from him. He's got a prior
42    J:   Well we know he spent ten hours and uh maybe
43         (            ) some more. And what do you think
44         would be reasonable, Jeffrey
45         (6.0)           ((DA looks through files))
46   DA:   Seventy five dollar fine
47   PD:   Why don't we compromise and make it fifty
48   DA:   It's done
49   PD:   Arright
```

At line 8, the DA responds to the PD's proposal with a turn initiation that projects disagreement. After the DA's incomplete turn, there is a pause, followed by the PD's withdrawal of his offer (lines 10–11). Through his abandonment of the proposal, the PD not only oriented to its rejection but also to the avoidance of argument so that the rejection never became explicit. The PD seems to attempt to maintain the negotiation open for a new solution and in so doing he also displays his willingness to make a concession. At that point the judge starts to work for a re-entry to a proposal. He opens the issue concerning the charges against Bryan and suggests that the charge of resisting public officers (section 148 of the penal code) might be dropped if the defendant would plead guilty to disorderly conduct (section 647f of the penal code). The judge thus proposes which of the charges would be appropriate, thereby narrowing down options for sentences and bringing the negotiators closer to each other. After the clarification of his view of the appropriate charge, which the DA and PD seem to accept by not rejecting it, the judge asks the PD to make a new proposal (at line 16). The PD, however, passes this possibility to the DA. Possibly, the PD does not want to publicly compromise the position he had just stated, instead asking the DA (Jeffrey) to be responsible for making the new offer. The PD's refusal to make a new proposal may also involve a complaint against the DA, as the PD describes himself as the person who goes along with what Jeffrey says, i.e., he is the one who is flexible and able to accept compromises though the other party does not seem to reciprocate. The judge is alive to a potential conflict, and takes the turn after the PD at line 20, before giving the DA a chance to respond. In this fashion, the judge withdraws his view that that the case would have already be ready to settle, but instead opens up another dimension of relevance which he suggests be gone through before re-entry to bargaining. At lines 20–29, the parties resolve how long the defendant has already been in jail. After they do this, the DA volunteers to bring up the issue that may have been his basis for disagreement. He notifies the other parties about the defendant's prior conviction (30–33). Consequently, he claims that the defendant is not such a nice person as has been claimed (36–37). As a counter argument, the PD pleads that there is an increased statistical likelihood for a black person to have had contact with the police (38–41). After this post-proposal prenegotiation, the judge solicits a proposal from the DA, and the parties are able to compromise (as already discussed, see extract 9).

Extract 14 comes from a hospital finance meeting, and includes many interesting post-proposal expansions. The discussion moves back and forth between concrete and hypothetical proposals. In the meeting Hal, the chief of physicians, introduces a new revenue-based budget practice to induce cost-saving measures on some laboratory tests (called BVRL). At the beginning of the extract, Hal introduces his budget vision but does not gain aligning responses. Instead he exits to a hypothetical example as a vehicle to move away from a rejected proposal (a new budget vision) to reshape ground for a new proposal.

(14) Boden 1995, 87–88 ((Hospital/Finance Meeting))

```
1    Hal:    ... Y- your bu:dget is based on charges, I mean you take
2            a look at revenues
3    Paul:   Hmhmm
4    Hal:    And when revenues fa:ll? (0.5) you make adjustments
5            for it. You don't ma:ke adjustments for co::sts first.
6            (0.6) You know what I mean- you don't say=
7    Paul:   =(I do.)
8    Hal:    NO, no, no, but- but- let me jus' say that if- that
9            if you: (0.7) I mean if you say yer expe::nses::
10           (1.0)
```

11	Paul:	[average out]
12	Hal:	[A hundred] dollars inna lab=ratory and you're
13		getting a hundred an' ten dollars in revenue, arright?
14	Paul:	Hmhmm.
15	Hal:	And revenues fall to a hundred an 'five do:llars- you
16		don't say: We::ll, c-costs really weren't a hundred,
17		I mean- let's readjust it down t'real dollars (0.3)
18		you don't do tha:t. You say look we're living onna
19		revenue- onna revenue base. [Bud] gets are built=
20	Paul:	[Mm,]
21	Hal:	=up that way, an' that's what we've do:ne. So, ra:ther
22		than saying: well it's no s::ense in takin' out a BVRL
23		because it only co:st a nickel
24		(0.7)
25		We say there's sti:ll a sense taking it out because
26		we're cha:rging (.) five dollars for it. And in the-
27		in the revenue discussion (.) twenny thousan' versus
28		fifteen thousand?
29	Paul:	(Hmhmm)
30	Hal:	It means so:mething to the doctor to change his
31		behavior. (0.8)
32		Arright?
33	Paul:	Hmhmm
34	Hal:	Now it ma:y not mean as much to you in terms of
35		a cost function, but in fa:ct (.) the lab'ratory has
36		built their BUDGET!
37		up on revenue? not on cost. (0.4) Arright?
38	Paul:	Well, that's not exactly- that's not really true: (.)
39		though, because we- we have looked- y'know we've done
40		efficiency studies t'see ho:w (.) many hou:rs it takes to
41		run some of these te[:sts]
42	Hal:	[No-]
43		I know [that]
44	Paul:	[So] that's- tha:t's the way that we bu:dget
45		[(for various percentages 'n tha:t)]
46	Hal:	[But- but- you still- but you- look] look- and again WE:
47		use a cost-of-charge (0.2) figure (0.2) for the laboratory of-
48		let's say eight point se:ven (0.8) when we ta:ke ou:t a BVRL
49		(0.3) we don' kno:w whether that's a point ni:::ne or a
50		point o:ne
51		(0.9)
52		Arright, we don't go: into tha::t detail … ((continues))

At line 8, Hal reacts to the lack of response and expresses sharp disagreement with his repetition of "no's". In sequential terms, the turn-initial repetition among disagreeing parties displays the speaker's attempt to keep the floor and to continue the turn. A turn-initial, disagreeing repetition is a pre-turn component which projects continuation, as it does not work toward satisfying the pragmatic completeness of the sequentially-implied activity in that position. The turn initial repetition of "no's"[5] does not make relevant the perspective implied in the previous turn, in contrast to items like "you do?", "really?", or "you think so?". In contrast "NO no no" projects the speaker's own perspective by denying the relevance of the other's perspective. In this way, Hal reserves place for persuasive communication through constructing an opportunity for an extended multi-unit turn (see Arminen 1998, 40–47).

Hal locates his new argument in the hypothetical realm, "if you say" (lines 8–9). The use of hypothetical examples is a common persuasive device in negotiations, see also extract 12a, lines 6–15. The hypothetical realm has several functions in negotiations. It simplifies and abstracts contingencies prevalent in real circumstances; it may also allow neutrality and distance from real persons and personalities involved; and also enable a construction of tendential arguments. From line 15 on Hal builds an imaginary dialogue between parties so as to construct a tendentious version of the recipient's perspective. After the imaginary, hypothetical example, Hal makes a generalized conclusion that is presented as fact (lines 19 and 21). At line 21, Hal moves to a concrete level and suggests that the use of some laboratory tests (BVRL) should be made dependent on case-based decisions rather than being an automatic routine. Finally, at lines 30–31, Hal spells out the practical implication of his argument: doctors should be sparing in their use of procedures that create costs for the hospital. Significantly, the same argument in principle but on a higher level of abstraction was already put forward at line 4. Here the hypothetical example has bridged an abstract principle and an implementable practice. In terms of principles, Hal's suggestion is radical: he proposes a shift away from a traditional way of thinking of costs as pre-calculated and budgeted entities to a finance-driven analysis directed towards the elimination of all unnecessary costs. The hypothetical example is used as a device to disconnect a radically ideological vision from its mundane meanings. It allows seemingly neutral talk about a highly conflictual issue. Furthermore, it provides a one-dimensional account of a complicated matter, narrowing it down to a single perspective and leaving out all the potentially problematic practical aspects that the change of patterns of medical work may involve. The ability to delimit and define the perspective on the negotiable issues is thus a key dimension of negotiation practices. The power to define dimensions and relevancies of the objects of a negotiation also bears on the outcome evolving from the negotiation process.

7.5 Formal Constraints

Negotiations may also include formal constraints on how to act and talk. In particular, if a negotiation concerns emotionally-charged issues, it may be pertinent to constrain parties' behavior to minimize the risk of uncontrolled affective outbursts that would jeopardize the orientation to the negotiation process. In formally organized institutional interactions, procedural limitations may be imposed on parties to enhance dispute resolution without disputing. Negotiations may be organized under formal constraints that will slow down the process and diminish the chance that arguments erupt. Garcia (1991) has noted that the emergence of a dispute in everyday life relies on adjacently positioned actions that aggravate a disagreement. The escalation of argument trades on the speech exchange system of ordinary conversation in which the selection of the next speaker is done on a turn-by-turn basis without systematic constraints preventing a disputant from giving a disputational response. Consequently, exchanges of oppositional turns involve the potential for an aggravation of the argument and, finally, to the eruption of an uncontrolled fight. In ordinary conversation oppositional turns may cumulate, leading to the disputants' loss of affective control, as in the following family dispute: Stan accuses his ex-wife (Karen) of writing a rude comment on his last support check (15).

(15) Garcia 1991, 820

```
1 Stan:  I want to talk to you ( )=
2 Karen: =I DI:DN'T: (0.3) HAVE ANY THING,=
3   Stan:  =YOU HAD ( RIGHT) TO DO WITH=IT!
4           [(YOU ARE ALWAYS)]
5 Karen: [YOU KNOW THAT IS ]
6          BULL I DIDN'T
7   Stan:  [YOU ALLOWED IT]
8 Karen: [ ( see  it  )        ]=I DIDN'T EVEN DO
9          THAT CRAP I DIDN'T SEE THAT.
```

In the first line, Stan still maintains a degree of emotional control, but receives an aggravated denial in response. In his counter accusation at line 3, Stan matches his volume and tenor to Karen's aggravated tone in the preceding turn. At lines 4 and 5, Stan and Karen not only argue with each other but also compete over the floor still raising their pitch. After the charges are met with counter charges, in addition to the ongoing competition over the floor, Karen ends up in a high-pitch scream at lines 8–9. Through a fast circle of aggravating accusations and denials the parties have developed an emotional crescendo, in which their affective self-control has loosened and they have lost the orientation towards mitigating their argument.

Institutional environments enable the development of specialized speech exchange systems that constrain what types of contributions are regarded as appropriate, thereby also tilting the speech event toward a particular social outcome. For example, the mediation hearings analyzed by Garcia (1991) involved constraints on the positioning and formulation of accusations and denials. The mediation program serves as an alternative to the small claims court and was planned to facilitate negotiations in which the disputants are supposed to reach an agreement with the help of a third party. These mediation hearings involve a clear division of roles between the mediator (M), the complainant (C) and the respondent (R). The mediator acts as a chair, who distributes turns between the parties and in that way controls the evolving relationship between the disputants not to open a family strife (16).

(16) Garcia 1991, 823

```
  1    R_A:   She was: very very upset about that!=and
  2           (0.1) .h (0.4) made it perfectly clear that
  3           she=didn't want (0.1) anything °that had°
  4           to do with Ben! (0.3) °after tha:t?°=
  5→   C:     =COULD=I- (0.1) could=I a:sk a question
  6           °at this point?°
  7           (0.1)
  8    Mn:    °Sure!°
  9           (0.2)
 10    C:     Was: (0.3) wa:s: (0.2) he:r: (0.9) u::h inte:nt,
 11           in °you=know?, uh° (0.3) Did it SOU:ND
 12           to you: that she was TE:LLing you:?, ...
```

At lines 5–6, the complainant displays his orientation to the distribution of participation rights and requests permission from the mediator to ask the respondent a question (see Chapter 2; Heritage and Greatbatch 1991, 103). As long as the disputants orient to and acknowledge the mediator's role in distributing turns, the mediator has several resources to maintain control over the discussion. As a chair, the mediator may not only get a chance to control who speaks next, but as a primary recipient also controls the direction of talk. Consequently, the affective tension between the disputants is held under control.

Mediators also defend the formal rules of turn-taking and their privileged right to distribute turns. If the disputants try to return to oppositional argumentation and start to challenge each other, the mediator may sanction the institutional rules and forbid departures to open arguments. In extract 17, a father (R) is giving a critical depiction of the way the stepfather (C) has treated their children.

(17) Garcia 1991, 824

```
  1    R_A:   ... the CHILDren coming ho::me and
  2           him (0.4) ta:king them into the
  3           BA::throom, (0.4) and looking in their
  4           EYE:S!, because their: pupils might be
  5           di=h=lated 'cause they've
  6           had=too=many- (0.1) too much sugar from
```

```
 7         milkshakes that they drink in at my HOU:SE!
 8         (0.2)
 9  →C:    °That's [not true at all°]
10  R_A:          [And=MY- M]Y KI:DS: (0.2) my kids
11         have cry: (0.1) cried over [ that. ]
12→M_A:                              [Excuse] me for interrupt for just=
13         a=minute.=I forgot to, (0.1) mention,
14         one=of=the GROU:ND ru:les!, (0.2) and
15         that i:s when- (0.2) you're telling your
16         story, (0.7) you say nothing.
```

At line 9, after a brief pause the stepfather denies what he hears as an accusation about his mistreatment of the children. The father comes in and continues his account in overlap with the stepfather at line 10. Already at that point the volume of speech is rising as the disputants compete over the floor. At line 12, the mediator stops the discussion to tell the parties not to take turns during the other's story. In this fashion, the mediator prevents the potential aggravation of the argument.

The maintenance of a formal participation framework not only works toward minimizing the outbursts of open conflicts, but also influences the style and tenor of the discussion. To the extent that the disputants direct their talk to the mediator, they orient to designing their talk for an unknowing recipient to whom they have to detail their cases in an institutionally adequate way. The cases become presented as accountable facts in which claims have to be justified and in this way ungrounded accusations may be precluded. In extract 18, the complainant orients toward building his claims in a vehicle repair case as objective facts.

(18) Garcia 1991, 824

```
 1    M_A:   Okay, .h Dan?, If you'd like to go ahead
 2           then=and (0.2) and tell us your side of the story?
 3           (0.6)
 4    C:     Okay. (0.3) U:::h, (0.5) think=it=was
 5           approximately: u:h (0.1) °think it was in
 6           eighty six° (1.9) the date was u::h (0.1)
 7           FI::ve uh seven eighty °seven I believe
 8           an' I-° took the: motor ho::me, to u:h
 9           Mark's Auto. (1.0) .hh chuh! (0.1) for:=a
10           see (0.1) replace fan belts, repla:ce upper=
11           radiator hose, (0.2) inspect the air conditioning:, unit.
```

In telling his side of the story, the complainant starts from the verifiable facts that may serve as basis for his claims. In presenting their cases to the third party, the disputants also reconstruct the facts concerning their cases that may help them establish a common ground for their negotiation. In this way, the formal constraints of the mediation contribute to excluding unnecessary and unjustified accusations that might lead to an unproductive quarrel. Through the participation framework the disputants also address each other in the third person, thereby maintaining the objectivity of their accounts. In extract 19, the respondent responds to the complainant's claims in the car repair dispute (see above), which preserves factuality and the adequacy of detail as the focus of discussion. The complainant is addressed in the third person as Dan.

(19) Garcia 1991, 824

```
1     R_A:   Whe::n (0.7) DAN was ca:lled, and was
2            told that the water pump housing:, (0.2)
3            was lea:king,…When he came dow:n
4            and he picked up the car:, right before=the coach (0.4)
5            °uh° before it was adequately road tested.
```

The successful management of the participation framework contributes toward the maintenance of the suitable negotiation tenor that may keep the participants directed toward the resolution of a dispute. However, the participation framework does not exist automatically, nor is it a threshold that has to be established just once. Instead, the participants, and the mediator in particular, have to work toward maintaining the participation framework, not to slip into uncontrolled debate. Mediators have to display their recipiency actively to live up to their role as the primary recipients of talk. Also, this demonstration of active recipiency might be highly influential for the negotiation process. Many small but not insignificant activities may thus contribute to the outcome of the negotiation, although the minute details may have escaped the participants' conscious attention. In extract 20, the mediator displays his recipiency through a minimal response at line 5.

(20) Garcia 1991, 824

```
1     C:     At tha:t sta:g:e, (0.2) it is true that (0.1)
2            volunteer=help=that I=had (0.2) sugge:sted
3            could be- (0.2) available, (0.1) didn't - (0.1) didn't work out.
4            (0.2)
5 →M_B:      °um=hmh.°=
6     C:     =But- the=eh- (0.6) she was NOT- (0.4)
7            SHE: nor=anybody=in=my family
8            was=the pri:mary, (0.3) volunteer help on
9            which the- budget was (0.2) ma:de …
```

In her analysis, Garcia points out that through the minimal response the mediator invites the complainant's gaze. Through his shift of gaze direction between mediators (M_A and M_B), he displays his treatment of them as the primary recipients of his talk. Through small gestures and minimal responses, mediators thus sustain their participation status as the primary recipients of the talk moment by moment. The participation framework that forms the basis for the negotiation process is an achievement that relies on the parties' ongoing monitoring of the situation and reflexive reshaping of their activities. If they fail to do so, so-called "butterfly effects" in talk-in-interaction may emerge. In the worst case scenario, the lack of a minimal response may open up a chance for eye-contact between the disputants, which may disrupt their orientation to the formal participation framework and intensify the tension between them, occasioning a sudden shift of tenor allowing an open attack. Talk-in-interaction is both an accountable achievements but also highly unpredictable; each turn at talk carries the potential to recontextualize the sense of the ongoing interaction. Negotiations can be intense and burdensome, indeed: there is no time out during a negotiation, and each and every action is potentially fateful.

7.6 Mediator's Role

In negotiations the mediator's role can be crucial. The mediator may be critical in facilitating the interactional organization of the negotiation, which may contribute toward limiting and defining the ways in which opposing parties' represent their positions. In addition, mediators may participate in the negotiation process through representing the negotiators' positions. A mediator's degree of involvement in negotiations varies. Mediators may restrict their role to an outwardly neutral position and "limit themselves to rephrasing, restating, or elaborating a disputant's position" (Garcia 1995, 23). In any case, these reformulations may be consequential for the negotiation in that they allow subtle changes in the representation of positions. Occasionally, mediators may also depart from a neutral position and put forward arguments to a negotiating party. Giving up neutrality allows the mediator to engage in the negotiation and may create pressure for finding a resolution, but it also risks the mediator's impartiality and respective moral authority. Let us next examine the mediators' various degrees of involvement in the representation of the negotiators' positions with the help of Garcia's (1995) study of mediation.

Reformulations allow the mediator to make slight changes in the parties' positions. Extract 21 is from a dispute between a divorced couple concerning visitation arrangements for their three children. The first part of the extract is a segment from the complainant's story through which he announces his offer to give away two Thursdays of his monthly visitation days. Some minutes afterwards the mediator rephrases the offer.

(21) Garcia 1995, 32 ((First segment: the complainant's offer))

"The twins said well what happened to Thursdays they,
you know they specifically brought that up to me and I
said well, it looks like Mom wants to spend more time
with you two. So if you know you want to do
Thursday, Friday one week, and then just a Friday the
next week, that's compromising a little bit ..."

((mediator's reformulation of the offer a few minutes later.))

```
1      M:   And then what I hear, is the last month or so,
2            it's been every other Thursday, and then that
3   →        next week is uh for the Friday, and you're not
4   →        willing
5      R:   Uh=
6   → M:   =to he's willing to relinquish! He used the
7            word. Uh one of those Fridays.
8      C:   No=
9      M:   =Instead of making it
10           cons[iste]nt I MEAN THURSDAYS!
11     C:        [No]
12     C:   Thursdays ri:ght.
13     M:   Instead of [mak]ing it I just
14     C:              [I  ]
15           I'm willing to go along with the schedule that
16           she said just to keep the status quo and keep
17           her happy that she's you know,
18     M:   Urn hmh. He's offering the two Thursday night.
```

In restating the complainant's position, the mediator effectively characterizes both disputants in terms of their willingness to agree. While addressing the respondent, she notes her unwillingness (lines 3–4) and contrasts that with his willingness to relinquish (line 6). In this way, even if the mediator does not alter the disputants' positions, she characterizes them in a consequential fashion. Her representation of positions places responsibility on the respondent to make a move. In depicting the complainant's willingness to make a concession in contrast to the respondent's unyieldingness, the mediator puts pressure on the respondent without saying that in so many words. Consistently, at line 18 the mediator characterizes the complainant's proposal as an offer that puts the respondent in the position to accept or reject the offer. Thus, the mediator works towards the resolution even if she may just seem to be a go-between who merely relays the disputants' positions to each other.

Without sacrificing outward neutrality, the mediator may also elaborate a party's position. In rephrasing the party's position the mediator may clarify or enrich the stated position and in that way go beyond the original phrasing. The elaboration of a party's position may contribute toward the resolution as it may reshape the positions closer to an agreement. Extract 22 continues the dispute between the divorced couple. The respondent's reasoning about why she feels that their children should spend more time with her first receives the complainant's (Stan) disputational response, after which the mediator starts representing the disputants' positions.

(22) Garcia 1995, 34

```
 1      R:   That I got the base, the home, family, and I feel that
 2            Thursday, Friday, and Saturday without them be:ing,
 3            consistently at home, is too much. I feel that it's too
 4            much. Even though you don't get to see them,
 5            they're not at home, and they're at school, and
 6            they're on the road,=
 7      C:                        =They're home
 8            seventy five percent of the time.
 9   →  M:   Stan wait.
10           C: Okay.
11   →  M:   That's your feeling,
12      R:   Right.
13   →  M:   And you have every right to that. That is not his
14            feeling, a[nd that's] not how he sees his home base.
15      R:            [ I know ]
16      R:   I know.
17      M:   You know he sees it very loving, very whole, very
18            . consistent, very disciplined.
19      R:   I know!
20   →  M:   Okay. For him that's what he sees and what we have
21   →        to discuss.
22      R:   I know.
23      M:   And he's a fifty percent a parent, and you're fifty
24            percent a parent.
```

The mediator first states that both disputants have a right to their feelings and then represents what she thinks the complainant feels. Through her portrayal of the complainant's feelings, which she says are as justified as the respondent's, the mediator grounds her claim that their discussion is originally about the complainant's concerns (lines 20–21). Then, since the mediator states that both parents are fifty percent parents, she implicitly takes a stance in the dispute. Through the elaboration of the parties' positions, the mediator – without explicitly resigning neutrality – backs the complainant's view that their visitation arrangements are unequal. Here, the elaboration of the parties' positions works toward a resolution in which the respondent is asked to make some concession.

On occasion, a mediator may also act as if he were a principal in the debate. The mediator may overtly take a stance and either put forward an argument for a party or refute a party's claim. Extract 23 concerns a dispute between neighbors concerning the location of the boundary line between their properties. The respondent, who has had an expensive culvert built between the properties to solve an erosion problem, claims that he should get compensation from his neighbors. The respondent gets a response from the mediators.

(23) Garcia 1995, 36

```
1     RA:  Damned for my troubles that I went through, and the
2          money that I paid the county to improve his property
3          and getting the base rock fill, and everything else,
4          that he should compensate me for part of my expenses.
5   →MB:  Let's try to understand one thing, Mister Cartel,
6   →      the work and the money that you expended in
7   →      putting in this culvert, and actually rescuing your
8   →      property from destruction, you did it, for your sake.
9     RA:  I went with a compromise with the county,
10    MA:  Yes.
11    MB:  Yes.
12    RA:  That I would take my fences and they would accept the
13    MA:  You went with the compromise with the county, not
14         these folks. You went there. You did it.
15    RA:  They wouldn't have done it,
16    MA:  You decided it was worth it to you to do it, otherwise
17         you wouldn't [have   ]
18    RA:                [It's not] only to my advantage, though
19         I'm protecting my neighbor's advantage also.
20    MA:  THAT is something you were giving your neighbors
21         unwittingly. You were between a rock and a hard
22         place. I will agree! But you can not, you could not
23         have committed them to something they didn't agree
24         to. Now, if you feel that equity is on your side. Then
25         you can after the fact sue them for their share. If you
26         feel that you want to do arbitration on that you can do
27         that. But we're talking about something else here.
28         Remember we defined the area. You put five thousand
29         dollars in there but that wasn't his statement of the problem.
```

At lines 5–8, mediator B refutes the respondent's proposal, and presents grounds why the proposal is not appropriate. Subsequently, mediator A replies to the respondent's further challenges providing further arguments for their inadequacy. Consequently, mediator A narrows down the area of conflict between disputants and proposes limits on what they should be talking about. Here, the mediators constrain the allowable topical area of the dispute by turning down the respondent's proposal. In this fashion, they effectively prevent a quarrel of issues that they define as not belonging to the case. In ruling out conflicts they may contribute to the resolution of the dispute. However, they also risk being seen as partial, and thus jeopardize their neutrality and the moral authority crucial for the success of a mediation. Actions that can be seen as taking a stance in a conflict are hazardous, even if they are aimed at contributing to the conflict's resolution.

7.7 Conclusion

Negotiations are a distinct activity type, which are nevertheless grounded in mundane behavior. Various types of proposals project their acceptance or refusal as the next activity. By studying proposals, we are able to scrutinize the modifications and complications of basic sequences that may take place pre- or post-proposal, or may occasion a co-construction of proposal. In institutionally distinct negotiations, the bargaining sequence is the nucleus of negotiation work. In practice, however, most negotiation work either precedes or follows bargaining. During the preliminary stage of negotiations the agenda for the negotiation proper is set up. Setting the agenda involves making decisions about the range of issues to be dealt with in negotiation, the timetable and decisions concerning the relationships between issues: which issues belong together, which can be dealt with separately. Ultimately, pre-negotiations give negotiations a reflexive shape involving decisions about what the negotiations are about. Thus, pre-negotiations are highly consequential for the outcome of the negotiations concerning the status of issues, what issues are put on agenda now, hypothetically, or in the future, etc. Formulations are a key negotiation device which enable negotiators to force an unwilling opposing side to display its position, or assess its alleged position. Negotiations are also prone to post-proposal expansions, as the golden rule of negotiations forbids the negotiator ever to accept the first offer. During these post-proposal expansions, negotiators have to rework their understanding concerning the case, settle the facts and relevancies to make possible re-entry to bargaining. Post-proposals involve recurrent interactional practices, such as the use of hypothetical examples. Hypothetical examples are used to abstract contingencies prevalent in real circumstances and bridge abstract principles and implementable practices. Negotiations can also involve formally distinct interactional practices so that the speech exchange system may be modified to prevent the outburst of arguments. The mediator may have a crucial role to maintain a distinct negotiation mode that excludes affective overloads. Mediators may also have a critical role in representing the opposing parties' positions. Generally, mediators are constrained in terms of maintaining their neutral role vis-à-vis negotiating parties. As a high risk strategy, mediators may engage in the negotiation by taking a stance between the parties thereby creating further pressure for the acceptance of a resolution, but risking their impartiality and respective moral authority.

Further Reading

– Firth's collection (1995b) on negotiation includes many articles used in this chapter.

– Douglas Maynard's (1984) *Inside Plea Bargaining* is a thorough study of a particular kind of American juridical negotiation.

– Boden's (1994) workplace study also pays attention to negotiations at workplaces.

– Garcia (1991) concerns the role of formal constraints in negotiations.

– Kangasharju (1996) addresses a special question about aligning in multiparty negotiations.

– For exercises, see http://www.uta.fi/laitokset/sosio/project/ivty/english/sivut/exercises.html

Notes

1 Though "sometimes" could be heard as an increment, if "see" is a pre-closing pitch peak and then "sometimes" would be a "post-proposal" component that follows the lack of immediate response after "me" (cf. Schegloff 1996a). "Sometimes" mitigates the proposal and makes it lighter. More careful analysis would demand access to the tape, which I did not have.
2 Preference organization differs from mundane talk, where a disagreement would be delayed.
3 Section 148 of the penal code: resisting public officers.
4 Section 647f of the penal code: disorderly conduct.
5 It is also salient that the repetition is done in response to a disagreement, projecting a rejection of the disagreement. A repetition done in an agreement with a prior speaker would allocate the turn back.

Chapter 8

Information Systems and Organizational Interaction

When I got my first TV set, I stopped caring so much about having close relationships with other people. I'd been hurt a lot to the degree you can only be hurt if you care a lot. So I guess I did care a lot, in the days before anyone ever heard of "pop art" or "underground movies" or "superstars".

So in the late 50's I started an affair with my television which has continued to the present, when I play around in my bedroom with as many as four at a time. But I didn't get married until 1964 when I got my first tape recorder. My wife. My tape recorder and I have been married for ten years now. When I say "we", I mean my tape recorder and me. A lot of people don't understand that.

The acquisition of my tape recorder really finished whatever emotional life I might have had, but I was glad to see it go. Nothing was ever a problem again, because a problem just meant a good tape, and when a problem transforms itself into a good tape it's not a problem any more.

(Warhol, 1975)

Computerized data-processing has become more and more ubiquitous in various types of social interactions, and is being studied in new fields such as human-computer interaction (HCI) and computer-supported co-operative work (CSCW). In this chapter, I will introduce an applied conversation analysis for the scrutiny of computer-mediated communications (CMC) and computer-assisted work activities.[1] Earlier, ethnomethodologically-inspired studies have addressed the discrepancy between user assumptions and design assumptions built into machines (Suchman 1987). These studies not only reveal problems in interface design and provide practical suggestions for system design, but on a more fundamental level amount to a comparison of human and computational logic, thereby illuminating distinctive human features in contrast to artificial, computational systems. Another profound question concerns the tension between standardization and recipient design. When an information system is designed for a standardized response with a wide variety of recipients, a potential conflict emerges between situated recipient needs and the requirements of the standardized system. On a more general level, CA studies can appraise the modifications and also possible complications brought by computer assistance to the practical realization of tasks in institutional environments. For instance, computer-mediated classroom interaction can be compared with traditional classrooms. Complex hi-tech environments pose specific questions. In particular, settings saturated with technology, responsible for large numbers of people, with high work intensity and a potential for fatal errors, benefit from the analysis of collaboration-as-an-achievement and the scrutiny of routine troubles. As a whole, CA looks at the social dimension[2] of how technology is used, a dimension too easily missed if technology is seen only as an exterior fact without considering the intimate connection between technology and meaning-making processes as part of work activities and other practices. Let us begin by examining key dimensions of this emerging, multifaceted field. Then we will address the elementary properties of human-computer interaction, and progress towards more complicated applications of the approach.

8.1 Overview

The high speed of technical development and the rapid increase of interest in studies of technology-in-action make it difficult to compose a systematic view of the field. To make it easier for you to come to terms with such a hybrid field, I will summarize some of the main types of studies in Figure 8.1, which also gives you an idea of the prevailing and potential research questions in the area. Studies are organized into six groups in terms of the scope and complexity of the research objects, from more microscopic and less complex research settings to more macroscopic and more complex settings. To begin with, studies may focus on the elementary properties of human-computer interaction and address the user's inferential and sequential work in using the artifact through its interface. Second, studies may address technologically-assisted work processes in which information has to be standardized, such as computer-assisted emergency dispatch or (computer-assisted) survey interaction. Third, technologically-assisted multi-party communications, such as videoconferences or computer-assisted classroom interactions, offer particular contingencies to study. Fourth, focused hi-tech environments, such as various co-ordination centers, are information-intensive, high-risk and stressful workplaces offering unique settings in which precise co-ordination of interaction is matched with increased technological complexity. Fifth, elaborating requirements for future systems through the analysis of existing systems offers a new challenge for studies on interaction. Finally, co-operative design processes themselves also offer an important area for scrutiny, allowing us to examine the ways the designer team interacts to create new artifacts.

I User interface research
    L. Suchman: Use of "intelligent" copy machine;
    P. Raudaskoski: Software tutorial;
    I. Arminen: Use of Internet-linked mobile devices
        Goal: understand user's logic, evaluate the situated usability of the
        interface, if possible, in natural, non-laboratory settings

II Computer-assisted interaction
    J. Whalen, M. Whalen and D. Zimmerman: Emergency centers and their
    information systems;
    L. Suchman and B. Jordan, H. Houtkoop-Steenstra, D. Maynard, P. ten Have:
    Survey interaction and computer-assisted telephone interviews;
    D. Martin: telephone banking
        Goal: evaluate the impact of standardization and information packaging
        for interaction

III Computer-supported co-operative multi-party communication
    A. Garcia and S. Jacobs: computer-mediated classroom interaction
    P. Raudaskoski: video conferences
        Goal: assess the social/functional usability of the system

IV Computer-supported co-operative work in hi-tech settings:
    C. Heath and P. Luff: subway control room;
    L. Suchman, C. Goodwin, M. Goodwin: Airport ground operation control
    room
        Goal: develop ways to describe and account for interaction in complex
        technical environments

V Requirements specification for future systems
    D. Martin: design of internet banking service;
    R. Wooffitt et al.: airport timetable service
        Goal: assess the competencies involved in the type of interaction, evaluate
        the requirements for the future system on the basis of the current system

VI Co-operative design processes
    G. Button and W. Sharrock, Hughes et al.: software design process
        Goal: understand the software design process as a situated action (approach
        has mostly been ethnographic)

Figure 8.1 Types of Research on Technologically-Assisted Interaction

In this chapter I will cover the first four areas described above. On an elementary level, conversation analysis may not only afford an intricately detailed account of what people appear to be doing while interacting with artifacts, or what they claim they are doing, but reverse-engineer how they have oriented to accomplishing what they have done (Martin 2001). That is, interaction between humans or between a human and a machine is not seen as the mechanical outcome of a plan, but as an emergent property of the interactant's orientation to the emerging objects of interaction that recontextualize the sense of ongoing action moment by moment. In her study of users' interactions with a photocopier, Lucy Suchman (1987) was the first to criticize the idealized plan-based model of human-computer interaction, as she demonstrated that users' actual interaction with the machine did not fit with the design ideal derived from the plan-based approach. Consequently, CA studies may also enable us to show that the affordances of a given technology differ from the designers' intentions. The actual uses and meanings of technology in action may be crucially different than those intended by the designers, engineers and marketers. In this way, CA may also amount to a criticism of premature technological visions, which neglect the situated, contextual uses of technology affording a particular range of meanings.

CA may also focus on computer-assisted work processes. These studies address the requirements of a computerized system assisting interaction between humans. A systematic feature is that some discrepancies between interactional demands and system requirements arise. The question concerning the relationship between standardized information systems and unique, situated user needs covers a wide range of situations, from expert systems assisting agent/customer interaction in call centers to the organization of emergency dispatch and survey interaction. In the final instance, the issue remains how the standardized system can be fitted to talk-in-interaction, which has its own internal, autonomous logic.

Collaborative computer-mediated multi-party communication creates particular challenges for the participants in maintaining a shared focus with communicative resources that may have different properties than taken-for-granted mundane expectations. Systematically, participants trade on mundane expectancies, such as adjacency organization of turns so that a turn is "automatically" treated as a response to a previous one unless otherwise stated, even if technical constraints may have partially restricted the operation of adjacency (Garcia and Jacobs 1998). People's unease in artificially-transformed participation frameworks, such as those of video-conferencing, may explain why predictions of their rapid expansion have proved false (Raudaskoski 1999; Heath and Luff 2000).

Information-rich, complex technological environments, like control rooms, provide multiple simultaneous communication flows whose value partially depends on their mutual linkage. Consequently, parties' individual actions in hi-tech contexts may be embedded in their real-time co-ordination with others' actions. CA research can focus on the collaborative construction of actions both when it is an explicit aspect of co-operative work, but also when it is a tacit, underlying dimension of work activities that may seem separate and individual. CA can help respecify the nature of work processes, which may clarify work tasks and their requirements for the information systems to be used or designed (Heath and Luff 2000; Luff et al. 2000).

8.2 User Assumptions/Design Assumptions

The study of human-computer interaction poses specific methodological challenges since the parties of interaction – human and computer – do not share similar operating principles. Indeed, scholars have discussed to what degree conversation analysis can be applied to human-computer interaction. Luff et al. (1990) applied the metaphor of "conversation" to human-computer interaction, and suggested that CA findings could be applied to the design of interactive devices. These kinds of straightforward applications received a cautious response from Button et al. (1995), who claimed that computers are not and cannot be conversing agents in any ordinary sense and that no conversation between a human and a machine can take place. Nevertheless, you can *interact* with a computer. Human-computer interaction is from the outset asymmetrical. Despite speedily growing computational powers, computers are not intentional agents which would reciprocate with humans, infer the sense of human actions, and base their activities on the interpretation of meaningful, goal-oriented human acts. Further, human-computer interaction consists of several knowledge domains whose epistemological status differ from each other (Figure 8.2).

THE USER		THE MACHINE	
Actions not available to the machine	Actions available to the machine	Effects available to the user	Design rationale

Figure 8.2 Knowledge Domains in Human-Computer Interaction (Suchman 1987, 116)

Mutually available activities between the user and machine take place in the interface between the middle two columns. In addition, the observer may take into account the user's other actions, such as talk and visual gestures that are not available to the machine (though speech recognition would make at least some verbal actions available to the machine). For the observer, the user's actions that are not available to the machine may provide crucial cues for grasping the user's aims, orientations and interpretations of the machine's activities. The machine, in turn, is informed by its design rationale, which may or may not be available to the user depending on the user's (and respectively the analyst's) level of expertise. Suchman's (1987) analytic framework allows us to develop a systematic analysis of human-computer interaction in which CA may be applied and different knowledge domains kept separate.

We can generalize Suchman's (1987) analysis of the interaction between a user and a copy machine to account for any human-computer interaction which seems to follow a basic sequence: any single user's action which causes a change in the system state emerges on the interface as a shift in the display. This process can be broken down into a three-step model:

User's domain	Interface	Design domain
1 User browses contents, locates and interprets activities	DISPLAY 1	Contents and collection of activities #1
2 User makes a choice	User performs an activity	An activity causes a change in a system state
3 User evaluates the outcome of the activity	DISPLAY 2	Contents and collection of activities #2
**********		
(4 User browses contents, locates and interprets activities for the next activity)		

Figure 8.3 The Basic Sequence in Human-Computer Interaction

The user's basic step consists of taking action with respect to the current state of the device (Arminen 2002a; see also Silverman 1998, 177-178; Suchman 1987, 107; 148-67), and we can define this step as any action that alters this state. These steps may be preceded by work within a current state, so that the user may read and use the prevailing information and perform allowed activities, such as writing, in the current state. But to change the activity domain, the user needs to alter the state. This simple model allows us to distinguish between reasoning about and negotiating what action should be taken next and evaluations of the outcomes of the user's actions. The model also allows us to understand the reflexivity of user-device interaction, since receiving new information through browsing redirects the user's actions. It allows us to distinguish talk and actions taking place during the pre-monitoring of the action, i.e., before any action is selected, and post-monitoring of the action, i.e., after an action has been taken. This is an economic way to account for iterative steps of user-device interaction. It is also both context-free and context-sensitive, so that it can be applied to any moment and any situation, but it is sensitive in that it allows us to distinguish between different types of interaction both vis-à-vis types of devices and users. In this way, it becomes possible to account for the position structure of the interactional use of a device.

Each selection of the next activity consists of sub-tasks such as recognizing referents, for instance hypertext items, locating functions through which activities may be carried out and inferring outcomes of activities. In particular, if a device is used in pairs much of the users' reasoning may become transparent. CA is useful for several reasons. For one, it not only traces usability problems, but may also reveal the cultural expectations and conventions that have occasioned the patterns of use and possible difficulties in usage. Also, by explicating the user's orientation, CA allows us to focus on how technical properties operate in use, rather than seeing these properties and the users' reasoning as separate entities. All this can be shown through a couple of extracts. Extract 1 comes from a session of a tutorial program for DOS Word 5.0 in the early 1990s. Both users (A and B) are novices. Instructions for users displayed on the computer screen are marked with the symbol C. In the excerpt, A and B are practising using the mouse, B "types" and A discusses with him what to do next. The extract starts from the "instruction" the computer (C) offers to the users. B, who is doing the "typing", fails to follow the instruction, occasioning a repair initiation by A. Here the users "negotiate" about the meaning of the instructions and struggle their way toward the next move. Extract 1 consists of a single action in human-computer interaction.

(1) (Raudaskoski 1999, 115-116)

1	C:	**[Move the mouse pointer to the "d" in "due". Click-L**
2	B:	[o-oh
3	A:	move the (.) mouse
4	B:	mouse
5	A:	first
6	B:	oh [(move the mouse pointer)] ((whistle))
7		[((moves mouse))]
8		(2.0)
9	B:	y[eah (1.0)] click l
10		[(((gaze: screen, keyboard))]
11		((hand to l on kb, gaze up, hand to rest, knits eyebrows))
12	A:	did you click l?
13 B:	[	no]
14		[((hand towards l on the keyboard))]
15	A:	[the left button?]
16		[((gaze to B))]
17	B:	((hand to rest, gaze: mouse, hand to mouse, clicks mouse))
18	C:	**((instruction on the screen disappears))**

At lines 3–6, A and B orient to the first part of the computer's instructions and display their understanding of it before B carries out the first part of the instruction and moves the mouse at line 7. At line 9, B orients to the latter part of the instruction to "Click-L". But since B does not carry out the latter part of the instruction, A asks him to do so (12). At line 14, B displays his understanding of the term "Click-L" by moving his hand towards 1 on the keyboard, and occasions a repair initiation by A "the left button?" (15). Subsequently, B moves his hand to the mouse and clicks the left button of the mouse, thus completing the action that A's repair initiation had made relevant.

In this sequence, the referent recognition became troublesome for B. Consequently, the repair sequence highlights a routine task that we might have taken for granted if the trouble had not appeared. Further, through the failed recognition of the referent, B falsely locates the next action. For the analyst, this again makes accountable a routine procedure, the locating of functions (mouse vs. keyboard). In all, this analysis shows that objects of human-computer interaction, like "Click-L", are embedded in the parties' sense making so that they gain situated, context-sensitive meanings that may differ from the inscribed design rational. Further analysis of the wider sequence would also reveal the origin of B's trouble[3] (see Raudaskoski 1999, 112–129; Arminen 2000).

A user's general cultural assumptions and background knowledge also play a role in human-computer interaction. Interactional tasks such as referent assignment and inferences of the outcomes of activities (if not known in advance) are embedded in the user's tacit cultural knowledge. Users' cultural assumptions may also differ from the design ideas of the artifact, as we can see in the next example. Extract 2 is from a videotaped session of two novices using a WAP device (internet-connected mobile phone) in September 2000, when WAP services had been publicly available for some months in Finland. B is using the phone, holding it and pushing buttons, and A is assisting her. C is the test organizer who may interfere and ask the users questions about their understanding of their procedures. In a test-like situation, users were asked to find information about the stock market index of Helsinki (HEX). During the task B contacts Merita Bank, and the following sequence unfolds (for transcription conventions see note 4.

(2) (Arminen 2001b) [Kuitto and Miesmaa 1.27–31, 164–188] ((translated data, originals available from the author))

1		\<SELECTS MERITA BANK\>
2	A:	there we are
3		{SERVICE IS CONTACTED}
4	B:	I don't- uh no
5	A:	Maybe we better do something else than
6		(- -)
7	B:	where are we?
8	A:	no erm at the economy menu
9		{WELCOME TO MERITA}

10	A:	Now you went to [Merita
11	B:	[Merita
12		hhh
13	A:	NO we don't get [anything without those [user id's
14	B:	[don't get, don't get, don't get,
15		that's right [<EXIT>=
16		={ECONOMY}
17	C:	Have you been using wap before?
18		((scrolls))
19	A:	I haven't ever
20	C:	So anyhow you know that one needs those user id's
21	A:	=
22	B:	=Yes
23	A:	yes I know that in those bank services you need to
24		[have user id's]
25	B:	[Yes you need] Yes I know it too
26		((scrolls))

At line 7 when the display shows that it is contacting service, B asks "where are we?" displaying that the previous selection contacting Merita Bank had been fortuitous. After the users have recognized that they have entered the Merita Bank service (lines 10–11), A states her understanding that they are not allowed to use bank services without user IDs, i.e., without registering as service users (line 13). B backs A's assessment in overlap with her at line 14, and exits from the service immediately at line 15. This sequence occasions C, the test organizer, to ask questions about A's and B's competence (lines 17, 20). In passing, C's questions indirectly display her understanding that A and B had just made a mistake.[5] A and B, however, do not take C's hint and continue to believe that bank services are open to registered clients only. Clearly, A and B have some background knowledge; they know that there are banking services which require registering. However, because they knew that closed banking services exist, they (falsely) generalized that all bank services require registration. Notably this follows a common cultural reasoning through which cultural stereotypes of different entities such as ethnicity are formed[6]. Here the users' firmly held background assumption makes it practically impossible for them to get the stock market information they were supposed to find. This example also raises important methodological questions. Does the failure of the testees to find the required information only imply that the test was poorly organized? Should the organizers have provided a more extensive set of instructions for the test participants? Indeed, in many usability test situations the users are instructed much more carefully and, consequently, some profound basic problems are never found (for usability test interaction, see Koskinen and Kurvinen 2000). By contrast, there were good grounds here for bad testing results (cf. Garfinkel 1967; Maynard and Marlaine 1992). The test revealed a widely-held basic cultural assumption, that bank services are for registered clients only, which posed serious difficulties for users trying to navigate with the WAP device. These cultural assumptions should have informed the service interface design in the first place; at the very least, users should have been informed that the service was open to everyone, not just to registered bank clients.

Various types of false alarms (i.e., users believed they had made a mistake) as well as "garden paths" (i.e., users thought they were doing OK when, in fact, they had made a mistake, see Suchman 1987, 163–169) were quite common among novice users of WAP devices. In extract 3, the users have incorrect expectations of the outcome of the action, and therefore misperceive the activity that is taking place. The users (K=the user, N=the assistant user, O=the test organizer) are searching for stock market information in the WAP pages of the Trade Journal. At line 6, K selects the item "news", but is shocked by the device's response (lines 7–9).

(3) (Arminen 2001b) [Rytkönen 1.25–27, 41–44]

```
1                {TRADE JOURNAL}
2      N:       #Y[a:h#
3      O:         [what next
4      N:       news
5      K:       new[s
6                  [<SELECTS NEWS>            ←
7                {CALLING SERVICE}            ←
8      N:       No, no, [no                   ←
9                      [<CANCEL>              ←
10     K :      Sa[me
11                 [{NO RESPONSE FROM SERVICE}
12     N:       Let's put then let's go then [back
13     K:                                    [let's go
14              from some other place [then.
15                                    [{TRADE JOURNAL}
```

Here, the users panic after noticing the announcement "calling service" (line 7) on the device display. At this point the assistant user says "no, no, no" in a nervous tone (line 8), and the user instantly selects "cancel" at line 9. Again, the users reacted unanimously and without delay, thus displaying their shared understanding. Here the announcement "calling service" is the source of trouble: it is a hybrid form that can potentially mean two things: here the calling is meant to be understood in a technical sense as making a data-link connection to a service. Instead the users understood that the device was operating as a phone and making an ordinary telephone call. The users failed to understand the intended sense of the announcement. Consequently, the testees are unable to use the service as it was intended. Again, we might blame their failure on inadequate test instructions. Here it is important to note that part of their trouble derives from the variation in terminology between different service providers.

In extract 2, the phrase "service is contacted" (line 3) was used instead of the phrase "calling service". Forms like "service is contacted" or "contacting service" were not prone to similar misunderstandings as "calling" announcements, which might lead us to suspect that such usability problems derive from immature interaction design. Note, too, that neither of the problems in extracts 2 or 3 is a technical problem in a narrow sense, but rather stems from differences between assumptions made by these users and the designers. CA can help provide the necessary insights to avoid such interaction problems in product design (for parallel observations concerning the usage of mobile devices, see Palen and Salzman 2001).

8.3 Standardization vs. Recipient Design

When interaction is used for gathering standardized information, particular constraints and contingencies emerge for the way such interaction is organized. Consequently, such interactions take a particular shape, and are constituted as part of a series of "text-to-talk-to-text" (Whalen and Smith 1997; Houtkoop-Steenstra 2000, 58–61). In these settings, the institutional task does not only prescribe the goal of interaction but requires the institutional agent to collect information in a pre-specified format. However, this standardization of information is achieved only through local, situated interaction, in which the mundane resources of talk-in-interaction are mobilized in order to standardize verbally expressed information. Further contingencies for interaction may emerge when computer-assisted work practices are adopted. For instance, the operation of emergency dispatch services involves a standardization of information which may also be computerized so that the dispatch package can be transmitted electronically (Figure 8.4).

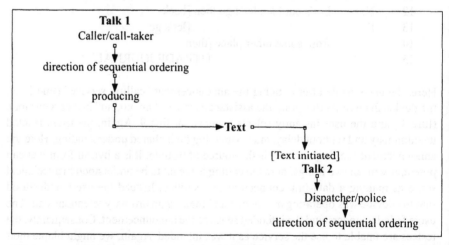

Figure 8.4 Emergency Services as Text Regulated Activities (Whalen and Smith 1997)

The call-taker's task is to collect the information required for the creation of the dispatch package. This involves categorizing the caller's problem according to standardized categories. Suspects of criminal activities are described using a list of pre-given criteria. The location has to be obtained in an appropriate, standard form. Additionally, computer-assisted dispatch systems may impose further constraints on the encoding of information, including restrictions on the order in which the information is entered into the computer terminal (see Whalen 1995; Zimmerman 1992; Wakin and Zimmerman 1999). At the other end of the continuum, the dispatcher decodes the information and announces it to the help provider (ambulance /police/fire department) who registers the call. This standardization of information is meant to guarantee uniform, fast service, but such standardization also trades on the parties' communicative competence and poses interactional challenges that may in fact cause problems (see Whalen et al. 1988)

Another common institutional practice aiming to achieve standardized information is a survey interview. A survey interview also has an interactional substratum which has been well-depicted by Paul ten Have (Figure 8.5).

(questionnaire) → [interview] → (recorded answers)

or in more detail:

(questionaire)   (recorded answers)
↓   ↑

['reading' questions, understanding questions, giving answers, understanding answers, recording answers; and possibly 'repairing' questions and/or answers]

Figure 8.5 The Interactional Substratum of Survey Data (ten Have 1998, 188)

Survey results are commonly understood to be objective expressions of respondents' opinions. Nevertheless, as Figure 8.5 shows, survey data involve an interactional substratum so that each answer to a question is an artifact accomplished through interaction and interpretative work. CA research can focus on this interactional dimension and allow us to understand inherent contingencies and uncertainties deriving from the interview situation, as these are a necessary, constitutive aspect of survey data. Generically, survey interview interaction highlights the issues and tensions inherent in any type of situated, recipient-oriented interactions which aim at creating standardized information, such as dispatch packages. The key interactional dimensions of survey interview interaction include the interpretation of questions, repairs of the ways the original question has been understood, including reformulations of the question, and the interpretation of answer options and a respondent's answers (Houtkoop-Steenstra 2000).

Part of the idea of standardized survey interviews is to ask respondents exactly the same questions in the same manner and order. Consequently, survey questions have to be designed to be free standing to reduce the need for clarification and elaboration. Through its questioning format, a survey interview departs from the conventions of turn-taking for ordinary conversation, which maximizes the shifts of speakership and minimizes the length of turns (Houtkoop-Steenstra 2000, 88–91). Due to their intended standardization, survey questions tend to be multi-unit turns that as such pose interactional challenges. For a recipient, these lengthy questioning turns are burdensome and may lead to difficulties in understanding, as in (4).

(4) ten Have 1999, 171–172 [CATI Transcr. RJM (Wisconsin Survey 01)]

```
 1   IV:    .hhhh okay(gh): a::[::nd? now we have some questions=
 2                            [##                    ((typing sound))
 3   IV:    =about government agencies. .hhh as you know:? every ten
 4          year there is a census of the population of the united
 5          states. .hhh how confident are you: (.) that the census
 6          bureau protects the privacy of personal information
 7          about individuals and does not share it with other
 8          government agencies. .hhh very confident (0.4)
 9          somewhat ↑confident (0.5) not ↑too confident? (0.2) or
10          not at all ↑confident.            (({q5} in a questionnaire))
11          (1.0)
12   FR:    share it with what other governments
13   IV:    (tch) .hh well the question doesn't specify: but (0.3) it just
14          says other government agen[cie ]s
15   FR:                             [oh ]
16   FR:    probably very confident
17          (0.5)
18   IV:    "oh kay" people have different ideas about what the
```

First, the interviewer projects an action by announcing the slot for questions concerning a particular topic (lines 1 and 3). Then the target of the question is developed (3–5) prior to delivery of the question proper (5–8). Finally, the response options are given for the respondent (8–10). Note that the strong inbreathe at line 8 immediately follows the question proper, indicating the interviewer's orientation to continue so that the response options are latched to the question. At line 12, the female respondent (FR) asks for clarification concerning an aspect of the question. The interviewer's response (13) treats it as a request for an elaboration of the original question. Subsequently, the interviewer repeats the part of the question that has been problematic for the respondent without any further elaboration. In this fashion, the interviewer maintains the participatory role as the relayer of questions, who just reads them without personal authorship. As a nice detail, FR receives the repetition of the part of the question with a news marker "oh" (15), thereby indicating that she had originally missed the latter part of the term "government **agencies**". After the trouble has been resolved, FR answers immediately, though she prefaces her answer with an uncertainty marker "probably" (16).

A question arises, what occasioned the respondent to miss the term "agencies" at line 8, and what enabled her to catch it at line 14? In the first instance, the term "agencies" is not only the last item of the third consecutive turn-construction unit, but it is also the last item of a very technical question. Notice that when the term is repeated, it is not in itself problematic for the respondent, and so it has been problematic due to the verbal construction it belonged to. These overtly elaborated survey questions clearly pose interactional dilemmas and occasion repairs as discussed (ten Have 1999). In addition, they may be prone to misunderstandings if the respondent's problems pass unnoticed. Also, in this extract the interviewer and the respondent lack an intersubjective understanding of the type of problem the respondent had with the question. Here, the respondent's problem was solved by fiat. Alternatively, the analyst might also suggest that the interviewer had indeed detected the nature of the respondent's problem at line 13. The sound "tch" displays the interviewer's realization of the respondent's problem, but due to her orientation to her narrow participation role, she withholds from a direct repair that would have interfered with the respondent's understanding of the question. Through her avoidance of corrections, the interviewer maintains neutrality and simply replaces the term "governments" with "government agencies". Nevertheless, the interviewer's limited participation role, aiming to guarantee the interview's objectivity, also restricts the repertoire used for maintaining intersubjectivity between interviewer and respondent, and thus further hinders the development of mutual understanding.

A possible strategy to solve the standardization problem of survey questions is to continue the elaboration of the question such that almost all the possible imaginable specifications have been spelled out. An example of this strategy is shown in an extract taken from a US national health interview survey.

(5) (Suchman and Jordan 1990, 233; see also Hutchby and Wooffitt 1998, 174)

```
1    I:      During those two weeks, did anyone in the family
2            receive health care at home or go to a doctor's
3            office, clinic, hospital or some other place.
4            Include care from a nurse or anyone working with
5            or for a medical doctor. Do not count times while
6            an overnight patient in hospital.
7    R:      (pause) No::
```

Here a question designed to be carefully elaborated has become almost impossible in terms of its interactional properties. The specifications carry the question far beyond what would have been the original transition-relevant place (did anyone in the family receive health care [at home] TRP.) Not only is a set of locations incremented, but also a new set of inclusive criteria (lines 4–5) and an exclusive criterion (lines 5–6) are added. Notice that the instructions on how to answer at lines 4–6 have been formulated as independent clauses so that they do not seem to project a suitable place for the respondent to answer the original question. The pause (whose length is not measured) seems to stand for the respondent's difficulty to answer at all. The pause, as it were, brings the original question back onto the action agenda. An immediate answer after the instructions might have been audible as an answer to the instructions and not to the original question. The overtly long specifications after the question proper pose daunting interactional problems.

Another set of contingencies derives from the assumptions built into the questions and the range of response options. In extract 6, the respondent comments on the question concerning whether an appropriate amount of money is being spent on solving the problems of big cities.

(6) (Suchman and Jordan 1990, 234–5; see also Hutchby and Wooffitt 1998, 176)

1	I:	...solving the problem of big cities
2	R:	hm:: ((long pause)) Some questions seem to be
3		((little laugh)) hard to answer because it's not
4		a matter of how much money, it's-
5	I:	Alright, you can just say whether you think it's too
6		much, too little or about the right amount, or if you
7		feel you don't know you can:: say that of course.
8	R:	Ah from the various talk shows and programs on TV
9		and in the newspapers, ah it could be viewed that
10		they're spending maybe the right amount of money.
11		but it isn't so much the money that they're spending
12		it's the other things that-
13	I:	Well do you think we're spending too much too little,
14		or about the right amount.
15	R:	Ahm, I'll answer I don't know on that one.

Here the question presupposes that the amount of money spent is decisive for solving the problems of big cities. The respondent, however, disagrees with the presupposition but the response options do not allow her to articulate her disagreement. Thus, the respondent has to choose the response option "I do not know", though her answer would have been that according to her the amount of money is not relevant for solving the problems. Even though the response options seem to cover all options, they in fact narrow down the scale of possible answers. In this way, potential variation is lost and the reliability of the study is weakened.

Given that respondents sometimes face similar problems answering survey questions, interviewers may also orient to these problems. As was shown in extract 4, the interviewer may respond to the respondent's repair initiation with a repetition of the relevant part of the original question. If the interviewer does not follow the survey etiquette strictly and blindly, the questions may also be reformulated to improve the respondent's ability to answer. In extract 7, the question and the response options are shown below, after which their transformation in the actual survey interaction can be detected. The data below is from interviews with people with a learning disability; nevertheless the interactional challenge is common to all interviews.

(7) (Houtkoop-Steenstra and Antaki 1997, 290–291)

Q9. How successful do you think you are, compared to others?

Probably more successful than the average person	*About as successful as the average person*	*Less successful than the average person*

```
1   I:    ↑how successful (0.2) d'you think you are (0.2)
2         compared to other ↓people (0.2) ↑yeh?
3         (0.5)
4   R:    ↑m
5   I:    ↑more successful than average (0.2) a↑bout as
6         successful as average (0.2) or ↓less successful
7         (0.5)
8   R:    °(      )°.
9         (0.5)
10  I:    gi'me one of them
11  R:    ↑yeh
12  I:    ↑which ↓one
13        (0.8)
14  I:    >↑d'you think you do< ↑better at things
15        than the [(public) (        )
16  R:             [↑better (0.8) better ↓now
17  I:    ↑yeh?
18        (0.2)
19  R:    yes
20        (2.0)
21        ((I asks next question))
```

In lines 1–6 the question is formulated as scripted. However, the respondent seems unable to provide an answer and consequently the interviewer revises the question radically (lines 14–15). Firstly, the question is altered to a candidate answer inquiry. Secondly, it is truncated so that the question component and response options are tied together as if the interviewer assumed that the respondent had a problem with a multi-unit turn involving a separate question and answer options. In any case, the question becomes drastically altered and though the interviewer succeeds in soliciting an answer, it is not an answer to the original question. Further, the respondent has reconstructed a time dimension to the question through his answer "better now" (line 16), which shows that the answer is given to a completely different question than what was asked.

In extract 8, an even more radical alteration of the question can be noticed. The interviewer jumps immediately to a candidate answer inquiry that enhances the respondent's ability to answer but also modifies the question thoroughly (extract 8 is from the same data set as the previous one).

(8) (Houtkoop-Steenstra and Antaki 1997, 303) [HB/MR/TT]

Q14 How do people treat you on your job?

The same as all other employees		Somewhat differently than other employees	Very differently

```
1   I:    ↑how a↓bout (0.2) getting ↑on with other
2         ↓people at work (0.2) is tha' (0.5)
3         is that ↑good
4   R:    yes:
5   I:    yeah?
6   R:    ↓yes
7   I:    o↓kay (0.5) °>two for ↑that<°
```

Here the interviewer manages to make the answering easy for the respondent, and successfully receives a prompt answer (line 4). However, the original question is lost through the modification. The scripted question concerns the respondent's idea whether he is treated equally in comparison to other employees, while the modified question concerns the respondent's overall sense of whether he is doing well with others at work, so the original sense is lost. Possibly, the modified question is designed not only to ease answering but also to save the respondent's face. Nevertheless, the intention of the question in the questionnaire never gets spelled out.

In all, survey interviews and other forms of standardized information collection suffer from the tension between standardization and recipient design. As far as the interviewer orients toward the maintenance of inter-respondent reliability through avoiding departures from the scripted questions, resources for achieving intersubjective understanding of the questions are severely restricted. On the other hand, if the interviewer opts for free interpretations of the questions to ease the respondent's burden to understand the intended meaning, the departures from the scripted questionnaire may guide the respondents to such an extent that reliability will be threatened. Standardization restricts the arsenal available for maintaining intersubjective understanding between interactants; such understanding, however, is a precondition for standardized coding of information.

8.4 Computer-Supported Co-Operative Multi-party Communication

Recently, various tools have been developed for computer-supported co-operative multi-party communication, such as conferencing facilities and chat lines (see Raudaskoski 1999; Hutchby 2001; Sellen and Harper 2001; Garcia and Jakobs 1998; 1999). In their technical details these computer-mediated communication systems vary, but invariably they modify or impose constraints on the sequential achievement of multi-party communication in comparison to face-to-face interaction. Even if these modifications, such as slight delays in the reception of messages, may seem minor, they indeed have a significant effect on the interactional organization of action. These modifications may affect the taken-for-granted sequential properties of interaction and seriously restrain the achievement of intersubjective understanding for ongoing action. Despite overwhelmingly optimistic technology visions, the success of multi-party communication tools for facilitating task-oriented work interactions has been limited, perhaps due to neglected details of intersubjective action not sufficiently addressed in the design of these technologies.

To consider these issues more fully, let us first examine technical features of the quasi-synchronic computer-mediated communication systems for classroom interaction (Garcia and Jakobs 1998; 1999). Quasi-synchronic computer-mediated communication (QS-CMC) enables all participants to simultaneously participate in a discussion through text messages, but the messages only become available for the group after they are completed and sent. QS-CMC thus differs in two crucial respects from ordinary multi-party communication. First, there is a delay between message production and transmission. Second, parties are prevented from monitoring the production of messages. Analysis of QS-CMC allows us to consider the implications of these technical constraints on the achievement of task-oriented interaction. Garcia and Jakobs have demonstrated that these restraints result in the emergence of new kinds of sequential objects, such as ghost adjacency pairs and phantom responsiveness that endanger the intersubjectivity of collaborative action. The data illustrate how pervasive the sequential orientation of interactants is, so that parties relied on the order of messages and used it as an interpretative resource even when technical systems had affected it. The tacit understanding of parties traded on procedures from conversation and did not enable them to pay attention to technical system constraints; as a corollary, confusions emerged. The following data comes from a college classroom involving three students (who had been using the program for eight weeks). In extract 9, two of the students (Silver and Fred) are engaged in discussion, and the third one (Mr. White) makes a clarification request at line 7. The response (at lines 8–9) perplexes him completely (line 10).

(9) (Garcia and Jacobs 1998, 311) ((Monitor Printout, line numbers changed))

1	Silver:	YOU SAISD THAT YOU CHANGED YOUR
2		POSITION SIND=CE THE FINAL DRAFT?
3	FRED:	INSTEED OF DEALING WITH ON A TOTAL
4		PERSONNAL LEVEL I INTEND TO GIVE
5		MORE COLD HARD FACTS, AS TO THE
6		SCHOOLS WRITTEN SOG'S
7	Mr White:	SOG'S?
8	FRED:	CHANGE MY POSITION NO FOCUSED MY
9		POSITION YES
10	Mr White:	WHAT?!!!

Garcia and Jakobs' analysis, based on videotapes of the students' monitors, shows that by the time Mr White's query "SOG'S?" was sent, Fred had almost completed her[7] turn at lines 8–9. Therefore Fred's turn could not possibly have been designed as a response to Mr White, who could not possibly know this as he lacked the possibility to monitor the production of others' turns. Indeed, Fred's turn at lines 8–9 was thus a continuation of her response to Silver's question at line 1. Through its adjacency to Mr White's query, it merely appears to be responsive to it. Consequently, Mr. White who appears to have traded on the procedures of ordinary conversation was completely lost (line 10). In this fashion, the technical constraints resulted in a phantom response and a ghost adjacency pair, which momentarily confused one of the parties. The extract also shows that parties in interaction may automatically rely on sequential orderliness, despite its limited applicability due to technical constraints.

Extract 10 gives another example of phantom responsiveness, and shows that the power of adjacency is so strong that at times it is difficult to make a difference between randomly and purposefully adjacent turns.

(10) (Garcia and Jacobs 1998, 308; Monitor Printout, Line numbers changed)

1	Silver:	SO YOU TRANSFERRED HERE FROM SU
2	FRED:	SO THEY HAVE TO ENSURE A CERTAIN
3		LEVEL OF SKILLS FROM THEIR
4		GRADUATES
5	Silver:	AND YOU ARE ANGRY THAT YOUR
6		CREDITS DID NOT
7		FOLLOW YOU

In the printout it appears as if Silver's lines 5–7 are a response to FRED's lines 2–4. The videotaping of their production, however, shows that they were written simultaneously, with Fred completing her turn just a second before Silver. The fact that parties in QS-CMC do not always necessarily know how their messages are related to each other opens the possibility for misunderstandings. Here, Silver knows that she meant her post at lines 5–7 to be understood as a continuation of her prior turn (and not of Fred's turn) but other group members do not have any resources to figure that out.

Of course, intersubjectivity may be momentarily lost in face-to-face conversations as well, but generally face-to-face interaction affords multiple resources both for detecting and repairing misunderstandings (see Schegloff 1992b). In QS-CMC intersubjectivity is more easily fractured and the misunderstandings may grow deeper and more difficult to repair. An instance of a complicated, deep misunderstanding in QS-CMC is shown in the next extract, a continuation of the prior one.

(11) (Garcia and Jacobs 1998, 305–306) ((Monitor Printout, Line numbers changed))

1	Silver:	AND YOU ARE ANGRY THAT YOUR
2		CREDITS DID NOT FOLLOW YOU
3	Mr White:	IS THAT IT?
4	FRED:	YES I AM ANGRY THAT I LOST A LOT OF
5		CREDITS BUT THATS WHERE I FELL
6		INTO A HOLE WITH THE FIRST FINAL OF
7		THIS PAPER I TENDED TO FOCUS IN ON
8		THAT ANGER AND NOT ON THE
9		LOGICALITY OF THE BIG PICTURE
10	Mr White:	AH HA
11	Mr White:	AND NOW YOU WILL CHOOSE TO FOCUS
12		ON THE LOGIC, INSTEAD OF THE
13		EMOTION ...
14	Silver:	OAKY SO YOU NEED TO BE DETACHED
15		FROM YOUR FEELINGS WHEN WRITING
16		THIS ESSAY ... EASIER SAID THAN DONE
17	FRED:	NO THATS NOT IT THEY DO HAVE
18		ALSORTS OF CRACKS IN THE SYSTEM
19		THAT IF YOU KNOW HOW TO PLAY THEM
20		YOU CAN GET MORE CREDITS TO
21		TRANSFER THAN YOU COULD IF YU
22		DID'NT KNOW HOW
23		TO DODGE THE SYSTEM

Reading this printout, it appears that parties are directly responding to each others' turns (except that Fred's "no that's not it" at line 17 may seem slightly awkward).

Analysis of the videotape of the production of messages, however, shows that Fred's turn at lines 4–9 was a response to Silver's candidate inquiry at lines 1–2. Consequently, Fred's turn at lines 17–23 responded to Mr White's "is that it?". However, parties who do not have access to each other's production of messages cannot possibly have followed the sequential ties between the messages. Mr White's turns at lines 10–13 display that he had at that point taken Fred's previous turn as a response to his question. Both Mr White and Silver lacked adequate resources at that point to decipher the sequential position of Fred's turn. Subsequently, their comments at lines 10–16 to Fred's response have again recontextualized the discussion before Fred launches her repair at line 17, which hence may again be misunderstood. The parties' inability to follow the production of turns and trace the sequential ties between the turns jeopardizes the achievement of collaboration, and so intersubjective action becomes fractured. This case study is supported by statistical findings which show that multi-party CMC tends to have a multiple amount of clarification sequences in comparison face-to-face interactions.

QS-CMC seems only partially to support real-time task-oriented interaction. It constrains the parties' ability to maintain the intersubjectivity of their action and to repair misunderstandings. However, as Garcia and Jakobs (1999) point out, QS-CMC also has merits in educational contexts. It enables parties more time to respond and infinite slots for answers to questions. In this way, it might turn out to be adequate for tasks demanding lengthy processing time and which do not critically depend on real-time co-operation. In addition, the immense popularity of chat lines shows their adequacy for the kind of interaction they are used for. It is also possible that in non-serious chat lines, the kinds of shortcomings described above are simply understood as "funny misunderstandings" which parties may even artfully exploit – though this would demand a study of its own.

8.5 Computer-Supported Co-Operative Work in Hi-Tech Environments

Air and subway traffic are examples of complex technically-sophisticated systems of late modern societies. Indeed, they may be typical of the late modern period just as railways characterized early modernity and the Internet may characterize future societies. They also provide a test bench for social scientific analysis aspiring to come to terms with late modernity. Any brief moment of social action in these settings involves an unforeseen complicity. All complex systems of transportation share a common feature: actions and the flow of work in these settings depends on the power of monitoring centers of coordination. These control rooms are scenes of intensive, information rich, and technologically-saturated work in which multiple flows of computationally-mediated data are used for monitoring and controlling the surrounding multidimensional networks of actions. Work activities in these settings are characterized as having responsibility for a large number of people, high intensity and the potential for fatal errors. The management of work tasks depends on the smooth collaboration of agents through the use of various tools and technologies to respond to normal, natural troubles and difficulties in maintaining schedules and coordinating activities in these overtly complex settings. Recently, control rooms have become one of the central research topics in workplace studies informed by ethnomethodological and conversation analytical principles (see Suchman 1996; Goodwin and Goodwin 1996; Goodwin 1996; Heath and Luff 2000; Luff et al. 2000). Here I will introduce one detail of these studies.

Essentially, the work tasks in coordination centers consist of making sense of enormous flows of information to give quick, reliable instructions and orders to co-ordinate actions. At its grass root level, the management of information flows consists of recognizing technically-mediated representations of objects and interpreting their significance in the light of ongoing tasks. These work tasks also involve compiling and sharing data from various media, and maintaining collaboration with co-workers to enable smooth intersubjective understanding of the ongoing action. To discuss an aspect of these features I will introduce a brief glimpse of data in which the social constitution of "seeing" as an activity is clear. The data comes from a mid-size US airport control room that is the coordination center for ground activities servicing arriving and departing airplanes, including operations at gates, baggage ramps etc. Many of the work tasks are related to solving and amending routine problems, such as delays and minor technical faults.

Before we analyze a brief instance of work interaction mainly through Goodwin's (1996) study, some brief extracts will give you a flavor of the setting (see Figure 8.6).

Figure 8.6 The Operations Room [Goodwin 1996, 377; Fig. 8.3]

To co-ordinate ground operations, Ops workers are equipped with tools – telephones, radios, and computers of various types – which allow them access to events at various locations. In this way, Ops workers gain perception of distant settings relevant to their work. For the current piece of data an array of monitors at the front of the room is critical (Figure 8.7).

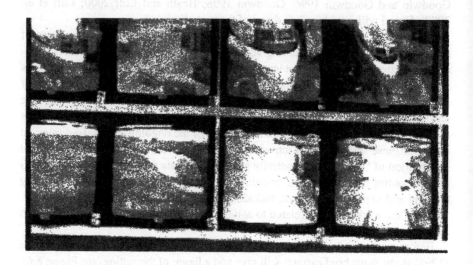

Figure 8.7 Gate Monitors in front of the Operations Room [Goodwin 1996, 378; Fig. 8.4]

Through the wall of monitor screens, the Ops workers see at a glance a partial representation of what is going on at the gates. Significantly, the visual information on the screens is constituted as part of the work activities it belongs to: the visual images do not possess any pure, objective sense, nor does the screen wall afford an intrinsic valence. Instead, the information on the screens is processed and transformed as part of work processes that constitute the monitors as tools. The information on the screens – as distorted and one-sided a representation of the object realm as it may be – offers a semiotic grid that is both an object and a tool of work: a plane visible/no, a plane moving/no (coming/going), jet bridge connected/no, type of plane, identificatory details (colors, numbers, etc.), servicing vehicles around the plane/no, visible deviations of normal courses of events, etc. The ability to make sense and distinguish relevant features of the visual information is part of the endogenous craft knowledge through which Ops work is practically achieved.

An overview of the participants and tools in the operations room is depicted in Figure 8.8. Even though participants have their own tools and work tasks, they are also ratified overhearers of each other's talk and possess a mutually co-present object of focus, such as the monitor screens and complex board conveying flight information. Through their copresense and mutually available objects of focus, Ops workers may balance between individual work and collaboration that may be improvised at any moment via their existing knowledge of each other's work tasks.

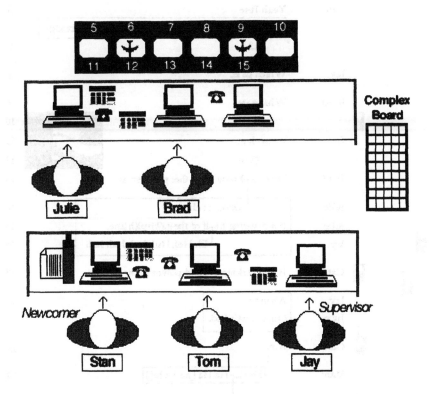

Figure 8.8 Participants and Tools in the Operations Room [Goodwin 1996, 379; Fig. 8.5]

The data instance here concerns the recognition and reception of a "routine" problem. The Ops center receives a radio call from a gate about a problem. In the data excerpt, radio conversations are in boxes and marked with walkie-talkie icons. The monitor picture of the gate in trouble is added on the relevant sequential location at the side of the discussion. Significantly, the problem is received collaboratively so that not only Brad who receives the radio call but also most of the co-present workers (Jay, Julie, and Stan) act upon the reported trouble.

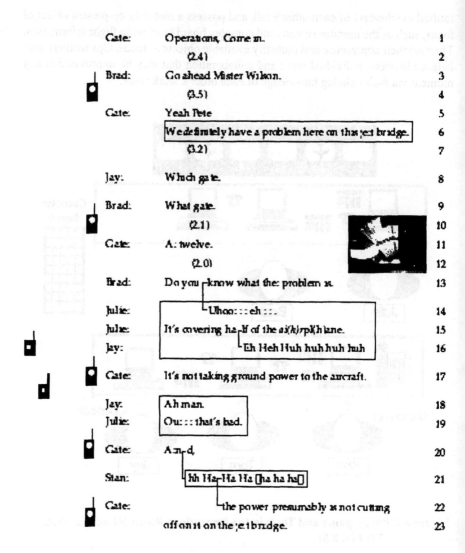

Gate:	Operations, Come in.	1
	(2.4)	2
Brad:	Go ahead Mister Wilson.	3
	(3.5)	4
Gate:	Yeah Pete	5
	We definitely have a problem here on this jet bridge.	6
	(3.2)	7
Jay:	Which gate.	8
Brad:	What gate.	9
	(2.1)	10
Gate:	A: twelve.	11
	(2.0)	12
Brad:	Do you ⌈know what the problem is.	13
Julie:	⌊Uhoo::: eh :::.	14
Julie:	It's covering ha⌈lf of the ai(k)rp(k)h lane.	15
Jay:	⌊Eh Heh Huh huh.huh huh	16
Gate:	It's not taking ground power to the aircraft.	17
Jay:	Ah man.	18
Julie:	Ou:::: that's bad.	19
Gate:	A.n⌈d.	20
Stan:	⌊hh Ha⌈Ha Ha ⌈ha ha ha⌋	21
Gate:	⌊the power presumably is not cutting	22
	off on it on the jet bridge.	23

Figure 8.9 Seeable Trouble [Goodwin 1996, s. 380; fig. 8.6]

At the outset, problem reception seems very economic and routinized. In lines 1–7, the problem announcement takes place. The problem is then located at lines 8–12. The elaboration and definition of the problem occurs at lines 13–23. Let us examine the problem reception process: first, the problem is received and dealt with collaboratively. Though Brad receives the radio call, it is actually Jay, the supervisor, who makes the first agenda move to locate the problem at line 8. Subsequently, after the locating the problem, Julie is the first to define the problem at lines 14–15. Moreover, Julie's affective nonlexical response cry invites Jay's collaborative laughter at line 16. Consequently, it is Jay and Julie who collaboratively treat the problem as being transparently visible through their laughing together at the monitor screen image. At this point, Jay and Julie have arrived at an intersubjectively available recognition of the problem, notably prior to the Gate's elaboration of the problem at line 17. In passing, Stan, the newcomer, also joins the laughter at line 21, thereby displaying the intersubjective validity of the problem recognition. The analysts, C. and M. Goodwin (1996, 84–5), note that briefly after this exchange Stan, the newcomer, asks what the problem is. Despite his laughter, Stan seems not to have shared Julie and Jay's understanding of the problem, but appears to have acted as if he had.[8]

The sequence also enables us to specify the nature of work activity at the control room. The Ops workers seem to be engaged in a motivated search to try to interpret problem announcements as swiftly as possible through all their tools at hand. In this fashion, communication with outsiders makes relevant the visual images on the monitor screens, and additionally provides interpretative resources to focus on aspects pertinent to the ongoing action. Talk is listened to as offering instructions for looking at monitors so that the "seeing" of images is influenced by communication that may then be redirected through new information. The exact sequential order of the activation of resources also seems critical for the work course.

Julie's exclamation at line 14 is a strong change of state token through which she displays publicly and consequentially her realization about her oriented object. In other words, not until at that moment has the visual image of gate 12 had any perceived relevance. As such the video image of the gate was not new, but had been available for some time (the jet bridge was no longer moving, but had been installed some time ago). The valence of visual information had been changed due to the call from the gate that had primed the Ops workers to attune to a specific image and to search for a problem. The information flows conveyed through different media have reflexive relationships through which they mutually shape the available meanings. Perception and knowledge of the external objects are thus socially constituted. Finally, the sequence displays the socially-distributed, context-dependent nature of action at the coordination center. The initial report from the gate enables the Ops workers to engage in the specification of the problem using the tools they have at hand. The gate monitors offer a particular perspective on the events at the gate. The staff at the gate have their own local resources for seeing and making sense of their own situation but they do not have access to the information on the gate monitor screens. Asymmetrically, the Ops workers only have access to monitor images as their perceptual data about the gates. Here, the asymmetric perspectives allow the parties, Ops workers and the staff at the gate, to gain somewhat differing perceptions of the problem. Julie and Jay treat the problem as being transparently clear to them through their access to the monitor screen image which affords them a particular sense of the problem even before the gate staff share their understanding of the problem (at lines 17, 22– 23). The socially organized and limited access to perceived objects of work shapes them and gives them a dynamic existence so that knowledge is perspective bound and unevenly distributed.

As a whole, the process of recognition and elaboration of the problem can be summarized with the help of Figure 8.10. The reporting of a problem is what Goodwin calls a prospective indexical, i.e., an expression whose meaning is not readily available to the recipients, but which implicates a further inquiry about its meaning. Here, the

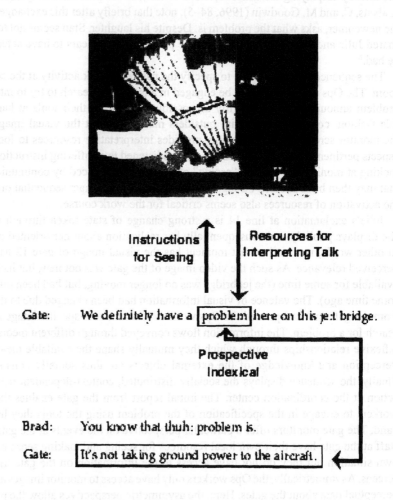

Figure 8.10 Mutual Shaping of the Prospective Indexical and the Event It Interprets [Goodwin 1996, 388; fig 8.11]

prospective indexical makes relevant for the Ops workers the visual image of gate, through which they aim to make sense of the indexical. Subsequently, the visual information allows the Ops workers to interpret further talk about the problem.

An interesting feature of this data, in fact, is that it is about the misrecognition of the problem. As Goodwin (1996) and Goodwin and Goodwin (1996) discuss, it turned out that the problem was the ground power unit and it had nothing to do with the visible shape of the jet bridge. Here, the original wording of the trouble had anchored it to the jet bridge that consequentially occasioned the Ops workers to see it in their available monitor image of the jet bridge. The wording of the problem was thus highly consequential for the subsequent recognition of the trouble. On a more general level, this brief episode clearly illustrates the distinction between information and knowledge. Since we know that the problem was not what it was believed to be, we can appreciate how information flows are connected to the social organization of knowledge. Information is transformed into knowledge only through its passing through distributed agents who are tied to their physical, cognitive, and perspectival limits. The technical and social resources that enable smooth co-ordination of activities also make possible socially-situated reasoning which may turn out to be erroneous. Technically-improved access to distant objects also engenders a fabricated participation framework where reciprocity of perspectives is not gained and intersubjectivity may be challenged. Technical facilitation of perceptions thus also enables the possibility of human error.

8.6 Conclusion

Currently, processor technology is becoming more and more ubiquitous, and will eventually also permeate most institutional settings. Information technology in practice also offers an increasing challenge for conversation analysis. CA can focus on a number of dimensions of work processes that are facilitated by or assisted with information technology. On a primary level, CA can be applied to the scrutiny of user interfaces, illuminating real-time, situated uses of technical artifacts. Analysis of a user's step-by-step actions with a device allows us to systematically approach human-computer interaction, enabling us to perform a detailed sequential scrutiny of the user's emergent understanding of the interaction with a device. We can thus begin to understand the basic sequences in human-computer interaction as well as the cultural reasoning models and conventions of use, providing us with valuable information both on systematic patterns of how technical artifacts are used and grounds for usability problems. This focus on computer-assisted work can reveal how actual work practices are affected by the adoption of information technology. Analysis, for instance, may focus on the encoding of information, and the potential implications of the interface solutions adopted. Computer-supported co-operative multi-party communication offers several intriguing research topics. In most cases, computer-mediated communication systems entail some smaller or larger modifications for the framework of multi-party communication vis-à-vis face-to-face interaction. Even small modifications, such as delays in the reception of messages, may bear significantly on the organization of social action. Finally, complex hi-tech settings, such as operation centers for traffic systems, have become an important topic for ethnomethodologically-attuned workplace studies. CA enables the analysis of the emergence of collaborative construction of actions both when it is an explicit aspect of work processes and when it is an implicit, tacit dimension of activities. The analysis of social organization of knowledge shows how activities are tied to their physical, cognitive and perspectival limits so that perceived objects at work gain a dynamic existence through the uneven distribution of knowledge. In technological settings, CA studies may be valuable both in understanding the maintenance of intersubjectivity under demanding circumstances and in enhancing the requirement specifications for technical systems through contextual knowledge.

Further Reading

– Suchman's (1987) classic study has been influential in directing research towards human interactions with technical devices.

– Current workplace studies are well introduced (see Heath and Luff 2000; Luff et al 2000), see: http://www.kcl.ac.uk/depsta/pse/mancen/witrg/.

– Some of Charles Goodwin's work deals with technically-mediated action in interaction, see his web page: http://www.sscnet.ucla.edu/clic/cgoodwin/publish.htm

– A special type of interaction also dealt with in this chapter is survey interaction (Houtkoop-Steenstra 2000; Maynard et al. 2002).

– For exercises, see http://www.uta.fi/laitokset/sosio/project/ivty/english/sivut/exercises.html.

Notes

1   Also the repertoire of available ICT devices is large and increasing, ranging from ordinary telephones and mobile phones to technically more sophisticated devices. Unfortunately the role of telephones has not been systematically studied in organizational interaction; nor are there systematic studies of interactional properties of mobile calls (for provisional studies, see Luke and Pavlidou 2002).
2   A critic might suggests that the phrase "social dimension" is unfortunate as technology is as such social. However, I would suggest that it is still tenable emphasis in contrast to viewing technology as such, or analyzing interaction as such without paying attention to the technological constraints and affordances in interaction.
3   In her analysis of the tutorial session, Raudaskoski (1999: 112–129) shows that both A and B had originally understood the given definition for "Click-L" (to press and release the Left

mouse button) and successfully connected "Click-L" with the left mouse button. B had not became confused about the referent for "Click-L" until the previous exercise in which he had been instructed to "Click-L" on the letter "l" in the word "lead". The reinforced association between "Click-L" and the letter L gave grounds for B to reshape the referent for "Click-L", a mistake that did not materialize until the extract discussed. This example again shows that the broader sequential context may turn out to be relevant for sensitive analysis of sequential details (here accounting for the origin of the trouble-source). This kind of knowledge may also be background knowledge given to parties outside the recorded occasion.

4   The speech is transcribed according to standard CA conventions. In addition, the transcripts include the user's activities and the main items of a menu or a display. I am indebted to Ilpo Koskinen for formulating this transcription system.

<SELECTS OPENING PAGE>   Performing an activity with the device
{SYDNEY 2000   Menu (or page or state) that is opened through the activity

In a more precise transcript the cursor location on the display could be shown through underlinings.

{UTILITY}   In the utility menu the cursor is put on "economy".
   {SHOPPING}
    {TRAVEL}
      {ECONOMY}

5   Because the test organizer knew that A and B had just made a mistake, she knew that they did not know what they were doing. Therefore, her utterance was ironic, and essentially questioned A and B's competence.

6   If you know that one case from the category A has the property X, a stereotypical claim generalizes the knowledge of this one case so that accordingly all cases belonging to the category A have the property X. (for the stereotype of the "Silent Finn", see Sajavaara and Lehtonen 1997).

7   It appears that Fred and Silver are female students; Mr. White is a male student.

8   Reviewer suggested that Stan's question may not be just a display of not-knowing, but a display of his doubts concerning the "transparent vision" of the others.

Chapter 9

Toward Applied Conversation Analysis

To wrap up, let us consider some of the future challenges of studying institutional interaction. As a whole, the field has already matured to a great degree. The elementary scientific procedures in data analysis and the basic ideas of study design have largely been established. However, there will be challenges in addressing new kinds of institutional environments and in adapting new principles of study design to respond to new kinds of knowledge demands. These challenges partly reflect the continual social changes impinging on institutional realities. Not the least important of these are globalization and the ever-increasing role of technology: both are directly relevant to studies of interaction and create different challenges for study design, as they raise questions about the possibilities for applied studies. This final chapter will discuss dimensions of interactional studies, which have potential for such applied studies.

New computational technologies promise to mediate and create new types of communications between/among persons, or interact themselves with users (persons). The role of new technologies is indeed salient in enhancing person-to-person communications. Telephones, videophones, computerized expert systems, and Internet applications, like Internet conferences, chat rooms and multi-user domains, are all technologies for communication. In future institutional environments, there will be few face-to-face interactions that are not somehow computationally mediated or enhanced. Therefore, studies of institutional interaction must address these technologies. In positive terms, these technologically-enhanced forms of social interaction and communication present specific challenges: can CA be systematically applied to new forms of interaction and cyber-agencies? Moreover, can CA contribute to technological research and development for system design?

Ethnomethodological and conversation analytical studies can become relevant for studies in technology insofar as they deal with the communicative affordances of technologies (Dourish 2001; Hutchby 2001), that is, if they address the possibilities technologies offer for action. By focusing on concrete usages of technology, the study of affordances opens up both the potential and the limitations of technologies. It addresses limitations, if a given technology impairs a set of actions in a specific context (see Heath and Luff 2000, e.g., the computerization of medical records, or the implantation of portable computer records in building sites), or shortcomings when technology fails to satisfy customers' needs. In all, these studies provide resources for or participate in the design processes in which the relationship between human parties and technology is addressed.

Globalization, in turn, makes salient knowledge about multi-cultured environments, as people increasingly encounter the cultural heterogeneity permeating new arenas of social action. The prevalence of cultural heterogeneity requires knowledge of how to deal with diversity. This challenge can partially be met with comparative studies addressing heterogeneity, the variety in registers. In terms of analytic strategies, comparative studies pose questions about how to quantify findings. Purely qualitative comparative studies are unsatisfactory, as they are promiscuous in terms of potential comparative dimensions. They do not allow rigorous comparisons. Quantification may help in solving this problem: you have to select a default aspect of the data which will then be presented in numerical form, allowing you to build a strict comparative dimension. Besides studies of technology, comparative studies are another step towards applied conversation analysis.

9.1 Communicative Technologies at Workplaces

As we saw above, the increasing role of technology in society and its deepening penetration into the details of everyday life, also known as ubiquitous computing, make technology increasingly important for studies of interaction. One development answering this challenge is what has become known as workplace studies, a new synthesis combining methods of ethnomethodology, CA and ethnography. Originally, this synthesis was pioneered by Lucy Suchman (1987). Her study is a misleadingly easy combination of background knowledge of the intelligent properties of the machine (computerized information system), an ethnomethodological account of situated human reasoning and a conversation analytical explication of the sequential flow of human-machine interaction.

Following Suchman's lead, the elementary steps of human-machine interaction can be subject to empirical scrutiny. In the application Suchman analyzed, the elementary sequence was a triad: a machine presents an instruction, the user takes an action, and the machine presents the next instruction. The study then exposes the user's reasoning about instructions and the assumptions upon which the reasoning is based, and contrasts them with the assumptions upon which the design of the machine is based. Consequently, Suchman reverse-engineers the logic of the user's problems with the machine, and introduces the differences between human assumptions and design assumptions. Thus an account of the situated logic of usability problems is given, and the design features that tend to lead users down the wrong track are depicted. On a theoretical level, Suchman develops an alternative to rule-based models of human conduct. She notes that these models neglect the human reasoning that takes place whenever rules or plans are applied to any concrete situation with contingent features. The application of rules is dependent upon the circumstances in which they are invoked. Consequently, rules do not determine conduct, but provide interpretative resources used in organizing conduct. This reflexivity of rule use has important implications for the study of technology use: such use cannot be separated out for formalized study, but must be studied as part of the social action in which it occurs. This is the theoretical imperative for workplace studies: to study the use of technology where the action is – in everyday settings and at work sites.

Workplace studies center on the production and coordination of workplace activities in real-time interaction through talk and visual conduct (Heath and Luff 2000; Luff et al. 2000). They analyze both face-to-face (inter)action and the coordination of work activities between distant parties mainly through various technological means. Typically, the analysis of work activities is based on ethnography and video recordings. The ethnographic materials provide background understanding for a more detailed scrutiny of videotaped work (inter)actions. As best, the use of several data sources may lead to a hermeneutic circle in which interactional details are interpreted vis-à-vis their ethnographic context, which itself is elucidated by reference to the actual interaction. Video recordings offer both a chance to test the validity of more "loose" ethnographic insights and provide reportable evidence of instances of the practices studied.

The analysis of videotapes combines the study of spoken interaction and visually observable physical actions. Spoken interaction is transcribed using conversation analytical conventions, and visual actions are linked with the stream of verbal actions. Consequently, the sequential flow of work activities is unraveled. In other words, these studies reverse-engineer the building blocks of the intersubjective understanding of social action in which parties' coordination of their activities itself displays the sense of action. The fundamental assumptions of the approach include that the contributions to actions are contextually oriented and structurally organized. Each activity is positioned with respect to previous activities, thereby displaying the actor's interpretation of the stage and sense of action. To conclude, even in work activities, there exists *order at all points*. Consequently, no detail of (inter)action at the work site should a priori be overlooked as trivial, irrelevant or accidental. For instance, one of the earliest workplace studies concerned the impact of the computerization of medical records on doctor-patient encounters (see Heath and Luff 2000). The study consisted of two sets of observations. First, it scrutinized how doctors used traditional medical record cards, and then how they used the computerized medical record system. Second, the study compared doctor-patient interactions in which either paper or computer records were used. The findings were quite revealing: they showed that traditional medical records are not a precise description of the consultation or the patient's illness, but a sketch that conveys the doctor's overall interpretation of the particular case to a knowledgeable recipient (i.e. to a doctor who would have a firm grasp of "how to read medical records"). Therefore a certain amount of idiosyncrasy and messiness in traditional records was not necessarily an obstacle for transmitting information, but could also be a means to convey the doctor's own medical sense-making process. Subsequently, when traditional paper records were replaced with computerized records, these subtle, tacit means of communication were irrecoverably lost. The new computerized records were systematic and consistent, not least to provide a database to allow bureaucratic follow-up of clinical work. The design of the new computer system had been based on two incompatible ideals: to aid individual general practitioners' consultative practices and to form a systematic database of medical treatment. Hence, it may not come as a surprise that many doctors ended up using the traditional paper records after the introduction of the new computer system. As a whole, the study looks at the social dimension of the use of technology, which is missed if technology is seen only as an exterior fact without considering the intimate connection of technology to meaning-making processes as part of work activities and other practices. The findings thus provide a detailed understanding of the ways in which medical records are used in practice and in encounters with patients, understanding which surpasses the practitioners' own understanding of such differences, as their ways of making notes or reading records while interacting with patients are largely such practical matters that they escape conscious attention, yet they form "an essential and accountable feature of everyday professional medical work" (Heath and Luff 2000, 58).

In terms of the type of work, a growing body of studies have concerned centers of co-ordination, such as emergency dispatch centers, the control rooms of rapid urban transport systems, and air traffic and ground control centers. These studies focus on how collaboration is achieved through the use of various tools and technologies to respond to normal, natural troubles and difficulties in maintaining schedules and coordinating activities in complex settings. Other studies have addressed work practices in large corporations, like financial institutions, in newsrooms, medical settings or in call centers and help desks. Some studies have analyzed train drivers' or pilots' work activities in real or simulated settings. In principle, any work practice can be studied, but the concentration is on settings saturated with technology, responsible for a large number of people, with high work intensity and a potential for fatal errors.

Another issue is the stage of technology deployment or organizational innovation: studies may address anticipatory stages, trials and experiments with new tools, or evaluate existing settings and the use of technology within them. The accelerated speed of technology development has raised decision-making problems about whether new tools, and which ones, should be adopted to assist work processes. Workplace studies may give an account of a work practice in the light of potentially available new assisting devices. The analysis of competencies involved in the actual details of work practices may inform decision-making concerning the choice of new technologies, though the salience of the researcher's advice for deployment is a complicated question. Trials and experiments with prospective technology provide the natural timing for studies. Experiments with prototypes also offer a point of contact between research and design. However, existing work settings are key for workplace studies, as analysis of the organization of work practices in "natural", "normal" circumstances can provide the essential background knowledge which may then be used in redevelopment or in experiments. Therefore, studies without any demand for immediate applications would provide a chance to develop workplace studies as a scientific field of its own.

The analytical focus of workplace studies may range from the organization of an entire work site, the collaboration of workers in a given setting, and finally to details of the work practice of an individual worker. Given the complexity of work settings, any individual study can scarcely address all aspects of a work process, so a selective design is a precondition for success. Studies with different focuses on a work process also employ different combinations of methods. Ethnography is the most suitable tool for depicting the overall organization of a workplace; the smaller the details addressed, the more critical CA and ethnomethodology become for the study. To get a flavor of a detailed study of work practices, let us take a look at the interactive use of expert systems in diagnosing copying-machine problems over the phone.

Whalen and Vinkhuyzen's (2000) studied the use of an expert system in a large corporation's customer support telephone center via two months of ethnographic observations and 36 hours of video recordings. The customers' service requests are answered and processed by customer service and support representatives (CSSRs), who enter the information into a computer with the help of expert system software. The study highlighted the use of an expert system in its social context to understand the competencies involved and the problems or inadequacies of the system for the particular tasks within the context. The findings include deciphering the users' logic in comparison to the system assumptions.

The expert system was based on the assumption that the diagnosis of a machine problem can be started from a single initial category, such as "blurry copies". The final diagnosis was to be made through refining the initial problem description. However, the analysis of actual interactions shows that customers were often unable to provide a single heading/description for the problem they were reporting. Consequently, the CSSRs often had to engage in analytic, sense-making work concerning the customer's problem, which is the work the expert system was initially designed for. The expert system did not relieve the CSSRs from reasoning and the use of expertise. At least in this respect the expert system failed; it does not seem to contain expertise in itself so that "anybody" could use it, but it seems to demand a considerable amount of knowledge from its users.

Further, the expert system also complicated CSSR/customer interaction. Its diagnostic questions were designed to be neutral. However, the CSSRs were not always able to use the questions since, even if neutral and logical, they were at times were clumsy or improper for actual interaction. For instance, one area concerned whether the originals (to be copied) were defective. The expert system proposed a question: "Is the defect also on originals?" (Whalen and Vinkhuyzen 2000, 120–121). The CSSRs were unable to use the question as phrased, as it would have implied that they thought the customers were stupid or completely ignorant. The fact that CSSRs had to deal with persons and not with "information providers" amounted to a series of complications that affected the use of the expert system. To sum up, the system was designed in such a way that it did not take into account the context in which it was to be used, leading to discrepancies between the steps suggested by the system and these steps as sensible moves in agent/customer interaction. Whalen and Vinkhuyzen argue that understanding the context in which a new technology will be used is essential for the design process.

Not coincidentally, Whalen and Vinkhuyzen's study was conducted in the Xerox research laboratories, who launched the most systematic, interaction-oriented studies on the appropriation of digital systems within prevailing working environment in the 1990s (Sellen and Harper 2001). These studies have paid attention to the properties of various artifacts in their social activity contexts and have in effect specified everyday intuitions about the requirements existing social practices set for the technologies to be appropriated. To compare paper and digital artifacts, for example, Sellen and Harper show that reading is not a unified category. Instead, they list ten different types of reading: reading to identify a document, skimming, reading to remind, reading to search for answers to questions, reading to self-inform, reading to learn, reading for cross-referencing, reading to edit or critically review a text, reading to support listening, and reading to support discussion. These different types of reading set different requirements for the digital tools appropriated for these activity contexts. In these contexts, the following issues are critical for digital technologies: the flexible real-time availability of separate sections in a working document; the capability to simultaneously work with several documents; the simultaneous reading and handling of a document; collaborative access to working documents; simultaneous access to work with and to read a document; the capability to make flexible alterations in a document that remain separate from the core document, various context-bound privacy issues, etc.

A key lesson Sellen and Harper (2001) offer is that activities, like reading, are often embedded in their activity context, and in different contexts they pose different requirements for supporting technologies. Therefore, although digital technologies have progressed immensely, and will continue to progress, it seems unlikely that one solution would be workable in all contexts; rather different artifacts are needed for different tasks. As a whole, Sellen and Harper show that the use of artifacts is embedded in the organization of work, and cannot be understood without detailed analysis of work processes in their organizational context.

9.2 Consumer Technologies in Everyday Life

The interactions supported by consumer technologies permeating everyday life provide a completely new field for research that has barely been opened. It would be worthwhile to consider a CA-inspired approach for the study of smart consumer products, i.e., information appliances, in particular, as the challenges in designing universal smart consumer products are generally acknowledged (Säde 2001; Ketola 2002). Portable, mobile consumer products may be used by anybody, anywhere, anytime. Still, the uses and contexts of use have an impact on a product's usability and likeability.

Ethnomethodological and CA studies may prove useful in showing the way adoption of innovative technologies is interwoven with taken-for-granted patterns of users' daily activities. For instance, Koskinen et al. (2002) have shown that mobile image messaging was embraced through mundane practices, such as teasing, joking and gossiping. Image messages with accompanying texts were sent to others in order to engage in and maintain social relations with others. In this way, the images sent were embedded in social activities. On the whole, users' own social innovations for how to use new technologies only develop within existing patterns of social action. Moreover, the minutiae of technology may prove salient for users. For mobile images, the capability to send text together with images turned out to be immensely valuable. It provided a possibility to enrich images through clarifications and insertions of background knowledge and also made possible plays of meaning through the use of attached ironical comments. In all, mobile image messaging seems to support person-to-person communication and add new dimensions to technologically-enhanced communication between persons.

CA can be applied even more straightforwardly to the analysis of emerging forms of verbal communication with new media. For example, mobile phone calls have not yet been systematically studied despite their increasing prominence in most parts of the world.[1] The preliminary findings of an ongoing study in Finland (Arminen and Leinonen 2003) suggest that at least the openings of mobile calls are drastically different from landline telephone openings. Finnish landline telephone calls are normally opened not with a generic "hello", but with a turn where answerers say their first name, family name or both. Callers usually respond symmetrically, except they can build intimacy by allowing answerers to recognize them by voice. One of the most remarkable new features of mobile calls, by contrast, is the disappearance of these articulated, explicit identifications. Almost unanimously callers have withdrawn from identifying themselves; saying your name in the traditional Finnish way now functions as "doing being a stranger", i.e., the caller does not belong to the sphere of people from whom the answerer could have expected to receive a call. Consequently, opening sequences seem to be systematically truncated. We should note that this truncation may reflect the technology: a quick glance at the phone reveals the identity of any caller who is entered in the digital phone book on the recipient's phone, so answerers know who is calling before they actually answer the phone. In addition, the discursive identities of "caller" and "answerer" have become more fluid: mobile conversationalists no longer unanimously orient towards the caller being accountable for delivering the reason for the call. Topic initiations are more equally distributed between caller and answerer. In general, there is more variability in the linguistic practices for introducing the first topic. A particular trajectory involves a "where are you" question following the truncated opening sequence, leading to a stepwise topic initiation. The specific sequential features also include a strong tendency toward a lengthy pause after the first turn (the answer to the summons).

We might next ask what do these differences tell us? In commenting upon the debates concerning the differences between call openings in different cultures, Schegloff (2002) states: "Where the surface appearance of openings is on the face of it different, we can ask whether, on the one hand, the parties nonetheless confront and work through the same issues in the opening, and in the same order, but do so differently, and if so what the consequences of those differences are, or whether, on the other hand, the very issues posed by opening a conversation on the phone in that cultural or institutional setting are different." Comparing landline and mobile conversations is somewhat different from comparing calls in different cultures, but such comparisons partly ask the same questions. Do the differences between landline and mobile conversations stand for some emerging development in interactional conduct? Or are these differences just stylistic, surfacing an immutable core of telephone call openings? Or can the differences be reduced to technical differences between media? It is not easy to answer these questions, but they open salient perspectives both for the analysis of talk-in-interaction and also for understanding the use of communicative media today. We are beginning to see that more and more everyday communication will involve some technical component in the future. Furthermore, these new forms of the technical mediation of communication, as innocent as they seem, may transpose the mundane patterns of interaction. CA is a potential research tool that may identify and specify these small but not necessarily insignificant changes in everyday communicative behavior. In this way, CA may also play a role in building understanding of social change in the era of ubiquitous computing.

9.3 Comparative Studies

CA is inherently a comparative approach. CA studies notably involve several layers and types of comparison (Drew 2003). On a rudimentary level, instances of data are compared to observe similarities, patterns, and invariances. Of course, as discussed in Chapter 4, in this respect CA is not that different from any other genuinely empirical scientific endeavor (see also Ragin 1987; 1994). Characteristically, CA studies of institutional interaction include comparisons between "ordinary conversation" and "institutional interactional practices". This has largely been the backbone of this book as well, though I have pointed out that institutional interactions are not necessarily formally distinct from mundane interaction and that generic mundane patterns of interaction may play a distinct role in institutional contexts (Chapter 2). Therefore, comparison between ordinary and institutional interaction may be a relevant but not yet sufficient step for exposing the meaning of institutional talk. Nevertheless, comparisons between ordinary talk and institutional interaction pave the way towards understanding the nature of practices in institutional contexts.

Comparisons between different types of institutional interaction can shed light on the particularities of institutional practices. For instance, Vehviläinen (1999; 2001) has analyzed argumentative use of the stepwise entry to giving advice in counseling, contrasting counseling within labor market training with counseling in health care and therapy settings. In the latter, a stepwise entry to advice enables the professionals to fit their advice with the clients' perspective, create alignment between them, and minimize resistance. In labor market training, a parallel pattern was used to evaluate a student's plans. Further, it enabled the counselor to gain an argumentatively advantageous position for giving advice. In this work practice, alignment and agreement with the client were not oriented to as much as in health care and therapy. As we can see, a comparative analysis between different types of institutional interaction can illuminate the characteristic nature of a specific kind of work practice. Paul Drew (2003) has noted how the differences between formulations, such as "you mean", "you suggest" or "you are saying", are telling in terms of the differences between institutional practices.

Cross-setting comparisons within the same institutional area, standard procedure in evaluative studies and in outcome measurements, in practice do not exist in CA. In cross-setting comparisons, the outcome or the nature of the process in units working in the same area are compared (the treatment outcome evaluations, etc.). In principle, CA would afford naturalistic, detailed observations that would bring a new level of accuracy to process evaluations. In some usability studies, for example, videotaping of sessions is a routine procedure that amounts to a high level of information from a small sample of cases (Rubin 1994; Dumas and Redish 1999). Hypothetically, CA studies could adapt similar study designs that would afford intensive cross-setting comparisons. In any case, cross-setting comparisons would offer a worthwhile strategy to enrich the methodological canon of study designs in CA.

Cross-cultural/linguistic comparative studies are already prevalent within interactional linguistics. Cross-linguistic studies can analyze the ways in which distinct linguistic resources contribute to the emergence of interactional procedures in different languages. It has been shown that the projection of turn-construction unit, repair and participation strategies vary among speakers of different languages. In this respect, there seems to be a form-function correlation. The fact that linguistic forms have a say in the variation of interactional formats between different languages opens vast prospects for inquiries (Selting and Couper-Kuhlen 2001). An area of cross-cultural studies a bit closer to institutional interactions is comparison of (landline) telephone call openings. Studies have found differences in the practices of call openings in different cultures, and have attempted to account for these differences by pointing to cultural differences. Schegloff (2002), however, has some reservations about the conclusions drawn from these findings, as he is generally critical of jumping too quickly from an observable interactional property (or here a difference in practices between cultures) to properties of culture (here cultural differences). Further, Schegloff accuses these studies of having an ecological fallacy, a faulty shift from one plane of analysis to another. For example, the fact that telephone calls are opened in a given culture in a different way than in the United States does not indicate differences in cultural values and commitments for Schegloff (2002). According to Schegloff, alternative practices in different cultures are not alternatives to one another (unless both practices exist in a given culture, and the speaker can make a choice between them). Though Schegloff raises a valuable point in warning against jumping too quickly from interactional practice to its cultural significance, it remains debatable whether cultural routines, such as culturally characteristic or specific telephone call openings, can be regularly oriented to cultural features, as they themselves constitute the possibility for such an orientation.[2] Eventually, all this comes back to the nature and interpretation of procedural relevance (Chapter 2). Further analysis will be needed to demonstrate the ways in which interactional practices are procedurally relevant for cultural practices. Studies of institutional interaction have not yet included many cross-cultural comparisons, but they will become increasingly important in the globalizing world.

Historical comparisons are a final extension for studies of institutional interaction. Clayman and Heritage (2002b), for example, have compared journalistic adversarialness in the press conferences of Eisenhower and Reagan, showing that journalists have become increasingly aggressive in their treatment of the president. They noticed substantial and significant differences in the journalists' initiative, directness, assertiveness and hostility. The study raises wider questions about the evolving relationship between journalism and government. More generally, historical comparisons are a valuable asset for studies of institutional interaction as they link the development of interactional practices to the evolution of institutions.

9.4 Quantification of CA and Combinatory Studies

Comparative studies also raise methodological issues, of which the quantification of findings is one. Though quantification has been debated in CA (see Schegloff 1993; Zimmerman 1993; Tracy 1993), it may be claimed that CA findings are incipiently statistical (Heritage 1999).[3] CA allows us to count the incidences of distinct patterns, and link the observed cases to other factors. Schegloff's (1968) classic study of telephone conversation openings included a count of cases, and also accounted for the anomalous case, the so-called deviant case analysis. Subsequently, this manner of study, first to seek regularity and then to account for deviant cases, has become a standard methodology (see Clayman and Maynard 1995). In short, CA applies analytic induction as its methodological policy (ten Have 1999). Analytic induction is particularly well-suited to the study of ordinary conversation in which the goal is to identify the interactional patterns constituting a specific action, but in which the frequencies of actions do not generally matter as they are contingently and not conventionally distributed. In addition to mainstream CA, which is not statistical, there have been some attempts to do statistical analyses of the interactional patterns of everyday language use, though these studies have not generally overcome the heterogeneity of local contexts and measured items (see Schegloff 1993; for exceptions, Ford and Thompson 1996). Study of institutional interaction, however, offers a different platform for statistical work.

Institutional practices are designed to produce measurable outcomes: to sell products, solve the client's problems, achieve a deal, prescribe an appropriate cure, etc. Clearly defined outcomes dominate institutional practices (in contrast to everyday life where outcomes are contingent). When interaction forms a part of the institutional practice, the interaction becomes accountable in terms of its outcome. This opens up the possibility to reverse-engineer the patterns of interaction that may turn out to have a bearing on the outcome. The analyst's task is first to identify the strategic moments of interaction that have an impact on the outcome. Secondly, the analyst singles out the range of activities used in these strategic moments and describes the recurrent patterns. Thirdly, the criteria are formulated so that the rate of incidence of each pattern can be counted. Fourth, counting allows us to present findings in a frequency table. Finally, the quantified CA findings can be correlated with various types of outcome measurements (the success rate, the client satisfaction, etc.). Additionally, quantified CA findings also allow historical or cultural comparisons of institutional practices; for example, the distributions of activity patterns from different periods or environments can be compared (Clayman and Heritage 2002b; Heritage 1999).

Some examples of work applying a combination of quantified CA and outcome measurements include an analysis of the impact of communication styles on the financing of medical treatment (Boyd 1998; Heritage 1999), and an analysis of doctors' ways of dealing with parental pressure to prescribe antibiotics (Heritage and Stivers 1999; Heritage 1999). Elizabeth Boyd (1998) has analyzed the interactional accomplishment of peer reviews of the proposed treatment procedure. Boyd's study shows that the reviewer's adoption of a "collegial communication style" increased the likelihood that the proposed procedure was approved. Significantly, she also discussed various alternative interpretations of this correlation (i.e., the possibility of intervening factors). Tanya Stivers has studied ways in which doctors' manage parental pressure to prescribe antibiotics. Preliminary results suggest that "online commentaries" – the physician's descriptions of what she or he sees, feels or hears during physical examination – may be a technique to counter demand for antibiotic medication.

The quantification of CA findings offers a new level of data for outcome measurements, thereby promising a more fine-grained analysis of the ingredients of the outcome. Furthermore, historical and cultural comparisons may also shed light on the distribution of activity patterns across cultures and times. However, some words of caution are necessary. Quantification can only be done after a careful analysis of the sequential patterns of interaction. Premature coding may obscure phenomena if the strategic sequential environments and patterns have not been adequately identified. Furthermore, the research procedure is even more laborious than in qualitative studies, as the amount of data must meet statistical criteria. Additionally, the research team must posses adequate knowledge both of the qualitative analysis of interactional data and of quantitative data analysis. Finally, the interpretation of correlations is risky;

in particular, supposed causal relations are always open to reinterpretations that may modify and even reverse the original assumptions (see, Boyd 1998; for a classical account, see Hume 1998 [1777]). The quantification of CA may not necessarily be the last word for studies on institutional practices, but it will definitely be a great asset that has hitherto been neglected.

9.5 Applied CA

The time is ripe for applied CA. In the early stages of CA, the efforts of Sacks and his colleagues concentrated on establishing a new autonomous field of study (Sacks et al. 1974; Schegloff and Sacks 1973). After the new field was established, questions about its links to other subjects started to evolve. In terms of CA's connection to the social sciences, studies of institutional interaction have been the most important. As we noted earlier, studies of institutional interaction always stand on the crossroads of two institutional realms (Peräkylä 1997a). In institutional interactions, interaction is the interface between the institution and its users, but by definition, interaction is also connected to the social order as it appears in institutions. CA studies may augment our understanding of institutional practices by respecifying their interactional substratum. The linkage between CA and institutional realms opens a door for the emergence of applied CA that generates knowledge on selected aspects of interaction for purposes related to various institutional goals (whether official, unofficial, lay or professional).[4] CA may concretize, broaden, detail, and even correct our grasp of professional practices and intersubjective meaning making in institutions (Peräkylä and Vehviläinen 2003).

In terms of the research and development of technology, workplace studies provide a potential link between developers' practical interests and academic research. The renewal of interest in workplace studies is practical: the new multiplicity of technical tools, devices and applications not only increases the efficiency of work, but also leaves a string of underused or collapsed systems, frustrated clients, unfulfilled promises and workers resisting proposed changes. Some ask what is wrong with these people, why don't they cheer enthusiastically for all that technical ingenuity offers them? Against this background, workplace studies might offer a glimpse of what is actually going on at the work site, and provide the worker's point of view on how technological tools ought to work. This would amount to *usability problem-solving* for existing systems, and *requirements analysis* for future systems.

However, the practical applications of workplace studies are only part of their achievement. Workplace studies are up to *something more* than what a usability engineer would track as a repairable problem in a system, or what a requirements engineer would characterize as a desirable feature of a prospective system based on user interviews. Of course, this *something more* is both a promise and a problem.

It is a promise of a more complete understanding of the lived sense of the practice. But it is a problem as far as it concerns the accumulation of practical guidelines for developers.

More broadly, CA studies could also play some role within constructive technology studies that formulate scenarios to anticipate the development of future technologies and their patterns of use (Koskinen et al. 2002). This type of study first identifies existing trends, such as a visualization of the world. The trend, then, is opened up for research. Some version of the presumed future product is constructed (a prototype, mock-up, or an inventive combination of existing technologies). Simulated future products are then given to real users in order to monitor evolving patterns of usage, with analysis focusing on the social and temporal aspects of use. Consequently, a potential evolution of technology usage can be identified and articulated. CA or some alternative, sensitive microanalysis can provide key data on social and emotional communication to help developers understand the formations of users' preferences concerning technologies. Design of future services should be informed by an understanding of the practices of sociability, like joking, teasing, storytelling and gossiping, as services supporting these activities will also be useful in task-related contexts. Social and emotional behavior is an analyzable invariance that forms the bedrock for the adoption of technology and can inform technology research and design.

In addition to technology studies, comparative studies may also have a specific value from the applied perspective. Traditional CA studies are individualizing, idiographic in their orientation. Traditional methodological policies, like a strong version of the procedural consequentiality of the context (Schegloff 1991), guided the researcher to seek patterns of interaction specific to that context only, never raising the question about the distribution of patterns or their frequency.[5] In contrast, the weaker form of procedural consequentiality (Chapter 2) allows the analyst to consider all systematic, recurrent interactional patterns that may be pertinent for the institutional practice. Accordingly, it becomes possible to question the distribution of interactional patterns and their frequencies, as well as to quantify the findings. These invariances and regularities can then be linked with other measurements making possible combinatory studies in which quantified CA results are combined with measurements of outcome variables. These combinatory studies offer a more sensitive view of the interactional components of institutional practices that may be connected to outcomes. Quantified CA findings linked with statistical measures of institutional practice may also be relevant: comparisons of the distributions of activity patterns may be combined with information about cross-setting differences between practices to develop institutional procedures.

9.6 Conclusion

As a whole, my perspective has been integrative. Early CA soon became, if it was not already from its Sacksian start, a separationist project. From the perspective of the history of science, this separationism was a natural phase of the establishment of a new branch of science. Now, however, CA has come of age, and is strong enough to rebuild links to other fields of science. CA can benefit from recognizing the contributions made in related fields of science, and this recognition can help CA to fulfill its original promise to invigorate our understanding of social actions.

CA can make a threefold contribution to social and human sciences. First, it has established a systematic way to study interactional behavior as an emergent property of social actions. Second, the study of interaction topicalizes the purposefulness and intelligibility of social actions, and it may discern tacit understandings and assumptions revealing parties' identities and their hidden rationalities. Third, it opens social actions as situated activities that emerge from their practical management within their realization.

The aim of this book has been to provide a conceptually-informed way to understand interaction in institutional contexts. In terms of methodology, I have addressed the ways in which the analyst's knowledge of the context is pertinent for making observable the critical dimensions of institutional practice. In this way, the study of institutional interaction may shed light on particular practices through which the institution in question is constituted. This context-sensitive way of analyzing institutional interaction is also one of the ways in which CA is connected to other human and social scientific enterprises. Another way to connect CA to other sciences is by quantifying results and designing combinatory studies linking quantified CA results with other data sources, allowing analysis of the ways interactional outcomes are connected to concrete interactional practices.

Throughout the book, I have discussed various areas of institutional interactions. I have tried to identify, specify and to some degree compare salient forms of interactional patterns that constitute or contribute to establishing key institutional practices in the fields in question. In the final chapter, I have tried to identify thematic areas for future development. Naturally, I have not been able to discuss all the different types of interactions in society. Also, many conceptual issues still need further work. For instance, I was only able to briefly consider the infinite richness of context in Chapter 2. Currently, much interesting work has been carried out on gender in interaction that would be salient for further development in this area (Stokoe and Smithson 2001; McIlvenny 2002). Another area I have only mentioned in passing is the interactants' competence, and in particular analytic issues related to the analysis of communication involving parties with restricted competence (Goodwin et al. 2002). If this book helps to identify gaps in the studies on institutional interaction, it will have served one of its most important goals, outlining new research questions to be investigated. As a whole, this book may have contributed toward our grasp of the diversity in institutional practices. Unexplored regions in the sequential organization of institutional activities appear still to be rich. Further investigations may provide potential applications but also enrich our understanding of human beings in society.

Notes

1   For provisional studies, see Katz and Aakhus 2002; Licoppe and Relieu 2002.

2   Routines as such are achievements (Schegloff 1986), but they stand for "apparently" neutral bedrock of culture. At times, a person may become conscious of routines, and may enact various roles including cultural stereotypes. However, if routines are constantly only enacted, they stop being routines. A person may "do being a Finn" or "do being an American", but if one constantly traverses between various identities that may be considered anomalous (Sacks 1984; Goffman 1974).

3   I am grateful to John Heritage who has given a number of lectures on these issues.

4   Notably, this involves ethical questions concerning for whom this knowledge will be utilized. CA as a reverse-engineering discipline is essentially open for different usages. These ethical questions would be worth addressing separately to inform subsequent study designs.

5   Schegloff, of course, has been the key person developing the collection-based research strategy, which also distinguishes CA from ethnomethodology, which has even more strictly remained an idiographic enterprise. Analytic induction in the form Schegloff has pursued it involves comparisons of instances of data. In any case, Schegloff has been consistent in keeping the participants' orientation as the only form of evidence. Comparative and applied studies differ from this ideal. Comparative studies also discuss differences as positive data; applied studies seek potential practices that may not yet be actualised.

References

Alasuutari, Pertti. (1996) *Researching Culture: Qualitative Method and Cultural Studies*, London: Sage.

Anonymous. (1952) *Twelve Steps and Twelve Traditions*. New York: Alcoholics Anonymous World Services.

Arminen, Ilkka. (1996) 'On the Moral and Interactional Relevancy of Self-repairs for Life Stories of Members of Alcoholics Anonymous', *Text* 16: 449–80.

Arminen, Ilkka. (1998) *Therapeutic Interaction: A Study of Mutual Help in the Meetings of Alcoholics Anonymous*. Helsinki: The Finnish Foundation for Alcohol Studies.

Arminen, Ilkka. (2000) 'On the Context Sensitivity of Institutional Interaction', *Discourse and Society* 11: 435–58.

Arminen, Ilkka. (2001a) 'Work Place Studies – Practical Sociology of Technology', *Acta Sociologica* 44: 2, 185–189.

Arminen, Ilkka. (2001b) 'A Simplest Systematics for the Organization of User–Device Interaction', paper presented at the 11th *Conference on Discourse Studies*, Santa Barbara, July 14th 2001.

Arminen, Ilkka. (2002a) 'Emergentes, Divergentes? Les cultures mobiles', *Réseaux* 20: 112–13, 107–38.

Arminen Ilkka. (2002b) 'Design-oriented Sociology', *Acta Sociologica* 45: 4, 315–322.

Arminen, Ilkka. (2004/forthcoming) 'On the Weakness of Institutional Rules – The Case of Addiction Group Therapy', *Discourse and Society* 15: 6.

Arminen, Ilkka and Mia Halonen. (Forthcoming) 'Conversation Analysis: Studying Talk at Work in Addiction Treatment', in Tim Rhodes (ed.) *Qualitative Methods in Drugs and Alcohol Reasearch*. London: Sage.

Arminen, Ilkka and Anna Leppo. (2001) 'The Dilemma of Two Cultures in the 12-step Treatment: The Professional Responses for Clients Who Act Against Their Best Interests', in Michael Seltzer et al. (eds) *Listening to the Welfare State*. Aldershot: Ashgate, 183–212.

Arminen, Ilkka and Riikka Perälä. (2002) 'Multiprofessional Team Work In 12-step Treatment: Constructing Substance Abusers to Alcoholics', *Nordic Studies on Alcohol and Drugs* 19: [English supplement] 18–32.

Arminen, Ilkka and Minna Leinonen. (2003) 'Mobile Phone Calls – Reflecting a New Type of Openings as an Emergence of a New Genre of Talk-in-Interaction?', paper presented at the conference on *Pragmatics*. Toronto, July.

Atkinson, J.M. (1984) *Our Masters' Voices: The Language and Body Language of Politics*. London: Methuen.

Atkinson, J.M. and P. Drew. (1979) *Order in Court: The Organisation of Verbal Interaction in Judicial Settings*. London, UK: Macmillan Press and Atlantic Highlands, NJ: Humanities Press.

Atkinson, J.M. and J. Heritage, eds. (1984) *Structures of Social Action: Studies in Conversation Analysis*. Cambridge: Cambridge University Press.

Austin, J.L. (1962) *How to do Things with Words*. Oxford: Clarendon Press.

Baker, Carolyn D. (1992) 'Description and Analysis in Classroom Talk and Interaction', *Journal of Classroom Interaction* 27: 2, 9–14.

244   *Institutional Interaction*

Baker, Carolyn, Mike Emmison and Alan Firth. (2001) 'Discovering Order in Opening Sequences: Calls to a Software Helpline', in Alec McHoul and Mark Rapley (eds) *How to Analyse Talk in Institutional Settings: A Casebook of Methods*. London: Continuum, 41–56.

Bateson, Gregory. (1972) *Steps to an Ecology of Mind*. New York: Ballantine Books.

Beattie, Geoffrey. (1981): 'Interruption in Conversational Interaction and its Relation to the Sex and Status of the Interactants', *Linguistics* 19: 15–35.

Becker, Howard. (1998) *Tricks of the Trade – How to Think about Your Research While you are Doing It*. Chicago: Chicago University Press.

Bellack et al. (1966) *The Language of the Classroom*. New York: Teachers' College Press.

Bergmann, Jörg R. (1992) 'Veiled Morality: Notes on Discretion in Psychiatry', in P. Drew and J. Heritage (eds) *Talk at Work: Interaction in Institutional Settings*. Cambridge: Cambridge University Press, 137–62.

Billig, Michael. (1999) 'Whose Terms? Whose Ordinariness? Rhetoric and Ideology in Conversation Analysis', *Discourse and Society* 10: 4, 543–58.

Bilmes, J. (1995) 'Negotiation and Compromise: A Microanalysis of a Discussion in the United States Federal Trade Commission', in A. Firth (eds) *The Discourse of Negotiation: Studies of Language in the Workplace*. Oxford: Pergamon, 61–82.

Bleiberg, Susanne and Lindsay Churchill. (1975) 'Notes on Confrontation in Conversation', *Journal of Psycholinguistic Research* 4: 3, 273–78.

Boden, Deirdre. (1994) *The Business of Talk: Organizations in Action*. Cambridge: Polity Press.

Boden, D. (1995) 'Agendas and Arrangements: Everyday Negotiations in Meetings', in A. Firth (eds) *The Discourse of Negotiation: Studies of Language in the Workplace*. Oxford: Pergamon, 83–100.

Boden, Deirdre and Zimmerman, Don. (1991) (eds) *Talk and Social Structure*. Cambridge: Polity Press.

Boyd, E. (1998) 'Bureaucratic Authority in the "Company of Equals:" the Interactional Management of Medical Peer Review', *American Sociological Review* 63: 2, 200–24.

Button, Graham, ed. (1991) *Ethnomethodology and the Human Sciences*. Cambridge: Cambridge University Press.

Button, Graham. (1992) 'Answers as Interactional Products', in P. Drew and J. Heritage (eds) *Talk at Work – Interaction in Institutional Settings*. Cambridge: Cambridge University Press, 212–34.

Button, Graham et al. (1996) *Computers, Minds and Conduct*. Cambridge: Polity Press.

Camp, Jim. (2002) *Start with No: The Negotiating Tools that the Pros Don't Want You to Know*. New York: Crown Business.

Cazden, Courtney. (1988) *Classroom Discourse. The Language of Teaching and Learning*. London: Heinemann.

Clavarino et al. (1995) 'Assessing the quality of qualitative data', *Qualitative Inquiry* 1: 2, 223–242.

Clayman, S.E. (1992) 'Footing in the Achievement of Neutrality: The Case of News-interview Discourse', in P. Drew and J. Heritage (eds) *Talk at Work: Interaction in Institutional Settings*. Cambridge: Cambridge University Press, 163–98.

Clayman, S.E. (1993) 'Reformulating the Question: A Device for Answering/Not Answering Questions in News Interviews and Press Conferences', *Text* 13: 159–88.

Clayman, S.E. (2001) 'Answers and Evasions', *Language and Society* 30: 403–42.

Clayman, S.E. and J. Heritage. (2002a) *The News Interview: Journalists and Public Figures on the Air*. Cambridge: Cambridge University Press.

Clayman, S.E. and J. Heritage. (2002b) 'Questioning Presidents: Journalistic Deference and Adversarialness in the Press Conferences of Eisenhower and Reagan', *Journal of Communication* 52: 4, 749–75.

Clayman, S.E. and D.W. Maynard. (1995) 'Ethnomethodology and Conversation Analysis', in P. ten Have and G. Psathas (eds) *Situated Order: Studies in the Social Organization of Talk and Embodied Activities*. Washington, DC: University Press of America: 1–30.

Clayman, S.E. and J. Whalen. (1988/89) 'When the Medium becomes the Message: The Case of the Rather-Bush Encounter', *Research on Language and Social Interaction* 22: 241–272.

Coulter, J. (1990) 'Elementary Properties of Argument Sequences', in G. Psathas (ed.) *Interactional Competence*. Washington: University Press of America, 181–203.

Davidson, J.A. (1984) 'Subsequent Versions of Invitations, Offers, Requests, and Proposals Dealing with Potential or Actual Rejection', in J.M. Atkinson and J. Heritage (eds) *Structures of Social Action: Studies in Conversation Analysis*. Cambridge: Cambridge University Press, 102–28.

Davidson J.A (1990) 'Modifications of Invitations, Offers and Rejections', in G. Psathas (ed.) *Interaction Competence*. Lanham: University Press of America, 149–180.

Dennett, Daniel, C. (1991) *Consciousness Explained*. Boston: Little, Brown and Company.

Dersley, Ian and Anthony Wootto.n (2000) 'Complaint Sequences Within Antagonistic Argument', *Research on Language and Social Interaction* 33: 375–406.

Dersley, Ian and Anthony Wootton. (2001) 'In the Heat of the Sequence: Interactional Features Preceding Walkouts from Argumentative Talk', *Language in Society* 30: 611–38.

Dourish, Paul. (2001) *Where the Action Is: The Foundations of Embodied Interaction*. Cambridge: MIT Press.

Drew, P. (1984) 'Speakers' Reporting in Invitation Sequences', in J.M. Atkinson and J. Heritage (eds) *Structures of Social Action: Studies in Conversation Analysis*. Cambridge: Cambridge University Press, 129–51.

Drew, P. (1987) 'Po-faced Receipts of Teases', *Linguistics* 25: 219–53.

Drew, P. (1991) 'Asymmetries of Knowledge in Conversational Interactions', in I. Marková and K. Foppa (eds) *Asymmetries in Dialogue*. Hemel Hempstead: Harvester Wheatsheaf, 29–48

Drew, P. (1992) 'Contested Evidence in Courtroom Cross-examination: The Case of a Trial for Rape', in P. Drew and J. Heritage (eds) *Talk at Work: Interaction in Institutional Settings*. Cambridge: Cambridge University Press, 470–520.

Drew, P. (1997) '"Open" Class Repair Initiators in Response to Sequential Sources of Troubles in Conversation', *Journal of Pragmatics* 28: 69–102.

Drew, P. (2003) 'Comparative Analysis of Talk-in-Interaction in Different Institutional Settings: A Sketch', in Phillip Glenn, Curtis D. LeBaron and Jenny Mandelbaum (eds) *Studies in Language and Social Interaction: In Honor of Robert Hopper*. Mahweh, NJ: Lawrence Erlbaum, 293–308.

Drew, P. and J. Heritage, eds. (1992a) *Talk at Work: Interaction in Institutional Settings*. Cambridge: Cambridge University Press.

Drew, P. and J. Heritage. (1992b) 'Analyzing Talk at Work: An Introduction', in P. Drew and J. Heritage (eds) *Talk at Work: Interaction in Institutional Settings*. Cambridge: Cambridge University Press, 3–65.

Drew, Paul and Marja-Leena Sorjonen. (1997) 'Institutional Dialogue', in Teun A. van Dijk (ed.) *Discourse: A Multidisciplinary Introduction. Vol 2. Discourse as Social Interaction in Society*. London: Sage.

Dumas Joseph and J. Redish. (1999) *A Practical Guide to Usability Testing*. Exeter: Intellect Books.

Duranti, Alessandro. (1997*) Linguistic Anthropology*. Cambridge: Cambridge University Press.

Duranti, A. and C. Goodwin, eds. (1992) *Rethinking Context: Language as an Interactive Phenomenon*. Cambridge: Cambridge University Press.

Edwards, Derek and Jonathan Potter. (1992) *Discourse Psychology*. London: Sage.

Edwards, Derek and Jonathan Potter. (2001) 'Discursive Psychology', in Alec McHoul and Mark Rapley (eds) *How to Analyse Talk in Institutional Settings: A Casebook of Methods*. London: Continuum, 12–24.

Fairclough, Norman. (1989) *Language and Power*. London: Longman.

Fairclough, Norman. (1992) *Discourse and Social Change*. Cambridge: Polity Press.

Firth, A. (1995a) 'Talking for a Change: Commodity Negotiating by Telephone', in A. Firth (eds) *The Discourse of Negotiation: Studies of Language in the Workplace*. Oxford: Pergamon, 183–222.

Firth, A. ed. (1995b) *The Discourse of Negotiation: Studies of Language in the Workplace*. Oxford: Pergamon.

Ford, Cecilia E. and Sandra A. Thompson (1996) 'Interactional Units in Conversation: Syntactic, Intonational, and Pragmatic Resources for the Management of Turns', in E. Ochs, E.A. Schegloff and S.A. Thompson (eds) *Interaction and Grammar*. Cambridge: Cambridge University Press, 134–84.

Ford, Cecilia E., Barbara A. Fox and Sandra A. Thompson, eds. (2002) *The Language of Turn and Sequence*. New York: Oxford University Press.

Forsythe, Diana. (2001) *Studying Those Who Study Us – An Anthropologist in the World of Artificial Intelligence*. Stanford: Stanford University Press.

Frankel, R.M. (1984) 'From Sentence to Sequence: Understanding the Medical Encounter through Micro-interactional Analysis', *Discourse Processes* 7: 135–70.

Frankel, R.M. (1989) '"I Wz Wonderinguhm Could *Raid* uhm *E*ffect the Brain Permanently D'y Know?": Some Observations on the Intersection of Speaking and Writing in Calls to a Poison Control Center', *Western Journal of Speech Communication* 53: 195–226.

Frankel, R.M. (1990) 'Talking in Interviews: A Dispreference for Patient-initiated Questions in Physician-patient Encounters', in G. Psathas (eds) *Interactional Competence*. Washington: University Press of America, 231–62.

Garcia, A. (1991) 'Dispute Resolution Without Disputing: How the Interactional Organization of Mediation Hearings Minimizes Argument', *American Sociological Review* 56: 818–35.

Garcia, Angela. (1995)'The Problematics of Representation in Community Mediation Hearings: Implications for Mediation Practice', *Journal of Sociology and Social Welfare* 22: 23– 46.

Garcia, A.C. and J.B. Jacobs (1998) 'The Interactional Organization of Computer Mediated Communication in the College Classroom', *Qualitative Sociology* 21: 3, 299–317.

Garcia, A.C. and J.B. Jacobs (1999) 'The Eyes of the Beholder: Understanding the Turn-taking System in Quasi-synchronous Computer-mediated Communication', *Research on Language and Social Interaction* 32: 4: 337–367.

Gardner, Rod. (1997) 'The Conversation Object Mm: A Weak and Variable Acknowledging Token', *Research on Language and Social Interaction* 30: 131–56.

Garfinkel, Harold. (1963) 'A Conception of, and Experiments with, Trust as a Condition for Concerted Stable Actions', in O.J. Harvey (ed.) *Motivation and Social Interaction*. New York: Ronald Press.

Garfinkel, Harold. (1967) *Studies in Ethnomethodology.* Englewood Cliffs, NJ: Prentice-Hall.

Garfinkel, Harold. (2002) *Ethnomethodology's Program: Working Out Durkheim's Aphorism.* Lanham, MD: Rowman and Littlefield.

Gibson, James J. (1979) *The Ecological Approach to Visual Perception.* Boston: Houghton Mifflin.

Giddens, Anthony. (1984) *The Constitution of Society: Outline of the Theory of Structuration.* Cambridge: Polity Press.

Goffman, E. (1964) 'The Neglected Situation', *American Anthropologist* 66: 6, part II: 133–6.

Goffman, E. (1969) *Strategic Interaction.* Oxford: Basil Blackwell.

Goffman, E. (1974) *Frame Analysis: An Essay on the Organization of Experience.* New York: Harper and Row.

Goffman, Erving (1981) *Forms of Talk.* Philadelphia: University of Pennsylvania Press.

Goffman, E. (1983a) 'The Interaction Order', *American Sociological Review* 48: 1–17.

Goffman, E. (1983b) 'Felicity's Condition', *American Journal of Sociology* 89: 1–53.

Goodwin, C. (1981) *Conversational Organization: Interaction Between Speakers and Hearers.* New York: Academic Press.

Goodwin, C. (1994a) 'Recording Human Interaction in Natural Settings', *Pragmatics* 3: 181–209.

Goodwin, C. (1994b) 'Professional Vision', *American Anthropologist* 96: 606–33.

Goodwin, C. (1996) 'Transparent Vision', in E. Ochs, E.A. Schegloff and S.A. Thompson (eds) *Interaction and Grammar.* Cambridge: Cambridge University Press, 370–404.

Goodwin, C. (2000) 'Action and Embodiment within Situated Human Interaction', *Journal of Pragmatics* 32, 1489–522.

Goodwin, C. and M.H. Goodwin. (1996) 'Seeing as Situated Activity: Formulating Planes', in Y. Engeström and D. Middleton (eds) *Cognition and Communication at Work.* Cambridge: Cambridge University Press, 61–95.

Goodwin, C., M.H. Goodwin and D. Olsher. (2002) 'Producing Sense with Nonsense Syllables: Turn and Sequence in Conversations with a Man with Severe Aphasia', in Cecilia E. Ford, Barbara A. Fox and Sandra A. Thompson (eds) *The Language of Turn and Sequence.* New York: Oxford University Press, 56–80.

Haakana, Markku. (1999) *Laughing Matters. A Conversation Analytical Study of Laughter in Doctor–Patient Interaction.* Department of Finnish Language, University of Helsinki.

Have, P. ten. (1991) 'Talk and Institution: A Reconsideration of the "Asymmetry" of Doctor–patient Interaction', in D. Boden and D.H. Zimmerman (eds) *Talk and Social Structure: Studies in ethnomethodology and Conversation Analysis.* Cambridge: Polity Press, 138–63.

Have, P. ten. (1999) *Doing conversation analysis: a practical guide.* London: Sage.

Heath, C. (1986) *Body Movement and Speech in Medical Interaction.* Cambridge: Cambridge University Press.

Heath, C. and P. Luff. (2000) *Technology in Action.* Cambridge: Cambridge University Press.

Heritage, J. (1984a) *Garfinkel and Ethnomethodology.* Cambridge: Polity Press.

Heritage, J. (1984b) 'A Change-of-state Token and Aspects of its Sequential Placement', in J.M. Atkinson and J. Heritage (eds) *Structures of Social Action: Studies in Conversation Analysis.* Cambridge: Cambridge University Press, 299–345.

Heritage, J. (1985) 'Analyzing News Interviews: Aspects of the Production of Talk for an Overhearing Audience', in T.A. van Dijk (eds) *Handbook of Discourse Analysis.* London: Academic Press. Vol. 3: 95–117.

Heritage, J. (1989) 'Current Developments in Conversation Analysis', in D. Roger and P. Bull (eds) *Conversation: an Interdisciplinary Perspective.* Clevedon: Multilingual Matters, 21–47.

Heritage, J. (1990/1991) 'Intention, Meaning and Strategy: Observations on Constraints on Interaction Analysis', *Research on Language and Social Interaction* 24: 311–32.

Heritage, J. (1997) 'Conversation Analysis and Institutional Talk: Analysing Data', in D. Silverman (ed.) *Qualitative research: Theory, method and practice.* London: Sage, 161–82.

Heritage, J. (1999) 'CA at Century's End: Practices of Talk-in-Interaction, their Distributions and their Outcomes', *Research on Language and Social Interaction* 32.

Heritage, J. (forthcoming) 'Accounting for the Visit: Giving Reasons for Seeking Medical Care', in J. Heritage and D. Maynard (eds) *Practicing Medicine: Structure and Process in Primary Care Encounters.* Cambridge: Cambridge University Press.

Heritage, J., E. Boyd and L. Kleinman (2001) 'Subverting Criteria: The Role of Precedent in Decisions to Finance Surgery', *Sociology of Health and Illness* 23: 701–28.

Heritage, J. and D. Greatbatch (1991) 'On the Institutional Character of Institutional Talk: The Case of News Interviews', in D. Boden and D.H. Zimmerman (eds) *Talk and Social Structure: Studies in Ethnomethodology and Conversation Analysis.* Cambridge: Polity Press, 93–137.

Heritage, J. and D. Maynard, eds. (forthcoming) *Practicing Medicine: Structure and Process in Primary Care Encounters.* Cambridge: Cambridge University Press.

Heritage, J. and S. Sefi. (1992) 'Dilemmas of Advice: Aspects of the Delivery and Reception of Advice in Interactions between Health Visitors and First-time Mothers', in P. Drew and J. Heritage (eds) *Talk at Work: Interaction in Institutional Settings.* Cambridge: Cambridge University Press: 359–417.

Heritage, J. and M.L. Sorjonen. (1994) 'Constituting and Maintaining Activities Across Sequences: And-prefacing as a Feature of Questioning Design', *Language in Society* 23: 1–29.

Heritage, J. and T. Stivers. (1999) 'Online Commentary in Acute Medical Visits: A Method of Shaping Patient Expectations', *Social Science and Medicine* 49(11): 1501–17.

Hester, S. and D. Francis, eds. (2000) *Local Educational Order: Ethnomethodological Studies of Knowledge in Action.* Amsterdam/Philadelphia: John Benjamins [Pragmatics and Beyond NS 73].

Hester, Stephen and David Francis. (2001) 'Is Institutional Talk a Phenomenon? Reflections on Ethnomethodology and Applied Conversation Analysis', in Alec McHoul and Mark Rapley (eds) *How to Analyse Talk in Institutional Settings: A Casebook of Methods.* London: Continuum, 206–17.

Holstein, James A. (1993) *Court-ordered Insanity – Interpretative Practice and Involuntary Commitment.* New York: Aldine de Gruyter.

Houtkoop-Steenstra, H. (1991) 'Opening Sequences in Dutch Telephone Conversations', in D. Boden and D.H. Zimmerman (eds) *Talk and Social Structure: Studies in Ethnomethodology and Conversation Analysis.* Cambridge: Polity Press, 232–252.

Houtkoop-Steenstra, H. (2000) *Interaction and the Standardized Interview. The Living Questionnaire.* Cambridge: Cambridge University Press.

Houtkoop-Steenstra, H. and Ch., Antaki. (1998) 'Creating Happy People by Asking Yes–No Questions', *Research On Language and Social Interaction* 30: 4, 285–315.

Hume, David. (1998/1777) *Enquiries.* Oxford: Oxford University Press.

Hutchby, I. (1996a) 'Power in Discourse: The Case of Arguments on a British talk Radio Show', *Discourse and Society* 7: 481–97.

Hutchby, I. (1996b) *Confrontation Talk: Argument, Asymmetries and Power on talk radio.* Hilldale, NJ: Erlbaum.

Hutchby, I. (2001) *Conversation and Technology: From the Telephone to the Internet.* Cambridge: Polity Press

Hutchby, I. and R. Wooffitt. (1998) *Conversation Analysis: Principles, Practices and Applications.* Oxford: Polity Press.

Hymes, Dell. (1964) *Language in Culture and Society: A Reader in Linguistics and Anthropology.* New York: Harper and Row.

Hymes, Dell. (1972) 'Models of the Interaction of Language and Social Life', in John J. Gumperz and Dell Hymes (eds) *Directions in Sociolinguistics: The Ethnography of Communication.* New York: Holt, Rinehart and Winston.

Jacoby S. and E. Ochs. (1995) 'Co-construction: An Introduction', *Research on Language and Social Interaction* 28: 3, 171–184.

Jayyusi, L. (1984) *Categorization and the Moral Order.* Boston: Routledge and Kegan Paul.

Jayyusi, L. (1991) 'Values and Moral Judgement: Communicative Praxis as Moral Order', in G. Button (ed.) *Ethnomethodology and the Human Sciences.* Cambridge: Cambridge University Press, 227–51.

Jefferson, G. (1984a) 'Notes on a Systematic Deployment of the Acknowledgement Tokens "Yeah" and "Mm hm"', *Papers in Linguistics* 17: 197–206.

Jefferson, G. (1984b) 'On Stepwise Transition from Talk about a Trouble to Inappropriately Nextpositioned Matters', in J.M. Atkinson and J. Heritage (eds) *Structures of Social Action: Studies in Conversation Analysis.* Cambridge: Cambridge University Press, 191–222.

Jefferson, G. (1987) 'On Exposed and Embedded Correction in Conversation', in G. Button and J.R.E. Lee (eds) *Talk and Social Organisation.* Clevedon: Multilingual Matters, 86–100.

Jefferson, G. (1990) 'List-construction as a Task and a Resource', in G. Psathas (eds) *Interaction Competence.* Washington, DC: University Press of America, 63–92.

Jefferson, G. (1993) 'Remarks on "Non-Correction" in Conversation'. Unpublished ms.

Kangasharju, H. (1996) 'Aligning as a Team in Multiparty Conversation', *Journal of Pragmatics* 26: 291–319.

Katz, J.E. and M. Aakhus, eds. (2002) *Perpetual Contact: Mobile Communication, Private Talk, Public Performance.* Cambridge: Cambridge University Press.

Ketola, Pekka. (2002) 'Integrating Usability with Concurrent Engineering in Mobile Phone Development'. Acta Electronica Universitatis Tamperensis; 185, http://acta.uta.fi.

Klippi, Anu. (1996) *Conversation as an Achievement in Aphasics* (Studia Fennica Linguistica 6.) Helsinki: Finnish Literature Society.

Komter, M.L. (1991) *Conflict and Cooperation in Job Interviews; A Study of Talk, Tasks and Ideas.* Amsterdam: Benjamins.

Koskinen, Ilpo, Esko Kurvinen and Turo-Kimmo Lehtonen (2002) *Mobile Image.* Finland: IT Press.

Kusch, Martin. (1989) *Language as Calculus vs. Language as Universal Medium: A Study in Husserl, Heidegger, and Gadamer.* Kluwer: Synthese Library.

Laakso, Minna. (1997) *Self-initiated Repair by Fluent Aphasic Speakers in Conversation* (Studia Fennica Linguistica 8.) Helsinki: Finnish Literature Society.

Lerner, G. (1991) 'On the Syntax of Sentences-in-progress', *Language in Society* 20: 441–58.

Levinson, S.C. (1988) 'Putting Linguistics on a Proper Footing: Explorations in Goffman's Concepts of Participation', in P. Drew and A.J. Wootton (eds) *Erving Goffman· Exploring the Interaction Order*. Cambridge: Polity Press, 161–227.

Levinson, S.C. (1983) *Pragmatics*. Cambridge: Cambridge University Press.

Levinson, S.C. (1992) 'Activity Types and Language', in P. Drew and J. Heritage (eds) *Talk at Work: Interaction in Institutional Settings*. Cambridge: Cambridge University Press, 66–100.

Liberman, K. (1985) *Understanding Interaction in Central Australia: An Ethnomethodological Study of Australian Aboriginal People*. London: Routledge and Kegan Paul.

Licoppe, Christian and Marc Relieu, eds. (2002) *Mobiles*. Paris: Hermes Science revue Reseaux N. 112–13.

Lindesmith, Alfred. (1947) *Opiate Addiction*. Evanston: The Principia Press.

Livingston, E. (1986) *The Ethnomethodological Foundations of Mathematics*. London: Routledge and Kegan Paul.

Llobera, Josep. (1998) 'Historical and Comparative Research', in. C. Seale (ed.) *Researching Society and Culture*. London: Sage, 72–81.

Lloyd, Robin. (1992) 'Negotiating Child Sexual Abuse: The Interactional Character of Investigative Practices', *Social Problems* 39: 2, 109–24.

Luff, P., G.N. Gilbert and D.M. Frohlich, eds. (1990) *Computers and Conversation*. London: Academic Press.

Luff, P., J. Hindmarsh and C. Heath, eds. (2000) *Workplace Studies: Recovering Work Practice and Informing Systems Design*. Cambridge: Cambridge University Press.

Luke, K.K. and T.S. Pavlidou, eds. (2002) *Telephone Calls: Unity and Diversity in Conversational Structure Across Languages and Cultures*. Amsterdam: John Benjamins.

Lull, J. and S. Hinerman, eds. (1997) *Media Scandals. Morality and Desire in the Popular Culture Marketplace*. Oxford: Polity Press.

Lynch, M. (1993) *Scientific Practice and Ordinary Action: Ethnomethodology and Social Studies Of Science*. New York: Cambridge University Press.

Macbeth, D. (1991) 'Teacher Authority as Practical Action', *Linguistics and Education* 3: 281–313.

Macbeth, D. (1994) 'Classroom Encounters with the Unspeakable: "Do You See, Danelle?"', *Discourse Processes* 17: 311–35.

McHoul, A. (1978) 'The Organization of Turns at Formal Talk in the Classroom'. *Language in Society* 7: 183–213.

McHoul, A. (1990) 'The Organization of Repair in Classroom Talk', *Language in Society* 19: 349–77.

McIlvenny, Paul eds. (2002) *Talking Gender and Sexuality*. Amsterdam/Philadelphia: John Benjamins.

Martin, David. (2001) *Ethnomethodology and Computer Systems Design: Interaction at the Boundaries of Organisations*. Manchester University, Department of Computer Science.

Matoesian, Gregory M. (1993) *Reproducing Rape – Domination Through Talk in the Courtroom*. Oxford: Polity Press.

Maynard, D.W. (1984) *Inside Plea Bargaining: The Language of Negotiation*. New York: Plenum.

Maynard, D.W. (1989a) 'Perspective-display Sequences in Conversation', *Western Journal of Speech Communication* 53: 91–113.

Maynard, D.W. (1989b) 'Notes on the Delivery and Reception of Diagnostic News Regarding Mental Disabilities', in D.T. Helm, W.T. Anderson, A.J. Meehan and A.W. Rawls (eds) *The*

Interactional Order: New Directions in the Study of Social Order. New York: Irvington, 54–67.

Maynard, D.W. (1991a) 'On the Interactional and Institutional Bases of Asymmetry in Clinical Discourse', *American Journal of Sociology* 97: 448–95.

Maynard, D.W. (1991b) 'The Perspective-display Series and the Delivery and Receipt of Diagnostic News', in D. Boden and D.H. Zimmerman (eds) *Talk and Social Structure: Studies in Ethnomethodology and Conversation Analysis*. Cambridge: Polity Press, 162–92.

Maynard, D.W. (1992) 'On Clinicians Co-implicating Recipients' Perspective in the Delivery of Diagnostic News', in P. Drew and J. Heritage (eds) *Talk at Work: Interaction in Institutional Settings*. Cambridge: Cambridge University Press, 331–58.

Maynard, D.W. (1996) 'On "Realization" in Everyday Life: The Forecasting of Bad News as a Social Relation', *American Sociological Review* 61: 109–31.

Maynard, D.W. (2003) *Bad News, Good News – Conversational Order in Everyday Talk and Clinical Settings*. Chicago: University of Chicago Press.

Maynard, D.W. and C.L. Marlaire. (1992) 'Good Reasons for Bad Testing Performance: The Interactional Substrate of Educational Exams', *Qualitative Sociology* 15: 177–202.

Maynard, D.W. and D.H. Zimmerman. (1984) 'Topical Talk, Ritual and the Social Organization of Relationships', *Social Psychology Quarterly* 47: 301–16.

Maynard, D.W. et al. eds. (2002.) *Standardization and Tacit Knowledge. Interaction and Practice in the Survey Interview.* New York: John Wiley.

Mehan, H. (1979) *Learning Lessons: Social Organization in the Classroom*. Cambridge, MA: Harvard University Press.

Mill, J.S. (1976/1843–1883) *A System of Logic*. London: Longmans.

Miller, W.R. and S. Rollnick. (1991). *Motivational Interviewing: Preparing People to Change Addictive Behavior*. New York: Guilford Press.

Mitchell, Peter. (1977) *Introduction to the Theory of Mind*. Oxford: Oxford University Press.

Moerman, M. (1988) *Talking Culture: Ethnography and Conversation Analysis*. Philadelphia, PA: University of Pennsylvania Press.

Muller, Johan. (1989) '"Out of Their Minds": An Analysis of Discourse in Two South African Science Classrooms', in D. Roger and P. Bull (eds) *Conversation: An Interdisciplinary Perspective*. Clevedon: Multilingual Matters, 313–338.

Mäkelä, Klaus et al. (1996) *Alcoholics Anonymous as a Mutual Help Movement – A Study in Eight Countries*. Wisconsin: Wisconsin University Press.

Mäkelä, Klaus. (1997) 'Moraaliset ilmiöt sosiologian tutkimuskohteena', *Sosiologia* 34: 3, 250–253.

Nevile, Maurice. (2001) 'Understanding Who's Who in the Airline Cockpit: Pilots' Pronominal Choices and Cockpit Roles', in Alec McHoul and Mark Rapley (eds) *How to Analyse Talk in Institutional Settings: A Casebook of Methods*. London: Continuum, 57–71.

Nikander, Pirjo. (2002) *Age in Action. Membership Work and Stage of Life Categories in Talk*. Helsinki: Finnish Academy of Science and Letters.

Ochs, E. (1988) *Culture and Language Development: Language Acquisition and Language Socialization in a Samoan Village*. Cambridge: CambridgeUniversity Press.

Ochs, E., E.A. Schegloff and S.A. Thompson, eds. (1996) *Interaction and Grammar*. Cambridge: Cambridge University Press.

Palen, L and M. Salzman. (2001) 'Welcome to the Wireless World: Problems Using and Understanding Mobile Telephony', in B. Brown, N. Green and R. Harper (eds) *Wireless World. Social and Interactional Aspects of the Mobile Age*. London: Springer.

Parsons, Talcott. (1937) *Structure of Social Action*. McGraw Hill.

252 *Institutional Interaction*

Peräkylä, A. (1995) *AIDS Counselling: Institutional Interaction and Clinical Practice.* Cambridge: Cambridge University Press.

Peräkylä, A. (1997a) 'Institutionaalinen keskustelu' [Institutional Conversation] in L. Tainio (ed.) *Keskustelunanalyysin perusteet.* Tampere: Vastapaino, 177–203.

Peräkylä, A. (1997b) 'Reliability and Validity in Research Based on Transcripts', in D. Silverman (eds) *Qualitative Research: Theory, Method and Practice.* London: Sage, 201–20.

Peräkylä, A. (1998) 'Authority and Intersubjectivity: The Delivery of Diagnosis in Primary Health Care', *Social Psychology Quarterly* 61: 301–20.

Peräkylä, A. and Sanna Vehviläinen. (2003) 'Conversation Analysis and the Professional Stocks of Interactional Knowledge', *Discourse and Society* 14: 6, 727–50.

Peyrot, Mark. (1987) 'Circumspection in Psychotherapy: Structures and Strategies of Counselor–Client Interaction', *Semiotica* 65:3/4, 249–268.

Plato. (1977) *Dialogues.* Penguin Books.

Pomerantz, A.M. (1980) 'Telling My Side: "Limited Access" as a Fishing Device', *Sociological Inquiry* 50: 186–98.

Pomerantz, A.M. (1984a) 'Agreeing and Disagreeing with Assessments: Some Features of Preferred/Dispreferred Turn Shapes', in J.M. Atkinson and J. Heritage (eds) *Structures of Social Action: Studies in Conversation Analysis.* Cambridge: Cambridge University Press, 57–101.

Pomerantz, A.M. (1984b) 'Giving a Source or Basis: The Practice in Conversation of Telling "How I Know"', *Journal of Pragmatics* 8: 607–25.

Pomerantz, A.M. (1986) 'Extreme Case Formulations: A Way of Legitimizing Claims', *Human Studies* 9: 219–30.

Pomerantz, A.M. (1987) 'Description in Legal Settings', in G. Button and J.R.E. Lee (eds) *Talk and Social Organisation.* Clevedon: Multilingual Matters, 226–43.

Pomerantz, A.M. (1988) 'Offering a Candidate Answer: An Information Seeking Strategy', *Communication Monographs,* 55, 360–73.

Pomerantz, A.M. (1990/1991) 'Mental Concepts in the Analysis of Social Action', *Research on Language and Social Interaction* 24, 299–310.

Pomerantz, A.M. (1998) 'Multiple Interpretations of *Context*: How Are They Useful?', *Research on Language and Social Interaction* 31: 1, 123–132.

Pomerantz, A.M. and B.J. Fehr. (1997) 'Conversation Analysis: An Approach to the Study of Social Action as Sense Making Practices', in T.A. van Dijk (eds) *Discourse as Social Interaction: Discourse Studies 2 – A Multidisciplinary Introduction.* London: Sage, 64–91.

Popper, Karl. (1935/1977) *The Logic of Scientific Discovery.* London: Hutchinson.

Psathas, G. (1995) *Conversation analysis: the study of Talk-in Interaction.* Thousand Oaks: Sage [Qualitative Research Methods 35].

Ragin, Charles. (1987) *The Comparative Method: Moving beyond Qualitative and Quantitative Strategies.* Berkeley: University of California Press.

Ragin, Charles. (1994) *Constructing Social Research. The Unity and Diversity of Method.* Thousand Oaks/London/New Dehli: Pine Forge Press.

Raudaskoski, Pirkko. (1999) *The Use of Communicative Resources in Language Technology Environments.* Oulu: University of Oulu.

Rawls, J. (1955) 'Two Concepts of Rules', *Philosophical Review* 64: 3–32.

Rorty, Richard, ed. (1967) *The Linguistic Turn.* Chicago: University of Chicago Press.

Rostila, Ilmari. (1995) 'The Relationship between Social Worker and Client in Closing Conversations', *Text* 15: 1, 69–102.

Rubin, Jefrey. (1994) *Handbook of Usability Testing: How to Plan, Design, and Conduct Effective Tests*. New Jersey: Wiley.

Ruusuvuori, Johanna. (2000) *Control in the Medical Consultation: Practices of Giving and Receiving the Reason for the Visit in Primary Healthcare*. Acta Electronica Universitatis Tamperensis 16.

Sacks, H. (1963) 'On Sociological Description', *Berkeley Journal of Sociology* 8: 1–16 .

Sacks, H. (1984) 'On Doing "Being Ordinary"', in. J.M. Atkinson and J. Heritage (eds) *Structures of Social Action: Studies in Conversation Analysis*. Cambridge: Cambridge University Press: 413–29.

Sacks, H. (1987) 'On the Preferences for Agreement and Contiguity in Sequences in Conversation', in Graham Button and J.R.E. Lee (eds) *Talk and Social Organisation*. Clevedon: Multilingual Matters, 54–69.

Sacks, H. (1992a and b) *Lectures on Conversation*. 2 vols. Edited by Gail Jefferson with introductions by Emanuel A. Schegloff. Oxford: Basil Blackwell.

Sacks H., E.A. Schegloff and Gail Jefferson (1974) 'A Simplest Systematics for the Organization of Turn-Taking for Conversation', *Language* 50: 4, 696–735.

Sajavaara, Kari and Jaakko Lehtonen. (1997) 'The Silent Finn Revisited', in Adam Jaworski (ed.) *Silence: Interdisciplinary Perspectives*. Berlin: Mouton de Gruyter.

Sarangi, S. and C. Roberts. (1999) *Talk, Work and Institutional Order: Discourse in Medical, Mediation and Management Settings*. New York: Mouton de Gruyter.

Sargant, William. (1961) *Battle for the Mind. A Physiology of Conversion and Brain-Washing*. Baltimore, MD and Hammondsworth: Penguin Books.

Schegloff, E.A. (1968) 'Sequencing in Conversational Openings', *American Anthropologist* 70: 6, 1075–1095.

Schegloff, E.A. (1972) 'Notes on a Conversational Practice: Formulating Place', in D. Sudnow (ed.) *Studies in Social Interaction*. New York: Free Press: 75–119

Schegloff, E.A. (1980) 'Preliminaries to Preliminaries: "Can I Ask You a Question?"', *Sociological Inquiry* 50: 104–52.

Schegloff, E.A. (1982) 'Discourse as an Interactional Achievement: Some Uses of "Uh Huh" and Other Things That Come Between Sentences', in D. Tannen (eds) *Georgetown University Roundtable on Languages and Linguistics 1981; Analyzing Discourse: Text and Talk*. Georgetown University Press, 71–93.

Schegloff, E.A. (1986) 'The Routine as Achievement', *Human Studies* 9: 111–52.

Schegloff, E.A. (1987) 'Between Macro and Micro: Contexts and Other Connections', in J. Alexander, B. Giessen, R. Munch and N. Smelser (eds) *The Macro-Micro Link*. Berkeley and Los Angeles: University of California Press, 207–34.

Schegloff, E.A. (1988) 'On an Actual Virtual Servo-Mechanism for Guessing Bad News: A Single Case Conjecture', *Social Problems*, 35: 442–57.

Schegloff, E.A. (1988/89) 'From Interview to Confrontation: Observations on the Bush/Rather Encounter', *Research on Language and Social Interaction* 22: 215–240.

Schegloff, E.A. (1991) 'Reflections on Talk and Social Structure', in D. Boden and D. Zimmerman (eds), *Talk and Social Structure*. Cambridge: Polity Press, 44–70.

Schegloff, E.A. (1992a) 'Introduction', in Harvey Sacks, *Lectures on Conversation*, Vol. 1. Oxford: Basil Blackwell, ix–lxii.

Schegloff, E.A. (1992b) 'Repair After Next Turn: The Last Structurally Provided Defense of Intersubjectivity in Conversation', *American Journal of Sociology* 98: 1295–345.

Schegloff, E.A. (1993) 'Reflections on Quantification in the Study of Conversation', *Research on Language and Social Interaction* 26: 1, 99–128.

Schegloff, E.A. (1995) 'The Sequence Organization'. Unpublished ms.

Schegloff, E.A. (1996a) 'Turn Organization: One Intersection of Grammar and Interaction', in E. Ochs, E.A. Schegloff and S.A. Thompson (eds) *Interaction and Grammar*. Cambridge: Cambridge University Press, 52–133.

Schegloff, E.A. (1996b) 'Confirming Allusions: Toward an Empirical Account of Action', *American Journal of Sociology* 104: 161–216.

Schegloff, E.A. (1997) 'Whose Text? Whose Context?', *Discourse and Society* 8: 2, 165–87.

Schegloff, E.A. (1999) 'Discourse, Pragmatics, Conversation, Analysis', *Discourse Studies* 1: 4, 405–35.

Schegloff, E.A. (2002) 'Reflections on Research on Telephone Conversation. Issues of Cross-Cultural Scope and Scholarly Exchange, Interactional Import and Consequences', in K.K. Luke and T.S. Pavlidou (eds) *Telephone Calls: Unity and Diversity in Conversational Structure across Languages and Cultures*. Amsterdam: John Benjamins.

Schegloff, E.A. and H. Sacks (1973) 'Opening Up Closings', *Semiotica* 8: 4, 289–327.

Schegloff, E.A., G. Jefferson and H. Sacks (1977) 'The Preference for Self-Correction in the Organization of Repair in Conversation', *Language* 53: 2, 361–82.

Schieffelin, Bambi. (1996) 'Creating Evidence: Making Sense of Written Words in Bosavi', in E. Ochs, E.A. Schegloff and S.A. Thompson (eds) *Interaction and Grammar*. Cambridge: Cambridge University Press, 435–460.

Seale, Clive. (1999) *Quality of Qualitative Research*. London: Sage.

Sellen, Abigail and Richard Harper. (2002) *The Myth of the Paperless Office*. Cambridge: The MIT Press.

Selting, Margret and Elizabeth Couper-Kuhlen, eds. (2001). *Studies in Interactional Linguistics*. Amsterdam: Benjamins.

Silverman, David. (1987) *Communication and Medical Practice: Social Relations in the Clinic*. London: Sage

Silverman, David. (1997) *Discourses of Counselling. HIV Counselling as Social Interaction*. London: Sage.

Silverman, David. (1998) *Harvey Sacks: Social Science and Conversation Analysis*. Oxford: Policy Press

Silverman, David. (2000) *Doing Qualitative Research*. London, Sage.

Silverman, David and A. Peräkylä. (1990) 'AIDS Counselling: The Interactional Organisation of Talk about "Delicate Issues"', *Sociology of Health and Illness* 12: 293–318.

Sinclair, J. and M. Coulthard. (1975) *Towards an Analysis of Discourse*. Oxford: Oxford University Press.

Sorjonen, M.-J. (1996) 'On Repeats and Responses in Finnish Conversation', in E. Ochs, E.A. Schegloff and S.A. Thompson (eds) *Interaction and Grammar*. Cambridge: Cambridge University Press, 277–327.

Stokoe, Elisabeth H. and Janet Smithson. (2001) 'Making Gender Relevant: Conversation Analysis and Gender Categories in Interaction', *Discourse and Society* 12: 243–69.

Suchman, L. (1987) *Plans and Situated Action: The Problem of Human-machine Communication*. Cambridge: Cambridge University Press.

Suchman, L. (1996) 'Constituting Shared Workspaces', in Y. Engeström and D. Middleton (eds) *Cognition and Communication at Work*. Cambridge: Cambridge University Press, 35–60.

Suchman, L. and B. Jordan. (1990) 'Interactional Troubles in Face-to-face Survey Interviews', *Journal of the American Statistical Association*, 85: 232–41.

Sudnow, D. (1978) *Ways of the Hand: The Organization of Improvised Conduct*. London: Routledge and Kegan Paul.

Säde, Simo. (2001) *Cardboard Mock-ups and Conversations. Studies in Usability in Industrial Design*. Helsinki: Taideteollinen korkeakoulu.

Tanaka, Hiroko. (2000) 'Turn-Projection in Japanese Talk-in-Interaction', *Research on Language and Social Interaction* 33: 1–38.

Tracy, Karen. (1993) 'It's an Interesting Article', *Research on Language and Social Interaction* 26: 2, 195–202.

Travers, M. and J.F. Manzo, eds. (1997) *Law in Action: Ethnomethodological and Conversation Analytic Approaches to Law*. Aldershot: Dartmouth.

Turing, Alan. (1950) 'Computing Machinery and Intelligence', *Mind* 49: 433–60.

Vehviläinen, Sanna. (1999) *Structures of Counselling Interaction. A Conversation Analytical Study of Counselling Encounters in Career Guidance Training*. Helsinki: University of Helsinki.

Vehviläinen, Sanna. (2001) 'Evaluative Advice in Educational Counseling: The Use of Disagreement in the "Stepwise Entry" to Advice', *Research on Language and Social Interaction* 34: 3, 371–98.

Vygotsky, L.S. (1978) *Mind in Society: The Development of Higher Psychological Processes*. Cambridge, MA: Harvard University Press.

Wagner, J. (1996) 'Conversation Analysis of Foreign Language Data', *Journal of Pragmatics* 26: 215–35.

Wakin, W.A. and D.H. Zimmerman. (1999) 'Reduction and Specialization in Emergency and Directory Assistance Calls', *Research on Language and Social Interaction* 32: 4, 409–37.

Walker, E. (1995) 'Making a Bid for Change: Formulations in Union/Managment Negotiations', in A. Firth (ed.) *The Discourse of Negotiation: Studies of Language in the Workplace*. Oxford: Pergamon, 101–40.

Watson, D.R. (1990) 'Some Features of the Elicitation of Confessions in Murder Interrogations', in G. Psathas (ed.) *Interactional Competence*. Washington: University Press of America, 263–96.

Whalen, J. (1995) 'A Technology of Order Production: Computer-aided Dispatch in Public Safety Communication', in P. ten Have and G. Psathas (eds) *Situated Order: Studies in the Social Organization of Talk and Embodied Activities*. Washington, DC: University Press of America, 187–230.

Whalen, J. (1999) 'The Discipline of Endless Wonderment – an Interview', *Dialog on Leadership* http://www.dialogonleadership.org/interviewWhalen.html.

Whalen, J. and Dorothy Smith. (1997) 'Texts in Action'. Unpublished ms.

Whalen, J. and Eric Vinkhuyzen. (2000) 'Expert Systems in (Inter)action: Diagnosing Document Machine Problems over the Telephone', in P. Luff, J. Hindmarsh and C. Heath (eds) *Workplace Studies: Recovering Work Practice and Informing Systems Design*. Cambridge: Cambridge University Press, 92–140.

Whalen, J., D.H. Zimmerman and M.R. Whalen. (1988) 'When Words Fail: A Single Case Analysis', *Social Problems* 35: 333–62.

Wilson, Thomas. (1991) 'Social Structure and the Sequential Organization of Interaction', in Deirdre Boden and Don Zimmerman (eds) *Talk and Social Structure*. Cambridge: Polity Press.

Winn, Denise. (1983) *The Manipulated Mind: Brainwashing, Conditioning and Indoctrination*. London: Octagon Press.

Wittgenstein, Ludvig. (1958) *Philosophical Investigations*, translated by G.E.M. Anscombe. Basil Blackwell, Oxford.

Woolgar, S. and Pawluch, D. (1985) 'Ontological Gerrymandering', *Social Problems* 32: 214–27.

Wootton, Anthony. (1976) 'Sharing: Some Notes on the Organization of Talk in a Therapeutic Community', *British Journal of Sociology* 10: 333–50.

Zimmerman, D.H. (1992) 'The Interactional Organization of Calls for Emergency', in P. Drew, J. Heritage (eds) *Talk at Work: Interaction in Institutional Settings*. Cambridge: Cambridge University Press, 418–69.

Zimmerman, D.H. (1993) 'Acknowledgement Tokens and Speakership Incipiency Revisited', *Research on Language and Social Interaction* 26: 179–94.

Zimmerman, D.H. (1998) 'Identity, Context and Interaction', in C. Antaki and S. Widdicombe (eds) *Identities in Talk*. London: Sage, 87–106.

Zimmerman, Don and Melvin Pollner. (1970) 'The Everyday World as a Phenomenon', in Douglas Jack (eds) *Understanding Everyday Life*. Chicago: Aldine.

Yalisove, Daniel. (1998) 'The Origins and Evolution of Disease Concept of Treatment', *Journal of Studies on Alcohol*. 59: 469–76.

Appendix 1:
Transcription Symbols

In the transcripts, the speakers' names, and possibly some other details, have been commonly changed in order to secure the anonymity of the persons involved.

Transcription symbols and conventions of conversation analysis are used throughout the extracts (see Atkinson and Heritage, 1984), unless otherwise stated. The contributions are identified with the speakership symbols, like A:, i.e., A: Hi::,, often with the initial of the speaker's name or institutional role.

Extracts have been identified with the following code: [identifying symbol of the data corpus; possibly details indicating the position of the extract in the corpus], (reference to a source where the extract has been initially discussed).

Some of the extracts are translations. In some of the translated data three lines are used: the first line is the original speech, the lowest line is an 'idiomatic' translation, and most analyses can be followed with the help of that line only. The line in between is a 'glossary', which is used when the idiomatic translation diverts syntactically from the original speech. The glossary provides the reader a possibility to follow word-by-word the proceeding of the original speech. Interpretations are added if necessary. Principles of data translation are discussed in Chapter 1.

[ ]	simultaneous speech and voices, its start and end
=	immediately continuous talk, no interval
(0.6)	pause and its length in seconds
(.)	micropause, shorter than 0.2 seconds
.h	in-breath
hh	out-breath
―	emphasis
:	stretch
YES	loud
.	falling intonation
,	continuing intonation
?	rising inflection, not necessarily a question
?,	weak rise in intonation
↑	marked rise in pitch
↓	marked fall in pitch
da-	production of word is cut off
word<	abruptly finished, but not cut off
> <	pronounced faster than the surrounding speech

< >	pronounced slower than the surrounding speech
$	laughter in the voice
@ @	animated voice
° °	diminishing voice
# #	shivering voice
hah	laughter
(word)	unclearly heard
(( ))	researcher's comment
→	target line; crucial instance for the analyzed speech

Some further symbols may be used to mark special features. These symbols have been defined separately.

Appendix 2:
On the Weakness of Institutional Rules

Introduction

Setting, Data and Methods

Contextualizing the rules

Extract 1 (VR4,8,7–12)

```
 6  S:[Ok., (.) I'll (.) bit >explain t'you< the rules of the firm.
 7  →[S leans forward and looks at the table of rules
 8  (1.4)
 9  →S:      that's confidentia[lity in the group. (.) that's what we talk
10  →                          [P turns and looks at the table of rules
11  →        about here. (.)[what crooks   you see here and. (0.6)
12  →                       [P turns towards S
13  →        it's absolutely our own thing th't, (.) don't chat about them
14  →        there at the dinnertables and and (.) in smoking room th't,
15          (1.2)
16  →S:      if som'thin' comes up then we'll ask like here.
17  →        let's talk those things among (.) us.h° (0.3) .hhhh
18          erm we'll speak one at a time. (1.3) and morning round, (.)
```

Extract 2 (VR8, 26, 11-18)

```
 1  S:       erm we'll speak h (.) at least we try to speak one at a time h
 2           (1.0)
 3  →S:      and morning rounds about comments on turns at talk during
 4  →        round that's we're used to here?, (0.4) that Tea is with
 5  →        us [here?, (.) .nff always in mornings those two first hours
 6  →           [L turns and looks at S
 7  →S:      erm we'll have in the first hour such?, (0.8) a feeling round
 8  →        about the last evening and?, (.) we'll talk hh (0.8) them?, (.)
 9  →        comment on them not until afterwards to not cause such a
10  →        hubbub. h
11           (2.0)
```

```
12   S:    and?, (.) we won't bring any foodstuff drinks here?,
13         (2.6)
```

Extract 3 (VR4, 9, 13-14)

```
12   S:    respect others' views and other people.
13         (1.3)
14 →S:    >and erm< you may express your emotions freely,
15         (0.8)
16 →S:    it's if you're pissed off you're pissed off and you may tell it.
17 →      (.) and you may tell if (.) you are happy.
18         (2.1)
19   S:    and VIOLENCE AND THE THREATS TO USE IT ARE FORBIDDEN,h
20         (1.0)
```

Downgrading the Rules

Downgrading the Rules through Reformulations

Extract 4 (VR3,32,15-4; S = senior member, T = newcomer, E = other group member)

```
1    S:    that's y'know is somewhat clear °though
2          t[hat°,
3    T:    [Of course yeah,=
4          [T turns towards table of rules
5    S:    =.hhhhh E:rm (0.3) we'll talk one at a time,h
6          (0.5)((T turns towards S))
7    S:    of course °and,° hhh
8          (0.7)((T nods))
9  →S:    ↓No one I guess has
10 →      become mad here if someone has commented on things.=
11 →      =[but it's that way that:#,=
12   E:    [°#yea#hh°
13   T:    =$hmy$
14 →S:    Not necess- that  [@I and that and@, (.) you and
15                          [S animates his talk by gesturing hands
16 →      [tha:t
17   E:    [$hhoehe[hh
18   S:          [$or I me(h)an that$,=
19   T:    =$ssm smm [smm
20   E:              [$.hh[hh$,
```

```
21   S:              [.hhhh,
22   T:              [T turns towards table of rules
```

Extract 5 (VR8, 26, 18-19)

```
 9                   comment on them not until afterwards not to cause such a
10                   hubbub. h
11                   (2.0)
12   S:             and?, (.) we won't bring any foodstuff drinks here?,
13                   (2.6)
14  →S:             °at least° we won't gorge on anything,
15                   (.)
16   S:             and? (.) we follow the day program and group times?,
17                   (1.6)
```

Stating Exceptions to the Rules

Extract 6 (VR6, 16, 1-3)

```
 1   S:             in mornings we always go #through# E>(what)<E feelings are and
 2                   so on °hhh°,
 3                   (1.0)
 4   S:             there then?
 5                   [we won't bring food or drinks here?
 6                   [S turns towards table of rules
 7                   (.)
 8  →S:             throat pastils they say you may eat if you've a cough?
 9                   (1.4)
10  →S:             [°o(h)r li(h)ke thathhh°,
11   E:             [((E whispers something to S))
```

Interpretative Work Concerning the Salience of the Rules

Reading the Rules Plainly

Extract 7 (VR3, 35, 5-6; S = senior member, T = newcomer)

```
 1   S:             Then in the next hour we can take here notebooks and
 2                   write up.
 3                   (0.5)
 4   T:             [Mm:
```

5 →S: [.hhh (.) Respect other people and their
6 →   views, hh
7   (1.0)
8   and (0.3) .hhh you may express your emotions freely,hhh that's?,

Deviations from the Pattern Observed

Extract 8 (VR3,36,17-5; S = senior member, T = newcomer)

1   S: Yea:h. (0.8) .hhh (0.3) And violence and
2   threats are ↑forbidden, (0.8)
3   T: $hnä$=
4   S: =Listen to others without pre#judice#.
5   (1.2)
6 →S: <This was the hardest for me this last one> when I came like?,
7 →   (1.8)((All except R turn looking at S))
8 →S: As I had the thing that alcoholics =↑As they don't
9 →   understand my things that, (0.3) I talk nothin'
10 →   with them and (th) I fretted at a bit in the beginning
11 →   b't $surely(h) it then went by# .hh .hhh hhb by
12 →   bit by bit, (0.3) .hhh But I: (0.5) was$
13 →   in a such #condition in any case that, (0.9) °y'know it
14 →   was just the same who'd have been around there°#.
15   .hhhhh ↑Yeah,mhh And ↑then there aside was is the

Extract 9 (VR8, 26, 20-21)

12 S: and?, (.) we won't bring any foodstuff drinks here?,
13   (2.6)
14 S: °at least°B we won't gorge on anything,15   (.)
16 →S: and? (.) we follow the day program and the group times?,
17   (1.6)
18 S: and notes are taken only if ag[reed
19 ?:   [.nff

The tension between two rule authorities on surface: laughter
see extract 4.

Author Index

Subject Index

Printed in Great Britain by Amazon

If you have ordered this title please contact our
Customer Service Department on (+44) 1235 400 524
Verlag GmbH, Rothingstraße 37, 35781 Marktlaben, Germany